Mirror of

TWENTIETH-CENTURY JAPAN:
THE EMERGENCE OF A WORLD POWER

Irwin Scheiner, Editor

Mirror of Modernity: Invented Traditions of Modern Japan

EDITED BY

Stephen Vlastos

UNIVERSITY OF CALIFORNIA PRESS
Berkeley   Los Angeles   London

University of California Press
Berkeley and Los Angeles, California

University of California Press, Ltd.
London, England

© 1998 by
The Regents of the University of California

Library of Congress Cataloging-in-Publication Data

Mirror of modernity: invented traditions of modern Japan / Stephen
    Vlastos, editor.
        p.   cm. — (twentieth-century Japan ; 9)
    Includes bibliographic references and index.
    ISBN 0-520-20621-5 (alk. paper). — ISBN 0-520-20637-1 (pbk.:
alk. paper)
    1. Japan—Civilization—1868– .   I. Vlastos, Stephen, 1943– .
II. Series.
DS822.25.M57   1998
952.03—dc21   97-7897
                                                    CIP

Printed in the United States of America
9 8 7 6 5 4 3 2 1

To
Gabriella

Japan is a treasure house of tradition.

When tradition thus becomes master, it does so in such a way that what it "transmits" is made so inaccessible, proximally and for the most part, that it rather becomes concealed.

MARTIN HEIDEGGER

It is as ridiculous to yearn for a return to that original fullness as it is to believe that with this complete emptiness history has come to a standstill. The bourgeois viewpoint has never advanced beyond this antithesis between itself and this romantic viewpoint, and therefore the latter (the "childish world of antiquity") will accompany it as legitimate antithesis up to its blessed end.

KARL MARX

CONTENTS

PART THREE • FOLK

PART FOUR • SPORTS

PART FIVE • GENDER

PART SIX • HISTORY

ILLUSTRATIONS

FIGURES

ACKNOWLEDGMENTS

Publication of *Mirror of Modernity* brings to a close five years of collaboration on this project with sociologist Hashimoto Mitsuru of Osaka University, one of my oldest and closest friends. Professor Hashimoto took the initiative in launching the project, and he deserves full credit for the strengths (not the weaknesses) of this volume.

In 1990 Professor Hashimoto organized a research group comprised of sociologists from Osaka University, Kyoto University, and Osaka Gakuen University on the theme "invention of tradition in modern Japan." Obtaining funding from the Matsushita Foundation of Japan, in September 1991 he convened a conference in Kyoto at which his research group, joined by Irwin Scheiner and myself, presented proposals for future research. The discussions over the next three days were lively, challenging, and convivial: so much so that I proposed expanding the project to bring in more American scholars. With funding from the Japan Foundation of New York, the University of California Center for Japanese Studies, and the University of Iowa Center for Asian and Pacific Studies, in December 1992 I convened a planning workshop in Berkeley. The workshop was followed by a conference in Iowa City in October 1994. This conference was funded by the Japan Foundation of New York and co-sponsored by the American Council of Learned Societies and Social Science Research Council Joint Committee on Japanese Studies and the University of Iowa Center for Asian Pacific Studies. I received valuable institutional support from the History Department, the Graduate College, and the Liberal Arts College of the University of Iowa. The introduction was written in fall 1996 while I was a fellow at the National Humanities Center, Research Triangle Park, North Carolina, and was supported by a fellowship from the National Endowment for the Humanities. I thank them all most sincerely for such generous support.

Without the financial support of these foundations and academic institutions, the project could not have gone forward. But without many people's guidance, time, and labor, always generously given, progress would have been slower and the results poorer. The list is long.

First, the staffs of the foundations, departments, and programs that sponsored the project or lent support at various stages. Michael Paschal at the New York Japan Foundation office patiently steered me through the administrative thickets of the grant application process and financial accounting procedures. I detected only the faintest traces of fatigue in his voice when I called late in the day with some emergency. I also want to thank Mary McDonnell, program associate of the Social Science Research Council and her able assistants. Jae-on Kim, the director of the University of Iowa Center for Asian Pacific Studies, and Peggy Pick-Sutton, the administrative assistant, helped at every turn. Jeffrey Cox, then chair of the University of Iowa History Department, was continuously supportive of my many requests, and Mary Strottman, Ginny Ockenfels, and Ginny Miller sent fax after fax and mailing after mailing. Finally, there was a small army of graduate students at the University of Iowa. Jean Rasmussen carefully read the final manuscript. Akiko Anson, Beth Jerde, Kazuko Shimizu, and Michael Raine labored long and hard on the translations: this is perhaps the most demanding, and the least rewarded, task in any academic collaboration across native languages. Michael Raine and David Tucker recorded and usefully summarized the discussions of the Iowa City conference; David Obermiller helped with logistics and suggestions; and Christopher Gerteis handled a myriad of tasks, giving truly indispensable attention to software, disk conversion, and other computer matters. At a later stage, David Alexander and Christopher Rose did valuable work checking citations. They all did so much and did it so well.

As discussants Deirdre McCloskey and Laura Hein contributed a great deal to the success of the Iowa City conference, hence to the intellectual merit of this volume. It was only after the fact that I realized how much I had asked them to take on. The Afterword contributed by Dipesh Chakrabarty is a model of intellectual engagement with material outside one's specialization. It spurred me to rethink some very large issues.

The greatest satisfaction for me as editor has been the ongoing engagement with the scholars whose essays are collected here. Some were close friends from way back, some recent acquaintances, others I met for the first time when they arrived at the airport. In every case, intellectually and personally, they have been an extraordinary group to work with. I feel the richer for it. The only regret, which is very deep, is that Takasawa Atsuo, professor of sociology at Kyoto University, passed away shortly after returning to Japan following the planning workshop in Berkeley. He is not with us today but is fondly remembered.

A few special contributions to the volume should be acknowledged. Jennifer Robertson helped with the illustrations; Harry Harootunian supplied the wonderful quotations from Marx and Heidegger; Carol Gluck came up with the phrase "mirror of modernity," and Hashimoto Mitsuru recommended its use in the title; and Arif Dirlik, Dipesh Chakrabarty, and Irwin Scheiner critically commented on the Introduction. Two people made unusual contributions. Hashimoto Mitsuru deserves full credit not only for launching the project but also for keeping it going. He worked tirelessly, helping at every turn. Ostensibly my research assistant in the spring and summer of 1995 but in every other way a colleague, Michael Raine helped enormously in editing the final drafts of the essays and the translations. I wish to thank my editors at the University of California Press, Sheila Levine, Laura Driussi, and Jean McAneny, for their support and encouragement, with special thanks to my friend Betsey Scheiner for the wonderful copy editing. Finally, I thank Junko Kobayashi, Linda Fisher, and Joan Kellogg for their careful reading of the page proofs.

It is almost obligatory to acknowledge the love and support of one's family. This is unfortunate, since the repetition of this important gesture threatens to vitiate it. But I have no choice in the matter. My wife, Mary Ann Rasmussen, and my daughter, Gabriella Vlastos, have been so much a part of the whole process that this fact too must be recorded with gratitude and love.

NOTE ON TRANSLITERATION

Japanese words that appear in standard English-language dictionaries are rendered in roman type and without macrons; for example, judo and sumo but *kyūdō* (Japanese archery), and shogun but *yokozuna*. Common place names are also rendered without macrons except as they appear in the titles of Japanese publications. Japanese names are given in the Japanese order, family name first, except in citations to authors' works published in Western languages, where they appear in the English order.

ONE

Tradition

Past/Present Culture
and Modern Japanese History

Stephen Vlastos

Modern Japan is widely regarded as a society saturated with customs, values, and social relationships that organically link present generations of Japanese to past generations. Especially since 1945 and the eclipse of the ideology of the emperor-centered family-state, Japanese have come to know themselves, and to be known by others, through their cultural traditions. Group harmony, aversion to litigation, the martial arts, industrial paternalism: these and other "traditional" values and practices are assumed both to predate Japan's modernization and to have contributed to its unparalleled success. It was not that long ago, in fact, that Japan specialists ascribed Japan's successful modernization to the utility of its premodern values and institutions, on the assumption "traditions" were direct cultural legacies.[1]

Readers will be surprised to discover the recent origins of "age-old" Japanese traditions. Examined historically, familiar emblems of Japanese culture, including treasured icons, turn out to be modern. Much of the ritual and the rules of Japan's "ancient" national sport, sumo, are twentieth-century creations. Prince Shōtoku's enshrinement as an icon of Japanese communal harmony dates from the 1930s and wartime spiritual mobilization. There is little evidence of Japanese

---

I want to thank Dipesh Chakrabarty for his challenging Afterword and subsequent e-mail exchanges; Arif Dirlik and Irwin Scheiner for their valuable input; and the anonymous readers for the University of California Press.

1. For example, see Donald H. Shively, ed., *Tradition and Modernization in Japanese Culture* (Princeton: Princeton University Press, 1971), xii–xvii. Uncritical use of tradition was a conspicuous feature of modernization studies and provided the theoretical framework for the influential, multivolume series of the Conference on Modern Japan, 1959–1969, published by Princeton University Press under the general editorship of John W. Hall and Marius B. Jansen. Early on, Robert J. Smith pointed to the perils of "invented history" and "an imagined past" in the social sciences. See his "Town and City in Premodern Japan," in A. Southall, ed., *Urban Anthropology* (Oxford: Oxford University Press, 1973), 164.

cultural aversion to litigation before the twentieth century; a misnomer, the Japanese "weak legal consciousness" is largely the legacy of institutional innovations of political elites since World War I. The rhetoric of "warm-hearted" worker-management relations was invented in the 1890s by capitalists seeking to fend off government regulation. At that time labor relations on the shop floor tended to be strife-ridden and chaotic; the labor practices that today constitute "Japanese-style labor management" were introduced piecemeal decades later. Some were even borrowed from abroad.

What does it mean that so much of Japanese "tradition" is a modern invention? The essays in this volume build on the critical historical approach to tradition developed by Eric Hobsbawm and employed to startling effect by the contributors to *The Invention of Tradition*.[2] The methodological breakthrough of Hobsbawm and his collaborators was to historicize modern British and British colonial traditions and thereby reveal the ideological and constructed nature of modern tradition—an aspect of tradition scholars had only dimly perceived.

Social scientists have conventionally used tradition in two overlapping and somewhat contradictory senses. First, tradition designates a temporal frame (with no clear beginning), which marks off the historical period preceding modernity. Used in this way tradition aggregates and homogenizes premodern culture and posits a historical past against which the modern human condition can be measured. Thus Anthony Giddens contrasts the pervasive condition of "radical doubt" institutionalized by modernity with the "ontological security" and "moral bindingness" of life in traditional society, where kinship, religion, custom, and ceremony impart feelings of belonging.[3] Used in this way tradition is discontinuous with, and stands in opposition to, modernity.

Tradition in the second and more frequent usage represents a continuous cultural transmission in the form of discrete cultural practices of "the past" that remain vital in the present. In Edward Shils's formulation, tradition is "far more than the statistically frequent reoccurrence over a succession of generations of similar beliefs, practices, institutions, and works." The core of tradition is strongly normative; the intention (and the effect) is to reproduce patterns of culture. Shils writes, "It is this normative transmission which links the generations of the dead with the generations of the living."[4] In this conception, rather than representing culture left behind in the transition to modernity, tradition is what modernity *requires* to prevent society from flying apart.

Both conceptions of tradition are resolutely ahistorical, reproducing the linked binaries of premodern/modern and stasis/change central to the Western conception of modernity that achieved a kind of apotheosis in post–World War II

2. Eric J. Hobsbawm and Terence O. Ranger, eds., *The Invention of Tradition* (Cambridge: Cambridge University Press, 1983).

3. Anthony Giddens, *Modernity and Self-Identity* (Stanford: Stanford University Press, 1991), 3.

4. Edward Shils, *Tradition* (Chicago: University of Chicago Press, 1981), 24.

modernization theory.[5] Yet scholars who would reject out of hand the notion of timeless culture and a static past have often failed to problematize the historicity of tradition, for the normative status and repetitive practice of invented traditions powerfully naturalize them. Thus the provocative title of Hobsbawm's volume, and especially the lead essay by Hugh Trevor-Roper debunking the Scottish highland tradition, served as a wake-up call.[6] The timing was just right. The broad movement across the humanities to deconstruct culture had just been launched, and Hobsbawm's ironic representation of tradition as invention made an important fact unmistakably clear: tradition is not the sum of *actual* past practices that have perdured into the present; rather, tradition is as a modern trope, a prescriptive representation of socially desirable (or sometimes undesirable) institutions and ideas thought to have been handed down from generation to generation.[7]

The choice of the subtitle of this project, "Invented Traditions of Modern Japan," explicitly acknowledges our intellectual debt to the conceptual model developed in Hobsbawm and Ranger, which mandates skepticism with regard to the historical claims of tradition. Nevertheless, a word of caution is in order. "The invention of tradition," rather like the now-ubiquitous concept of "imagined communities," is both the title of a well-known book whose thesis broke new intellectual ground and a mobile and elastic concept, captured in a seductive title phrase, which has been adopted, used, and criticized, sometimes without close attention to the specificity of the original concept. Because the contributors to this volume both borrow from and revise Hobsbawm's conception of the invention of tradition, a short sketch of its salient features is useful.

In the introduction to *The Invention of Tradition*, Hobsbawm lays out a rigorous sociological definition of tradition (practically identical to Shils's) in which invariance is the salient characteristic.[8] Hobsbawm does this in order to distinguish invented tradition, which he identifies with superstructural institutions and elites, from custom, which he conceives as popular and capable of being mobilized by groups at society's base. Drawing out the contrast, Hobsbawm argues that while traditions impose fixed practices, custom is flexible, capable of accommodating a certain amount of innovation while still providing the sanction of "precedent, social continuity and natural law as expressed in history." Accordingly, in a world

---

5. See, for example, Robert A. Scalapino, "Ideology and Modernization: The Japanese Case," in David E. Apter, ed., *Ideology and Its Discontents* (London: Free Press of Glencoe, 1964), esp. 97–100.

6. Hugh Trevor-Roper, "The Invention of Tradition: The Highland Tradition of Scotland," in Hobsbawm and Ranger, *Invention*.

7. See also Jennifer Robertson, "It Takes a Village: Internationalization and Nostalgia in Postwar Japan," in this volume.

8. Dipesh Chakrabarty, "Afterword: Revisiting the Tradition/Modernity Binary," in this volume. Chakrabarty's insightful discussion singles out this feature of Hobsbawm's model and explores the conceptual and epistemological difficulties it entails.

marked by constant change, the invention of tradition functions "to structure at least some parts of social life within it as unchanging and invariant." Finally, invented traditions are distinguished from other (genuine?) traditions by the fact that continuity with a historical past "is largely fictitious."[9]

A frequent criticism of the concept of the invention of tradition is that *all* traditions are (and always have been) socially constructed, and hence in some sense invented. The invention of tradition, in this view, at best restates something everyone should already know, and at worst improperly denies the possibility of authentic tradition by collapsing the distinction between (legitimate) agency and artifice. A second and related criticism of the model arises from the dichotomy drawn between tradition and custom. Tradition, unlike custom, is said to be rigid—and must be so since the intent, Hobsbawm insists, is to represent some part of modern life as unchanging. Speaking from the theoretical position of postcolonial studies, Dipesh Chakrabarty raises an important epistemological issue in the Afterword related to the attribution of invariance in Hobsbawm's model. The point I will pursue is different: the conspicuous disjuncture between the rhetorical aspect of tradition represented in the claim to invariance, and the continually shifting substantive aspect, which is institutionalized in practices and texts that are reorganized and reformulated over brief spans of time without apparent forfeiture of authority. This observation leads to a third and final criticism. The elite/popular typologizing of tradition/custom is useful only up to a point, especially when applied to cultural, rather than to political, traditions. It is true, of course, that most traditions are instituted and regulated by elites; in fact, it is exactly this feature that makes their study so revealing of how discourse is constituted in relation to social power in specific historical contexts. But even when elites make tradition "just as they please," the practices and ideas they authorize have a tendency to take on a life of their own. Traditions, like customs, are embedded in larger social structures that are continuously reshaped by the very forces of change endemic in capitalist modernity that they aim to arrest.[10]

Each of these points warrants further discussion, both to develop a better understanding of the uses and misuses of the invention of tradition, and to indicate with reference to specific cases how the concept is deployed by the contributors to this volume. I began by noting the common criticism of the invention of tradition, which is also the most sweeping, that the concept itself is theoretically naive since everyone should know by now that culture is socially constructed. What if anything, then, is gained by conjoining invention with tradition?

---

9. Eric Hobsbawm, "Introduction," in Hobsbawm and Ranger, *Invention*, 2. Hobsbawm is interested in the appearance of new or newly configured cultural practices that claim, or are accorded, the status of traditions. He does not develop criteria to differentiate "invented" from other traditions.

10. Arif Dirlik pointed out to me the similarity of this conception of tradition to Bourdieu's concept of *habitus*. Pierre Bourdieu, *The Logic of Practice* (Stanford: Stanford University Press, 1990), especially chap. 3, pp. 52–65.

The criticism misses the point. The primary value of the invention of tradition to the critical study of culture is heuristic rather than theoretical; it raises new and important historical questions concerning the formation of culture, even if it does not in the end produce criteria capable of sustaining a new, or rigorous, typology. Even if one were to assume (which would be foolish) common knowledge of the comparatively recent origins of most modern traditions, establishing the fact of their invention is only the first step. The significant findings will be historical and contextual. How, by whom, under what circumstances, and to what social and political effect are certain practices and ideas formulated, institutionalized, and propagated *as tradition?* Take, for example, the Japanese tradition of "weak legal consciousness," which is the subject of Frank Upham's essay.[11] It is instructive (perhaps even startling) to learn, as Upham argues in the first part of the essay, that before the modern era Japanese apparently demonstrated little cultural aversion to litigation as a means of resolving conflicts. More instructive, though, is his account of the historical process through which Japanese political elites produced what, after the fact, became the tradition of weak legal consciousness. Finally, he offers an analysis of the larger implications of successful invention. The *political* decision to channel dispute resolution away from courts, Upham argues, imposed on subsequent generations a "choice" of legal cultures, whose primary effect has been to restrict the latitude and initiative, not only of citizens as private actors but also of the judiciary, in the implementation of legislation, while increasing those of the bureaucracy and the executive branches of government.

There are potential pitfalls inherent in the problematic of the invention of tradition, however. When "invention" is narrowly construed as artifice, the possibility of a legitimate exercise of agency is erased, leaving only manipulation and mystification. Quite apart from producing boring history, such a reading entails real political costs. As Arif Dirlik recently noted in relation to the history making of indigenous peoples, a theoretical position that ignores the social conditions of the production and reception of invented traditions (and other tropes of identification) denies to marginal and oppressed populations legitimate recourse to the authority of the past in their ongoing struggle to fashion counterhegemonic cultural identities.[12] Though not as forcefully as Dirlik, Marilyn Ivy also expresses reservations in the introduction to her study of popular traditions of Japan's Tōno region with "the now common critique" that all tradition is invention. Ivy makes an important point: "To say that all tradition is invented is still to rely upon a choice between invention and authenticity, between fiction and reality, between discourse and history."[13]

11. Kawashima Takeyoshi introduced the phrase "weak legal consciousness" to characterize the presumed long-standing cultural aversion of Japanese to the formal legal processes. See Frank Upham, "Weak Legal Consciousness as Invented Tradition," in this volume.

12. Arif Dirlik, "The Past as Legacy and Project: Postcolonial Criticism in the Perspective of Indigenous Historicism," *American Indian Culture and Research Journal* 20, no. 2 (1996): 1–3.

13. Marilyn Ivy, *Discourses of the Vanishing: Modernity, Phantasm, Japan* (Chicago: University of Chicago Press, 1995), 21.

The essays in this volume take account of the double meaning of "invention," which the dictionary tells us signifies both imagination and contrivance, creation and deception.[14] Every tradition trades between these two poles; and if traditions are to retain their vitality under changing historical conditions, one can expect to find constant shifting and overlapping of signifying positions. Traditions of any duration are diastrophic rather than flat and unified; hence they function as multivalent and somewhat unstable cultural signifiers.

This aspect of the invention of tradition, which is not sufficiently recognized, is well illustrated in Itō Kimio's discussion of one of Japan's most celebrated traditions, *wa no seishin* ("the spirit of peace and harmony"). *Wa*, one hears repeated tirelessly, has regulated Japanese community life since the misty beginnings of Japanese civilization. The injunction "Harmony is to be valued" is indeed recorded in the first article of Prince Shōtoku's "Seventeen-Article Constitution," a foundational document dating to the seventh century. But as Itō shows, this famous precept has traversed a circuitous path in arriving at the present "traditional" meaning. Looking at shifts of meaning in the modern period alone, one sees that in Meiji (1868–1912) *wa no seishin* signified the ethical basis of the state and prescribed a hierarchical social order. Under the pressure of wartime mobilization in the 1930s and during the Pacific War, *wa*, Itō argues, first came to signify *communal* unity, as in the ubiquitous slogan "All People, One Mind." However, it was only in the radically altered political, social, and economic conditions of the postwar era that *wa no seishin* acquired its current meaning of cooperation among equals. Finally, as marvelously illustrated by the spatial ordering of the employees' faces in a bank's New Year's greeting card from the era of high economic growth (see fig. 1) the earlier hierarchical meanings of *wa* have not been completely erased but are partially retained in the spatial order.

It is not hard to explain why, despite the strong rhetorical claim to represent unchanging culture, the signifying functions of traditions turn out to be anything but invariant over time. Like other modern institutions, traditions are shaped by everything from capitalist markets to technological innovation in the ongoing process of incorporating and reorganizing new knowledge and information that Anthony Giddens usefully characterizes as "institutional reflexivity."[15] Formalized and strongly ideological, traditions are not, of course, as plastic as commodities of mass consumer capitalism. Adjustments are likely to be "sticky" rather than continuous and may provoke moments of resistance. Nevertheless, it would be difficult to differentiate tradition from custom solely on the basis of degree of substantive rigidity. Both appear to be remarkably flexible.

---

14. According to Gaurav Desai, "Invention is at once a process of taking and making." Desai, "The Invention of Invention," *Cultural Critique*, no. 24 (Spring 1993): 122.

15. Giddens, *Modernity*, 2.

The puzzle posed by modern traditions is the disjuncture between the rhetorical posture of invariance—the strong claim at the heart of every tradition to represent "time-honored" beliefs and practices—and their actual historicity. Why is it that startlingly recent origins, frequent "tailor[ing] and embellish[ing],"[16] and even shifting signifying functions, do not, as a rule, impair traditions' authenticity and authority? The essays in this volume reveal, but do not address, this paradox, which is deeply implicated in the related but separate problematic of public memory. Nevertheless, promoted by Dipesh Chakrabarty's well-warranted criticism of the neglect of affect, it is worth reconsidering, as one relevant example, the invented tradition of the *yokozuna*, the highest rank in sumo.

As Lee A. Thompson notes, authoritative histories of sumo date the origin of the *yokozuna* system to November 1789, when two wrestlers were allowed to perform a ring-entering ceremony wearing a white rope around the waist. This privilege continues today. Thompson argues, however, that the modern *yokozuna* is very much the product of the tournament champion system—a twentieth-century innovation that placed new emphasis on objective and quantifiable measures of sumo wrestlers' performance. Today the criteria for appointment to *yokozuna* rank, and the expectations for performance once promoted, bear faint resemblance to those of the historic institution. New rules have been added and a good deal of the ritual is new, including the archaizing gestures of the referee's costume and the Shinto-style roof suspended over the wrestling ring, which frame the spectacle. In less than a century the substantive aspect of the *yokozuna* tradition has been transformed. Nevertheless, the fact of slim continuity with the original practice has not undermined the status of the *yokozuna* as a powerful signifier of this "ancient" and uniquely Japanese tradition of physical prowess. Hence, the prospect of an American-born sumo wrestler meeting the existing requirements for promotion to *yokozuna* precipitated a moment of cultural crisis, which, Thompson argues, led to a tortured reformulating of the criteria for promotion.

The case of the *yokozuna* lends force to Chakrabarty's critical reminder—which applies to all of the essays—of the importance "of smelling, tasting and touching, of seeing and hearing," the sensory dimension of cultural practices such as traditions. Noting that "ideas acquire materiality through the history of bodily practices, they work not simply because they persuade through their logic," Chakrabarty warns against reducing memory to "the simple and conscious mental act. The past is embodied through a long process of the training of the senses." The *yokozuna* provides a particularly striking reminder of the importance of the performative aspect of invented traditions. Substantive continuity with the historic institution of the *yokozuna* may be slender. But the dignified ring-entering ceremony

16. The phrase is from Jocelyn Linnekan, "The Politics of Culture in the Pacific," in Jocelyn Linnekan and Lin Poyer, eds., *Cultural Identity and Ethnicity in the Pacific* (Honolulu: University of Hawaii Press, 1990), 161. Cited in Nicolas Thomas, "The Inversion of Tradition," *American Ethnologist* 19, no. 2 (May 1992): 213.

repeated each day at the opening of the senior division matches provides the audience with a convincing sensory spectacle of continuity with an "age-old" past.

The third point to be discussed in relation to invention of tradition is the complicated relationship of modern traditions to social power. Most (though not all) traditions are produced by elites, and some are consciously fashioned as instruments of control. This process is quite clear in the political sphere. In Japan as throughout the industrialized world, the rise of the nation-state in the late nineteenth century produced an outpouring of new national symbols and rites such as flags, anthems, and holidays, as well as new (e.g., public health) or reorganized (e.g., armed forces) state institutions that created and imposed their own discourses of social control. The idea of "the nation," after all, stands as the mega invented tradition of the modern era.

The essays in this volume examine developments *in the cultural sphere.* Here, too, one finds new traditions that served hegemonic interests. Several of these have already been introduced in other contexts. Perhaps the clearest example, however, is provided in Andrew Gordon's discussion of the tradition of Japanese-style management. In the 1890s industrialists opposed to factory legislation, Gordon pointedly observes, had to concoct the neologism *onjō-shugi* ("warm-heartedness") to give a name to the purportedly timeless Japanese custom of benevolent workshop relationships. Yet examination of even this clear-cut case of invention soon produces a complicated picture. Gordon's discussion, which does not stop with the fact of the invention at the turn of the century but follows its progress down to the bubble economy of the late 1980s, reveals sharp swings at the level of discourse. Not once but twice, managers' passionate insistence on preserving Japan's "beautiful customs" of workplace cooperation and harmony rapidly dissipated when it appeared that greater economic advantage was to be had by adopting Western models. Still, during the periods when *onjō-shugi* was out of favor, industrial elites were not able to remake the workplace; to a large degree, management was constrained by the normative, as well as the institutional, inertia of the discourse of Japanese-style management it had initiated.[17]

Inoue Shun's discussion of the modern martial arts tradition shows how easily the inventors of traditions lose control of their progeny. Kanō Jigorō, the founder of Kōdōkan judo on which the twentieth-century martial arts tradition is modeled, was an unapologetic rationalist committed to modernizing the techniques, mode of instruction, philosophy, and organization of the Tokugawa-era martial arts. A patriot, Kanō was not a narrow nationalist or a social conservative; he opened the Kōdōkan to women and worked hard to make judo an international sport. Yet with the rise of militarism in the 1930s and the ascendancy of a xenophobic ethos of Japanese exceptionalism, the idea of the martial arts Kanō had

---

17. See also Robert J. Smith, "The Cultural Context of the Japanese Political Economy," in S. Kumon and H. Rosovsky, eds., *The Political Economy of Japan* (Stanford: Stanford University Press, 1991), 3:17–19.

pioneered was reinvented by ultranationalists and promoted as a counterweight to Western values, with the express purpose of infusing Japan's burgeoning modern, and largely Western, sports culture with "Japanese spirit."

Up to this point I have primarily addressed conceptual issues related to the use of invention of tradition as a historical problematic with the aim of revising, and perhaps extending, the original model. Here my emphasis shifts from the model to several larger historical themes that emerge from the essays in this volume. The appearance and trajectories of new traditions are "important symptoms and therefore indicators" of larger social developments.[18] Constitutive of modern cultural formation, they also mirror modern society's anxieties, fissures, and ruptures. The discussion that follows is organized around two themes: the relationship of invented traditions to social conflict and to national identity.

Capitalism drives the production of new cultural practices, just as the nation-state mobilizes the production of modern political traditions. In Japan the beginnings of industrial capitalism can be dated to the last decade of the nineteenth century, consumer capitalism to the decade following World War I. The discourses of tradition analyzed in this volume are infused with anxiety over new, more sharply delineated and disturbing social divisions. Tenant militancy, rural impoverishment, industrial strikes, sprawling urban slums, periodic violent protests (culminating in the massive rice riots that swept through 368 cities, towns, and villages in the summer of 1918): these and other signs that capitalism was remaking the social landscape in new and frightening ways fueled deep apprehensions. Not surprisingly, new traditions attempted to contain these social divisions by imagining a society made whole.

One such discourse was the invented tradition of *kyōdōtai*, Japanese village community, whose origins Irwin Scheiner locates in the mid-nineteenth century and the development of capitalistic social relations in villages. Following the opening of major ports to unrestricted trade in 1859, a development that greatly stimulated farm by-employments and rural manufacture, villages increasingly became polarized between the poor (insecure wage-laborers and small holders) and the wealthy (rural manufactures, middlemen, moneylenders, and landlords). But the phenomenon of *yonaoshi* (world renewal) uprisings, Scheiner suggests, cannot be adequately grasped by Sasaki Junnosuke's influential theory of the revolutionary struggle of the "semi-proletariat." Scheiner argues, rather, that it should be seen as the attempt by the new rural poor to renegotiate the village, via "world renewal," as a community in which norms of mutuality and unity are enforced.

By the end of the nineteenth century, the transition to industrial capitalism increasingly accentuated the disparity between the rural and urban sectors and, at the same time, sharpened class divisions within both. The unevenness of capitalist development produced two overlapping but distinct discourses, which addressed

18. Hobsbawm and Ranger, *Invention*, 12.

(and refigured) the rural/urban divide: agrarianism (*nōhōnshugi*) and native ethnology (*minzokugaku*). Both reified the difference between country and city—though to quite different ends. Louise Young's essay on the still-born tradition of Manchurian colonization and my essay on the radical agrarianism of the Ibaragi Aikyōkai examine the bureaucratic and popular streams of agrarianism in the tumultuous interwar period. The former emanated from the highest levels of the bureaucracy and the latter from village-level activism bitterly critical of the central government, but both imagined the Japanese farm village as (the only) social space within Japan's capitalist modernity capable of transcending class divisions.

While to agrarianists of all stripes the relative poverty of the village was a sign of backwardness, a deplorable social condition that impelled spiritual and political mobilization, Yanagita Kunio and the native ethnology movement he founded *celebrated* cultural unevenness. As discussed in the essays of Hashimoto Mitsuru and H. D. Harootunian, Yanagita reacted to the social indeterminacy of capitalist modernization by constructing an imaginary folk (*jōmin*) and space (*chihō*) free of social division. Hashimoto argues that Yanagita, unable to go back in time to recover a unified "Japan," rendered the diachronic dimension of culture synchronically as center/periphery, thereby creating a space where the "true" Japan lived on. In Harootunian's striking formulation, Yanagita, Orikuchi Shinobu, and legions of followers "searched out practices they believed predated modernity and constructed an imaginary folk, complete, coherent, and unchanging in lives governed by immutable custom." Many scholars read Yanagita as a critic of capitalist modernity, which in some sense he was. But Harootunian's analysis shows that despite a rhetorical opposition, native ethnology actually worked to stabilize capitalism by offering the *appearance* of an alternative to capitalist modernity.

Strenuous denial by capitalists of conflict in Japan's new factories was, of course, the principal impetus to the invention of the discourse (and later the practice) of Japanese-style management. But anxiety over class also appeared in other, more unlikely places. Jordan Sand's analysis of the invention of "home" in the late Meiji period primarily revolves around the gendering of domestic space but also reveals the insecurity of Japan's nascent middle class hemmed in by the masses of new urban poor on one side, and on the other by the still culturally influential aristocracy of birth. The discourse and architectural practices that promoted the new progressive ideal of the intimate conjugal family (which quite quickly became established as "traditional") was part of a broader effort to make middle-class values normative of "Japan." Thus, one such reformer at the turn of the century insisted, against all evidence, that Japan was "65 percent middle class."

The second theme that emerges with great clarity is the role of new traditions in the formation of Japanese national identity. Japan specialists, at least, now recognize that below the level of the politically active samurai and wealthy peasant classes (and even here one must speak in qualified terms), Japan did not enter the modern era with a strong or unified sense of national identity.[19] Despite a comparatively high degree of common ethnicity, language, material culture, and religious practice, in Japan no less than in the newly formed nation-states of Europe and America, a sense of "being Japanese" developed after, rather than before, the building of the modern state. Following the first phase of economic, social, and cultural modernization, which ended in the late 1880s, the oligarchy launched a broad effort to push the imperial institution to the forefront of the people's consciousness. Drafted at the highest levels of government, such celebrated texts as the Preamble to the 1889 Meiji Constitution and the 1890 Imperial Rescript on Education made unbroken dynastic succession the cornerstone of the family-state ideology. Their success, Carol Gluck has shown, is partly explained by the fact that provincial officials and local notables played a key role in interpreting and disseminating the "modern myths" of a continuous emperor-centered polity.[20] More recently, Takashi Fujitani has expanded our understanding of the mechanisms of imperial myth making by focusing on "material vehicles of meaning" such as national ceremonies, holidays, emblems, and monuments, which created "a memory of an emperor-centered national past that, ironically, . . . had never been known."[21] Fujitani extends his analysis to "a torrent of policies" regulating everything from hair styles to hygiene, which "aimed at bringing the common people into a highly disciplined national community and a unified and totalizing culture."[22]

Yet it is important to remember that instilling a consciousness of being imperial subjects was only part of the process of (mis)using history to create a cohesive Japanese identity. The process involved—in fact it required—the wide circulation of common practices that claimed to represent continuous and stable culture. In other words, "tradition" contributed to the formation of national identity though the ideological function of collapsing time and reifying space. Troping new or newly configured cultural practices as tradition removed these practices from historical time. They were read back into the undifferentiated time of "the Japanese past," to be recuperated not merely as values and practices that had withstood the test of time, but as signs of a distinct and unified Japanese culture.

19. Marilyn Ivy, citing Naoki Sakai, *Voices of the Past: The Status of Language in Eighteenth-Century Discourse* (Ithaca: Cornell University Press, 1991), writes, "It is arguable that there was no discursively unified notion of the 'Japanese' before the eighteenth century, and that the articulation of a unified Japanese ethnos with the 'nation' to produce 'Japanese culture' is entirely *modern*" (*Discourses*, 4). Mariko Tamanoi notes that Western theorists of the nation-state such as Benedict Anderson and Ernest Gellner tend to assume Japan's ethnic and cultural homogeneity prior to modernization (*Politics and Poetics of Rural Women in Modern Japan: Making of a National Subject* [Honolulu: University of Hawaii Press, 1998]).

20. Carol Gluck, *Japan's Modern Myths: Ideology in the Late Meiji Period* (Princeton: Princeton University Press, 1985).

21. T[akashi] Fujitani, *Splendid Monarchy: Power and Pageantry in Modern Japan* (Berkeley and Los Angeles: University of California Press, 1996), 11.

22. Ibid.

I am not suggesting that the historical past played no role in the formation of modern Japanese identity. None of the "traditional" cultural practices we have discussed was cut from whole cloth; rather, as in the case of the invention of the modern emperor system, cultural traditions were fashioned from both material and discursive antecedents. Even in the clearest cases of instrumental and self-interested invention—that is, the discourse of industrial paternalism—the capitalists who coined the neologism *onjō-shugi* did not invent the concept of *onjō*, an old and celebrated norm whose prescriptive meaning was widely understood.[23] The point, rather, is that cultural traditions are "chosen," not inherited.[24] Fabrication enters when the rhetoric of Japanese "tradition" functions to deny the historicity of cultural production; when it authorizes communalism and cultural particularism while obscuring the "strategic" character of the process through which the past enters the present.[25]

Yanagita Kunio's native ethnology is not only an immensely influential tradition in its own right, as demonstrated by its followers. As Hashimoto Mitsuru shows, Yanagita invented *the tradition* of Japanese tradition by claiming that Japan's preservation of its original culture made Japan unique among modern nations. Countries of the West, Yanagita argued, were disconnected from their past; in Japan, however, tradition lived on in the latent but ubiquitous world of the "abiding folk." Citing James George Frazer's classic study *The Golden Bough*, Yanagita boasted that only in Japan, where traditional culture lived on, was it possible to have "nation-specific folklore studies" (*ikkoku minzokugaku*).[26]

Like the invention of the "abiding folk," Yanagita's remarkable assertion that Japan alone had achieved modernity without cutting itself off from its original culture has meaning only as the assertion of an ideological position. Nevertheless, it draws attention to the specificity of the historical conditions of Japanese modernity. Unlike most of Asia, the Middle East, and Africa, Japan was never colonized; infringement on Japanese sovereignty through the "unequal treaty system" was largely limited to the commercial sphere. Its retention of sovereignty, in turn, accelerated political, social, and economic modernization, creating the material basis for new forms of cultural production, including "tradition," which appeared only after modernization was well under way. More directly, sovereignty ensured that Japanese elites (rather than colonial administrators) did the inventing. The result: in Japan the invention of tradition furthered the national project of modernization. Here Japan presents a striking contrast with India, where "the British were . . . implicated in the production of those very components of Indian tradition that have in postcolonial times been seen as the principal impediments to full-

23. Cf. Smith, "Cultural Context," 17–19.

24. The very useful concept of "choosing a tradition" is taken from Upham, "Weak Legal Consciousness."

25. Andrew E. Barshay, "'Doubly Cruel': Marxism and the Presence of the Past in Japanese Capitalism," in this volume.

26. Hashimoto Mitsuru, "*Chihō*: Yanagita Kunio's 'Japan,'" in this volume. See also Ivy, *Discourses*, especially 66–97.

scale modernity."[27] Simply put, Itō Hirobumi, the principal architect of Japan's modernization project in the latter part of the nineteenth century, enjoyed a luxury denied to Jawaharlal Nehru more than a half century later. Nehru, because of the powerful, prior Orientalizing of precolonial Indian culture by the British, had to find evidence of modernity in Indian tradition; for example, he went to pains to argue the "scientific temper and approach" of Indian thought.[28] Itō, Andrew Barshay tellingly observes, had the freedom to look upon Japan's "feudal" legacy as an "enormous historical opportunity" for promoting, for example, "the bond between patron and *protégé*" in Japan's modern factories.

The strategic use of tradition did in fact further the state's modernization project. The discourses of "the spirit of peace and harmony" and industrial benevolence are only the most obvious examples, but there were others. Kären Wigen analyzes the forging of a shared, primordial "Shinano" identity among residents of the newly drawn prefecture of Nagano. The invention of regional identities in Meiji, she suggests, played a critical role in extracting financial sacrifices from prefectural residents by giving them an affective stake in the progress of their prefecture.

It is sobering to discover how broadly the notion of Japan's particularity was shared. It invaded, and partially disarmed, even oppositional discourse. Andrew Barshay's analysis of prewar Marxist historiography shows how Yamada Moritarō's seminal text, *Nihon shihonshugi bunseki* (Analysis of Japanese capitalism) (1934), inadvertently participated in the discourse of a unique Japanese modernity. Outraged by the social costs and imperialist agenda of the forced march to "national wealth and power," Yamada hinged his analysis of Japanese capitalism on "semi-feudal" land tenure in Japan's villages and the "serf-like" regime of workers in Japan's dual-structure manufacturing sector. Yamada's text, Barshay argues, forged "an iron link" between discourses of Japanese particularism and historical backwardness whose influence extended far beyond Marxist circles.[29] On this point, at least, the Marxists converged with Japanese-style management: both asserted that capitalism in Japan was sui generis because the core consisted of premodern values and social relations. By constructing tradition at the heart of Japanese capitalism, the preeminent sign of modernity, Yamada unwittingly joined his intellectual enemies in fashioning the myth that capitalism in Japan wasn't really capitalism after all because of the strength of Japan's tradition. Despite enormous intellectual achievement and moral passion, Barshay concludes, Yamada's analysis "missed the invented—and *strategic*—character of the process" through which "tradition" entered the present.

---

27. Nicholas B. Dirks, "History as a Sign of the Modern," *Public Culture* 2, no. 2 (Spring 1990): 28.

28. Ibid., 27

29. Barshay, "'Doubly Cruel.'" It should be pointed out that Marxism was obviously anything but normative in the prewar period. But in the postwar period the *Kōza* school of historical economics wielded great influence, at least until the 1970s, in intellectual circles, in the labor movement, and within the left political parties. In this sense, one can speak of Yamada as having invented a tradition.

Traditions, I noted early on, are normative and establish themselves through repetition. Two essays on gendered cultural practices of the prewar period suggest that tradition is amenable to reform but not to radical change. Jordan Sand analyzes the new gendering of domestic urban space initiated in the late Meiji period by social reformers and middle-class professionals. Focusing equally on architecture and ideology, Sand traces the evolution of the concept of *katei*, a neologism for home / home life, from its origins in nineteenth-century Japanese Protestant reformers' moral criticism of "feudal" family life, to the point where it became a societal norm. A great deal had to be invented: for example, architectural innovations such as the interior corridor (*nakarōka*), which divided interior residential space into separate spheres, and the short-legged dining table (*chabudai*) which introduced the common dining table into the Japanese house and made it possible for the family to eat together. While conservative state ideologues wrote the patriarchal family into the Meiji Civil Code, a more democratic, affect-centered family prevailed in the redesigning of actual living space. What became the iconic (and today nostalgic) image of the "traditional" Japanese family—consanguine members seated on *tatami* and gathered around the *chabudai* to share tea or a meal—in fact originated in turn-of-the-century discourses of architectural and social reform, which drew heavily from the West.

In the decade following World War I, Japanese capitalism entered a new stage, characterized by the explosive growth of modern media technologies, mass marketing of items of personal consumption, and new forms of entertainment and pleasure seeking. The stylish *moga* (modern girl) of the 1920s represented bourgeois women's challenge to established gender norms. As Miriam Silverberg argues, the cafe, where rural and urban lower class young women sought employment as waitresses, created a narrow but new social space for the renegotiation of gender relations. But while the cafe and the cafe waitress drew from a long history of female sex workers in food service occupations, the social indeterminacy of the cafe waitress, whose role allowed seduction to go both ways, posed too radical a challenge to gender norms. First restricted, and finally prohibited, in the period of wartime mobilization, the culture of the cafe and cafe waitress, Silverberg claims, died out. It never became a tradition.

In Jennifer Robertson's critical analysis, contemporary *furusato-zukuri* (native place-making) represents more than a nostalgia for rootedness and wholesome living associated with the farm village. Robertson argues that the affective pull of *furusato-zukuri*, especially to the males who engineer these projects, resides in the equation of *furusato* with mother, as illustrated in the quite amazing statement of the director of the 1983 movie *Furusato*: "*Furusato* is the ancestral land [*sokoku*]. My/our [*waga*] ancestral land is Japan, it is Gifu prefecture, it is Saigō village, it is the village's subsection [*aza*] . . . , it is [my] household, it is mother." This association, Robertson suggests, points to the recuperative aspect of native place-making in the paternalistic attempt to reconstruct an authentic, ontologically secure representation of stable gender relations in the much less certain present.

I noted that tradition is used in two distinct, though overlapping senses: on the one hand, "the past" against which the modern is measured and on the other, specific cultural practices believed to represent cultural continuity. The Edo period (1600–1867), Carol Gluck argues, has functioned since early Meiji as the invented past in relation to which Japan's modernity defined itself. Identified as "tradition," Edo was to Meiji Japan what the *ancien régime* was to revolutionary France: a historical imaginary that evoked the past to get to the future. The original invention of Edo occurred in the late nineteenth century, when commentators conceived the national project in terms of a telos of progress on an East-West axis and made Edo the obverse of the Meiji vision. They mapped Edo using tropes like feudalism, the cultural and economic energies of commoner society, the era of great peace, and *sakoku,* "a closed country." Depending on the vision of modernity, images of Edo sometimes affirmed and sometimes opposed the direction of the Meiji state. Whatever the initial political and social valence of the tropes, they constituted an allegedly indigenous tradition. In every case, from the anti-Edo of the fascist 1930s to the rose-colored Edo of the postmodern 1980s, the period is constructed as the mirror image of a particular modern future.

A final point concerns the ideological modalities of the invention of tradition. One of the interesting issues that Chakrabarty raises in his Afterword concerns the tropes of temporality and affect. Addressing the articles on Yanagita Kunio by H. D. Harootunian and Hashimoto Mitsuru, he distinguishes two modes of temporality in Yanagita's writing: "nostalgic" and "epiphanic." The nostalgic mode corresponds to the familiar sense of belatedness in invented traditions, the ideological construction of a past that must be recovered by adherence to practices of quite recent origin. However, the epiphanic mode rejects the figure of loss and recovery. It escapes from historical time and constructs a vision of eternity, a "modern nationalist epiphany" produced by a performative agency resistant to state institutions. Citing the examples of Mahatma Gandhi and Rabindranath Tagore, and carefully noting that "the shadows of both capitalism and the nation-state fall much more heavily and lengthily on our discussion of Japanese history" than in South Asian studies, Chakrabarty argues against the notion that the romantic/aesthetic nationalism leads inexorably to statist and jingoist fascism.

Certainly not everywhere at all times, and probably not again in Japan. The changes in domestic and world political economy since the Pacific War have been epochal, and historical coordinates are always decisive. The evidence of the essays in this volume is sobering, however. In the 1930s and during the Pacific War only Marxism, with all its modernist baggage, held its ground as an oppositional discourse. Judo, harmony, industrial paternalism, folklore studies, "home": these and the other new cultural practices of the prewar period either actively collaborated with militarism and imperialism or were severely compromised by not resisting. The subject of my essay, the populist strain of agrarianism, is illustrative in this respect. I characterize the social imagination of Tachibana Kōzaburō and Aikyōkai as romantic and utopian— epiphanic, in Chakrabarty's formulation. In its populist phase—that is, prior to Tachibana involvement in the Incident of May 15, 1932—the rhetoric of the Aikyōkai was neither nostalgic nor jingoistic, suggesting that utopia posits new social relations in imaginary political space. But

Tachibana held this posture only as long as his politics remained local. When he superimposed the ideology of native place on the nation, he allied with fascist elements in the military. H. D. Harootunian's analysis of Yanagita's representation of the Japanese folk is similar—and equally bleak. "Yanagita was never able to sufficiently differentiate the native place from the boundaries fixed by the state; his communitarian discourse was never able to articulate a sufficiently different narrative from that other place—from the outside—that might lastingly challenge the state's capacity to appropriate whatever version it wished to project as its own." In the end, Harootunian concludes, Yanagita's project of native ethnology supplied ideological support to imperial and colonial policies.[30]

The case of India may suffice to show that romantic/aesthetic nationalism need not end up in fascism, and there surely are others. But this observation only confirms the potential peril of the rush in historical studies toward a history of subjectivities—particularly if the subject position comes to occupy so much of the historical frame that powerful historically determined structures such as the nation, state, capitalism, and the world systems to which they are inextricably linked fade out of the picture. It *was* different in Japan between the turn of the century and the Pacific War. To varying degrees but with discouragingly few exceptions even outside the political sphere, invented traditions aided—or did little to obstruct—the mobilization of Japanese affective identification with a pernicious vision of the modern nation-state whose demise as a consequence of defeat in the Pacific War was the only welcome consequence of that historic tragedy.

Nevertheless, it would be wrong to view the invented traditions of modern Japan only in terms of the ultimate failure in the prewar period to establish intellectual and cultural autonomy from the state. One also sees many examples of creative responses by ordinary people who resisted the norms and values that conservative elites and the state sought to impose. Upham shows how the Burakumin of Hozu village turned the state-sanctioned norm of cooperation and the mechanisms of informal dispute resolution to their advantage in winning restitution of their ancestors' property. Gordon observes that Japanese workers have taken the grant of "warm-hearted" labor-management relations to resist changes inimical to their interests. Sand shows how the ideal of the emotionally bonded residential family promoted by social reformers and given material expression by progressive architects compromised the coldly hierarchical and patriarchal *ie* family system beloved by conservative ideologues. Finally, Scheiner shows that notions of community have remained a conflicted discourse in the postwar period. These are only a few examples of the significance of individual agency in cultural production. They are all the more meaningful in light of the unrelenting efforts of conservative social forces to monopolize the invention of tradition.[31]

30. H.D. Harootunian, "Figuring the Folk," in this volume.
31. Irwin Scheiner contributed to the writing of the final paragraph.

PART ONE

Harmony

TWO

The Invention
of Japanese-Style Labor Management

Andrew Gordon

The idea that labor-management relations in Japan were based on unique social traditions appeared almost simultaneously with the advent of modern industry. Oddly enough, although members of Japan's industrial elite declared that traditions of mutual respect between superior and subordinate were ancient "beautiful customs" that made factory life in Japan unique, when they pinned general descriptive labels on these practices they turned to clumsy neologisms: *kazoku-shugi*, or "family-ism," and *onjō-shugi*, often translated "paternalism" but literally "warmheartedness-ism."[1] That capitalists had to use invented words to describe reputedly ancient customs is a good sign that we are in the presence of hastily invented ideas about a "traditional" social practice.

The invention of industrial paternalism in Japan was a dynamic process that has continued for a full century, and ideas about unique traditions of management have been articulated in uneven fashion. Japan's rulers first claimed that the nation's factories were exceptional sites of warm-hearted social relations in the 1890s. Over the following century, moments in which capitalists and bureaucrats vigorously affirmed the value and vibrance of distinctly Japanese traditions of managing work have alternated with times in which they presented industrial paternalism as part of a dying past and denied its efficacy or even its existence. Events such as mobilization for war, sudden defeat, unexpected economic "miracles," or the sudden bursting of economic "bubbles" marked sharp breaks in the dominant modes of discussing industrial relations; across these breaks, elements of the invented tradition of industrial relations were recast and reassembled. This essay seeks to describe and explain the protean character and durability of the discourse on Japanese-style management.

---

1. On the origins of the terms *onjō-shugi* and *kazoku-shugi*, see Hazama Hiroshi, *Nihon no rōmu kanri shi kenkyū* (Tokyo: Ochanomizu Shobō, 1978), 45–46, nn. 1 and 2.

An alternative approach to this topic would be to analyze the invented tradition of labor management as a social practice. With varying degrees of detachment or irony, many observers have noted the presence of "three sacred jewels" in the institutional arrangement of Japanese workplaces: long-term (or "lifetime") employment, seniority-based wages, and factory- or enterprise-based unions. How, one might ask, did these practices come into existence? I have written on the social history of these practices at length, arguing that systems of management in Japan most resembled those in the more advanced factories of Europe or North America during the early days of Japan's industrial revolution.[2] Over a contentious century in which workers resisted managerial innovations or appropriated and inverted them, one can identify several discrete though related systems of labor-management relations, marked by varying degrees of job and wage security and shifting forms of factory-based unionism. Some of these practices have been, and remain, quite distinctive when compared to systems elsewhere.

But my concern in this essay is with the ideological dimension of this topic, primarily because the tradition of Japanese management was invented first as a discursive structure. In particular, I will consider the way in which concepts of so-called traditional, paternalistic, or Japanese-style management were discussed among owners, managers, and people outside the firm.[3] The threats of a factory law in the early twentieth century and of a trade union law in the 1920s, the mobilization for the hot war of the 1930s and 1940s, and the trade wars of the 1980s and 1990s, have provoked voluminous public discussions, attacks, and defenses of Japanese industry that reveal to us how traditions were invented, denied, and then reconfigured. Looking at cases where Meiji-era capitalists argued in defense of their "beautiful traditions" of management against state intrusion, or where postwar professors of business administration earnestly explained Japan's unique traditions to foreigners, helps us to understand the politics of invented traditions and offers some insight into why modernity "fabricates its 'past' even to the extent of inventing a contrived 'tradition.' "[4]

INDUSTRIAL PATERNALISM INVENTED: THE FACTORY LAW DEBATE

The pioneering sociologist of Japan Ronald Dore pointed out several decades ago that some of Japan's modernizing elites were proudly and improbably boasting of

2. Andrew Gordon, *The Evolution of Labor Relations in Japan: Heavy Industry, 1853–1955* (Cambridge, Mass.: Harvard Council on East Asian Studies, 1985).

3. Neither dialogue between workers and their bosses within the firm nor the social practice of labor management in the factory is central to this inquiry. Our focus is on "Japanese-style management" as a discursive practice rather than a social one. Yet the relationship between these two realms of practice is important, and I will address it briefly in conclusion.

4. Hashimoto Mitsuru, "Kindai Nihon ni okeru dentō no hatsumei shinpojiumu," *Soshioroji* 37, no. 1 (May 1992): 65.

the nation's unique, traditional management practices as early as the 1890s. He examined a series of discussions among bureaucrats, politicians, and business leaders in the mid-1890s that asked whether Japan needed a law to ameliorate factory conditions. The first of these took place at a conference of bureaucrats, politicians, and business leaders convened in 1896, and this initial round of debate on worker protection and paternalism continued for fifteen years, until passage of a factory law in 1911.[5]

In these early debates, businessmen dismissed the idea of factory legislation with contempt. Textile industrialists were among the most vociferous, for a factory law banning night work for female or child labor would have restricted their operations and cut off a critical source of workers. But industrialists in all sectors joined the chorus condemning a law as they articulated a powerful collective plea: Japan possessed time-honored "beautiful customs" (*bifū*) of obedience and loyalty from below matched by sympathetic understanding from above that would suffice to solve problems such as resistance to factory discipline, low morale, or poor health. A law, by contrast, would legally sanction the interests of workers, thereby undermining the emotional basis of the old, integrated social order. As they made this claim, they invented the notion that warm-hearted paternal relations rooted in pre-Meiji society pervaded modern industry as well.

One of several eloquent spokesmen for this view was Shōda Heigorō, for many years director of the Mitsubishi Shipyard in Nagasaki, the nation's largest. In a magazine column published in 1910 he offers a succinct summary of the paternalistic ideology of Japan's first-generation managerial elite:

> Since ancient times, Japan has possessed the beautiful custom of master-servant relations based firmly on a spirit of sacrifice and compassion, a custom not seen in the many other countries of the world. Even with the recent progress in transportation, the development of ideas about rights, the expansion of markets, and the growing scale of industrial society, this master-servant relationship persists securely. It is not weak like that of the Western nations but has its roots in our family system and will persist as long as that system exists. Because of this relationship, the employer loves the employee and the employee respects his master. Interdependent and helping each other, the two preserve industrial peace. . . . Today, there exist no evils and we feel no necessity [for a factory law]. We cannot agree to something that will destroy the beautiful custom of master-servant relations and wreak havoc on our industrial peace.[6]

Bureaucrats were not convinced. They viewed paternalism as a dying tradition, not a vibrant one. They argued that capitalists were motivated by profits, not

5. Ronald P. Dore, "The Modernizer as a Special Case: Japanese Factory Legislation, 1882–1922," *Comparative Studies in Society and History* 11, no. 4 (October 1969).

6. Shōda Heigorō, "Kōjōhō seitei no riyū ikan," *Tōyō keizai shinpō*, March 5, 1910; cited in Sumiya Mikio, "Kōjō hō taisei to rōshi kankei," in Sumiya Mikio, ed., *Nihon rōshi kankei shi ron* (Tokyo: Tōkyō Daigaku Shuppankai, 1977), 26.

love for employees. Thus, Oka Minoru, chief of the Industrial Bureau of the Ministry of Agriculture and Commerce and the most active proponent of the law, worried that inadequate facilities and overwork would cause excessive rates of turnover inimical to the interests of the industrialists themselves.[7] Soeda Juichi, a high-ranking Finance Ministry official and important backer of a law, made it clear at the 1896 conference that the goodwill of the Japanese people as a whole did not mean the nation possessed a viable tradition of labor-management relations:

> We cannot find security in the fact that our nation's people are rich in compassion. If the state does not take some slight role in employer-employee relations, there will be no way to protect the interests of the employed, and as a result there will be increasing cases of social illness, disturbance, and struggle.

In precocious fashion, he went on to raise the specter of a British disease:

> If we leave things as they are today, we will see a process producing extreme social illness much like the one that befell England at the beginning of this century. . . . We will have unavoidable problems ending in social evils such as strikes. . . . My fervent hope is that we can solve this problem before it develops and save ourselves from the disease of the advanced countries of Europe.[8]

Soeda here presented Japan as a modernizing nation on a course no different from any other, where traditions of the old order were dying inevitably and a new legal system was needed to build a modern industrial order. With the passage of a rather watered-down factory law in 1911 (the law would not take effect until 1916, and the key provisions banning night work for women were deferred until 1926), his argument had seemingly prevailed.

But if the bureaucrats won a political battle, capitalists such as Shōda won the ideological war. The bureaucratic view of "traditional" management practice moved sharply in the direction of the business position. Rather than push factory legislation as a substitute for paternalism, as they had in the 1890s, state bureaucrats by 1911 saw the law as compatible with, or a condition for, the survival of "beautiful customs" of paternalism. Together with opponents of the law, they now defended paternalism as a progressive concept that took the best of Japan's past and applied it to insure an economically and socially healthy future. Finance official Soeda offers the best example of this shift. In 1896 he had found no solace in the "compassion" of his countrymen, so he had called for a law. In 1907 he supported a factory law as before, but he saw it as a complement to a living tradition, not a replacement for a dying one.

> The old, beautiful customs existing in Japan are concepts of mutual love and respect from employer and employee. This master-servant relationship is not an evil feudal

---

7. Oka Minoru, *Kōjō hōan no setsumei* (1910), cited in Sumiya Mikio, "Kōjōhō taisei to rōshi kankei," in Sumiya Mikio, ed., *Nihon rōshi kankei shi ron* (Tokyo: Tōkyō Daigaku Shuppankai, 1977), 7.

8. Obama Ritoku, ed., *Meiji bunka shiryō sōsho* (Tokyo: Kazama Shobō, 1961), 1:38, 55.

remnant but a benefit gained from feudalism. Will not these beautiful customs, namely compassion from above for those below, and respect from below for those above, be greatly helpful in harmonizing labor-capital relations?[9]

Thus, by the eve of World War I, Japanese government, business, and intellectual elites had accepted the idea that Japan possessed a unique tradition of paternalistic management of labor, based on "warm master-servant relations" and reinforced by law. They agreed this "tradition" would be a key to heading off the social ills of industrialization before these erupted as a full-blown social disorder. To be sure, they formed no consensus on the particular social practices that would define this relationship; in this sense, warm-hearted management was a rhetorical device of little substance.[10] Yet they did agree on the basic virtue of "traditional" management. More than an ability to produce profit, they saw the essence of Japanese-style management as a capacity to insure a harmonious social order, more or less hierarchical in different renditions, which would avoid or contain conflict.

INDUSTRIAL PATERNALISM FORGOTTEN?—
THE UNION LAW DEBATE

Soeda's newly found respect for the power of beautiful traditions to inoculate Japan against European infections already stood on shaky grounds the day he stated it at the first annual meeting of the Social Policy Association in December 1907. This body convened at the end of a year that saw more strikes than ever in Japan's history, and just ten months after the nation's most tumultuous labor protest ever, the three-day riot at the Ashio copper mine.[11] Events in Japanese workplaces, villages, and city streets of the next two decades made state officials unwilling to accept, and capitalists unable to sustain, the illusion that Japan possessed a stable tradition of labor-capital relations. Especially after the nationwide rice riots of 1918, a new surge of strikes in 1919, the increasing formation of unions, the founding of the Japan Communist Party in 1922, and a brief flowering of anarchism in the early 1920s, few bureaucrats or politicians any longer extolled the efficacy of warm-hearted managerial care for workers.

In these years state officials and party politicians only rarely argued that native traditions supported by Western-style laws would suffice to prevent labor-capital

---

9. Shakai Seisaku Gakkai, ed., *Kōjōhō to rōdō mondai* (1908), 96, cited in Hazama, *Nihon rōmu*, 52–53. Soeda made this statement at the first annual meeting of the newly founded Social Policy Association (Shakai Seisaku Gakkai), modeled on the German body of the same name (Verein für Sozialpolitik). The theme of the meeting was "The Factory Bill and the Labor Question," and the gathering served as an important moment in the development of the consensus described here.

10. Gordon, *Evolution*, chaps. 2–3.

11. On numbers of disputes, see Rōdō Undō Shiryō Iinkai, ed., *Nihon rōdō undō shiryō* (Tokyo: Chuō Kōron Jigyō Shuppan, 1959), 10:440–41. On the Ashio dispute, see Nimura Kazuo, *Ashio bōdō no shiteki kenkyū* (Tokyo: Tōkyō Daigaku Shuppankai, 1986). Trans. as *The Ashio Copper Mine Dispute* (Durham: Duke University Press, 1997).

conflict; in the twenty years after round one (roughly 1890–1911) of the discourse on "beautiful customs" in the workplace, they claimed instead that Japan faced problems common to the advanced West and would need to explore common solutions as well. Public discussion and policy-making on labor issues in these years focused on the virtues or defects of numerous Western models, implicitly or explicitly nontraditional ones. These included a health insurance law (passed in 1922, effective 1927), a revised factory law (1923, 1926), and a labor disputes conciliation law (1926). But the most important and controversial item on the public agenda was a law to recognize (and regulate) labor unions. Between 1920 and 1931, nine drafts of such a law were presented to the Imperial Diet, although no law was ever enacted.[12] The 1931 bill actually passed the lower house of the Diet but was killed in the House of Peers.

Although the Ministry of Agriculture and Commerce introduced one bill in 1920, the most energetic official proponents of social legislation in the 1920s were bureaucrats in the Home Ministry, especially those in its new Social Bureau. Allied to these men were politicians in the Kenseikai/Minseitō party. Harking back to the rhetoric of the earliest official calls for a factory law, some thirty years before, these advocates lamented the absence of a viable tradition of labor management, admitting that in Japan, as in the West, "the rapid growth of the so-called labor movement by which workers organize themselves to assert their interests is, in fact, a natural economic trend."[13] In the face of such global trends, most bureaucrats agreed that recognizing and nurturing "healthy" moderate unions would insure social harmony. Even the home minister of the Seiyūkai party from 1919 to 1922, Tokonami Takejirō, among the most reluctant to grant any sort of rights to workers, admitted that the development of unions was a "natural" trend, in Japan as elsewhere. His practical solution, and that of his subordinates, was to look away from native traditions and build on British, German, or American institutions such as works councils and shop committees to promote cooperative "vertical unions."[14]

Also in sharp contrast to the first round of debate on the social problem in industry, numerous businessmen were ready to recognize labor unions. A survey of Osaka factory owners conducted in 1919 counted 132 men who favored recognition of unions, 17 who felt the time was too soon, and just 12 entirely opposed. Two important business federations, the Osaka Industrial Association and the

---

12. Sheldon Garon, *The State and Labor in Modern Japan* (Berkeley and Los Angeles: University of California Press, 1987), appendix 5, pp. 254–55, describes eight of these. Miwa Ryōichi, "Rōdō kumiai hō seitei mondai no rekishiteki ichi," in Andō Yoshio, ed., *Ryōdaisenkan no Nihon shihonshugi,* (Tokyo, Tōkyō Daigaku Shuppankai, 1979), 242–43, lists nine (including one from the Social Masses Party).

13. Garon, *State and Labor*, 68, cites this 1922 Kenseikai party endorsement of a union bill.

14. Nishinarita Yutaka, *Kindai Nihon rōshi kankei shi no kenkyū* (Tokyo: Tōkyō Daigaku Shuppankai, 1988), 243, for Tokonami's view of unions as a "natural development." Garon, *State and Labor*, 53–54, on his use of Western models.

Tokyo Federation of Business Associations, issued calls for the recognition of horizontal labor unions and state creation of a body to mediate labor-capital disputes in statements that breathed not a word about traditional customs of mutual affection.[15] These two bodies primarily represented owners of small-to-medium-sized firms, a fact that itself supports the view that industrial paternalism was an invented tradition. That is, to the extent that paternalism evolved in some organic fashion out of practices and ideas of the past, one would expect it to be more vibrant among precisely these men, the less-educated owners of small firms, who lived in close quarters with workers recruited through friends and relatives. Yet it was more often the managers of huge enterprises, who had experienced Western-style university education and overseas travel and possessed a sense of themselves as the modernizing pioneers of the nation, who sang the praises of Japanese tradition in the factory.

Thus many capitalists, especially executives in zaibatsu firms, resisted these foreign-inspired initiatives in the 1920s, as they had opposed passage of the factory law before 1911 and continued to oppose its full implementation. But even their opposition was now conditional, not absolute. Their statements against social legislation contained none of the confident bombast of earlier paeans to Japan's "beautiful customs" as practices that made any law superfluous. Rather, the idea that Japan might possess "traditions" to guide managers appears only in an undertone of concern to insure that "if there is truly a need for a labor union law in Japan today [1925] . . . it should be a magnificent Japanese-style law that is truly appropriate to our country."[16] Especially in debates over the various union bills proposed between 1920 and 1926, the Japan Industrial Club and the nation's most powerful businessmen most typically claimed either that a union bill was premature (rather than unthinkable) or that a modified bill "appropriate to our nation's feelings" was acceptable.[17]

Such claims are intriguing. What did these men mean by a law "appropriate" to Japan? The Japan Industrial Club argued in 1925 that an acceptable law must allow civil suits against unions for damage incurred in disputes, could not contain sanctions against discriminatory dismissals, and must not recognize a closed shop. To this extent, "appropriate" had nothing to do with tradition; it simply meant a weak law appropriate to allow a purportedly fragile economy to develop. But at the same time, as capitalists brandished opaque references to "our nation's feelings" (kokujō) or "magnificent Japanese-style" legislation in order to protect their privilege, a notion lurked beneath the surface of their rhetoric that

15. Nishinarita, *Rōshi kankei shi*, 255, on the Osaka survey; pp. 254–56, for statements in favor of recognizing unions.

16. Nishinarita, *Rōshi kankei shi*, 270, cites Mitani Jūni, chairman of Mitsubishi Mining Corporation.

17. The expression was *jikoku no kokujō ni teki suru*, made by the Japan Industrial Club, drawing on language of the Versailles Peace Treaty. Nishinarita, *Rōshi kankei shi*, 269.

Japan possessed native traditions that must be respected by any law. While few bureaucrats any longer affirmed this view, and although business claims were more muted than those made during the factory law debate, this idea—that Japan's social traditions were relevant to industrial life—appears to have been submerged but not banished from public discussion of social policy and labor-capital relations. In the debate over social legislation of the 1920s, the view that Japan's modernity partook of a global character that made unions and a union law inevitable was entwined with a suggestion by some capitalists that the nation's industry was somehow anchored in unique native "feelings."

In a similarly complex way, when businessmen and some bureaucrats proposed *alternatives* to social legislation, they modeled these on Western practices but sometimes repackaged or represented the alternatives as traditional. The best example of such a maneuver is offered by the energetic Home Ministry bureaucrat and politician Tokonami Takejirō. As noted above, Tokonami quite purposefully and consciously derived his proposals for "vertical unions" and works councils from Western models, but he cloaked them in the nativist rhetoric of a masterful inventor of tradition. He argued that "we should not thoughtlessly imitate the examples of foreign nations" because in contrast to the West "we have special ideals based on the conditions of our country." In the West "the boundary between capitalist and worker is a broad line, drawn horizontally to separate the higher and lower strata," while Japan possessed "a spirit of cooperation and harmony that pervades the unit of work in a vertical fashion."[18]

Tokonami's rhetoric was unusual among the social policy bureaucrats, most of whom doubted that native traditions had much to offer the modern capitalist. The notion that Japan possessed a living tradition of organizing the social and economic life of the industrial workplace was invented in the 1890s and 1900s and then partially eclipsed in the 'teens and 1920s. Some businessmen hinted that such traditions might exist, but like Tokonami they put most of their energy into searching for usable models abroad, in the welfare capitalism of the United States or the workplace councils of Britain and Germany.[19] And in the final round of debate over a union law in 1930–31, during a newly unprecedented round of labor-capital confrontation in numerous industries, the eclipse was nearly total. Unlike both the factory law debates before 1911 and the union law discussions of 1919 through the mid-1920s, one finds barely a word on "beautiful customs" or "national feelings" in the extensive parliamentary debates on this law.[20]

---

18. Tokonami's ideas and policies are thoroughly described in Garon, *State and Labor*, 50–54. He cites the quote of Tokonami's position in Watanabe Tōru, "Nihon ni okeru rōdō kumiai hōan no tōjō o megutte," pt. 1, *Nihon rōdō kyōkai zasshi*, no. 87 (June 1966): 4, in turn citing *Ōsaka asahi shinbun* (December 30, 1918).

19. Nishinarita, *Rōshi kankei shi*, 271.

20. Nihon Gisei Kyōkai, *Nihon gikai shi* (Tokyo: Nihon Gisei Kyōkai, 1953), 10:448–66, 11:768–77.

PATERNALISM REVIVED:
THE INDUSTRIAL PATRIOTIC SERVICE MOVEMENT

The eclipse passed in 1931. The following fifteen years saw the reaffirmation of an acclaimed "traditional" Japanese labor-management relationship. This was articulated for public consumption in the debates over a retirement and severance pay law, enacted in 1936, and over the Industrial Patriotic Service Movement (Sangyō Hōkokukai, abbreviated below as Sanpō) from 1937 onward. In many ways, these debates represent a return to the consensus reached among bureaucrats and businessmen with passage of the factory law in 1911. The two parties differed in their sense of urgency but agreed on their ultimate objective: they would use a law, or a state-sponsored campaign, to bolster "traditional" industrial relations.

The retirement and severance pay law was explicitly conceived as a "Japanese-style" alternative to unemployment insurance. In contrast to the latter, described by Home Ministry officials as too much a "translation" of Western social policy, bureaucrats felt a law requiring firms to give lump sum severance or retirement benefits, already a fairly common practice in large companies, would play a critical role in defending and improving vital Japanese traditions of industrial paternalism.[21] Businessmen were dubious at first. The nation's major business federation dealing with labor issues, Zensanren, strongly opposed early drafts of the law in 1935 on grounds that it would "destroy Japan's unique beautiful customs" of master-servant relations.[22] But Zensanren eventually accepted the proposal as "appropriate Japanese-style" legislation. Its defensive declaration in the wake of the failed coup of February 26, 1936, reveals the cautious shift in its position:

> In our country, thanks to our country's unique industrial spirit, we have traditional labor-capital relations based on intimate feelings, and we must do all we can to nurture these. . . . [But] in cases where it appears difficult to solve problems of the healthy development of industry together with the increased welfare of employees through our own endeavors and group solidarity and cooperation, we will cooperate gladly to realize appropriate social legislation.[23]

Here we see the powerful return of a claim that "our country," a phrase repeated twice in the same sentence lest anyone miss the point, possessed unique "traditional labor-capital relations."

The Industrial Patriotic Service Movement began the following year. The Sanpō program eventually created a pyramid of workplace, regional, and national councils

---

21. For a more extended discussion of this law, see Andrew Gordon, "Business and the Corporate State: The Business Lobby and Bureaucrats, 1911–1941," in William D. Wray, ed., *Managing Industrial Enterprise: Cases from Japan's Prewar Experience* (Cambridge, Mass.: Harvard Council on East Asian Studies, 1989), 66–68.

22. Ōhara Shakai Mondai Kenkyūjo (Ohara Institute for Social Research), ed., *Nihon rōdō nenkan* (1937), 408.

23. Ibid., 379–80.

of employees intended to meet regularly to build trust among workers and their managers, raise morale, and boost the war economy. Leading advocates had traveled to Germany in the 1930s to seek new ideas for social policies. They carefully modeled their project on the Nazi Labor Front (DAF), but they rarely mentioned this ideologically inconvenient fact. Rather, the Welfare Ministry's official "prospectus for the Industrial Patriotic Movement" of November 1939 claimed that Sanpō would resolve labor-capital problems by "constructing Japanese-style enterprises in which the true form of Japanese industry would be manifest." Yet this same manifesto, with its frequent use (so common in all public discussion of these years) of terms such as "construct" and "reorganize" reflects a state belief that it must recast (reinvent) traditional Japaneseness in a new state-centered mold. The next sentence of this manifesto essentially admits that "Japaneseness" in the workplace was not easily or organically emerging from past traditions. Rather, Sanpō must both "eliminate the evil capitalist ideas that make profit an absolute value and overcome the evil of Marxism that exalts the manual laborer, by perfecting the true spirit of our imperial nation's industry."[24]

In the half-century from the 1890s through World War II, the idea that Japan possessed unique and usable traditions of industrial management had become deeply rooted and widespread, a discursive tool available to varied users for diverse ends, from businessmen resisting state intrusion, to bureaucrats trying to insure social order as they mobilized for war, to workers demanding material confirmation of the bosses' paternalistic solicitude. Much of the power of this idea came from its malleability. As first described in the 1890s, this tradition was a fundamentally hierarchical "master-servant" relationship. In the wake of intense social protest at home and revolution in Russia, Tokonami's notion of "special ideals" appropriate to Japan was ever-so-slightly less hierarchical; he claimed that factories were sites of "cooperation," albeit implemented "in a vertical fashion." Then, in the late 1930s, bureaucrats restated the relationship between bosses and workers with more egalitarian metaphors: "two wheels of a cart, two wings of a bird."[25] Across eras of affirmation and denial, concepts of warm-hearted paternalism or national feelings serving the cause of social order were reassembled in new contexts.

OVERCOMING TRADITION: FEUDAL PATERNALISM DENIED

Since the end of World War II, two views have alternately dominated the way Japanese publicly discuss their "traditional" industrial management. One vision, pervasive from 1945 through the 1960s and resurgent in very recent years, recognizes that "traditional" labor management exists but casts it as an obstacle to be overcome. In the early postwar years this perspective, common among business

---

24. Ōhara Shakai Mondai Kenkyūjo, ed., *Nihon rōdō nenkan* (1940), 382–83.
25. Ōtsubo Yasuo of the Home Ministry's Police Bureau, quoted in *Shakai undō ōrai* (December 1933): 15.

leaders as well as intellectuals, state officials, and leaders of the newly legitimized union movement, was a more forceful statement of the Western-inspired reformism of the 1910s and 1920s. The other view, which came into its own in the 1970s and 1980s, presents Japanese tradition in the workplace as something valuable and viable, to be preserved, developed, and even exported.

The decades from the occupation era through the 1960s witnessed a feverish drive to "modernize" Japan's labor relations on an American model; much of the business establishment as well as the state spoke of paternalism as an impediment to modernization. To be sure, a few stubborn guardians of the old order never abandoned their conviction that Japan's warm-hearted traditions were a viable basis upon which to rebuild the industrial economy. Inoue Jutoku, a personnel manager at the Nippon Kōkan (NKK) steel works from the 1930s through 1960, still held this view in a 1992 interview. With utmost conviction, he asserted that NKK viewed itself as "one big family" (kōkan ikka) and that his mission was to insure a good working environment for employees, whom he regarded as kin. All his initiatives as manager stemmed from this belief, he said, and most all the workers, "except of course the ideological ones," appreciated his efforts.[26] In this view both conflict and modern or foreign institutions such as unions are rendered as destructive intrusions.

But Inoue did not represent mainstream managerial opinion, especially in the 1950s and 1960s. Orii Hyūga, his younger subordinate and rival in the NKK personnel division, was a Western-oriented graduate of the law faculty at Tokyo Imperial University and a thoughtful spokesman for the early postwar consensus. He insisted that Japan must overcome its feudal past, including its practice of labor management, by adopting the "enlightened" human relations techniques of American industrial sociologists. Writing in a 1954 publication of Japan's new postwar business federation, Nikkeiren, whose primary concern was labor policy, Orii offered this succinct appraisal of his place (and that of Inoue) in the history of labor management in his country:

> It is said that "it used to be possible to get one's way by shouting, but today we must win understanding from the heart."... Let us examine the transformations of the fundamental principles of those in charge of labor management or personnel management. Long ago there was an era of so-called authoritarianism, when we constrained workers with penalties and regulations, and motivated them to raise productivity by making them fear dismissal or punishment. Next, the mode of warm-hearted paternalism (onjō-shugi) was implemented. And recently the methods of industrial psychology or the fruits of labor physiology research have been applied in labor management in order to ameliorate the difficulties imposed on workers in the process of rationalization.[27]

26. Author's interview with Inoue Jutoku, August 28, 1992.

27. Orii Hyūga, "Jyūgyōin no kaisha ni tai suru ittaikan wa ika ni shite takameru ka," in Nihon Keizai Dantai Renmei, ed., *Rōshi kyōryoku o meguru shomondai* (Tokyo, 1954), 100–101.

Written in the passive voice, this statement obscures the identity and location of the agents who "implemented" these modes. Possibly Orii means to say that the trajectory from authoritarian to paternal to modern management is a global one. But his essay is addressed to "those of us [in Japan] in charge of labor management," and it draws a clear contrast between implicitly indigenous "authoritarian" and "paternal" modes and explicitly foreign, new departures of the 1950s that were imported from the United States. Operating on the principle that "data is all," Orii engaged the American-trained sociologist Odaka Kunio to carry out a pioneering series of social surveys of NKK workers' attitudes, and he used these as the basis for NKK labor policies of the 1950s and 1960s.[28] In addition to such managers at individual firms, powerful organizations such as the Japan Productivity Center, the Japan Union of Scientists and Engineers, and Nikkeiren all looked to America in these years, as they sought to replace purportedly inefficient, feudal practices with modern, rational labor management. And indeed, American practices of quality control, wage determination, grievance procedures, and the overall framework of so-called "business unionism" had a major impact on postwar managerial practice in Japan.

JAPAN AS NO. 1 AND THE REINVENTION OF TRADITION

While most managers and a growing number of conservative labor leaders were intent on learning from the American masters of mass production in the 1950s and 1960s, the workplace social practices that they developed over these decades were distinctive. A new Japanese system of labor-capital relations emerged through a process of learning from abroad and bitter conflict between unions and companies at home.[29] As this happened, and as the pupil seemed to be outshining the teacher, many people in Japan decided their "miraculous" postwar growth was neither an illusion nor a fragile blossom and reversed once more the dominant rendition of tradition. Among managers, among foreign observers, and among some intellectuals, the belief that Japan's "traditional" labor relations were outmoded simply evaporated. The new social practices—quality control circles, union-company consultation and cooperation, or flexible deployment of workers—were largely foreign-inspired and the product of turbulent confrontation. But as confidence in the efficacy of these practices increased, ideas about unique Japanese institutions of management rooted in harmonious native traditions were reassembled yet again, with one important difference. Spokesmen now not only

28. Orii Hyūga, *Rōmu kanri nijūnen: Nippon kōkan ni miru sengo Nihon no rōmu kanri* (Tokyo: Tōyō Keizai Shinpōsha, 1973), describes the surveys and related policies in detail.

29. For an overview, see "Contests for the Workplace," in Andrew Gordon, ed., *Postwar Japan as History* (Berkeley and Los Angeles: University of California Press, 1993). A more detailed account of this process in the 1950s at NKK is in Andrew Gordon, *The Wages of Affluence* (Cambridge: Harvard University Press, 1998).

claimed that Japan should preserve and improve its "traditions" of labor management; they began to promote their export.

We can trace the emergence of such views in the pages of a number of new English-language publications of the high-growth era and beyond. In these journals, Japanese establishment figures explained and justified themselves to the outside world. But as many of these articles were originally published in major Japanese magazines, they reflect the character of domestic discussion as well.

One early example can be found in Toyota's public relations journal in 1972. The author is relatively cautious in his judgment, noting that "until recently" the "dominant view" of Japanese scholars was that Japan had modernized in a deviant, incomplete fashion. He demurs from celebrating traditional Japanese managerial practice: "I agree with the people who believe that the Western form of modernization is not universally applicable, especially in view of the impasse that Western industrialism has come to. But I disagree with scholars who over-evaluate the Japanese experience."[30] Even so, he goes on to argue that "the Japanese management approach, by contrast, is more human [than Western individualism or Social Darwinism]. In this country a subordinate is treated not as a peon but as if he were a member of his superior's family. I do not mean to suggest that the Japanese paternalistic system does not have disadvantages as well as advantages, however, and there is much room for doubting whether or not the humanity Japanese managers display is genuine."[31] But finally he abandons restraint: "To a Japanese worker, his relationship with his company is not merely one association among many he might have. His company is his community, even his family. . . . Corporate feudalism and the resultant fierce competition among companies is behind the awesome spirit that made Japan's postwar economic growth possible."[32]

As this reevaluation of "feudal" traditions gained momentum, it co-existed for a time with the earlier postwar view that "feudal" traditions were impediments to economic success that had to be overcome. But around the end of the 1970s, such critical appraisals lost ground dramatically to the celebratory onslaught. One sociologist who analyzed this shift wrote in 1980 that "a consensus appears to be emerging affirming the unique vitality and adaptability of Japanese corporations, a view point that is taking hold throughout Japan regardless of how these corporate strengths are understood and explained and irrespective of the depth of comprehension and the phraseology."[33]

One ambitious 1980 statement of this consensus is offered by Takeuchi Hiroshi, a director of the Long-Term Credit Bank of Japan and the author of several books,

30. Yoshimatsu Aonuma, "The Japanese Corporation: Its Structure and Dynamics," *The Wheel Extended: A Toyota Quarterly Review* 2, no. 2 (1972): 3.

31. Ibid.

32. Ibid., 7.

33. Imai Ken'ichi, "Hard Work Is Not Enough," *Japan Echo* 7, no. 2 (1980): 35. Trans. from *Kikan Chūō Kōron* (Spring 1980).

including *The True Face of the Arab Oil-Producing States* and *Japan's Economic Flexibility*. He anchors the economic dynamism of contemporary Japanese society securely in traditions of the Tokugawa era, supposedly articulated in the late 1700s by the economic thinker Satō Nobuhiro:

> Many Westerners wonder what drives the Japanese employees of today to work so hard that they forget to eat and sleep. As is apparent from the passage from Nobuhiro's pamphlet paraphrased above, methods for encouraging employees to work hard had been thought out 200 years ago and seem to have been actually put into practice. Nobuhiro's management theory as outlined here differs not at all from present day management principles.[34]

Among the similarities Takeuchi finds between Satō's manual and the "present day" is the egalitarian pay scale: "Also similar to today is the fact that there is little difference between pay for the white-collar workers and the blue-collar workers. As is well known, Japan's pay scale is the most egalitarian in the world. . . . Nobuhiro's pay scale, which was created in Japan 200 years ago, is far more egalitarian than the pay scales seen in industrialized nations other than Japan today."[35]

By the mid-1980s, declarations elevating Japan's traditional mode of management to the status of a universal, thus exportable, model, were common. One grand, almost euphoric statement came from Itami Hiroyuki, a professor of management at Hitotsubashi University. He wrote, "I believe that the time has come for those concerned with Japan's long-term prosperity to consider seriously the feasibility of exporting certain elements of Japanese civilization that have resulted in Japan's leadership in the production of goods—most notably, its corporate system."[36] Where did these elements come from? Clearly, from something conceived of as "traditional," as we learn indirectly when Itami answers an imagined skeptic who objects that a social form specific to the unique tradition of one culture cannot be exported. He counters that the resulting system is founded on underlying principles that have universal validity, even though "traditional patterns of Japanese culture have played a role in the evolution of Japanese-style management."[37] In the same year (1986), the eminent sage of Japanese-style quality control, Karatsu Hajime, made a similar claim. "I believe that the results of Japan's experimentation [in industrial management] should be disseminated throughout the world. . . . More fundamentally, Japan should offer a positive challenge to the Cartesian assumptions underlying Western business methods."[38]

---

34. Takeuchi Hiroshi, "Satō Nobuhiro, Father of Japanese-Style Management Principles," *Japan Echo* 7, no. 4 (1980): 48. Trans. from *Shokun!* (October 1980).

35. Ibid., 49.

36. Itami Hiroyuki, "The Humanistic Corporation—An Exportable Concept?" *Japan Echo* 12, no. 4 (1986): 57. Trans. and abridged from "Bunmei o yushutsu suru toki," *Asuteion* (Autumn 1986).

37. Ibid., 59.

38. Karatsu Hajime, "Japanese Know-how for American Industry," *Japan Echo* 13, no. 4 (1986): 64. Trans. from "Beikoku keizai no hatan" (The collapse of the American economy), *Voice* (October 1986). Note the sharp change in title for the English version.

OVERCOMING "TRADITION" ONCE MORE?

For a historian it is dangerous and uncomfortable to discover the beginning of a new long-term trend in events of five years ago. But it seems clear that an era in which many voices confidently promoted a Japanese style of management (*Nihongata keiei*) rooted in traditional social values, even informed by a unique non-Cartesian mode of thinking, ended with Japanese responses to unceasing international criticism and the prolonged recession of the early 1990s. A key moment in this turn came in February 1992, when Morita Akio, co-founder and (at the time) chairman of Sony corporation, drew international attention with an essay titled "Japanese-Style Management in Danger."[39] In this rather complex piece, Morita argued that Japanese management had been too successful for its own good and needed to temper its relentless drive for markets over profits by carrying out a "fundamental change in corporate behavior."[40] At first glance, this was not a simple call to overhaul practices described as "traditional." Morita noted that "Japanese corporate management created the lifetime employment system in the postwar period, and based upon this, it also created fate-sharing management practices."[41] But his rhetoric, this final phrase in particular, inevitably linked his views to the discourse of invented traditions. The term "fate-sharing" is fundamentally identified in Japan with prewar and wartime images of Japanese society as a harmonious "community of fate," in which managers and workers were commonly likened to "two wheels of a cart, two wings of a bird" in their functional and organic interdependence.[42]

Morita and others who have echoed his tune are claiming that practices invented in the early postwar era, now imbued with an aura of traditional Japaneseness, are no longer appropriate. Basic change in corporate behavior, Morita concluded with a flourish, "cannot be achieved without a thorough reform of the entire Japanese social and economic system."[43] Such a position recalls the stance common in the interwar years or the early postwar decades, when many observers saw traditions of paternalistic management as something to be replaced or rejected. But the framing of Morita's call for reform also holds within it the inevitable

---

39. Morita Akio, "A Critical Moment in Japanese Style Management," *Japan Echo* 19, no. 2 (Summer 1992). Trans. from "Nihon gata keiei ga abunai," *Bungei shunjū* (February 1992). Quotes are from the translation.

40. Ibid., 14.

41. Ibid. His claim that the Japanese system of labor management was created in the postwar era is no afterthought. He makes the same statement on p. 11 as well: "The lifetime employment system in Japanese corporate society, which was created as a consequence of the postwar liberalization of Japanese labor practices by the Occupation authorities, brought about a tremendous reform of the Japanese management system. A fate-sharing consensus between management and employees emerged from the lifetime employment system."

42. For example, this phrase was used by the Home Ministry police official Ōtsubo Yasuo, writing in *Shakai undō ōrai* (December 1933): 15, on the need for social policy that would support a Japanese-style system of industrial relations.

43. Morita, "Critical Moment," 14.

promise that when future observers identify the next new Japanese system, they will anchor this, too, in some notion of tradition and Japaneseness.

CONCLUSIONS

As of the 1990s, talk about Japanese-style labor management had a varied history of about one century. One rather obvious conclusion to be drawn from these discussions is that invented traditions of industrial relations, from notions of a "beautiful custom of master-servant relations," through calls for social legislation "appropriate to our nation's feelings," to recent praise for uniquely efficient "Japanese-style management" have been articulated in specific historical contexts as sticks to beat upon political opponents. Once articulated, the idea that unique ancient social traditions were manifest in modern labor-capital relations has proved both malleable and durable, functioning in diverse ways in response to fluctuating political dynamics. In the prewar and wartime years, capitalists and bureaucrats, in particular, flailed each other by invoking tradition, either to protect business from legal regulation or to justify such intervention. And from an early point, these debates were engaged in an international environment as well, beginning when Japanese elites sought to fend off application of the conventions of the International Labor Organization in the 1920s.[44] More recently, spokesmen for Japan made claims for uniquely Japanese habits of mind and business practice to defend themselves in a context of trade wars and chronic political friction with the United States and Europe. To return to a question raised at the outset, one reason why modernity fabricated its past to the extent of inventing traditions resides in the power of such "traditions" to legitimate the endeavors of those who initiate, support, and gain from "modern" projects.

But something in addition to political convenience explains why people kept coming back to restate and reassemble this particular, transparently invented tradition. Why, for example, did Soeda Juichi so easily surrender his initial position that Japan's traditional compassion would be useless in the modern era? Why did Tokonami Takejirō, in promoting works councils in 1920, and later bureaucrats who pushed the wartime labor front in the late 1930s feel the need to disguise these Western-inspired programs in a cloak of ancient Japaneseness? An alternative would have been to justify their position or program by proudly presenting their Japan as a nation in the modernizing, universalistic vanguard, be it a form of liberalism in the 1910s–1920s or fascism in the 1930s, but these men shied away from such logic. Why? I think the answer lies in the ambivalent response of so many people, in Japan and elsewhere, to that which we call "modern." From the

---

44. Iwao F. Ayusawa, *A History of Labor in Modern Japan* (Honolulu: East-West Center Press, 1946), 127–235, discusses the efforts of bureaucrats and businessmen to avoid compliance with ILO requirements, in part by appealing to the special situation of Japanese industry.

moment they apprehended a "modern" condition in their midst, the people introduced in this essay anxiously identified it with the decay of social order. These people did not usually reject modernity outright, for they saw it as a source of power, wealth, or even welfare. But insofar as they also viewed (or still view) the modern as a carrier of social disease or disorder, they responded by reinforcing, reconfiguring, or simply fabricating what they defined as their "tradition."

This said, it remains to revisit briefly two further questions. What is the relation between the "rhetoric" of tradition and the "reality" of practice within companies, between invented tradition as a discursive practice and a social one? And what have those inside the organization—the workers described as "servants" in the early rounds of paternal discourse—made of this tradition-mongering?

Certainly we cannot take pious elite declarations about beautiful customs of reciprocal commitment as reliable indicators of social relations at work. For one thing, social practices are sticky; they could not have fluctuated as wildly as the prevailing attitudes did toward "traditional" or "Japanese-style" systems of management. But simply to dismiss the rhetoric of tradition as "unrealistic"—the self-serving concoctions of self-interested elites—is of limited value in understanding the relationship between what people said and what they did.

Once an ideology of traditional labor-capital relations had been articulated, the "reality" of the experience of workers as well as that of owners, managers, or bureaucrats willy-nilly included making sense of this ideology and responding to it. This does not mean workers accepted claims of paternal solicitude at face value. At times they sharply attacked the emptiness of the rhetoric of "beautiful customs." Japan's so-called worker representative to the ILO in 1919, Masumoto Uhei (in fact a managing engineer selected by the government), quite frankly acknowledged that "workers view the shipyard as a place that, even if it provides work, by no means does so with the workers' interests at heart."[45] But workers who scorned paternalism as empty talk were obviously aware of the claims made on its behalf. Whether calculated lies or sincere solicitude, the pronouncements of men such as Mutō Sanji of the Kanebō textile mill, Shōda Heigorō at the Mitsubishi Shipyard, and their many like-speaking colleagues in the early twentieth century constituted a critical part of the ideological environment inhabited by mill girls and lathe workers.[46]

What, then, did these workers make of such messages? In the years before and during World War II, their most important response was to appropriate and manipulate or invert the language of paternalism or Japaneseness to the ends of winning improved treatment by superiors, enhanced job security, more stable wages, and greater respect as human beings. For example, a union activist at the

45. Masumoto Uhei, *Kokka no shōrai to rōmu kanri no hyōjun* (Tokyo: Waseda Daigaku Shuppankai, 1923), 47. For background on Masumoto's selection as ILO representative, see Garon, *State and Labor*, 44.

46. On Mutō Sanji, the designer of Kanegafuchi Textile Company's (Kanebō) paternalistic system of management, see Hazama, *Nihon rōmu*, 48–49, 307–17.

Shibaura Engineering Works (forerunner of Tōshiba) in 1923 wrote in his union's magazine:

> One day, a supervisor got hold of me and asked whether I thought community life was important. "In order to live in this community, everyone must take responsibility. If you only do what you want, or freely do whatever comes to mind, we can't maintain a community." All this talk about community spirit is amusing. I can't recall ever voting for a foreman. . . . The motto here is supposedly, "We all eat from the same pot." Since none of us has ever shared a meal with any of the big shots, it's no wonder the message doesn't get across.[47]

While he scoffed at his supervisor's use of the adage about eating from a common pot, this man nonetheless implied that if the bosses were ever willing to respect workers by sharing a meal with them, the community message would find a sympathetic audience.

In postwar history, notions of Japanese traditions of mutual respect and harmony facilitated the accommodation that evolved from the 1950s through the 1970s between the right wing of the labor movement, business management, and the state. In ideological terms, this accommodation was founded on a consensus about the elements of a modernized Japanese style of "cooperative labor-capital relations." Unions are recognized in rhetoric as equal partners in a cooperative endeavor of production and shared benefits, a settlement accepted by many employees as a Japanese way of replacing an older paternalism in which workers had to accept what they were given.[48] Critics of this labor-capital accord have written with insight on the gap between the ideology of shared benefits under "Japanese-style" management and the reality of meager distribution of corporate profits to workers.[49] And the left wing of the labor movement has consistently refused to join the chorus that celebrates harmonious workplace life. But in the postwar history of worker interactions with employers, as in the prewar era, the invented and reconfigured concepts of cooperation and Japaneseness have been prominent features of the cultural landscape. In addition to framing Japanese explanations of their society directed at outsiders, they have informed union and employee self-conceptions that lead workers to accept their place inside the system.

47. *Shibaura rōdō* (April 1923): 7–8; related discussion on pp. 110, 119–21. Also, Thomas C. Smith, "The Right to Benevolence," in Smith, *Native Sources of Japanese Industrialization* (Berkeley and Los Angeles: University of California Press, 1988).

48. Yamamoto Kiyoshi, "Sasebo jūkō sōgi (1979–80)," in Yamamoto Kiyoshi, ed., *Nihon no rōdō sōgi, 1945–1980* (Tokyo: Tōkyō Daigaku Shuppankai, 1991), especially pp. 415–17, has an interesting discussion of a rare private-sector strike of the 1970s in large measure motivated by outrage among workers at the violation of this implicit agreement on what constituted "Japanese-style" labor-management cooperation.

49. Matsuzaki Tadashi, *Nihon tekkō sangyō bunseki* (Tokyo: Nihon hyōronsha, 1982), 164–75, describes the relatively limited benefits to employees in the steel industry's 1972 union-management agreement to "share profits" from productivity gains with workers.

THREE

The Invention of *Wa* and the Transformation of the Image of Prince Shōtoku in Modern Japan

Itō Kimio

I have long doubted the existence of Japanese collectivism as a historically transcendent cultural trait. Also, I have a long-standing personal interest in Prince Shōtoku and his image in Japanese society. The purpose of this paper is to reconsider the changing historical meaning of the spirit of *wa* (harmony) and Shōtoku's image together in relation to their symbolic function in the national integration of modern Japan.

Today *wa* is a ubiquitous signifier of Japanese collectivism. The character often appears on decorative scrolls and is explicitly cited in the management policies of many companies (see fig. 1). Anyone reading the word will recall the "Seventeen-Article Constitution" laid down by Prince Shōtoku (572–621), which, it is believed, evokes *wa* as a guiding principle. Yet despite these historical connotations, the spirit of *wa* associated with the name of Prince Shōtoku may in fact be a modern invention.

As developed by Eric Hobsbawm, the "invention of tradition" is closely related to the formation of modern nation-states.[1] I will interpret the invention of *wa* as a process through which members of the ruling class revised and reorganized part of Japan's ancient history into new symbols at a time when they faced the challenge of integrating the nation and inculcating a national consciousness. This paper proposes to think through the invention of tradition in modern Japan by viewing *wa* and the changing image of Prince Shōtoku through the lens of Hobsbawm's work.

The question of the modern nation-state has become a controversial issue recently, since the nation-state itself is in crisis. Following Benedict Anderson's *Imagined Communities*,[2] I will approach the nation-state from a cultural viewpoint and

---

1. Eric J. Hobsbawm and Terence O. Ranger, eds., *The Invention of Tradition* (Cambridge: Cambridge University Press, 1983).

2. Benedict R. Anderson, *Imagined Communities* (London: Verso, 1991).

will argue that modernization always involves the invention of new traditions to stabilize itself. Modernization and the invention of tradition proceed together in a nested relationship. There are many examples of this process in modern Japan's political development—for example, the image of the Meiji emperor and the modern imperial ideology that grew from it are invented traditions. I would also argue that, on a more quotidian level, *shichi-go-san* (the ritual celebrating children's reaching the age of seven, five, and three), the Shinto marriage ceremony, and indeed state Shinto itself are traditions that were invented after the beginning of the Meiji era.

First of all, let me cite some current examples of the spirit of *wa*. Takagiwa Hiroo variously describes *wa* as "a traditional practice of mutual assistance embedded in everyday life"; "freedom and equality in a community"; "a decision by consensus"; and "a nonidealistic and emotional tie."[3] These descriptions, I believe, are very close to what most Japanese think about *wa* today. Tamaki Koshirō says:

> *Wa* can be seen as a basic spirit regulating the way of life in a community. This spirit permeates our families, and our workplaces, not to mention our villages, cities, states, and today, the whole world. Needless to say, it is important to maintain *wa* in each of these communities. Today, maintaining world peace has become a basic condition for the survival of human beings. This fact reminds me that the spirit of *wa* advocated by Prince Shōtoku has never been so relevant to our world as today.[4]

This quotation exemplifies the prevailing sense of *wa*'s centrality among Japanese people today. Some even insist that this spirit is part of the Japanese genetic heritage. Below I will argue that, on the contrary, this spirit is an invented tradition and a product of modernity.

THE CHANGING IMAGE OF PRINCE SHŌTOKU IN STATE-DESIGNATED HISTORY TEXTBOOKS

School textbooks published in the Meiji era reveal subtle shifts in the positioning of *wa*. Because the Japanese ruling class was using these textbooks to construct a unified national consciousness, we can assume that they reflected the sanctioned ideas of each period.

The first textbook, *Shōgaku Nihon rekishi*, published in 1903, contains the following description:

> Prince Shōtoku was the child of Emperor Yōmei. He was a brilliant child, and as he became older, he made great progress in learning. Shōtoku became the crown

3. Takagiwa Hiroo, *Nihonjin ni totte wa to wa nani ka: Shūdan ni okeru chitsujo* (Saitama-ken, Niiza-shi: Shōgaku Kenkyūsha, 1987), 42, 46, 59, 83–84.

4. Tamaki Koshirō, "Shōtoku taishi to Nihon bukkyō," in Shitennooji Joshi Daigaku, ed., *Shōtoku taishi sangyō* (Osaka: Kangakuin, 1979), 65.

prince in the reign of Empress Suiko and dictated all the issues of the government . . . The prince also believed in Buddhism; he made great attempts to spread
the faith with his minister Soga no Umako (?—626), by ordering the construction
of a large number of temples and statues of Buddha. . . . Shōtoku also enacted the
Seventeen-Article Constitution and thus provided a moral basis to people of all
ranks.[5]

Here, although there is no mention of *wa*, the Seventeen-Article Constitution is
credited with establishing a common morality. *Jinjō shōgaku Nihon rekishi* of 1909
shows the beginning of a greater emphasis on Prince Shōtoku as a nationalist
figure:

Prince Shōtoku was a grandchild of Emperor Kimmei. . . . The prince adopted
some of the strengths of China for our benefit and enacted various new laws.
Among them, the Seventeen-Article Constitution is the most famous.[6]

The tendency, reflected in this passage, to emphasize Prince Shōtoku's nationalism was retained in later textbooks. The 1920 *Jinjō shōgaku kokushi* went one step
further. It preserved the sense of previous texts by noting that "the prince enacted
the Seventeen-Article Constitution and provided a moral basis to both bureaucrats and citizens," yet it added a new passage: "The prince of the country of the
rising sun wrote to the prince of the country of the setting sun. What a noble action!"[7]

The emphasis on Shōtoku's nationalism increased following Japan's occupation of Manchuria in 1931 and reflected Japan's growing feeling of superiority
over China. The 1934 edition of *Jinjō shōgaku kokushi*, for example, contained a description of the Seventeen-Article Constitution—"The prince enacted a moral
basis for all people, bureaucrats and commoners alike"—that is almost the same
as in previous textbooks. But it lavishly praised the prince's effort to renegotiate
Japan's relationship to China: "At that time, China was a powerful nation because
of its advanced learning. As such, it tended to be arrogant and dealt with other
nations as its colonies. But Prince Shōtoku was not in the least afraid of its
power."[8]

Even the *Shōgaku kokushi* of 1940 did not explicitly link Prince Shōtoku to *wa*.
Rather, it emphasized his role as a forceful leader: "The prince enacted the
Seventeen-Article Constitution and thus instructed his subjects." It also stressed the
role of Prince Shōtoku as a proponent of nationalism: "He showed how powerful
our nation was."[9] It was only after the onset of the Pacific War (1941–45) and mobilization for total war that Prince Shōtoku is depicted as instructing his country in

5. *Shōgaku Nihon rekishi* (Tokyo: Monbushō, 1903), 17–18.
6. *Jinjō shōgaku Nihon rekishi* (Tokyo: Monbushō, 1909), 17–18.
7. *Jinjō shōgaku kokushi* (Tokyo: Monbushō, 1920), 23.
8. *Jinjō shōgaku kokushi* (Tokyo: Monbushō, 1934), 25–26.
9. *Shōgaku kokushi* (Tokyo: Monbushō, 1940), 26, 27.

the importance of *wa*. The *Shotō-ka kokushi*, published in 1943, contains the following passage:

> Then the prince carefully instructed his subjects by enacting the Seventeen-Article Constitution. In this constitution, the prince gave the strict instructions: "If you are given a decree by the emperor, be sure to follow it"; "All people are subjects of the emperor. Rulers must not torment their people by taking willful actions." He also preached the importance of *wa* . . . [showing] his wish to bring peace to the people at court who were in conflict.[10]

This is the first appearance of *wa* in elementary Japanese history textbooks. The textbook also described Prince Shōtoku not as the founder of Japanese Buddhism but as an advocate of Shinto: "The prince ardently worshiped the gods [*kami*], following the example of the emperor. . . . At that time some people tended to slight the worship of the gods in favor of Buddhism, which came from abroad. . . . The prince examined Buddhism thoroughly and in promoting it, adjusted it to the special characteristics of our country."

Surprisingly, *wa*, which first appeared in 1943, survived in postwar textbooks. The last state textbook published in 1946, *Kuni no ayumi* contained the following description of Prince Shōtoku:

> Things had changed inside and outside the country. Seeing this, the prince thought of a way to improve the system of inherited offices, which emphasized family rank. He ordered the ranks so as to promote able people. Then the prince enacted the Seventeen-Article Constitution and preached its precepts to the officials. The Constitution began by teaching the importance of *wa*, which contained the message that people at Court should cooperate with one another in harmony. Further, the Constitution elaborated the moral principles of politics that men in power should not impose taxes arbitrarily on people; they should listen to the people and deal fairly in political matters; they should not decide important issues by themselves, but by consulting many people.[11]

These two state history textbooks, published in 1943 and 1946, both introduced *wa*—but their connotations differed considerably. The first stressed the importance of national integration under the emperor; the second conveyed a message of harmonious cooperation in re-creating Japan as a peaceful nation.

THE HISTORICAL
TRANSFORMATION OF THE IMAGE OF PRINCE SHŌTOKU

At most, textbooks provide signposts indicating shifts in the ideological terrain. We cannot conclude that the collectivist spirit of *wa* is a modern invention simply on the basis of elementary history textbooks. Therefore, I will trace the broader

10. *Shotō-ka kokushi* (Tokyo: Monbushō, 1943), 31.
11. *Kuni no ayumi* (Tokyo: Monbushō, 1946), 6–7.

historical development of the image of Prince Shōtoku and the spirit of *wa* in the Seventeen-Article Constitution. Here too we will find that the nexus between the prince and the spirit of *wa* is most distinct in the modern period.[12]

In the Nara period, the earliest "history" of Japan, *Nihon shoki* (720), described Prince Shōtoku as a saint. During this period, the image of the prince changed from a worshiper of Buddha to an object of religious worship himself. *Jōgū kōtaishi bosatsuden* (754) described the prince as a reincarnation of the Chinese prelate Nangaku Eshi, who succeeded the founder of Tendai Buddhism.[13] Another text, *Shichidai ki*, written in 771, introduced the theory that the prince was an incarnation of Buddha, who had transformed himself for the seventh time to become Prince Shōtoku.

In the Heian period, various books described the prince as a savior, the reincarnation of Kuze Kannon.[14] In Kamakura, after the Mongolian invasions of 1274 and 1281, veneration of the prince stressed his role as a prophet. Taishikō, a popular cult devoted to worshiping the prince, developed at this time among carpenters, plasterers, and stone craftsmen. Taishikō became quite active in the Edo period. Yet in the Edo period there was a countertrend, as some scholars severely criticized the prince for introducing Buddhism into Japan and accused him of being a disloyal minister. For instance, Kumazawa Banzan (1619–91), a Confucian and Shinto scholar, claimed that Prince Shōtoku had assassinated the Emperor Sujun (?–592), even though Shōtoku's kinsman, Soga no Umako, had done the deed. On the same grounds, the Confucian scholar Nakai Riken (1732–1817) even refused to enter Shitennōji temple, claiming that he would be defiled by doing so. Hayashi Razan (1583–1657), advisor to Tokugawa Ieyasu and chief exponent of the Shushi (Chu Hsi) school of Neo-Confucianism, and Hirata Atsutane (1776–1843), a leading *kokugaku* (nativism) scholar, also asserted that the prince had assassinated Emperor Sujun. Further, a critique added by the Mito School editors of *Dai Nihon shi*[15] described the prince as follows:

> The prince said, "Even gods did not dare to violate the ways preached by Buddha."
> This statement denigrated the worship of the gods. Emperor Yōmei fervently worshiped Buddha. Before that time, no prince had worshiped Buddha, but the prince recommended such a practice to the emperor. This action destroyed our national religion. . . . The prince was more interested in Buddhism than in laws. Therefore, he

12. Sources cited in the following discussion are drawn primarily from Shōtoku Taishi Hosankai, ed., *Shōtoku taishi zenshū* (Tokyo: Ryūginsha, 1942–44). Hereafter, *Zenshū*.

13. *Zenshū* 3:50.

14. For example, Sugawara Michizane and Fujiwara Kanesuke, *Shōtoku taishi denryaku* (917); Minamoto no Tamenori, *Sanpō eshi* (984); and Yoshishige no Tatsutane, *Nihon ōjō gokuraku ki* (ca. 986).

15. The Mito School was a school of nativist historical studies centered in Mito-han. It was known for its chauvinism, emperor-centered historiography, and hostility toward foreign culture. The writing of *Dai Nihon shi*, which was completed in 1715, was initiated by Tokugawa Mitsukuni, the second daimyo of Mito-han, in the mid-seventeenth century.

worked to enthrone an empress who was easy to control, and he spoke boldly. As a result, Buddhism's power came to rival that of the emperor; the rituals of the court included Buddhist services. This was what the prince and Umako wanted.

In this way nationalist scholars severely condemned Prince Shōtoku for disrupting the basic structure of the nation by introducing Buddhism. In the period leading up to the Meiji Restoration (1868), when imperial sentiment reached a feverish pitch, Shitennōji became the site of violent protests, including suicides and an incendiary attack that burned twelve buildings on its grounds.

Ironically, Prince Shōtoku's image at the end of the Edo period was deeply divided. Although worshiped by artisans, he was despised by nationalist intellectuals. How then, in the modern era, did Prince Shōtoku become a paragon of virtue and an icon of *wa*, the essence of the Japanese spirit of harmony, in spite of the criticism of learned scholars in the Edo period? How was their criticism defused? How was his image recast and made compatible with state Shinto and the modern imperial tradition?

Sonoda Muneemi's *Shōtoku taishi*, the first modern study of Prince Shōtoku, appeared in 1893. Yet interest in Shōtoku increased dramatically only after 1903, the 1,300th anniversary of the promulgation of the Seventeen-Article Constitution. Kume Kunitake, a Tokyo University professor of history expelled in 1891 for declaring that Shinto was no more than a folk religion, published *Shōtoku taishi jitsuroku*—"a true record of Prince Shōtoku"—in that year. The number of works published on Prince Shōtoku reached a peak in the years between 1903 and 1921, the 1,300th anniversary of the prince's death.

Kume Kunitake gave a relatively factual account of Shōtoku's life, but by 1921 the image of the prince had begun to take on a distinctly nationalist coloring. Previously, the prince had been seen as the introducer of Buddhism in Japan—the benevolent founder of Buddhism, as it were—or as a hero endowed with mystical power. From this point on, however, his image as an enlightened and forceful statesman was emphasized. Behind this new image stood the social turbulence that followed the Russo-Japanese War of 1904–5, which extended into the 1920s. The new image of the prince responded to the rise of nationalism in Japan.

According to Hanayama Shinshō's *Shōtoku taishi to Nihon bunka*, it is possible to trace the following trajectory:

> Especially in 1903, the 1,300th year since the publication of Prince Shōtoku's Seventeen-Article Constitution, and in 1921, the 1,300th anniversary of his death, . . . enthusiasm for the prince rose suddenly throughout the society. It was not necessarily a coincidence that one of these years was just before the Russo-Japanese War, when our national consciousness was most intense, and the other was a time when our nationalism was at its zenith because of the enormous victory in World War I. Around 1904–5 and around 1921, lectures and Buddhist meetings in praise of Prince Shōtoku became frequent. At the same time, a number of excellent books were written by scholars and people in all fields: in Japanese history, law, Buddhism, Shinto, arts, crafts, and architecture. The true value of the prince became increasingly appreciated.

In 1921 the prince was depicted as a mixture of cultural promoter, patron of Buddhist art, Buddhist thinker, poet, and politician. But the image of Prince Shōtoku as "the prince of the land of the rising sun" gradually acquired new salience, as did his relationship to the imperial tradition. Article 3 of the Seventeen-Article Constitution ("If you receive a decree from the emperor, be sure to follow it") was emphasized during this period because of its advocacy of unconditional obedience to the emperor's will. Significantly, Article 1, which espoused the principle of *wa*, was of comparatively little importance at this time.

With the approach of war, this patriotic image of Prince Shōtoku was gradually strengthened to emphasize his embodiment of the national spirit. Ōkawa Shūmei (1886–1957), a right-wing politician who lent support to the Incident of May 15, 1932 and supported Japanese expansionism in Manchuria, wrote the following in *Nihon nisenroppyaku-nen shi* (1941), a book commemorating the mythical 2,600th anniversary of the imperial state:

> Prince Shōtoku laid down decisive principles for solving the national problems of his turbulent age. The prince proposed Shinto as the basic principle in politics, Confucianism to improve the moral life of his nation, and Buddhism to regulate its religious life. Thus the prince relied on a spirit of unity, which sought to embrace the new without losing the old, and in so doing, adopted the principles of the Asian civilization appropriate to our national life, which came to our shore one after another. In this way he opened the door to a new age.[16]

As this passage demonstrates, Prince Shōtoku was now described as the synthesizer of three religions and moral traditions of religion, with Shinto at the core, surrounded by Confucianism and Buddhism. Prince Shōtoku was said to have created the Japanese spirit by assimilating Confucianism and Buddhism to indigenous Shinto at a time when the concepts of state and national consciousness needed support. In this way, the prince's historic role of introducing Buddhism to Japan was recast in terms of support for state Shinto and the worship of the emperor. In 1940 Hanayama Shinshō expressed his enthusiasm for the prince:

> Recently, our country has withdrawn from the League of the Nations. As the Japanese spirit increasingly came to be emphasized, voices were raised for the third time in memory and praise of the prince. In fact, almost every day we find excellent papers and books that have been published to extol the great works of the prince.

The evolution of the image of Prince Shōtoku from early Meiji to the end of World War II can be divided into three periods. As I have mentioned, the first wave of the Shōtoku boom began in 1903, the 1,300th anniversary of the publication of the Seventeen-Article Constitution. The image presented during this period was of Shōtoku as an enlightened and forceful cultural reformer. However, in 1921, the 1,300th anniversary of his death, the image of the prince as a politician

---

16. Ōkawa Shūmei, *Nihon nisenroppyakunen shi* (Tokyo, 1941), 15–16.

came to be stressed. The latter half of the 1930s saw a third wave, in which the prince came to be associated with both *wa* and worship of the imperial family.

As Hanayama Shinshō has stated, one of the central ideas relating to the prince in the latter half of the 1930s was the worship of *kami*, Japan's national gods. The prince did in fact discuss worship of the "three treasures,"[17] but without specific reference to the worship of *kami*. Nevertheless, sympathetic commentators simply attributed *kami* worship to him on the assumption that it was something which, because it had been taken for granted, did not require comment; indeed, it followed logically from the assumed centrality of Shinto. Commentators also found ways to explain away his silence on the subject of the emperor. And scholars in the 1930s argued, with regard to his supreme loyalty to the emperor, that the prince had to promote Soga no Umako, who assassinated Emperor Sujun, simply because the Soga clan was too powerful to be ignored. He had no choice. These scholars claimed, however, that in practice Prince Shōtoku resisted the Soga clan and made tremendous efforts to conduct politics under the emperor. Accordingly his loyalty to the imperial system was firm.

Commentators also found reason to praise Prince Shōtoku in his role as a nationalist. One letter addressed by the prince to the Sui dynasty court bore the subscription "From the Son of Heaven of the Land of the Rising Sun to the Son of Heaven of the Land of the Setting Sun."[18] Scholars used this phrase to argue that the prince worked to establish equal foreign relations, advocated nationalism (both of the state and of the people), and promoted the power of the nation. Such viewpoints dominated the image of the prince as a representative of Japanese culture and national spirit.

WA AND INTERPRETATION
OF THE SEVENTEEN-ARTICLE CONSTITUTION

Like the image of Prince Shōtoku, the spirit of *wa* advocated in Article 1 of the Seventeen-Article Constitution was transformed during the modern period. I will analyze the shifting interpretations of Prince Shōtoku's constitution with special reference to *wa*. We will see that this principle came to the fore (with various interpretations) only during the first four decades of this century.

Until the Meiji Restoration, scholars interpreted the Constitution as "a basic moral code for the princes who have reached enlightenment." Many seized on the word *wa* in the passage from the Confucian *Analects* that reads, "To practice *rei* (social decorum) is to promote *wa*," or they simply interpreted it as peace of mind. We find such passages as "*Rei* is the form, *wa* is the practice"; and "*Wa* is the fusion of

17. The "three treasures" refer to Buddha, Dharma, and Sangha—the Buddha, the Law, and the Priesthood.

18. Quoted in Ryusaku Tsunoda, ed., *Sources of Japanese Tradition* (New York: Columbia University Press, 1958), 39.

two things into one idea. When good and evil are separate, we do not achieve *wa*"; and "*Kokoro* [heart/mind] is the form; *wa* is the practice." I have not found a single discussion of *wa* in relation to the Seventeen-Article Constitution that posited that Article 1 advocated *wa* as the basic idea of the Constitution itself. Rather, they regarded *wa* as merely one element within the Constitution as a whole.

A gradual change appeared after the Meiji Restoration. In 1893 Ariga Nagao's *Shōtoku taishi jūshichijō no kenpō* discussed *wa* as "the basic principle for governing a nation and achieving peace for its people."[19] A little later, in 1916, Kuroita Katsumi's *Shōtoku taishi no jūshichijō no kenpō ni tsuite* stressed the theme of "peace among the ruling class and harmony among the ruled."[20] Here, as in Okada Masayuki's 1917 work, *Kenpō jūshichijō ni tsuite*, *wa* was constructed as part of a hierarchical relationship rather than an equal and harmonious one.[21]

It is worth noting that while most commentators emphasized the achievement of order and harmony in a vertical and hierarchical relationship, they did not identify *wa* as Prince Shōtoku's basic principle. Rather, they stressed Article 3, which advocated loyalty to the emperor, as the central theme of the Constitution. This trend continued through the Taishō period. In the 1930s, however, as war approached, the concept of *wa* and its place in the Constitution began to change. In this time of national emergency, *wa* suddenly began to be represented as the basis of national consciousness. It took on the ideological function of state integration.

According to Suzuki Masayuki of Kobe University, the rise of nationalism and the development of party politics in the Taishō period produced the "organ theory of the emperor."[22] This new ideology balanced party politics and monarchism. The image began to alter in the early Shōwa period, however. At a time when the conflicts among the world's superpowers were beginning to take on special importance, it did not seem to be able to portray Japan's special features that could match those of the United States and Europe. A sense of crisis prevailed in the latter half of the 1920s and the ensuing Great Depression. In early Shōwa, for instance, the Christian educator Nitobe Inazō stated: "Japan has nothing to be proud of except its national polity [*kokutai*]." The notion of "national polity" was paralleled by an increasing emphasis on the concept of *wa*. The idea became firmly established that the Japanese spirit, the emperor system, and *wa* constituted unique traditions that could stand against those of the United States

19. *Zenshū* 1:440.

20. *Zenshū* 1:451.

21. *Zenshū* 1:467.

22. Suzuki Masayuki, *Kindai tennosei no shihai chitsujō* (Tokyo: Azekura Shobō, 1986). The "organ theory of the emperor" was advocated by Minobe Tatsukichi in 1912. Minobe argued that, although the emperor represented the supreme origin of government, he was also an organ of the state with governmental functions based on the Japanese Constitution. See Frank C. Miller, *Minobe Tatsukichi, Interpreter of Constitutionalism in Japan* (Berkeley and Los Angeles: University of California Press, 1965).

and Europe. An increasing emphasis on spiritual mobilization in the 1930s gave the idea of *wa* a new centrality. The most famous example is found in *Kokutai no hongi* (1937), edited by the Educational Bureau of the Ministry of Education:

> When we trace the development and history of our country, we never fail to find *wa*. *Wa* was born of great works done by our country; its spirit resides not only in the power to form history but also in the government of everyday life.[23] . . . In our country, we have observed a close unity between the emperor and the people. We have embodied beauty in such ideas as "all people united with the emperor as their leader," and in the assiduous cooperation by successive generations to maintain our nation. The sacred virtue of the emperor and the fidelity of his subjects have fused to create a beautiful harmony.[24]

Ono Seiichirō's *Kenpō jūshichijō ni okeru kokka to rinri* (1938) posits Prince Shōtoku's constitution not as a mere guide to everyday life but as "a theory for governing the nation"[25] and as "the ethical basis of the state." It was seen as "maintaining existing hierarchical distinctions, making them useful for affairs of state."[26] In this reading, the ethic of *wa* presupposed a hierarchical order in society and asserted the unity of the nation on this basis. This was an organic conception: *wa* was capable of maintaining harmony in a whole made up of distinctive and separate parts; it was hierarchical and holistic:

> *Wa* involves morals for individuals. Moreover, it is a supreme ethic for the community of a state. It is a manifestation of the ethical order on which the state of Japan should rely. What is *wa*? It is not merely peace achieved on the surface. It is inner and spiritual harmony and peace. This ideal brings about a unity of communal spirit by maintaining not only hierarchical distinctions but also the essential equality of an ethical order. It should be the ethic that will bring forth continuity, integration, and unity in the state. . . . Truly, the ethic of *wa*, or the ethic of "all people, one mind" is the supreme essence of our state.[27]

EPILOGUE: *WA* AND PRINCE SHŌTOKU IN POSTWAR HISTORY

This fascination with *wa* and the Seventeen-Article Constitution survived even in the postwar period. Questionnaires asking about people's favorite figures in

---

23. Japan Ministry of Education, *Kokutai no hongi: Cardinal Principles of the National Entity of Japan*; trans. John Owen Gauntlett; ed. with an introduction by Robert King Hall (Cambridge, Mass.: Harvard University Press, 1949), 50.

24. Ibid., 57–58.

25. *Zenshū* 1:609.

26. *Zenshū* 1:623.

27. *Zenshū* 1:622. As an additional example, I recently discovered an interesting item in a second-hand bookshop. It was a box containing a volume of the Seventeen-Article Constitution, distributed as a souvenir of the opening of the Research Center for National Spiritual Culture in 1935. The Constitution had become such a part of the center's propaganda in the 1930s that it was distributed as a souvenir.

Japanese history today usually discover that Prince Shōtoku or Minamoto no Yoshitsune is in first place. Yoshitsune's popularity is understandable, but how is it that Prince Shōtoku's reputation, and his association with the spirit of *wa*, survive to this day?

We should recall that Prince Shōtoku's renown is of relatively recent origin. According to Takeda Sawako's *Shinkō no ōken Shōtoku taishi*, when the government considered in 1887 whose image would grace its currency, the prince was excluded from the final list of historical figures. Only in 1930, the period when the prince became the icon of nationalist consciousness, was he included. After the Pacific War, the prince appeared on ¥1,000, ¥5,000, and ¥10,000 notes. The American occupation authorities had banned the publication of Shinto images and debated banning Prince Shōtoku's as well because he had been a patriotic symbol during the war. However, the director of the Bank of Japan managed to persuade the Americans that the prince was a pacifist, for the prince taught that "it is noble to achieve *wa*; make it a principle not to have conflicts."

In the postwar period, Prince Shōtoku survived as a symbol of *wa*, the principle that teaches harmonious cooperation. This *wa* signifies equality, as we have seen in the example of state textbooks. Today the image of the prince and the significance of *wa* are still being debated.

In sum, Prince Shōtoku and the spirit of *wa* became a newly created tradition in a time of national crisis—the turbulent decade of the 1930s and the Pacific War. It performed an ideological function by addressing the need for unification. The artificiality of this invention is pointed up by its variability: not only was Prince Shōtoku's reputation revised profoundly during Japan's modern period, but both the definition of *wa* and its place in the Constitution fluctuated wildly, depending on the ideological needs of the moment.

FOUR

Weak Legal Consciousness
as Invented Tradition

Frank K. Upham

In this paper I challenge the conventional wisdom that weak legal consciousness is a historical attribute of the Japanese people. Very few people anywhere enjoy conflict, and when a dispute becomes unavoidable, most people prefer to resolve it as amicably and quickly as possible. The Japanese are no exception, but to the extent that contemporary Japanese are unusual in their preference for informal dispute resolution, it is not because they lack a history of conflict or litigation. Like other societies, Japan has a rich history of formal law and litigation.[1] What is often

I have a more than ordinary debt to two people for help on the "Specific Part" of this paper. Prof. Igeta Ryōji of Doshisha University Law Faculty spent many hours with me in the late 1970s, explaining the Hozu dispute and helping me read and understand the documents. Then in the summer of 1994, my research assistant at NYU School of Law, Tomer Inbar, took my fifteen-year-old notes and prepared a detailed summary and chronology of all the events relating to the dispute. I could not have written this paper without their generous assistance.

1. For Kamakura Bakufu practice, see Jeffrey Mass, *The Development of Kamakura Rule, 1180–1250* (Stanford: Stanford University Press, 1979). This essay focuses on Tokugawa law. The Japanese-language classic on Tokugawa law is Ishii Ryōsuke, *Nihon hōsei shi gaisetsu* (Tokyo: Kōbundō, 1960). For other Japanese sources on Tokugawa law, see the bibliography of Dan Fenno Henderson, *Conciliation and Japanese Law, Tokugawa and Modern* (Seattle: University of Washington Press, and Tokyo: University of Tokyo Press, 1965), 2:319–63. Readers interested in collections of precedents in civil cases between 1702 and 1867 are directed to *Saikyodome* (records of judgments) in *Shihō shiryō bessatsu*, vol. 19 (Tokyo: Shihōshō Hishoka, 1943), and *Tokugawa jidai minji kanrei shū* (collection of civil customary precedents of the Tokugawa period) in vols. 187, 192, 205, 213, and 216 of *Shihō shiryō* (Tokyo: Shihōshō Chōsaka, 1936). For commercial cases, see Takimoto Seiichi, ed., *Shōji kanrei rui shū* (Tokyo: Hakutōsha, 1932). Henderson, *Conciliation*, vol. 1, remains the classic and best account of Tokugawa law and legal process in English. On pp. 99–125, Henderson describes the types of suits brought before the shogunate courts in Edo and the processes developed to deal with what he characterizes as "the flood of money suits" (p. 107) that plagued these courts beginning as early as 1622. Money suits (*kanekuji*), i.e., commercial disputes, were the lowest on the hierarchy of social importance, but they were the most common and in-

lacking in the Western language literature on Japanese law, however, is a knowledge of this history and a recognition of the choices of "tradition" open to contemporary Japanese legal culture.

The paper is divided into specific and general parts. In the former I describe a dispute in Hozu village that first arose in the Tokugawa period (1802), recurred twice in the Meiji period (1871 and 1888), and was resolved in the middle Shōwa period (1962). I pay particular attention in this narrative to the procedures chosen by the parties and find that they were more likely to choose litigation or its equivalent in the earlier instances of the dispute than they were in the later. In the general part, I contrast these choices to the view that Japanese naturally prefer informal, consensual means of dispute resolution to the formality and contentiousness of litigation to a greater degree than people in other industrialized societies. Not an ineluctable legacy of the distant past, the contemporary strength of this "tradition," I contend, is the product of a series of conscious political choices by elites beginning in the early twentieth century.

Official action to suppress litigation has been standard practice throughout most of Japanese history, but as the Hozu dispute and general court statistics illustrate, it was not until after World War II that government efforts achieved a dramatic and seemingly permanent decrease in litigation rates. Although accompanied by the rhetoric of a traditional preference for consensus and harmony, present litigation rates are at least as attributable to official efforts to discourage litigation as to the preferences of individual Japanese. The history of the Hozu dispute is illustrative, if not in itself probative, of the continuing tendency of Japanese to look to formal processes to resolve their disputes and of the relatively recent success of the government in discouraging this tendency and strengthening what Kawashima Takeyoshi called Japan's "weak legal consciousness."[2]

The Hozu conflict originated in a complex struggle between wealthy farmers and their small farmer tenants. The aspect that interests us concerns the proper utilization of the village commons and the degree of access enjoyed by village Burakumin, who had become allied with the landlords. The conflict thus implicated both social status and land ownership, perhaps the two most important legal issues in Tokugawa Japan, and was representative of the status litigation that occurred throughout the period.

Although conflicts over status and land were not the most numerous disputes in Edo Japan—by far the largest number of lawsuits concerned the repayment of debts—they were treated with the greatest concern by the authorities. Control of land meant wealth and power, and a stable social hierarchy was the goal of Edo

---

terfered throughout the Tokugawa period with the shogunate's ability to deal effectively with the more important land and water suits (*ronsho*). For a chronology of Japanese legal history, see Kumagai Kaisaku, Igeta Ryōji, Yamanaka Einosuke, and Hashimoto Hisashi, *Nihon hō shi nenpyō* (Tokyo: Nihon Hyōronsha, 1981).

2. Kawashima Takeyoshi, *Nihonjin no hō ishiki* (Tokyo: Iwanami Shoten, 1967).

law and political ideology. The Burakumin occupied the lowest rung of the hierarchy, but disputes over their status vis-à-vis small farmers were no more distinctive than disputes brought by small farmers over the status privileges of wealthy farmers or complaints by villagers over a headman's abuse of the privileges of his office. In this important sense the Hozu litigation was typical of how Japanese citizens and authorities dealt with the issues of most fundamental importance to them.

THE SPECIFIC PART: THE HOZU VILLAGE *IRIAIKEN* DISPUTE

The Bunka Period Dispute

Hozu, now part of Kameoka City, Kyoto Prefecture, was part of Kameyama *han* when this dispute began in 1802. The litigation that we examine was a small part of a broader conflict over village forests among wealthy farmers, or *gōmyō*, who were allied with the daimyo in wanting to log the forest, and the small farmers, or *kobyakushō*, who rented land from the wealthy farmers and relied on the forests for fuel and fertilizer. The parties to the actual litigation were the small farmers and village Burakumin, whom the small farmers tried to prevent from using the commons.

The Burakumin were originally brought into the dispute by the wealthy farmers, who invited them to farm land that the small farmers had refused to cultivate. The latter had initiated a tenants' strike in response to complex changes in rural society that had enhanced the wealthy farmers' status and power at the expense of the *kobyakushō*. The alliance between the daimyo and the wealthy farmers had led to a division of the mountain commons and the exclusion of the small farmers from certain sections. The daimyo had also granted thirty-nine of Hozu's *gōmyō* the status of country samurai in 1801, enabling them to increase their control over village affairs. The response of the *kobyakushō* was to demand a reduction in the rent they owed on the wealthy farmers' fields. When they did not receive any reduction, they refused to cultivate the land and returned it to the *gōmyō*, who then hired the Burakumin to take their place.

The specific dispute of interest here began in 1808, when a group of small farmers interfered with a group of Burakumin children who were cutting brushwood in the forest. The *kobyakushō* harassed the youngsters and forced them to leave their bundles of cuttings behind. Over the course of the next few months, this type of incident reoccurred, and in August a Buraku representative appealed to the village headman and demanded an end to interference in their use of the commons. Attempts at conciliation apparently failed, and by January 1809 the Burakumin had filed a request under the village headman's seal requesting the intervention of a shogunate official. The representative of the *kobyakushō* filed an answer and by February 29, the Buraku representative had filed a formal suit at the administrative offices.

Throughout the litigation the Burakumin contended that they had had access to the mountain since ancient times, including unlimited use of the brush, and that this access had been confirmed by a 1802 settlement of previous conflicts. The defendants, they argued, had reopened the conflict by violating this agreement and had even interfered with access by plaintiffs entering at the behest of village officials. The *kobyakushō* countered by claiming that the Burakumin had originally neither farmed nor had access to the commons and that recent grants of access to portions of the mountain by village officials were limited to gathering fertilizer only. They further argued that the Burakumin had violated the boundaries of their allotted area, that they were using the mountain in a manner that would devastate it ecologically, and that their "trespass" illegally violated the appropriate social hierarchy within the village.

In September 1809 the magistrate granted temporary relief and allowed Burakumin access to the commons while the suit was pending. Over the next few years, several attempts were made to settle the litigation, but they all failed. Finally, in 1815 the daimyo increased the Burakumin's access to the commons and their allotted commons area. Their portion of the commons was still much less than that of other farmers and they were not allowed to sell brush, as were others, but the result ended the first stage of this dispute in at least a partial victory for the Burakumin and their *gōmyō* allies.

The Early Meiji Dispute

The second stage of the Hozu dispute arose from the disruption of Edo political and economic patterns, specifically a new regime of land holding and the legal emancipation of the Burakumin. In the first years after the Restoration, the five village *kumi* (wards) of Hozu (four small farmer *kumi* and the *gōmyō*—everyone except the Burakumin) succeeded in retaining village, as opposed to prefectural, ownership and control of the commons. After several years of experimentation with different means of management and controversy among the *gōmyō* and the *kobyakushō*, they divided most of the mountain into parcels allocated to each household of the five *kumi*. To deal with the Burakumin, "letters of agreement [*torikawashisho*]" were exchanged in 1876, reiterating the history of the ownership of the mountain and restating the Edo status quo setting aside an area of roughly 47 *chō* for exclusive Buraku use.[3]

The Burakumin were dissatisfied with this division. They claimed that the 1871 Emancipation Proclamation gave them total equality with the other villagers and

---

3. At this time, the mountain was divided into four sections: (1) an area of 789 *chō*, 3 *tan*, and 9 *se*, where the five *kumi* had exclusive use; (2) an area of 10 *chō*, 2 *tan*, and 4 *se*, where the five *kumi* had exclusive use of the trees while the entire village had access to the underlying brushwood and twigs; (3) an area of 33 *chō*, 3 *tan*, and 9 *se*, where the entire village had total access; and (4) an area of 47 *chō*, 4 *tan*, and 9 *se*, where the Burakumin had exclusive use. (It is not clear whether "entire village" included the Burakumin. The facts of later disputes seem to suggest that it might.)

therefore equal access to the mountain. Since the agreement with Kyoto Prefecture had been that the mountain belonged to the village as a whole and since they were now equal members of the village, they argued, it followed that they were entitled to use the mountain on an equal footing with the other villagers. Negotiations were attempted but the five *kumi* were adamant that an equal division was impossible, and in 1883 sixty-four Burakumin filed a petition with the prefectural authorities.[4] In response, 345 members of the five *kumi* brought suit against the Burakumin seeking an order compelling them to abide by the 1876 letters of agreement and its provisions for access to the commons.

The contentions of the parties were straightforward. The plaintiffs argued that the rights of the Burakumin to the commons had been determined in the 1811 settlement of the first stage of the dispute and that the 1876 letters of agreement simply reconfirmed those boundaries. Since the agreement was duly signed by authorized representatives, it was legally binding and the Burakumin must abide by its terms.

The defendants claimed that the 1811 settlement was legally void because it had been negotiated while the Burakumin were still unequal as a matter of law. Since in 1871 legal inequality was removed, it followed that all villagers would share equally in the commons. They attacked the 1876 letters of agreement on two grounds: First, it reflected the illegal inequality of the situation at that time, and, second, the representatives who had signed it were not authorized to bind the entire Burakumin group. Thus, the Burakumin should be treated equally and get the same rights as everyone else.

In 1885 the Kyoto District Court found that the boundaries delineated in the 1876 exchange of letters were controlling and ruled in favor of the plaintiffs. The court determined that (1) unless there was an express provision changing a long-standing custom or rule, the Emancipation Proclamation could not be seen as changing any such custom and therefore that custom must be maintained; and (2) the letters of agreement bound all Burakumin, as the signatories were properly acting in a representative capacity.

In upholding the district court, the Osaka High Court noted that the Burakumin's own actions belied their argument that they had received full equality in 1871. If that had been the case, the court reasoned, it did not make sense that they or their representatives would sign an agreement five years later curtailing their newly acquired rights. Thus, it was evident that they did not receive full equality in 1871 as regards the commons. Further support for this proposition was found in the fact that the Burakumin did not pay an equal share of the land tax, even after the mountain came into the possession of the entire village. Thus the court found that they obviously did not have equal usage rights. According to the court's view, emancipation gave the Burakumin full equality only so long as this equality did not interfere with anyone else's rights.

---

4. *Kyōto-fu chiji kikitagaki kokuzō.*

The Late Meiji Dispute

The third stage in the Hozu dispute also grew out of legal and institutional changes occurring on a national scale. In 1888 the Meiji government implemented a new local government system that stipulated that land titles and rights that had been granted to the village group were to become part of the public assets of the newly created local government. Up to this point, the *iriaiken* had been considered a private right belonging to the village as a group of private households. The government argued, however, that the 1888 reforms converted the *iriaiken* into a public right subject to local government control.[5]

In response to its supposed new power, the Hozu village council passed an ordinance regulating the use of Hozu Mountain in 1889, which was duly approved by the Home Minister. This ordinance reiterated the status quo as regards respective rights to the commons but was to be the first step in making the mountain public. In 1895 in an attempt to increase the financial assets of the village, the village council authorized the cutting and sale of a certain amount of trees from an area of the commons used by all villagers, including the Burakumin. The village then reforested this area and prohibited the gathering of brush and grass there as a conservation measure. The result was a significant decrease in the commons area available to Burakumin. Nor did the Burakumin receive a share from the sale of lumber, or any benefit from the increase in the village assets.

In 1906 the Burakumin sued the village in the Kyoto District Court for unjust enrichment, arguing that the village had no right to sell the trees privately—that is, to exclude the Burakumin from the profits—and that the ban on entering the forest to gather brush interfered with their private right to use the commons. Their claims were based on the theory that *iriaiken* had remained private despite the local government reforms and the government's attempts to make them public.

In April 1907 the District Court, in conformance with an earlier decision by the Daishin'in (roughly equivalent to the Supreme Court), declared that the *iriaiken* was a private right belonging to all the members of the village, rather than a public right subject to the control of the village government. It followed that the *iriaiken* was the Burakumin's private right and constitutionally protected from confiscation by the village. The court then ordered the village to pay each plaintiff his share of the proceeds from the illegal sale. The court further ruled that the

---

5. Sections 263 and 294 of the 1898 Civil Code consider the *iriaiken* as collective in nature, but Section 83 gave the local council the ability to regulate/control the *iriaiken*. Because the government at the time wanted to transfer certain administrative responsibilities to the localities, it had to establish a financial base for the localities to carry out these new functions. Therefore, the government wanted to consider the *iriaiken* public in nature. These two competing policies led to two theories of the character of the *iriaiken*: (1) The *iriaiken* was a purely private right, and (2) it was public in nature. The private theory was dominant in the courts, while the government advocated the public theory. A full discussion of this debate would be useful for understanding this stage of the Hozu dispute, but it is beyond the scope of this paper.

ordinance blocking Burakumin access to the reforested area was an illegal interference with their *iriaiken* and ordered the village to restore the area to its prior
state.

Unlike the 1880s litigation, where the courts had to interpret the effect of the
Emancipation Proclamation, the special status of the Burakumin played no substantial role in the 1907 decision. The key issue was the private or public nature of
the *iriaiken*, not only for the Burakumin, but for all villagers. It is notable, however,
that the Kyoto District Court was willing to find for Burakumin against the will of
their village council supported by the Home Ministry. It is also worth noting that
in 1910, presumably as a result of their successful suit, the Burakumin's commons
allotment was increased so that their shares were more than half those of members of the five *kumi*.

The Middle Shōwa Dispute

Like the second and third stages, the fourth stage in the Hozu dispute grew out of
national legal and political developments rather than out of any local changes. In
this case it was the 1947 Constitution of Japan, Article 14 of which explicitly prohibited governmental discrimination against Burakumin.

In 1951 Hozu Burakumin presented a list of demands to the village office relating to land and land use in the village. One of these demands was a reprise of
the dispute concerning the commons. Since by the 1950s the economic value
of the commons consisted primarily of revenue from lumber concessions, the
issue was less access to the commons than the equal division of its proceeds. Although in both the Bunka and the Early Meiji stages of the dispute, the share of
the commons allocated to Burakumin had been increased, it remained substan-
tially smaller than those of the other five *kumi*. This time the Burakumin used
their new constitutional rights to demand absolute equality with all other villagers.

The response to these demands was the creation of a *dōwa* ("harmony" or "assimilation," a term often used as a euphemism for "Buraku") committee of ward
representatives with the mayor as chairperson. The committee confirmed the factual allegations of past discriminatory treatment, including inequality in access to
and division of the commons, but resolution of the problem was put off ostensibly
first by floods in 1953 and then by the consolidation of Hozu into Kameoka City
in 1955. By 1958, however, the heads of the three Buraku wards petitioned the
local assembly for the end of discriminatory practices and submitted a draft for
the redrawing of the commons boundaries. This plan eventually became the basis
for the final settlement.

In the presentation of their petition, the Buraku leaders appealed for the cooperation of all citizens in resolving the problem. They made clear, however, that if
their demands were ignored, they would unilaterally take the following steps: (1) a

boycott of city taxes; (2) a physical blockade of the commons; (3) secession from Kameoka City; and (4) other "necessary actions." In October they put forward a detailed plan to reallocate the village land to eliminate discrimination and threatened to take control of the commons and put their plan into effect by force. They then declared that they would log whatever portion of the forest was necessary and announced, at the end of the year, that they were open to bids by lumber companies for logging concessions.

These threats got the desired attention, and in early 1959 the mayor of Kameoka City intervened personally with a proposed solution that was in essence the same as the Buraku plan. It called for the transfer of land from Hozu to the city and its subsequent retransfer to the Burakumin. The process took some time, but by 1961 the city had received the land and entered into a contract stipulating that this land would be for the exclusive use of the 2nd, 3rd, and 8th wards (the Burakumin). The correct legal registration of this land became a point of contention, but it was eventually registered in the name of 150 Burakumin from the three wards. In 1962 the land was granted to the Burakumin at no cost, and the 160-year-old dispute was finally settled.

THE GENERAL PART: CHOOSING A TRADITION

What is striking in the Hozu dispute is not only the repeated resort to formal litigation by both sides from the Bunka period through the late Meiji, but also its final resolution in the 1960s by nonlegal means. If an unusual aversion to formal legal dispute resolution were characteristic of Japanese historically, then the earlier stages of a prolonged dispute would be more likely to be consensually resolved than later stages. In Hozu we have the reverse. In 1809 and 1907 the Burakumin used the courts or their formal equivalent to seek equality in access to the commons; in 1883 non-Buraku villagers went to court to block Buraku demands for equality. It was only in the 1950s and 1960s, after the promulgation of the 1947 Constitution with its array of new legal rights, including the right of access to the courts, that neither party used litigation. If nonlitigiousness is a "traditional" value among Japanese, at least the Japanese of Hozu, Burakumin and non-Burakumin alike, seem to have become more traditional in the postwar period.

Of course the Hozu dispute alone proves nothing about historical tendencies of Japanese to use formal dispute resolution. First, it is only one series of events. Perhaps there was something singular about the village of Hozu that led to litigation when Japanese in other villages in similar circumstances would have relied on and been satisfied by the results of more consensus-based methods. Or perhaps the Hozu Burakumin or Edo- and Meiji-period Burakumin in general were more litigious than "ordinary" Japanese. Or perhaps there is some other unanticipated explanation that would demonstrate this case to be an anomaly.

Such speculation is beside the point, however, because there is ample evidence that formal dispute resolution was common in the Edo period.[6] In fact, in the late twelfth century when the English were still settling disputes by ordeal and the writ system was in its infancy, the Kamakura Bakufu had already developed a finely tuned set of formal legal procedures for adjudicating land claims.[7] By the seventeenth century litigation over money claims, which were particularly disfavored by the shogunate for Confucian ideological reasons and because the debtors were frequently samurai, so crowded Edo dockets that authorities could not deal with the more important land and water suits, and in 1622 the shogunate issued the first of nine decrees ordering money suits to be settled out of court.[8] Even many of the *ikki* that until recently have been portrayed romantically as peasant rebellions can be fruitfully interpreted as a form of litigation with an elaborate rhetoric of rights and obligations.[9] Even the majority of protests that did evolve into violence began with written appeals that functioned as what American law today would call administrative litigation.[10]

Of course one could argue that formal dispute resolution in the Edo period was so dissimilar to contemporary litigation that it can not really be considered litigation. And certainly the jurisprudential concepts used by commoners in collective protests were not identical to those of either current or past Western legal culture. But to demand formal or conceptual identity before one will acknowledge the use of law is to reduce the discussion to tautology. What is important is functional equivalence, with especial attention to procedures. The question that must be addressed is whether the procedures chosen by both parties involved in the Hozu dispute were consistent with a weak legal consciousness, predilection for

6. See the sources in n. 1 above. Henderson, *Conciliation* 1:132–62, has a fascinating and detailed description of the progress of one money suit. For an in-depth description of a set of protests from one geographical area in the mid-nineteenth century and the role that formal petitioning played in them, see William W. Kelly, *Deference and Defiance in Nineteenth-Century Japan* (Princeton: Princeton University Press, 1985). Commenting on "a general persistence of commoner litigation" in the Tokugawa period, Kelly anticipates my point in this paper when he notes (pp. 74–75) that "claims for present-day Japan as a non-litigious society find cold comfort in the 19th century." A third book-length description of Tokugawa litigation, which is of particular relevance to the Hozu dispute because it deals extensively with inter-status litigation, is Herman Ooms, *Tokugawa Village Practice: Class, Status, Power, Law* (Berkeley and Los Angeles: University of California Press, 1996). In his introduction, Ooms makes the following telling comment: "To change unwanted situations, the peasants relied far more frequently on suits and petitions than on mass protests or uprisings. One cannot avoid the impression that lawyerless Tokugawa Japan was far more litigious than the Japan of today" (p. 8).

7. See Mass, *Development*, chap. 5, n. 1.

8. Relieving pressure on the docket was not the only motive for such decrees. The fact that the defendants tended to be shogunate retainers was also important. See Henderson, *Conciliation* 1:107.

9. See Nanba Nobuo, "Hiyakushō ikki no hō ishiki," in Aoki Michio et al., eds., *Ikki*, vol. 4: *Seikatsu, bunka, shisō* (Tokyo: Tōkyō Daigaku Shuppankai, 1981), 43.

10. Stephen Vlastos, *Peasant Protests and Uprisings in Tokugawa Japan* (Berkeley and Los Angeles: University of California Press, 1986); James W. White, *Ikki: Social Conflict and Political Protest in Early Modern Japan* (Ithaca, N.Y.: Cornell University Press, 1995).

compromise, dislike of black-and-white decision making, antipathy to clear rules and logical reasoning, or a preference for the informality of mediation or concili-ation. While virtually anyone would prefer harmony to disharmony, informality to formality, mediation to litigation, and so forth, it is very hard to find in the nar-rative above any indication that the parties hesitated to use formal legal means to pursue their interests significantly more than would, for example, a citizen of con-temporary New Jersey, America's most litigious state.[11]

Avoidance of litigation is evident only in the fourth stage of the dispute, where the Burakumin, despite powerful new legal weapons in the 1947 Constitution, chose to threaten direct action rather than to use the courts. Similarly, the descen-dants of the five *kumi*, who had sued in 1883 to preempt an earlier move by Bu-rakumin, eschewed the courts and entered a process of committees and bargain-ing that one would have to characterize as more consensual, harmonious, and traditional than the choice of their ancestors.

The lurch toward "tradition" in the final stages of the Hozu dispute is consis-tent with other trends in Japanese legal culture since World War II. At least by the conventional standard of litigation rates, Japan in the 1990s is a dramatically less litigious society than it was seventy years ago.[12] While this fact alone casts doubt on any causal connection between current low litigation rates and historical prac-tice, it becomes all the more remarkable when one considers the extraordinary so-cial change that has occurred during this period. First, the volume of economic activity has grown several-fold and diversified to accommodate technological de-velopments that present economic choices totally unanticipated by "traditional" Japan. Social change has been equally dramatic, and it has been largely in a di-rection of increased individual freedom and power and social diversity that one would have expected to increase, rather than decrease, litigation rates.

This trend is anomalous of course only if one assumes that urbanization, in-dustrialization, the decline of extended families, and the legal empowerment of women, minorities, and labor universally increase societies' preference for imper-sonal, formal means of dispute resolution over consensual, informal means. Such is the conventional wisdom, and if Japan refutes it, as it appears to have done, it is worth asking how and why it has happened and what has made it so.[13]

Contemporary Japan has a low litigation rate and perhaps a "weak legal con-sciousness" not because of the influence of enduring cultural attitudes based on

---

11. *New York Times*, September 15, 1994, in an article about the New Jersey governor's attempt to reduce litigation.

12. Litigation rates peaked in the late 1920s and early 1930s. See Nihon Bengoshi Rengōkai, *Shihō hakusho* (Tokyo, 1974), p. 19, cited in John O. Haley, "The Myth of the Reluctant Litigant," *Journal of Japanese Studies* 4, no. 2 (1978): 359.

13. It is also quite worthwhile to ask whether the conventional wisdom is correct as it applies to other societies. There is reason to believe that Japan's increasingly "traditional" society is not so un-usual as it appears, but this question is well beyond the scope of this paper.

actual historical practice, but because various political elites have reified one among many historical practices as "tradition" while denying equally valid ones and have simultaneously created and maintained institutions that reinforce the chosen "tradition." The result is a society where litigation and resort to law is even more difficult, expensive, time consuming, and dishonored than it is in most societies.

I do not deny either the power of culture or the existence of consensual practices in Japanese history. I maintain that culture is inextricably intertwined with contemporary politics and that each is continuously re-creating the other. Hence a search for the political actors and social institutions that have shaped Japan's legal culture has no beginning point and will have no end. But since we are concerned with the "traditions" of the second half of the twentieth century, we might begin with the culture-shaping politics of the late nineteenth and early twentieth centuries.

Our story begins in 1889 with the opposition to the proposed adoption the next year of the newly drafted and European-inspired "old" civil code. Although often portrayed in legal literature as a battle between proponents of German and French law, the controversy revolved around Hozumi Yatsuka's essay "The Civil Code Appears and Loyalty and Filial Piety Die" and the sentiment that the new code would "destroy moral relationships and norms."[14] The controversy gathered steam in 1919 with the creation of the Rinji Hōsei Shingikai, a special legislative commission to study ways in which the "new" civil code, eventually passed in 1898, could be amended to correct what was perceived as its excessive liberalism.[15] Although the family law section of the code had originally been drafted to replicate traditional Neo-Confucian virtues and to provide a moral model for the social order, Hozumi Yatsuka and other opponents of liberalism believed that the code had to be further amended to stem the tide of social unrest most dramatically represented by the 1918 rice riots.

The members of the commission initially intended to revise the content of the code to conform to the "virtuous ways and beautiful customs" of old Japan. But deciding on what concretely constituted traditional virtue in a given factual or legal context turned out to be more difficult than anticipated, and the commission could not agree on changes in even one substantive provision of the civil code. Instead, commission members shifted their focus to the effects of the process of liti-

14. K. Mukai and N. Toshitani, "The Problems and Progress of Compiling the Civil Code in the Early Meiji Era," trans. Dan Fenno Henderson, *Law in Japan: An Annual* 1 (1967). The postponement faction won the battle and the French-inspired "old civil code" was discarded, but they may have lost the culture war since a German-inspired code was adopted in 1898. Beginning the story of the modern political opposition to legal rights in 1889 is arbitrary. It could be placed as easily in the 1870s and the debate on the correct translation of "right" into Japanese.

15. John O. Haley, "The Politics of Informal Justice: The Japanese Experience, 1922–1942," in Richard Abel, ed., *The Politics of Informal Justice* (New York: Academic Press, 1982), 2:125–47. Haley's account of this process is the best in English.

gation itself. John Haley contends that Japanese courts in the early twentieth century were remarkably successful in harmonizing novel legal norms with perceived customs and values, but to members of the commission litigation was in itself subversive of the moral order. The commission's final report, issued in 1922, concluded that "the existing system in which family disputes are resolved by means of formal trials fails to maintain the beautiful customs of old" and recommended that family litigation be replaced by conciliation.[16]

The commission had found, in other words, that the formal procedures of litigation were in themselves morally destructive, even when the substantive norms enforced by these procedures were not. What was important to its members and to bureaucrats and legislators who agreed with its reasoning was the suppression of the formal adjudication of individually asserted legal rights. It was not so much who emerged as the "winner" in a given social conflict but whether the process of conflict resolution had reinforced the harmony that now was asserted to be at the core of Japanese social morality.[17] As Dore and Ouchi put it in a political context: "The emphasis on harmony precluded the view of society as a balancing of conflicting self-interests. The demand for recognition of one's rights was itself unworthy."[18]

As a result of the commission's recommendations, in 1922 the Diet passed the Land Lease and House Conciliation Law (No. 41) to conciliate urban landlord tenant disputes, followed by the Farm Tenancy Conciliation Law (No. 18, 1924) for rural disputes, and eight more statutes culminating in the Special Wartime Civil Affairs Law of 1942 (No. 63). The early statutes simply provided conciliation as an option to litigation, presumably counting on the citizens' "natural" preference for conciliation to the un-Japanese practice of litigation. When this approach failed to stop the tide of litigation, the statutes became progressively more coercive until, by the time of the Special Wartime Civil Affairs Law, conciliation had been made compulsory and imposed settlements had the effect of final judgments. Not surprisingly, the number of new civil cases dropped precipitously from the mid-1920s to the mid-1930s[19] —a dramatic instance of the effect of deliberate government efforts to restore and maintain, if not invent, "traditional" behavior.

The postwar Constitution of Japan prohibits compulsory conciliation, but it has not prevented the Japanese government from providing a wide range of attractive alternatives to litigation. These devices are typically government-financed mediation services staffed either by officials or by volunteers and administered

16. Haley, "Politics," 130–31.

17. The chapters by Itō Kimio and Andrew Gordon in this volume describe other instances of the creation of traditions of harmony.

18. Ronald P. Dore and Ōuchi Tsutomu, "Rural Origins of Japanese Fascism," in J. W. Morley, ed., *Dilemmas of Growth in Prewar Japan* (Princeton: Princeton University Press, 1971). Cited in Haley, "Politics," 137.

19. Haley, "Politics," 141 (fig. 5.1).

within the responsible bureaucracy. In the Family Court, for example, a staff of volunteers, typically retired lawyers or law professors or their wives, mediate family disputes under the supervision of judges and the court staff.

In some instances, such as the Family Court or civil conciliation generally, the system has clear prewar antecedents, but others have been created in the postwar period to meet particular crises. The systems for mediating environmental disputes under the Law for the Resolution of Pollution Disputes[20] and for mediating employment discrimination complaints under the Equal Employment Opportunity Act are two prominent examples. From the 1960s through the '70s, pollution victims and female workers sued and won decisively and repeatedly. The result was not only incremental legal change as courts in case after case created doctrines favoring the plaintiffs; it was also political change as the repeated presentation in the courts of the victims' plight forced the government to respond to their grievances. This response included government-financed mediation schemes and attempts to discourage further litigation as well as relief for the plaintiffs' substantive injuries. Soon the pace of litigation in both areas declined, and the government was able to reestablish control of the political agenda in a way that would have been impossible had the leaders of these movements and their lawyers been able to continue to litigate successfully.[21]

I argue that a major goal of the creation and financing of mediation services in these instances, as in all instances of government-sponsored mediation in Japan, was the diversion of environmental or employment discrimination conflict and issues out of the judiciary and into the more easily controlled arena of bureaucratically managed conciliation. The Constitution prohibits the government from making these measures compulsory, but their establishment can and does shift the incentive structure for potential litigants away from the courts.

Postwar efforts to discourage litigation have not been limited to the provision of informal alternatives, however. Similar motives can be inferred, if not proven, in several other policies relating to the legal system. Perhaps most fundamental is the number of legal professionals in Japan. Commentators on the "litigation explosion" in the United States frequently bemoan the fact that the country has twenty times the number of lawyers in Japan, and Japanese themselves often point to the relative paucity of legal professionals as evidence of Japanese dislike of law and lawyers. While casual observers attribute the number of Japanese lawyers to custom or culture, it is instead the direct result of conscious political choice. One can argue about the demand for lawyers, but there seems little question that there is a large unfulfilled desire to become lawyers in Japan. Until a recent increase to 750, the government of Japan limited the number of legal professionals (judges, prosecutors, and private attorneys) trained each year to 500. Doing so meant keeping

---

20. Kōgai Funsō Shori Hō (Law no. 108, June 1, 1970).

21. For a fuller description of this process, see Frank Upham, *Law and Social Change in Postwar Japan* (Cambridge, Mass.: Harvard University Press, 1987), chaps. 2 and 4.

the passage rate on the exam to enter the Legal Training and Research Institute (LTRI) at or below 3 percent, meaning that for every successful lawyer, there were dozens of persons who had taken the exam to become a lawyer and failed.

The explicit justifications for this policy have at times strained credulity, at least from an American perspective. Before a shortage of prosecutors forced it to increase the number of trainees, the Ministry of Justice cited the expense of expanding the LTRI as justification of the low passage rate. There was enough money to finance informal dispute-resolution systems in virtually every field of potential civil litigation, but the ministry insisted that training additional lawyers or judges would be prohibitively expensive. It has also argued that training legal professionals would flood the profession with mediocrities. In American terms, this would mean that 90 percent of the graduates of American law schools each year are unqualified to practice. While a strong argument can be made that there are too many lawyers in the United States, nine times too many seems unlikely.

A more plausible reason, although not one officially cited by the Ministry of Justice, is the power of the private bar and the importance of preserving the legal services cartel that these restrictions have created. The doubling or tripling of the bar would mean not only increased competition, but also an influx of younger lawyers who had not had to take the exam six or seven times before passing. Both the increased competition and the younger demographics would change the culture of the bar. But it is unlikely that protecting the lawyers' cartel is the only reason for the low numbers. As long as the bar and the judiciary remain essentially the same size as they were in 1947, litigation will remain relatively expensive and slow, further insulating political issues from judicial intervention by tilting potential plaintiffs' incentive structure toward more informal means of pursuing their interests.

Surprisingly, those informal means occasionally include the use of force. The Hozu Burakumin's threat to take control of the commons by force was not an isolated incident. It is typical of a type of dispute resolution that is tolerated by Japanese elites in business, government, and politics, and perhaps even preferred to litigation. The Buraku Liberation League and its predecessor, the Suiheisha, have used forceful denunciation campaigns since the 1920s, and they are not alone in choosing this tactic. One faction of the Minamata mercury-poisoning victims eschewed litigation in favor of directly confronting Chisso executives, including physically occupying corporate headquarters for months at a time, and less extreme instances have not been uncommon in other types of conflict, including labor, land use, and environmental disputes. Even the top officers of Japan's most prestigious corporations have at least until very recently had no scruples about hiring quasi gangsters known as *sōkaiya* to shout down and harass dissident shareholders at annual meetings. While the police occasionally arrest and prosecute participants in these types of calculated instrumental violence, they do so relatively rarely from an American point of view, and the courts treat the defendants, even when convicted, with a great deal more sympathy than an American court would in similar circumstances.

While it is impossible to prove, Japanese officials and judges seem at times to prefer even violent informality to the legalization of social conflict. Thus, the Minister of Justice in 1976, when asked why he was not in favor of making discrimination against Burakumin illegal, stated that social issues like discrimination were "matters of the heart, not the law."[22] For the Ministry of Justice, apparently, the rigidity of legal doctrine and the cold formality of litigation would preclude the development of "harmonious" relations between majority Japanese and Burakumin. Perhaps the Diet and the Ministry of Labor felt similarly about discrimination against women in employment when they allowed most forms of employment discrimination to remain legal in the 1985 Equal Employment Opportunity Act but instead relied on cajoling companies to voluntarily treat women equally. The result of both these decisions and many similar ones, such as the refusal of both courts and the Diet to loosen the requirements for suing the government in administrative cases, has been to keep litigation difficult and relatively inaccessible while providing free and readily available informal means of dispute resolution.

CONCLUSION: A COMPARATIVE PERSPECTIVE ON POLITICS AND CULTURE

Litigation is a social construct. It cannot arise spontaneously from a culture and does not exist in a society without being consciously and deliberately created. Furthermore, it is expensive and complicated, requiring the education and training of a wide range of professionals, the creation and maintenance of courts with significant staffs and budgets, and the provision of institutional support to enforce judicial judgments. Nor is litigation popular. Even in the United States, the paragon of litigiousness according to conventional wisdom, litigation is considered difficult, expensive, time consuming, divisive, and shameful, and lawyers and litigation are blamed for a wide variety of social ills from the budget deficit to the disintegration of the family.

It may be useful at this point, to ask, therefore, not why Japan would have a low litigation rate, but rather why any society would ever make the political choice to create litigation as a means of dispute resolution. While a full treatment of this question is well beyond the scope of this article, a brief review of two types of incentives for civil litigation in the United States and the justifications given for them may offer additional insight into the relative disincentives created in the Japanese case.

Federal legislation in the United States grants plaintiffs treble damages in certain instances, most typically antitrust—that is, if successful, a plaintiff receives three times the monetary value of the actual injury caused by the defendant's illegal action. Similarly, in other instances, most notably civil rights cases, judges can

---

22. *Asahi shinbun* (December 10, 1976).

award successful plaintiffs the costs of bringing the litigation, "attorneys' fees" in legal jargon, in addition to compensation. The justification for this encouragement of litigation is what is known as the "private attorney general" rationale, that it is desirable to have legislative norms be enforced through private civil litigation as well as by the government through administrative, civil, or criminal litigation.

Private enforcement is considered desirable for two reasons. It lessens the demand on public resources if the government can rely on private parties to enforce the norm, and private enforcement through the courts prevents the executive branch from fully controlling the implementation of the legislation that created the norm. The former is about the public fisc; the latter is about the division of power among the branches of government and between the government and private actors. The judiciary is the obvious beneficiary of a private attorney general system. Its role as arbiter between the other branches of government is strengthened, and some degree of public power is shifted from both the executive and the legislature to the judiciary. Private citizens are also benefited, however, since businesses harmed by monopolistic action or individuals injured by racial discrimination, for example, need not rely solely on the government help to protect their interests. Conversely, such a system not only injures the interests of potential violators of the legislative norm but also limits the power and discretion of the government agency that would otherwise have a monopoly on the norm's enforcement.

The expressed rationale for avoiding the legalization of social and political issues in Japan, whether phrased as the "virtuous ways and beautiful customs" in the 1920s or as "matters of the heart not the law" in the 1980s, has been the creation, preservation, or nurturance of particular cultural values. The political decision to limit litigation, in other words, has been justified in cultural terms. If one posits, however, that a major goal of the Japanese bureaucracy and those in the private sector that it serves has been to control the pace and forms of social change, as well as influence its direction, the American perspective on litigation provides a complementary explanation for Japanese approaches to litigation specifically and to the development of legal institutions in general. Stated starkly and perhaps simplistically, the cultural goals of virtue and harmony are replaced by the instrumental goal of political control.

While I would argue that the choice in the early 1970s, for example, to provide elaborate alternative dispute-resolution machinery for environmental disputes while refusing to make pollution litigation easier or more effective was "political" by any definition, I do not need to untangle what are inevitably mixed motives to make my point. At the time that the Minister of Justice claimed discrimination for the realm of the heart, he could easily have done the reverse, as the Diet could in 1970 with the anti-pollution legislation or in 1985 with the Equal Employment Opportunity Act. Neither culture nor tradition dictated the choice of informality over law.

Culture will prevent choices when it makes them literally unimaginable, but these points in Japan's postwar history were moments of rapid social change, much of which had been accelerated by litigation and the courts. The narrative of Hozu's struggles over rights to the commons demonstrates, if nothing else, that litigation has been a continuing part of Japanese social behavior for centuries. What the reiterated choice of the government demonstrates equally conclusively is that it has never been a politically favored tradition.

PART TWO

Village

FIVE

The Japanese Village
Imagined, Real, Contested
Irwin Scheiner

We think in generalities but live in detail.
ALFRED NORTH WHITEHEAD

IMAGINED COMMUNITIES

Over the past several decades Japanese have shown a vast capacity to create an idealized past. Even more apparent has been their effort to establish this past as an ideological basis for present conceptions of the Japanese state and people. Playing a role in this conceptualization have been ideas of the continuous role of the *ie*, the household, as a peculiarly powerful means of political and economic organization. Ideas about the significance of the *kyōdōtai*, the Gemeinschaft, have also inspired the work of both populist critics of the contemporary state and new nationalists. Ideas about the ethos of the Japanese, echoing ideas of the prewar *kokutai*, have appeared in the works of government-sponsored academics and newly founded institutes for the study of Japanese culture and history. But nothing has perhaps touched the Japanese more deeply than the evocation of *furusato*, the old town or community. The call for the re-creation of the old community has not only been used as an instrument of national policy; it has also been encouraged by political agencies in various localities, particularly in the relatively recently created suburbs. This sort of past has most recently been invoked by the Tokyo metropolitan government in its effort to create museums and exhibitions to remind Japanese of the greatness of the culture of old Edo, at the very point when Japan and Tokyo have seemingly been internationalized.[1]

1. Murakami Yasusuke, "Ie Society as a Pattern of Civilization," *Journal of Japanese Studies* 10, no. 2 (Summer 1984); Jinnai Hidenobu, *Tokyo: A Spatial Anthropology*, trans. Kimiko Nishimura (Berkeley and Los Angeles: University of California Press, 1995); Jennifer Robertson, *Native and Newcomer: Making and Remaking a Japanese City* (Berkeley and Los Angeles: University of California Press, 1991), esp. Introduction and chaps. 1 and 2. See also Robertson, "It Takes a Village: Internationalization and Nostalgia in Postwar Japan," in this volume.

All of these efforts share an attempt to reify images of Japan as a community united by elemental themes of race and spirit and culture. All of these interpretations emphasize the group, group effort, and the ethical, cultural, and class homogeneity of Japanese society. Such a characterization ignores the problematic of the past, its authoritarianism and status hierarchy, and inevitably suppresses the role of conflict.

What is most significant about this recovered past is its deceptiveness. It willfully dismisses the impressive tension between group harmony and individual self-fashioning and between static conceptions of *kyōdōtai* and the dynamic *yonaoshi* (world-renewal) rebellions that characterized the late Tokugawa period. This retelling misses the real ambivalence about the acceptability of tradition and its prescribed role that was felt by both local elites and large parts of the peasant community in Tokugawa Japan. *Furusato* was as socially (politically) problematic in the past as it is socially (conceptually) idealized in the present.

The idealization of rural experience, with some sort of nostalgia and sentimental attachment to rural living and rural people, has characterized the modern history of much of the West as well as, of course, prewar Japan. In his *Age of Reform: From Bryan to F.D.R.*, for example, the American historian Richard Hofstadter characterized this complex of ideas and notions in the United States as the "agrarian myth . . . a kind of homage that Americans have paid to the fancied innocence of their origins." Politically active early twentieth-century English historians Richard Tawney, the Hammonds, and the Webbs, all liberals or social democrats, found in their study of English agrarian history the lost values of collectivism and communalism that could be emulated in the present: "a mirror by which the strengths and weaknesses of industrial society could be evaluated."[2]

Japanese agrarianists of the prewar period, scholars and activists, had no less an appreciation of the political significance and social instrumentality of their conceptualization of the value of Japan's agrarian past and present. The ethnologist Yanagita Kunio and the popular agrarianist of the 1930s Miyashita Itaru also commemorated agrarian communitarianism: the hamlet, Miyashita wrote, embodied "beautiful customs of mutual aid." But both assigned normative values to rural society (and Yanagita noted its regional variability as well) to combat the authoritarian intrusiveness of the imperial state and the domination of urban capitalists. The recognition that the individual farmer was vulnerable to exploitation, that individual interests could be defended only by collective action, and that, in the face of rural crisis, it was necessary to confront the urban capitalists led Miyashita to focus on the revitalization of community solidarity as the appropriate medium of struggle. For similar intellectual reasons, Yanagita described in his

2. Richard Hofstadter, *The Age of Reform: From Bryan to F.D.R.* (New York: Knopf, 1955), 24; Victor V. Magagna, *Communities of Grain: Rural Rebellion in Comparative Perspective* (Ithaca, N.Y.: Cornell University Press, 1991), 85.

analysis of traditional Japan a great variety of local popular religious practices and the distinctiveness of folk customs, thereby demonstrating the artificiality of state Shinto and resisting the spiritual colonization of rural Japan by the state.[3]

Yanagita and Miyashita, no less than contemporary Japanese populists and nationalists, invoked "imagined communities" for political purposes. But much like the Tokugawa nativists discussed by H. D. Harootunian in *Things Seen and Unseen*, they "interpreted events in a way that provided specificity to discourse as a suitable method for solving the contemporary dilemma of disorder and fragmentation." I, too (in homage to the work of nativists and populists alike), go back to the Tokugawa village. I do so with a recognition that the current ideology about the old community and its social cohesion, the "imagined community," has not been created out of whole cloth. Rather, the present myth of community was, for the Tokugawa village, but one part of a contested discourse in a fragmented and disordered world.[4]

"REAL VILLAGES": DETAIL

However they are classified in terms of class or status, the significant ties in villages of Bushū[5] and much of the Kantō region at the end of the Tokugawa period were between petty landholders or landless wage earners and their village employers. In the nineteenth century as in the eighteenth, Tokugawa Bakufu officials sought to prevent the "further pawning of land," seeing in the expropriation of small peasant holdings by the rich (as one officer of the Kantō Control Office argued in the 1820s) the specific cause of discontent that might lead to revolt. A magistrate in Nikkō in 1842 found that most of the dispossessed "had no choice but to become wage laborers . . . and some worked as farm laborers for rural merchants who had become involved in agriculture." "Untold thousands," he continued, had consequently lost their freedom, as they also became encumbered with debt. "Such an extreme situation called for firm legal measures."[6]

3. Ann Waswo, "The Transformation of Rural Society, 1900–1950," in Peter Duus, ed., *Cambridge History of Japan*, vol. 6: *The Twentieth Century* (Cambridge: Cambridge University Press, 1988), 594–96; Tetsuo Najita and H. D. Harootunian, "Japanese Revolt Against the West: Political and Cultural Criticism in the Twentieth Century," ibid., 750–52, 772.

4. H. D. Harootunian, *Things Seen and Unseen: Discourse and Ideology in Tokugawa Nativism* (Chicago: University of Chicago Press, 1988). The correction of disorder is a major theme in the book and is discussed thoroughly in chaps. 5–7.

5. Bushū: old name for the region in eastern Japan encompassing Tokyo, Saitama, and Kanagawa prefectures.

6. Fukaya Katsumi, *Hyakushō ikki no rekishiteki kōzō* (rev. ed.; Tokyo: Azekura Shobō, 1986), 337–41; Mori Yasuhiko, *Bakuhansei kokka no kiso kōzō: Sonraku kōzō no tenkai to nōmin tōsō* (Tokyo: Yoshikawa Kōbunkan, 1981), 225–27, 243–44, 248–54, 276–79, 309–13; Fukaya, *Hyakushō ikki*, 268; Ōdachi Uki, *Bakumatsu shakai no kiso kōzō: Bushū yonaoshi no keisei* (Saitama: Saitama Shinbunsha, 1981), 100–101, 163–64; Aoki Michio, *Tenpō sōdō ki* (Tokyo: Sanseido, 1979), preface and chap. 1.

Wage employment and the significance of a growing population of poor people and vagrants became critical issues for Kantō agrarian society because they were seen as offering the greatest potential for social disorder. Buyō Inshi, or Buyō the Hermit, as one eccentric samurai resident of Edo in the early nineteenth century called himself, found a portent of a coming crisis in Tokugawa rule in the tremendous disparity of wealth among the Kantō peasantry, particularly in the exploitation of the village poor by the village official class. And a Bakufu official in the 1820s tied the crisis more specifically to the "many who have been expelled from villages," taking particular note of "a rapid increase in the homeless and evil elements who have nowhere to go. . . . The land is truly upset." A village headman of Musashino agreed with this assessment, noting in his diary: "There is a great panic. People from Aome to Tokorozawa fear to travel on the roads and have taken to hiding their valuables in the forest." Bakufu and village officials took careful note of these troubling events, and Buyō the Hermit kept his eyes open for all signs of social and political disruption, proof for him of the general decline of Tokugawa rule.[7]

An examination of village employment patterns demonstrates quite effectively, if not as dramatically, the transformation of social economic relations. Let me illustrate with several examples. Residents of Kaminaguri village in Chichibu, notable as the igniting point of the 1866 *yonaoshi* rebellion, had depended on by-employments since at the least the 1810s. Kaminaguri, the *Shinpen Musashino fudoki* gazetteer reported, "had poor land and little of it arable." Out of 296 households in 1829, only 15 engaged solely in agriculture; the rest supplemented their income by raising silkworms, gathering firewood, weaving silk cloth, and so on. By 1838, of 153 households in one of the two divisions of the village, 143 had become employed by richer peasants and village officials to make charcoal or harvest and transport timber. By 1866 most villagers had become dependents of the rich, many as employees in the rafting enterprises of village headman, Machida Ryōnosuke. (The village carpenter charged with leading the 1866 rebellion described himself as an employee of Machida, who in turn sought his release from the Bakufu jail.) In neighboring Kamikodera, 119 villagers worked as paper makers for Matsumoto Ryūemon, patriarch of a money-lending and pawnbroking family that had appropriated most of the village land.[8]

Studies of Setagaya, an area near the borders of Edo itself, show that villages that in 1800–1810 had been dominated by small holders were split by mid-century between a few very wealthy families who monopolized the village offices and a mass of poor householders who, unable to subsist as farmers, turned first to by-employments and then to the sale of their labor. Here, as in Kaminaguri and in Kamikodera, many residents remained single, living in rented quarters.[9]

7. Fukaya, *Hyakushō ikki*, 331–39; Mori, *Bakuhansei kokka*, 236, 254, 281–89; Yasumaru Yoshio, *Nihon kindaika to minshū shisō* (Tokyo: Aoki Shoten, 1974), 241–44; Ōdachi, *Bakumatsu shakai*, 12.

8. Ōdachi, *Bakumatsu shakai*, 236–44; Mori, *Bakuhansei kokka*, 476–97.

9. Mori, *Bakuhansei kokka*, 230–38, 276–79, 280–91, 509–51, 616.

In 1842 the Nikkō magistrate argued that the remedy for "evil practices" was a restoration of "old customs" and called for "official measures to increase the number of taxable households and to protect the average farming family." But almost two decades earlier, in 1827, as part of the Bunsei reforms (1818–29), the Bakufu had chosen to accept the new status quo, co-opting the new elites of the villages into its administration, appointing them the leaders of leagues composed of as many as forty-five villages in a district. Calling them *yūtoku no mono*, "men of substance," the Bakufu transferred to them the administration of local society, allowing them to conscript the sons of wealthy peasants into a militia to contain malcontents. In 1863, for example, the Kantō Control Office urged a further strengthening of the leagues. "What really bothers us," the office indicated, "is the poor and the malcontents; out of benevolent concern for the welfare of the poor, the men of substance should watch out for and capture parties of the malcontented; by such means can rebellion be nipped in the bud."[10]

By the mid-nineteenth century, however, village headmen often did not distinguish between the poor and "the malcontents," describing both as "troublemakers." Rural society had become so fractured that "good villages" saw their duty as simultaneously to "provide allowances for the poor" and to arm their sons in defense against "troublemakers." A village leader in Shimotsuke complained that members of the lower class of the village assumed that they could always demand the aid of the rich. "The poor of the village, the *komae*," he wrote in his diary, demanded from the men of substance that "debts be adjusted, insisting that those with the means provide relief." This headman also described the anguish (*kokoro itami*) of the *yūtoku no mono* who believed that they stood to lose their lives as well as property. It was a situation, he concluded, "in which distinctions between high and low, rich and poor have been lost."[11]

CONTESTED VILLAGES

On the very day in the sixth month of 1866 that most of the peasants of Kaminaguri left their village to initiate the Bushū *yonaoshi* revolt, the Kantō magistrate in Iwahana warned of a potential rising. Rice prices had risen drastically, and "rich people's cornering the market," he argued, had contributed mightily to the inflation. " Village officials and the high born," he insisted, "must care for the poor and give them alms."[12]

---

10. Ōdachi, *Bakumatsu shakai*, 138–64, 191–96, 210–15, 223–25, 564–77, 572–73; Aoki, *Tenpō*, chap. 1; Sasaki Junnosuke, "Bakumatsu no shakai jōsei to yonaoshi," in Sasaki Junnosuke, ed., *Nihon no rekishi*, vol. 13 (Tokyo: Iwanami Shoten, 1977), 111–12.

11. Mori, *Bakuhansei kokka*, 564, 577–81; Fukaya, *Hyakushō ikki*, 417–35.

12. Mori, *Bakuhansei kokka*, 405–9, 412–51; Ōdachi, *Bakumatsu shakai*, 246–47; Kinsei Sonraku Kenkyūkai, ed., *Bushū yonaoshi ikki shiryō*, vol. 1 (Tokyo: Keiyusha, 1971), 35–43, 305–27.

Whatever the initial cause of the rebellion, the issue that appeared most prominently in Bushū, as it also did in a *yonaoshi* movement in the neighboring province of Shimotsuke in 1867–68, was the demand for relief. Most commonly the cry for "world renewal" was combined with a demand for "relief for the poor everywhere." Rebels also demanded price reductions and, particularly, the sale of cheap rice. Gizaemon, a figure conjured up as the "righteous" village headman leading the rebellion, allegedly took the lead after his fellow village leaders refused to aid the poor. Frequently, rebels demanded the return of all pawned articles (particularly work tools) and the destruction of all notes of debt. Occasionally, they destroyed the records of pawned land. Significantly, rebels never directed demands toward their lords for a reduction of either land taxes or corvée.[13]

The rebels' primary demand was that the rich accept their obligation to provide relief. Although they sometimes demanded the return of pawned land, they probably had little understanding of the reappropriation of farm land, other than as an issue of social leveling and hierarchy destroying. Most of them came from families that had been employed for generations as day laborers. The issue for them was the continued right to poor relief when impoverished. When the headmen or the wealthy were forced to concede to rebel demands the cry went up: "The leveling world-renewal divine rectifier." For the rebels, such concessions indicated not a return to a world where they labored as small-holding peasants but the achievement of a utopia where all statuses had been leveled.[14]

Headmen and the rich, leaders of the leagues of villages, did give relief. Machida led the rich of his village in granting 1,000 *ryō* to the rebels. (In the nineteenth century an agricultural laborer had a yearly income of about 6 *ryō*.) Under duress, most of the others did the same. One village notable, Ikota Jundō, declared that wealth "must be used to better the lot of the poor." He predicted that failure to do so would "flout the will of heaven " and bring about "a rebellion of the people."[15]

Machida and the many other rich villagers associated with him feared their peasants, much more, in fact, than they feared the wrath of heaven. For them, self-defense in the form of mutual aid alliances with others like them in neighboring villages offered the best means to deal with the danger of peasant revolt. Once the rebellion was quelled and the agreements it required revoked, Machida and

13. Fukaya Katsumi, "Yonaoshi ikki to shinsei hantai ikki," in Fukaya Katsumi and Yasumaru Yoshio, eds., *Nihon kindai shisō taikei*, vol. 21: *Minshū undō* (Tokyo: Iwanami Shoten, 1989), 410–12; Ōdachi, *Bakumatsu shakai*, 249–51, 256–62; Mori, *Bakuhansei kokka*, 417–27, 425–29, 443; Sasaki, "Bakumatsu no shakai," 84.

14. Ōdachi, *Bakumatsu shakai*, 251; Mori, *Bakuhansei kokka*, 268, 425–31; Yasumaru Yoshio, "Minshū hoki sekaizō," *Shisō* (April 1973): 114–16.

15. Mori, *Bakuhansei kokka*, 414–17, 431–35, 441–43, 451–55, 492; Ōdachi, *Bakumatsu shakai*, 71–72, 256.

his friends again granted relief. But they also took care to gather arms and build their defenses.[16]

A final and not, I believe, unsurprising twist is added to this essentially intra-village struggle by the actions of the Kantō Control Office. Not only did it arrest rebels and reprimand headmen (for, after all, it had been their responsibility to keep village peace). With the rebellion suppressed, the Kantō intendant ordered Machida as well as others of the rich elite who had been compelled to offer relief to renege on their promises to the *yonaoshi* rebels. Almost immediately afterward, however, the intendant directed Machida, as well as headmen from the many other villages attacked by the *yonaoshi* force, to offer official village aid to the peasantry of the village. These actions were a further indication, perhaps, of the Bakufu's desire to reestablish its control of the countryside. In this case, by reminding the agrarian elite that offering relief was a function of the role of the village headman as the agent of the Bakufu, the intendant reasserted his control of the village and of agrarian society.[17]

NORMATIVE HISTORY

Many Japanese national historians have characterized the peasant uprisings of much of the Tokugawa period as class struggles against feudalism. Hani Gorō, in the prewar period, emphasized the quantifiable intensification of this class struggle during the nineteenth century, sometimes pointing to the role and burden borne by an emerging proletariat in carrying out its own emancipation. Tōyama Shigeki, in his major study of the Meiji Restoration in the immediate postwar period, wrote that "the peasant uprisings and *uchikowashi* [smashing-and-breaking riots]" of the end of the Tokugawa era put Japan on the eve and at the stage of peasant war, invoking Engels's analysis of the potentially revolutionary German Peasant Wars of the sixteenth century.[18]

Since the 1960s, however, a number of Japanese historians have insisted that a qualitative distinction should be made between traditional peasant uprisings aimed at the lord and the *yonaoshi* disturbances that I have described. "The world-renewal condition," *yonaoshi jōkyō*, as Sasaki Junnosuke first characterized the period of *yonaoshi* rebellions, is, he argues, truly revolutionary and a situation of peasant war. Not only did class struggle intensify as the "fundamental class contradiction between lords and peasants." It was also the period of a widespread and intense struggle between the wealthy peasant and the newly emerging village semi-proletariat. The emergence of the proletariat, Sasaki further argues, "changed the

16. Ōdachi, *Bakumatsu shakai*, 215–17; Mori, *Bakuhansei kokka*, 446–61, 463–66, 473–76.

17. Mori, *Bakuhansei kokka*, 443–51, 464–66; Sasaki, "Bakumatsu no shakai."

18. Hani Gorō, "Bakumatsu ni okeru shakai keizaiteki jōkyō, kaikyū kankei oyobi kaikyū tōsō," in *Hani Gorō rekishiron chosaku shū*, vol. 3 (Tokyo: Aoki Shoten, 1967); Sasaki, "Bakumatsu no shakai," 108–9.

fundamental class contradiction. . . . [It became] the starting point for a social system following the Tokugawa" and made a true denial of feudalism possible.[19]

Sasaki's dramatic, tragic, and paradoxical narrative features a small cast, all of whom play multiple roles. His typology is complex and his discussion of potential, actual, and broken revolutionary alliances is intricate. Wealthy peasants, as usurers, merchants, and large landowners, could be held responsible for the deracination of the *komae*, the small landowning peasant. As such, they became the prime target of *yonaoshi* rebels. Also, as owners of small enterprises, they had a significant historical task: "the 'wealthy peasant,'" Sasaki writes, "as a special form of capital created the semi-proletariat as a special existing form of wage labor." Now describing the wealthy peasantry as a middle class or bourgeoisie, he asserts that they were anti-feudal—offering evidence for their clear recognition of both the incompetence of feudal rule and the economic and social alliances they established among themselves—and that they were the only class with the potential to develop a bourgeois nationalism based on a new vision of the economy.[20]

But, Sasaki writes, the wealthy peasants failed to carry out their historical role as a newly risen bourgeoisie. Although they struggled against feudal oppression, they could not be independent of feudalism: they would not, for example, align themselves with the "*yonaoshi* rebels" to challenge the feudal system of land ownership, ceding, therefore, to the "semi-proletariat" (who composed the major body of participants in these rebellions) the role of the revolutionary class.[21]

Let me sketch in (as Sasaki sees it) the "semi-proletarians'" qualifications to be the revolutionary class: Only they, he writes, "were qualified to play a driving role in the changes of the Bakumatsu-Restoration period." Excluded from the "feudalistic" landholding system and forced to seek employment beyond the village, this class of former small producers was transformed. They had escaped the fundamental characteristic of the peasantry, its "dispersion," or *bunsansei*. But as the rural semi-proletarians, they could form themselves into a class (a "class for itself" in the Marxian sense, I assume) and align themselves through *uchikowashi* with the emerging urban pre-proletariat. Also, as a result of their experience of "out-employment," they brought home ideas of village democracy that made it possible to challenge status distinctions within their community.[22]

In Sasaki's description the small-peasant–emerging-semi-proletarians appear as a protean force. In the *yonaoshi* rebellions, for example, they were proletarian

19. Yasumaru Yoshio, *Minshū undō no shisō*, vol. 58 of Shōji Kichinosuke, Hayashi Motoi, and Yasumaru Yoshio, eds., *Nihon shisō taikei* (Tokyo: Iwanami Shoten, 1971), 392–93; Sasaki Junnosuke, *Bakumatsu shakai ron* (Tokyo: Hanawa Shokyoku, 1969), 16–22, 27–34, 65, 258, 256; Sasaki Junnosuke, "Epilogue," in Sasaki Junnosuke, ed., *Murakata sōdō to yonaoshi*, vol. 1 (Tokyo: Aoki Shoten, 1972); Sasaki Junnosuke, *Yonaoshi* (Tokyo: Iwanami Shoten, 1979), 134–38.

20. Sasaki, *Yonaoshi*, 13, 17–18, 20, 36, 51–52.

21. Ibid., 48, 64, 138–39; Sasaki, *Murakata sōdō to yonaoshi*, 387; Sasaki, "Bakumatsu no shakai," 293.

22. Sasaki, *Bakumatsu shakai ron*, 18–22, 62–63, 267, 283, 286, 290; Sasaki, *Yonaoshi*, 36–37, 40–41; Sasaki, "Bakumatsu no shakai," 100–108, 22.

when they demanded a reduction in or refused to pay rents and taxes. When, however, they made further demands for the free circulation of commodities, they took on the role of the petty-bourgeois as well. But it is their ambivalence that best characterizes them. Sasaki writes that, ultimately, their status identity rooted them firmly in the village; they wanted to return to the land as small producers. They did not seek to eliminate the *kyōdōtai*; they merely wanted to reform it. Nor could they accept the revolutionary leadership of the urban pre-proletariat, Sasaki argues, since conflict between city and village precluded it.[23]

Sasaki's ultimate judgment of the *yonaoshi* rebellion and the semi-proletariat is melancholic. When the Tokugawa state was on the eve of collapse, *yonaoshi* "consciousness" and "energy" diffused into ecstatic movements such as *Ee ja nai ka* (Isn't it good!); the movement lacked a concrete and historically realistic program. Incapable of ever transcending their community or their status as small-producing peasants, the tragedy of the *yonaoshi* force, Sasaki indicates, is that they were subjugated by peasant troops and the town's self-defense force, the very groups they sought to represent and emancipate.[24]

Sasaki Junnosuke, like Engels in his *Peasant War in Germany*, writes normative history in which he openly judges what his historical subjects did by what their social roles indicate they should have done. The narrative parallels of the German Peasant Wars described by Engels and the *yonaoshi* reported on by Sasaki are quite striking: An embryonic bourgeoisie refuses to take on its historical task; betrays an awesomely energetic and revolutionary peasantry, which itself cannot transcend localism; and is, finally, subdued by powerful regional princes with the aid of peasant troops.[25]

I would like to shift the focus of the study of the *yonaoshi* from Sasaki's emphasis on class and revolution to one of village and community discourse.[26] Many years ago Thomas C. Smith described the gradual evolution of the Tokugawa agrarian economy from subsistence production to production for the market. Concomitantly, he noted, social and economic relations became freer, since workers and tenants become bound by contract rather than by status relations and ties of a real or putative familial type. Smith ultimately limited his analysis to structural changes and slighted their effects. He did write of the conflict over status between a newly rising economic elite and their traditional betters within the village. But it was historians like Sasaki Junnosuke who explored in great detail the village

23. Sasaki, "Bakumatsu no shakai," 299; Sasaki, *Yonaoshi*, 79; Sasaki, *Yonaoshi*, in *Nihon no minshū no rekishi*, vol. 5 (Tokyo: Sanseido, 1974), 281–83, 291–92.

24. Sasaki, *Yonaoshi*, in *Nihon minshū no rekishi* 5:14.

25. Friedrich Engels, *The Peasant War in Germany*, reprinted in Leonard Krieger, ed., *The German Revolutions: The Peasant War in Germany and Germany: Revolution and Counter-Revolution* (Chicago: University of Chicago Press, 1967), 8–9, 21, 28–32, 37–38, 62–64, 92–97, 104, 114, 117–18.

26. I will only suggest here how I will address this problem in a larger study entitled "*Yonaoshi* Rebellion and Its Enemies: The Contested Village in Nineteenth-Century Japan."

struggles between the newly emerging economic elite and the local *komae*, which, in a number of areas, later burst into *yonaoshi* rebellions. Both historians suggested that Japanese agrarian society in the nineteenth century was in turmoil; that attempts to redefine the village and its hierarchy were being conducted both by its elite and by its newly created landless small peasantry and wage earners. I would like to argue, furthermore, that in establishing their own peasant troop and entering into social, economic, and political alliances with others like themselves, the wealthy peasants were nurturing a new idea of the village and their relationship to it and, finally, that in the *yonaoshi* rebellions peasants were responding directly to these changes with what they believed was a legitimate conception of the village. *Yonaoshi* rebellion was not an attempt by the *komae* to retrieve their land and, thus, return to the status quo ante. The *kyōdōtai* was being restructured.

Evocative images of this polarization appear in official reports and village documents in Shimotsuke Province prior to the outbreak of a *yonaoshi* rebellion in the late 1860s. A Bakufu inspector, for example, identified the basic conflict within the village as that of the "poor" and the "distressed" against the "haves," or the *yūtoku no mono*. The "rich" of the village of Shioyama in the same province identified their enemies as the "poor leagued together." They had a firm sense of who the poor were: tenants, all who "lacked a permanent domicile," and less well-off members of the small-holding class. Facing what they believed to be an organized assault upon them by the mass of the village, the "rich" warned: "With the people of the village now joined together, we twenty-one households, who call ourselves the *yūtoku no mono*, fearing that we will be forced to make loans to the poor, have met and signed an agreement . . . to the effect that if an attempt is made to force us or one of us to make such loans to the poor, we will defend ourselves as a group." In response, the "poor" defined themselves quite simply as "the village united."[27]

THE VILLAGE RE-IMAGINED

Yonaoshi has become a contemporary political metaphor for anti-hierarchical and anti-establishment feelings, ideas, and movements of all sorts. The movements are characteristically populist, communitarian, and voluntaristic. Local citizens' movements against harbor or industrial pollution, created by the voluntary and horizontal association of hundreds of hamlets and neighborhood associations, for example, have been called *yonaoshi* movements. For the left-wing social critic Oda Makoto, the essence of the *yonaoshi* was expressed in the fraternal feelings and aspirations of student protesters of the 1960s and 1970s: the protests were liminal moments, when rebel students stood together as comrades in opposition to the university, the national government, and its police. Bin Akao, the late pre- and

27. Fukaya, "Yonaoshi ikki," 405–12; Fukaya, *Hyakushō ikki*, 428–31, 475–78.

postwar ultra-right-wing nationalist, equated *yonaoshi* with the millennium. In his posters he associated *yonaoshi* with the advent of a Japan freed of all of the encumbrances of postwar reform, including the presence of the United States.[28]

Nativist historian Irokawa Daikichi has argued that in the past when local village society became too stratified or a few accumulated too much wealth and power, "a self-purifying reaction would occur." Villages would carry out, he writes, "a leveling festival" (*yonaoshi matsuri*) to punish the wealthy. Irokawa, in fact, likens the historical process by which Tokugawa and Meiji *yonaoshi* erupted to the radicalization of contemporary local citizens' movements. In all cases, failed petitions to local officials, unsuccessful appeals to regional and national official bodies, accompanied by the movement's alienation from local notables (who either could not or would not sustain the demands of the petitioners), led to a fracture in all political relations, a distrust by the petitioners of all official bodies, and a social class crisis within the local community.[29]

Irokawa, no less than the official ideologues of the re-creation of the old community, *furusato-zukuri*, romanticizes the "natural community." For Irokawa, however, the "romance," the significance, of the "natural community" was that it offered the only organizational resources for popular resistance to external political or economic coercion. "The *kyōdōtai*," he wrote in his discussion of the Chichibu Incident of 1884, "became a base of insurrection and the villagers attempted to change its nature." He also recognized (and cherished) the difficulty of precisely defining the *kyōdōtai* itself: its institutional form depended on the elective affinity of its members to join together in egalitarian union; its substance and power were bound in the villagers' imagining of community itself. "The term 'village *kyōdōtai*,' " he argued in *The Culture of the Meiji Period*, "does not refer to any specific institution but simply to the ways the masses join together. . . . Its essence lies in the illusion of community that carries with it definite powers of social regulation."[30]

Irokawa's characterization of these *kyōdōtai* regulations ("[they] guaranteed the security of life and equality among its members") and his description of the real *kyōdōtai* ("alive with potential for change . . . [and from which] men of leadership emerged") powerfully evoke images of the *yonaoshi* movement and underlie, I believe, his belief in the vitality and significance of local citizens' movements. His interpretation gains political relevance by the likeness he offers of its opposites. He

---

28. Oda Makoto, *Yonaoshi no rinri to ronri*, vols. 1 and 2 (Tokyo: Iwanami Shoten, 1972). In the spring of 1976 I saw this Bin Akao proclamation posted near Tokyo's Roppongi crossing and across the road from the Self-Defense Forces Headquarters. Irokawa Daikichi, "The Survival Struggle of the Japanese Community," in J. Victor Koschmann, ed., *Authority and the Individual in Japan: Citizen Protest in Historical Perspective* (Tokyo: University of Tokyo Press, 1978).

29. Irokawa, "Survival," 257–62, 276–80.

30. Irokawa Daikichi, *The Culture of the Meiji Period*, translation edited by Marius B. Jansen (Princeton: Princeton University Press, 1985), 176, 274–76.

finds rural dystopia in imperial Meiji Japan: "A fictive communal village, an organization based in part on compulsion and dominated by landlords." Of its contemporary moral and political equivalent in rural Japan, he writes: "[The] spiritual degeneration has in turn given capitalists and bureaucrats free sway in polluting the nation and developing the land."[31]

Irokawa's idealization of the "old community" as a site of classlessness and group harmony resembles the assertions of many of the advocates of *furusato-zukuri*. But, as we have seen, in likening local citizens' movements to past village movements, he is emphasizing its significance as a site for individual creativity and social autonomy. In this case, the "imagined community" is the vital political other, the locus of civil society.

31. Irokawa, *Culture*, 222; Irokawa, "Survival," 277.

SIX

Agrarianism Without Tradition

The Radical Critique of Prewar Japanese Modernity

Stephen Vlastos

Responding to criticism of Japan's closed agricultural markets, Yamaguchi Iwao, executive director of the Central Union of Agricultural Cooperatives, concluded a ringing defense of the Japanese government's long-standing rice import ban with the following warning. "The principles developed in rice cultivation are the glue of Japanese society. They pervade our social structure, our culture, and our moral code. . . . Without its farms, our society might be fundamentally and irrevocably altered. The pernicious habit of bullying Japanese farmers and ridiculing Japanese agriculture can only lead our nation to ruin."[1]

Threatened by foreign competition, producers the world over are inclined to argue that protection of their industry is in the national interest. What distinguishes the protectionist rhetoric of Japanese farmers is its grandiose assertion of agriculture's historic contribution to Japanese culture. Yamaguchi's defense of the ban on rice imports draws on a "traditional" trope in the discourse on the social value of Japanese agriculture: the farm village as wellspring of Japan's cultural identity. So commonplace and uncontested is this notion that the lead-in to a recent highbrow journalistic piece on rice imports matter-of-factly reported that mandated reductions of paddy field acreage "deprived farmers of their sense of pride as creators of Japanese culture and history."[2]

This essay critically examines agrarian discourses in modern Japan from the perspective of the invention of tradition. I make three points. First, the idea that

I wish to thank my colleagues Deirdre McCloskey and David Arkush for reading and criticizing earlier drafts of this essay, and Totsuka Yoshihisa and Akiko Anson, who assisted my research.

1. Yamaguchi Iwao, "Don't Push Our Farmers Too Far," *Japan Echo* 14, no. 1 (1987): 26. Originally published in *Bungei Shunjū* (January 1987).

2. Ni'ide Makoto, "Rice Imports and Implications," *Japan Quarterly* 41, no. 1 (1993): 19.

Japan's farm villages function as a reservoir of national culture, reproducing the core values and habits that shape Japanese national character, is a relatively recent invention. Although one can find resonance in Tokugawa nativist thought (*kokugaku*), the valorization of the farm village as the heart and soul of Japan belongs to a modern discourse that developed in reaction to social cleavages and national anxieties attendant on industrialization.

The second point concerns the ideological permutations of agrarian thought in the modern period.[3] The dominant agrarian discourse was elitist and conservative, warning that the one-sided development of industry and a neglect of agriculture undermined society's natural bulwark against social revolution. There was also a radical, populist stream of agrarian thought that surfaced around World War I. Largely a discourse of angry outsiders, agrarian populists bitterly criticized the values, culture, and social relations of industrial capitalism. Appalled by the uneven development of the countryside, capitalism's inhumane social relations, and the moral corruption of "great Tokyo," they vehemently criticized Japan's trajectory of modern development.

Radical agrarianism, I argue, was a two-voiced discourse. Running parallel to the furious, apocalyptic polemic against industrial capitalism and urban culture was a utopian discourse on rural harmony and social cohesion. Radical in its critique of capitalism and bourgeois politics, it was not socially revolutionary. Affirming both existing property relations and the sanctity of the farm family, the values at the core of the visionary discourse were conservative.

The third point is analytical and concerns the rhetorical uses of tradition. In contrast to the dominant elite discourse on farm and nation, radical agrarianism did not invent a pre-capitalist golden age of Japanese agriculture. Its lack of nostalgia for the pre-Meiji village, in turn, points to the ideological valence of the trope of invention of tradition. "Tradition" uniquely evokes the authority of the past; it can be mobilized by any discourse of reform, or even of revolution, that hinges on a rhetorical construction of a national past. The rhetoric of utopia, however, posits new social relations in imaginary political space. Tradition, invented or real, has no place.

FROM TOKUGAWA TO MEIJI

Official praise of agriculture in the Tokugawa period (1600–1867), the historical era most closely associated in the popular mind with "traditional" Japan, may suggest that the modern valorization of farming possesses an unbroken lineage. In an often-quoted passage of *Seidan*, Ogyū Sorai (1666–1728), the most influential

---

3. Thomas R. H. Havens, *Farm and Nation in Modern Japan* (Princeton: Princeton University Press, 1974), 7. Readers are referred to Havens's comprehensive study of Japanese prewar agrarian thought and the lucid discussion of bureaucratic agrarianism and state policy.

political theorist of his time, used the Confucian botanical metaphor of root and stem in emphasizing agriculture's importance: "The sages teach us to prize the root and curtail the branches. Agriculture is the root, manufacture and commerce are the branches."[4]

Neo-Confucianism, the official ideology of Tokugawa feudalism, esteemed farming above other mundane occupations because of its social utility and presumed innocence of profit seeking. In the Neo-Confucian scheme merchants enriched themselves and impoverished others by their trade, while farmers supported the whole society by producing food and fiber to feed and clothe the entire population. Yet farmers were praised only to the extent they were law-abiding, diligent in their labor, and dutiful in paying taxes. In the world of Tokugawa feudalism, farming was never more than the mandatory occupation of a politically subordinate and morally inferior social class, and farmers' customs, beliefs, values, and communities were disparaged and viewed with suspicion. It was the warrior class, masters of the literary and martial arts, that embodied virtue.

The Meiji Restoration of 1868, which made economic modernization a top national priority, gave rise to a new discourse on agriculture shaped by the tenets of economic liberalism. Rejecting the notion that farming possessed special social value, Meiji statesmen promoted rural capitalism. In an often-quoted memorial to the emperor dated May 2, 1875, the architect of early Meiji modernization, Ōkubo Toshimishi, argued that enriching and strengthening the nation in the industrial age required "increasing production and building up enterprises" in all sectors, including agriculture.[5] Early Meiji reforms legalized private ownership of land and free movement of labor, imposed a modern land tax based on market values, and removed all barriers to interregional trade. Some farmers protested, but until the end of the nineteenth century the debate over agricultural policy was largely confined to two issues, technology and taxes.[6]

The first evidence of a counterdiscourse arguing agriculture's unique social value is found in the writings of Shinagawa Yajirō, a conservative member of the Meiji government's inner circle, who warned as early as 1884 against neglecting the countryside. "Agriculture," Shinagawa cautioned, "is the foundation of the

4. Cited in Tsunasawa Mitsuaki, *Nihon no nōhonshugi* (Tokyo: Kinokuniya Shinsho, 1971), 17; see also Havens, *Farm and Nation*, 18–21.

5. Quoted in Denda Isao, *Kindai Nihon nōsei shisō no kenkyū* (Tokyo: Miraisha, 1969), 59.

6. In the 1870s the Meiji government promoted the English-American model of large-scale, capital-intensive farming and encouraged the importation of Western farm machinery, but these efforts met with little success. By the mid-1880s advocates of small-scale farming prevailed, and the policy shifted to developing technologies suited to small-scale, labor-intensive farming and promoting their diffusion. See Havens, *Farm and Nation*, 36–41. The Meiji land tax was initially set at 3 percent of land value and was reduced to 2.5 percent in 1877 to appease restive farmers at the time of the Satsuma Rebellion. See Stephen Vlastos, "Opposition Movements in Early Meiji," in Marius B. Jansen, ed., *Cambridge History of Japan*, vol. 5: *The Nineteenth Century* (Cambridge: Cambridge University Press, 1989), 372–82.

family and the foundation of the country."[7] Shinagawa made his remarks in the midst of a massive dispossession of small farm families in the 1880s precipitated by the pro-industrial monetary and fiscal policies of Finance Minister Matsukata Masayoshi.[8] In the 1890s, war with China and the continued rise in farm tenancy again focused attention on the perils of uneven development. With one eye on the manpower demands of modern warfare and the other on the specter of social revolution, bureaucrats in the Ministry of Agriculture and Manufacture developed legislative initiatives—chiefly farm credit institutions and rural industrial cooperatives—designed to stabilize the middle stratum of family farmers who cultivated their own land.[9]

The most vocal apologist for Japanese farming at the turn of the century was Yokoi Tokiyoshi, a professor of agronomy at Tokyo University's agricultural college. A native of Kyushu who studied at the Kumamoto School of Foreign Studies, Yokoi matriculated at Komaba Agriculture College, where he specialized in soil chemistry. Employed first as a lecturer at the Fukuoka Higher Agriculture School and later as professor at his alma mater, Yokoi is remembered today as a pioneer of modern Japanese agronomy.[10] In the late 1890s, however, he took on a new role as the vocal critic of rapid industrialization and in 1897 published a short essay titled "Nōhonshugi," which articulated the main themes of the conservative agrarian critique of modern economic development.[11]

Yokoi couched his defense of agriculture in terms of farming's contribution to the nation-state. One-sided industrial development, he contended, jeopardized the social foundations of the nation. While industry produced greater wealth than agriculture, he conceded, industrialization frayed the social fabric by making the poor poorer and the rich fabulously rich. "Day by day, month by month," Yokoi warned, "the gulf between poor and rich expands." To his regret, Japan increasingly resembled the "advanced" nations of the West, countries where great disparity of wealth incited revolution.[12] Riches did not guarantee national health and security, he cautioned. On the contrary: "The vitality of a country is fostered

---

7. Quoted in Havens, *Farm and Nation*, 65.

8. According to data compiled by Paul Mayet, a German agricultural expert employed by the Japanese government, during the period from 1883 to 1890 some 367,744 farmers were forced into arrears in their payment of the land tax, resulting in foreclosure on more than 115,800 acres of farm land. Cited in E. H. Norman, *Japan's Emergence as a Modern State*, reprinted in John W. Dower, ed., *Origins of the Modern Japanese State* (New York: Pantheon, 1975), 251.

9. See Havens, *Farm and Nation*, 66–83.

10. Yokoi Tokiyoshi is primarily remembered today for developing techniques of brine seed assortment, fertilizer application, and tillage. The entry for Yokoi Tokiyoshi in *Nihon kin gendaishi jiten* (Tokyo: Tōyō Keizai Shinpōsha, 1978), for example, lists only his scientific achievements, not his writings on political economy. Yokoi's collected writings are published in *Yokoi hakushi zenshū* (10 vols.; Tokyo: Yokoi Zenshū Kankōkai, 1925). Hereafter, *Yokoi zenshū*.

11. Yokoi, "Nōhonshugi," in *Yokoi zenshū* 8:225–35.

12. *Yokoi zenshū* 8:227–28.

by its middle class families; it is particularly well developed among farm families."[13] Farmers, Yokoi contended, were physically and morally best qualified to be soldiers; being closest to the soil, they were naturally the most patriotic. Yet because agriculture could not compete with industry under conditions of unrestrained competition, inexorably the gap between urban wealth and rural poverty widened. "If this is allowed to go on," he warned, "the pitiful farmers will gradually be oppressed by the urban rich; sacrificed to their interest, they grow weaker and more impoverished year by year." As had already happened in Europe, in Japan the gap between rich and poor was growing. The social cleavage now observed in Japan, he concluded, would soon spawn socialism and violent social upheaval.[14]

Yokoi wrote "Nōhonshugi" in the decade bracketed by the Sino-Japanese War of 1894–95 and the Russo-Japanese War of 1904–5, a period of rapid urbanization and sustained industrial growth. Yokoi's essay, historian Thomas Havens has written, stands as the inaugural text of modern Japanese agrarianism.[15] But "Nōhonshugi" was not a radical text. Yokoi denounced "industrialism," not capitalism, and looked to the state for the remedy. "It is ultimately the responsibility of the nation-state," he advised, "to help the weak and prevent the strong from preying on the weak." If the state fulfilled its social responsibilities, he concluded, "commerce, industry and agriculture can all advance together."[16] This is the rhetoric of a dissenting insider. In 1897, when Yokoi wrote "Nōhonshugi," he spoke from the position of the loyal opposition. At this point he conceived of the problems of the countryside primarily in terms of the excesses of industrialization and believed in the efficacy of reform.

THE FIRST RADICAL TURN: YOKOI TOKIYOSHI'S THEORY OF THE JAPANESE "SMALL FARM"

If discourse is as much performance as written word, the November 1914 meeting of the Social Policy Association (Shakai Seisaku Gakkai) enacted the sundering of the Meiji consensus on agriculture's role in national development. Convened at Tokyo Imperial University, the eighth general meeting of the group adopted as its theme "The Problem of Protecting Small Farmers."[17] The first report, delivered by Takaoka Kumao (1871–1961), an eminent agricultural economist and educator, attributed the plight of Japan's small family farmers to their underutilization of household labor. Adopting Wilhelm Roscher's distinction between big and small

---

13. Ibid., 229. Quoted in Havens, *Farm and Nation*, 101.

14. *Yokoi zenshū* 8:228.

15. Havens, *Farm and Nation*, 101.

16. *Yokoi zenshū* 8:232.

17. Reprinted in Ōuchi Tsutomu, ed., *Shōnō hogo no mondai* (Tokyo: Nōsangyoson Seisaku Gakkai, 1976). Hereafter, *Shōnō hogo*.

farming, which hinged on the role of household labor in farm management, Takaoka began by observing that in Japan, 4–5 *chō* constituted the upper limit and 1.5 *chō* the lower limit of "small farmer" holdings.[18] The source of the distress of this class, he suggested, was rural overpopulation. Most owner-cultivators simply did not possess enough land to exploit the family's labor power fully, and because little land was left to reclaim, out-migration of farm families appeared the only solution. Invoking Gresham's law, the theory that bad money drives out good, he painted a bleak picture. "With advances in education and rising living costs, the most talented and enterprising will leave the countryside for cities, or will move away, so that those who remain in rural areas will be wives and children, the elderly and the very young, and those [adult men] who can't make a go of it."[19] While not a desirable end in itself, Takaoka hastened to assure the audience, out-migration was preferable to the alternative, birth control, which he strongly opposed as injurious to public morals and hygiene.

The second speaker, Soeda Juichi (1864–1929), was nearing the end of a distinguished career in public finance, having served as under-secretary of the Ministry of Finance and president of the Bank of Taiwan and the Industrial Bank of Japan. Soeda began by noting that from the standpoint of production, small-scale farming was not obviously superior to large-scale farming. From the political standpoint, however, small farmers best served the national interest. These farmers, Soeda confidently asserted, were "conservative, filled with loyalty and easily governed. They do not cause problems for political leaders." They were also an important military resource. Unlike the urban masses, farmers were physically fit; and unlike landlords, they did not buy their way out of military service. Sons of small family farmers "exert themselves unstintingly for the sake of their country." A large and economically viable stratum of small farmers, he concluded, provided an important buffer between the upper classes, who by necessity were few in number, and the growing masses of urban poor.[20] Urgent measures, Soeda warned, were needed to shore up the middle farmers, for "if the social disease flares up in Japan a ferocious force will be unleashed."[21]

While Takaoka and Soeda presented utilitarian arguments in the measured tones and reasoned voices of the statesman and scholar, Yokoi Tokiyoshi seized the occasion to issue a blanket condemnation of Meiji agricultural policy. The Meiji land tax reform of 1873, he declared, was "senseless" and the regulations of the Ministry of Agriculture and Forestry were "arbitrary and meddlesome." Rural credit institutions purportedly established to benefit farmers were in fact "not one wit different" from commercial banks. Subsidy of the sericulture industry only increased farm debt; and in any case, farm by-employment did more harm than

18. 1 *chō* = 2.45 acres.
19. Takaoka Kumao, "Hōkoku dai'ichi seki," in *Shōnō hogo*, 75.
20. Soeda Juichi, "Hōkoku daini seki," in *Shōnō hogo*, 80–81.
21. Ibid., 97.

good since quick profits promoted sloth and extravagance. The "incomparably stupid" state system of compulsory education only imposed an immense financial burden on farmers. The police "were hopeless," for instead of apprehending "shysters and gangsters" who ensnared village girls, they spent their time interfering with village culture, going so far as to prohibit *obon* dances, plays, and sumo contests. Politicians standing for election in rural districts were "cockroaches" who swarmed out at election time to buy themselves a seat in the Diet.[22] Every government official and agency with the exception of the emperor, it would appear, had a hand in creating the "present situation, where farmers had no choice but to leave in droves."[23]

How did the distinguished gentlemen of the Social Policy Association respond to Yokoi's tirade? The absence of the notation "applause followed" in the published proceedings provides a clue. At least one member, Dr. Fukuda Tokuzō, professor of economics at Tokyo Higher College of Business and Industry, was deeply offended. In his address the following day, Fukuda appended to his prepared remarks a blistering rejoinder to Yokoi's tirade. Dr. Yokoi's lecture, Fukuda asserted, violated all norms of "impartial scholarly inquiry" by interjecting such vulgar epithets as "gangster" and "cockroach" into the serious discussions of a "purely scholarly body like the Social Policy Association." Hadn't Yokoi, Fukuda asked sarcastically, "taken upon himself the role of physician administrating emergency care"?[24]

The bitterness, pessimism, and alienation that leap from Yokoi's text expose the limits of the generalization that a consensus on national priorities prevailed during Japan's modernization. Even within the elite membership of the Social Policy Association, deep divisions of opinion existed on the agricultural question—and this was in 1914, a decade before the onset of the interwar agriculture depression.

The vehemence of Yokoi's complaint and Fukuda's rejoinder strongly suggests that values rather than policy were being contested. Dripping with sarcasm, Fukuda's put-down of Yokoi deployed exactly the right metaphor: emergency-ward physician. Fukuda analyzed the problem of Japanese small-scale farming from the standpoint of market capitalism and questioned whether measures to shore up small-scale farming indeed addressed the urgent national task of "advancing" agricultural production. Yokoi viewed farming as a living organism struggling to survive in a hostile environment. In his last published work, *Shōnō ni kansuru kenkyū* (Studies concerning small farming; 1927), a book Yokoi proudly claimed to be the fruition of "research started fifty-two years ago," he plainly stated his conviction that agriculture held out the possibility of preserving a segment of Japanese

22. Yokoi Tokiyoshi, "Hōkoku daisan seki," in *Shōnō hogo*, 103–6.
23. Ibid., 111.
24. Ibid., 205, 208.

society from the dehumanizing forces of capitalism. "Japan is a country of small farmers," Yokoi wrote in the introduction, and "small-scale farming is not based on capitalism's profit motive; in fact, its essence is anti-capitalist."[25] In every other sector, "the profit motive prevails" and "one class exercises absolute control over other classes." Under capitalism, there are only two classes: the laboring classes, who "produce food and clothing," and capitalists, who "make others work to produce life's essentials." The capitalist entrepreneur, whether industrialist or landlord, is motivated exclusively by the profit motive. He treats "labor, property, and credit as factors of production, bending every effort to reduce costs and maximize profit."[26]

Shōnō ni kansuru kenkyū forcefully argued that Japan's small family farms resisted the dictates of capitalism. Coining the term "labor-power management" (*rōsaku keiei*), Yokoi categorically asserted that small-scale farming was governed by a fundamentally different logic: the maximum utilization of household labor. Only in the case of "big farming" did the principle of profit maximization prevail.[27] In Yokoi's formulation the size of holdings did not dictate the character of social relations in farming. The distinction between "big" and "small" farming was qualitative, reflecting the following criteria: Is a price attached to individual labor? Are farm products treated as marketable commodities?[28] Do farmers depend on capital for the factors of production?[29] In Yokoi's imaginary world of Japanese "small farming," the utilization of farm labor was a moral imperative, not a strategy of profit maximizing, which rendered farming free of compulsion, strife, and alienation. Everyone "willingly puts out the maximum labor, takes pleasure in work, is in sympathy with the environment, and finds happiness in nurturing the growth of plants and animals."[30] Japan's small family farms, in other words, were conceived as a social space immune to what Marx identified as the most dehumanizing effects of social relations under capitalism: exploitation and alienation.

Acknowledging that the husband exercised authority over his wife, Yokoi nevertheless claimed that in small farm households, in actual practice "there are no bosses or underlings; just plain workers who, without regard to status, will do what needs to be done."[31] Because value is calculated in terms of household production "reflecting the contributions of men and women, the weak and strong," farm villages do not show "the great gap between rich and poor evident in cities." Adding the qualification that too much equality can be socially debilitating, "only in the countryside," Yokoi claimed, "can one find people of more or less equal economic

25. Yokoi Tokiyoshi, *Shōnō ni kansuru kenkyū* (Tokyo: Maruzen, 1927), 1.
26. Ibid., 5–6.
27. Ibid., 3–4.
28. Ibid., 10–11.
29. Ibid., 34–35.
30. Ibid., 47.
31. Ibid., 48–49.

circumstances."[32] Where everyone, whether landlord or tenant farmer, is motivated by the single desire to utilize family labor fully, "a kind of spirit and a way of thinking" arise that bond villagers together in cooperation and harmony. This "spiritual element," the enabling condition of harmony and cohesion, frees farming from the social conflicts of capitalism "even within a developing capitalist economy." When the spiritual element is lost, however, "the cohesiveness of the farm community slackens, agriculture itself collapses, and noncapitalist farming is necessarily transformed into capitalist management."[33]

Yokoi developed his theory that "small farming" escaped the laws of capitalism at a time of sharply escalating conflict between tenant farmers and landlords over rents. In the five years preceding the publication of *Shōnō ni kansuru kenkyū*, more than ten thousand disputes between landlords and tenants were recorded; in 85 percent of the disputes, tenants demanded either permanent or temporary reduction in rents. Obviously, the issue of distributing farm profits was very much on people's minds. Village youths, moreover, appeared to be leaving the countryside in record numbers to take factory and service-sector jobs in cities. In some cases youths were forced out by their family's poverty and holdings so small their labor was largely redundant. But, increasingly, rural young people, and especially women, left voluntarily in search of an easier, more pleasurable and freer life than was possible within the patriarchal farm family. Yokoi's theory of "labor-power management," and his insistence that this principle generally prevailed, required a massive denial of the actual social divisions in Japanese agriculture.

Yokoi Tokiyoshi died in November 1927, five months after the first printing of *Shōnō ni kansuru kenkyū*. The year 1927 also marked the onset of the second agricultural recession of the decade. Farm commodity prices, which had just begun to recover from their post–World War I collapse, began a downward slide in 1926 that turned into free fall after 1929. One can only speculate how Yokoi's thinking might have developed in the crisis years of early Shōwa. As it was, Yokoi bequeathed a potent legacy. He developed a utopian theory of agricultural economy grounded in a moral critique of capitalism. Yokoi's later writings display the distinctive double voice that would characterize depression-era agrarian populism. One voice, angry and alienated, warned in apocalyptic tones of the imminent destruction of Japanese farming, hence of Japan itself. The other voice, urgent and exhortative, promised agricultural renewal, rural harmony, and national salvation.

THE SECOND TURN:
TACHIBANA KŌZABURŌ AND AGRARIAN POPULISM

In the context of the deepening agricultural crisis, agrarianism took a second turn around 1930. Agrarianism, we have seen, surfaced in Japan at the end of the

---

32. Ibid., 52, 252.
33. Ibid., 235.

nineteenth century as a minority critique of one-sided industrial development from within the Meiji establishment. The first turn in agrarian thought, which occurred in the Taishō period (1912–26), is illustrated by Yokoi Tokiyoshi's utopian conception of Japanese farming and his moral critique of capitalist social relations. At the end of the 1920s, however, embattled farmers and rustic intellectuals transformed agrarianism into a movement of economic renewal and political activism. Farmers desperately searching for practical solutions to the very real problem of economic survival, and rural polemicists certain that capitalism and city culture were the root causes of the crisis, developed their own brand of agrarianism.

Tachibana Kōzaburō (1893–1974) and the farm cooperative movement he founded exemplify the radical turn of agrarianism in the early Shōwa period. The son of a wealthy dye merchant in Mito City, the capital of rural Ibaraki Prefecture, Tachibana took up farming as a young man to find spiritual salvation. In February 1915, just before graduating from Tokyo First Higher School, the premier college preparatory institution in Japan, Tachibana dropped out. Foregoing matriculation that spring at Tokyo Imperial University, he returned home and began farming a seven-acre tract of fallow land that belonged to his family in nearby Tokiwa village. Tachibana married in 1916, and the next year his boyhood friend Hayashi Shōzō, who had just graduated from Tokyo Arts University, joined him at the farm. Over the next five years their brothers and sisters followed, creating a thriving farm commune known locally as Kyōdaimura.[34]

Looking back on his new life of relentless farm labor, Tachibana spoke in terms of religious conversion. "I saw God and, guided by the spirit of the divine, was received in the warm embrace of the great natural universe. My heart and whole being were filled with brotherly love for my neighbors and dear friends. In a word, I had at last found my spiritual home."[35] In the late 1920s, as the agricultural recession deepened, however, Tachibana was drawn into a life of political activism. Convinced that agricultural-production cooperatives organized and run by farmers held the key to revitalizing small-scale farming, and informed by a voluminous reading of world history and political economy, Tachibana began to publicize his ideas on the causes and cures of the farm crisis.

Believing that "only farmers can save themselves," Tachibana founded the Aikyōkai farm cooperative movement in 1929. The Aikyōkai quickly became the focal point of agrarian activism in northern Ibaraki. At its peak in 1932 it had 25 village chapters and 400–500 dues-paying members, and published a thick monthly journal, *Nōson kenkyū*. Both a newsletter with technical advice on new farming methods and a platform for political and cultural commentary by the

---

34. Havens, *Farm and Nation*, 234–237. The most detailed and insightful study of Tachibana Kōzaburō's life and thought is found in Matsuzawa Tetsunari, *Tachibana Kōzaburō: Nihon fuashizumu genshi kaiki ron ha* (Tokyo: San'ichi Shobō, 1973).

35. Tachibana Kōzaburō, *Nōsongaku* (Tokyo: Kensetsusha, 1932), preface, 4.

membership, *Nōson kenkyū* offers an intimate view of the thinking of Shōwa-era agrarianism at the grass roots (see figs. 2 and 3).

The tone of Tachibana's writings and many of the essays in *Nōson kenkyū* penned by village-level leaders is apocalyptic. Japan's farm villages confronted "imminent and total collapse," Tachibana warned in the lead essay of the first issue, and because "Japan and [its] farm villages are like fish and water," the nation itself was in peril.[36] Writing late in 1930 Tachibana attributed the "sick condition" of Japanese society to capitalism, arguing that historically capitalism caused "the destruction of villages and the decline of agriculture. While [capitalism] brings prosperity to industry and cities, it has precisely the opposite effect on farm villages."[37]

Passages like this demonstrate the polemical conflation by depression-era agrarian populism of capitalism, industrialization, and the modern city. Under capitalism, Tachibana insisted, the relationship of city to village could only be parasitic and destructive. Modern cities, "the very crystallization of modern capitalism's materialistic civilization," Tachibana declared, "demand the sacrifice of villages; there is absolutely no mutually beneficial developmental relationship."[38] This was a favorite theme. In an essay titled "The Age of Urban Tyranny," Yamakawa Tokio, a frequent contributor to *Nōson kenkyū*, identified the nineteenth century as the beginning of "the era of the capitalist state." How did farm villages fare under this regime? "Bourgeois scholars of agricultural science," Yamakawa warned, claimed the relationship between city and village was symbiotic. Although "a comforting theory," it was all a lie. In the age of the capitalist state, all economic transactions by farmers, whether trade, taxes, insurance, or even savings deposits, were means by which the city exploited the countryside. Cities, Yamakawa concluded, had become "the ruling class, the superstructure."[39]

The climactic metaphor of "The Age of Urban Tyranny" is a city likened to a "monstrous three-legged idol stained crimson with the blood of farmers." Not only the agent of rural economic exploitation and political domination, the city was also the producer of a mass culture of hedonism that attacked the village from within by colonizing farmers' minds. When Yamakawa sarcastically queried, "Is there anything more to cities than prostitutes, cafes, geisha houses, dance halls, cinemas, theaters, and department stores?" he gave voice to a deep and pervasive fear of Japanese farmers: the out-migration of village youths. The prosperity and luxury of cities represented more than wealth gained by an economic exploitation of the countryside. Cities stole away village youths by proffering a more exciting and easier way of life. An anonymous poem, "Guarding the Village," in the inaugural issue of *Nōson kenkyū*, for example, expressed the profound feeling of loss

36. Ibid., 10.
37. Tachibana, *Nōsongaku*, 142, 87.
38. Tachibana Kōzaburō, *Kōdō kokka nōhon kenkoku ron* (Tokyo: Kensetsusha, 1932), 9.
39. *Nōson kenkyū* (January 1931): 12–13.

experienced by a family whose only son fled the ancestral home for "the bright lights of the city."[40] Daughters, too, were being enticed away. "What is the world coming to," Tachibana Kōzaburō cried out in frustration, "when village maidens who are our pride and joy" desired only to become "servants in Tokyo, or, even worse, cafe waitresses?"[41]

In 1931, when *Nōson kenkyū* began publication, the crisis of Japanese farmers was real as well as imagined. Farm income declined steeply as prices of rice and raw silk, the largest cash crops, plummeted. The wholesale price of rice, which stood at ¥35 per *koku* in 1927 and ¥29 in 1929, fell to ¥18 in 1930. The decline of raw silk prices, which largely depended on exports to the United States, was even steeper. At the same time, taxes, interest payments, and fertilizers—farmers' principal costs—held steady or declined moderately.[42] Although not as deep or long-lasting as the agricultural depression, the industrial recession dealt an additional blow to poor farm families, especially tenant farmers who depended on remittances of sons' and daughters' factory wages. Escalating conflict between landlords and tenants added to the crisis atmosphere. Landlord-tenant disputes, which had declined somewhat in the latter half of the 1920s, exploded, more than doubling in number between 1928 and 1933.[43]

If material conditions fueled the apocalyptic tone of early Shōwa agrarianism, the crisis of the world capitalist system created in the minds of many Aikyōkai members the possibility of the birth of a new social order. Writing in January 1931 Yamakawa Tokio reassured readers that "the collapse of capitalism and also of the urban culture is not the same as the end of all civilization." In fact, the present crisis harbingered epochal change. "Necessarily, the road will open to a new age of local self-government and economic self-sufficiency. The nineteenth century was the era of the city, centralized polity, and large industry. But the twentieth century will be the age of agriculture, the farm village, and the devolution of political authority to localities."[44] In a postscript to the February 1931 issue of *Nōson kenkyū*, the editor, Sugiura Takashi, sounded the same theme. Capitalism had reached a historic impasse, and its self-destruction due to internal contradictions had already begun. "But rising from the ruins of capitalism is the banner of the agricultural cooperative movement, held high by the new-awakened farming masses, [who will] build a society with agriculture as the essence."[45] At the

---

40. Ibid., 30.

41. Tachibana, *Kōdō kokka*, 17.

42. Itō Masanao, Ōkado Masakatsu, and Suzuki Masayuki, *Senkan ki no Nihon nōson* (Tokyo: Sekai Shisōsha, 1988), 151–54.

43. Ann Waswo, *Japanese Landlords: Decline of a Rural Elite* (Berkeley and Los Angeles: University of California Press, 1977), 100.

44. *Nōson kenkyū* (January, 1931): 15.

45. Aikyōkai members dismissed the state-sponsored agricultural producers associations as "not real cooperatives but another form of capitalism." See the essay by Kawamata Sietarō in the inaugural issue of *Nōson kenkyū* (January 1931): 55–56.

vanguard of the historic movement of Japan's farmers, Sugiura boasted, was "our Aikyōkai," which had blazed the trail of farm village regeneration one year earlier by establishing the first true production cooperative, the Aikyōkai livestock cooperative.[46]

Agricultural-production cooperatives organized locally and managed entirely by farmers formed the core of the Aikyōkai program of farm village renewal. Production cooperatives offered farmers more than the economic advantages of market leverage and economies of scale. By bringing people together in collective labor, they made it possible to transcend the destructive ethos of acquisitive individualism. "When performed with a pure heart, diligent farm labor," Tachibana claimed, "spiritually and materially harmonizes the interests of self and other" and thereby "bestows the riches of true brotherhood." Unlike socialist alternatives to capitalist organization, production cooperatives arose "directly from human nature." A life of working and living together such as Tachibana experienced at Kyōdaimura, enabled people to grasp "the true meaning of human existence and its attendant joys. It fills people with virtue and secures their livelihood."[47]

Production cooperatives offered Aikyōkai members practical advantages, but the compelling attraction was their promise of spiritual fulfillment and new beginnings. It was a vision, moreover, that did not look to the past for legitimation or guidance. There was no talk of restoring a lost golden age. On the contrary, the figure of the traditional Japanese village in Aikyōkai discourse was uniformly negative. For example, an article in the March 1931 issue of *Nōson kenkyū* welcomed the "collapse of the old feudal village" and approvingly noted the "uninterrupted efforts of our Aikyōkai to build new farm villages." References to village tradition (*dentō*) were negative. In recounting the history of the Aikyōkai chapter in Yanagikawa village, the writer explained that as long as farmers "failed to free themselves from the shackles of tradition," no progress was possible.[48] In the November issue Shōji Hajime, a leader in Kuji district, where the Aikyōkai was particularly strong, praised Tachibana for showing the way to a bright future by "shucking off the old skin of traditional customs and habits and articulating a vision of rural renewal."[49]

If the Aikyōkai evoked an image of their past to explain the present, it was not a lost "golden age," but rather a history of "hundreds of years of exploitation of the feudal peasant."[50] Nor in the view of Kawamata Seitarō, director of the Aikyōkai production cooperative, did the Meiji Restoration bring much improvement. "The Meiji Restoration was a movement from the top down, carried out by a minority at the center." The Aikyōkai movement, he insisted, was the exact

---

46. *Nōson kenkyū* (February 1931): 52.

47. Tachibana, *Nōsongaku*, 20

48. *Nōson kenkyū* (March 1931): 20.

49. *Nōson kenkyū* (September 1931): 11.

50. *Nōson kenkyū* (February 1931): 55.

opposite: "a movement of farmers from the bottom up and from the provinces to the capital." While Meiji statesmen's goals were military strength and industrial development, the Aikyōkai's mission was "to build a truly free, unified, and equal Japan."[51] Until recently, another writer insisted, farmers lived lives of "blind obedience, not believing in themselves or taking the initiative." Now that farmers had become conscious of their historical condition, he continued, "[the] time when farmers can be hoodwinked by such pure cant as 'Farmers are the Treasure of the Nation' is long gone."[52]

Aikyōkai members imagined their movement as "the bright light of dawn breaking over the sleeping villages."[53] At times Tachibana spoke as if the new agrarian order spelled the end to capitalism, even predicting that "an international movement of farmers will sweep the world clean of capitalism." A few pages later, however, he defined his mission in terms of "the fundamental rectification of capitalism," implying that reform was possible.[54] Moreover, Tachibana and other writers explicitly rejected materialist solutions to the economic crisis and affirmed conservative gender relations. Private property and the patriarchal farm family still constituted the social foundations of the farm village.

Made up largely of owner-cultivators, the Aikyōkai insisted that rural renewal did not require land redistribution. The Marxist analysis of the rural crisis, Tachibana protested, was all wrong, since "tenants do not sell their labor and large landowners do not purchase labor power." Denying that social divisions based on capital were relevant in farming, Tachibana insisted that "we farmers are simply farmers, neither capitalists nor the proletariat." Because the tenant used the same technology as his landlord, Tachibana argued, "tenants do not need to look upon landlords as the enemy."[55]

The conception of the family, too, was ultimately conservative. "History," Tachibana wrote, "tells us that all culture is preserved within the family and all culture will dissipate when the family dissolves."[56] Tachibana's idea of the family was not the authoritarian *ie sei* based on lineage that Meiji conservatives advocated. Rather, he imagined the ideal farm family in terms of the late Meiji invented tradition of "home" (*katei*): domesticity as opposed to lineage, and cohesion arising from love rather than the legal authority of the male household head.[57] Nevertheless, in Tachibana's ideal farm family, order and harmony were achieved through a distinctly Confucian conception of a natural moral hierarchy,

51. *Nōson kenkyū* (September 1931): 23.
52. *Nōson kenkyū* (April 1931): 25–6.
53. *Nōson kenkyū* (February 1931): 62.
54. Tachibana, *Nōsongaku*, II, 45.
55. *Nōson kenkyū* (August 1931): 6–7.
56. Tachibana, *Nōsongaku*, 243.
57. For a discussion of *ie sei* and *katei* and the invented tradition of "home," see Jordan Sand, "At Home in the Meiji Period: Inventing Japanese Domesticity," in this volume.

not through relations of equality. The family and farming were, in fact, inseparable in this conception. "In the last analysis what most distinguishes farming [from industry] is the essential family element of small [farm] management. It is a fundamental principle that farm management cannot be separated from family life."[58]

The social construction of agriculture as an enterprise that uniquely fused family solidarity and economic production conveyed a strong message. Japanese agriculture anchored the entire society by reproducing both harmonious relations and gender hierarchy. "Japan," Tachibana warned, "must return to the sacred family system that nurtures the very life of the Japanese nation. This, I must insist, is the starting point for a fundamental reform of economic relations and [social] organization."[59]

This was a message that broad segments of Japanese opinion in the 1930s welcomed as an antidote to capitalism's erosion of the relations of social authority. The enshrinement of agriculture and village as the wellspring of authentic Japanese culture occurred in the context of military aggression in northeast Asia, international censure, and intensified ideological mobilization for war with America and England. But the 1930s was also a time of social and cultural turmoil: disputes between landlords and tenants reached unprecedented heights; rural youths poured into cities, attracted by service-sector employment; and in cities men and women experimented with new gender roles.[60] Under these conditions, the reassuring image of harmonious and productive farm families served the ideological needs of many sectors of Japanese society.

The underlying social conservatism of agrarian populism helps to explain its right-wing trajectory. Morally offended by capitalism's values, antagonistic to central authority, cool toward the military, and suspicious of overseas expansion, the Aikyōkai despised representative government, loathed Marxism, and feared social revolution. As long as the Aikyōkai stayed local, eschewing a broader politics, the movement managed to contain these contradictory ideological vectors. When Tachibana lurched into national politics, however, he pulled the movement hard to the right. In 1932, nineteen Aikyōkai members secretly enlisted by Tachibana joined army and navy officers in the Incident of May 15—attacks against government officials and installations in Tokyo intended to ignite a general insurrection. The army and navy officers assassinated Seiyūkai prime minister Inukai Tsuyoshi, whose murder brought down the last party cabinet of the prewar period.

The operational assignment of the Aikyōkai conspirators—to bomb power transmitters—was consistent with Tachibana's subsequent explanation of why he allied with the militarists. He desired, he later confessed, to awaken the metropolis to the desperate plight of villages by "plunging great Tokyo into darkness." The

---

58. Tachibana, *Nōsongaku*, 25.
59. Tachibana, *Kōdō kokka*, 244–45.
60. See Miriam Silverberg, "The Cafe Waitress Serving Modern Japan," in this volume.

Aikyōkai saboteurs failed to dim even one offensive neon sign with their primitive explosives. However, if Tachibana's goal indeed was to move the farm crisis to the center stage of national politics, the gambit succeeded. The mass media played an important role, sympathetically reporting the trial of the young army and navy assassins who claimed to have acted to save "village Japan." Political parties and the bureaucracy, which had given farmers short shrift before the spring of 1932, sprang into action. Appropriations for rural relief provided some material benefit—¥420 million between 1932 and 1934. Equally important, village representatives and government bureaucrats found common ground in a rhetoric of self-reliance and self-help on the one hand, and cooperation and collective effort on the other.[61] The public relations offensive that accompanied the campaign reinforced the identification of Japan's farm villages with conservative social core values. Soon afterward the bureaucracy launched a new campaign to recruit up to a million poor farmers to the imperial cause of colonizing Japan's new puppet state of Manchuria.[62] By the Pacific War the propaganda machine could persuasively identify Japan's villages as "spiritually and demographically the incubator of national strength."[63]

61. For an important revisionist interpretation of the farm village rehabilitation movement, see Kerry Douglas Smith, "A Time of Crisis: Japan, the Great Depression, and Relief Policy" (Ph.D. diss., Harvard University, 1994).

62. See Louise Young, "Colonizing Manchuria: The Making of an Imperial Myth," in this volume.

63. Furukubo Sakura, "Senzen, nōson ni okeru 'bosei' o meguru 'shisō,'" in Miyoshi Masayoshi, ed., *Shōnō no shiteki bunseki* (Tokyo: Fumin Kyōkai, 1990), 226.

SEVEN

Colonizing Manchuria

The Making of an Imperial Myth

Louise Young

Over the course of the 1930s Manchurian colonization became a social movement, a government program, and an icon of the imperial idea. Emerging from a
broad-based popular effort to resolve problems of social conflict and poverty in
the countryside, the Manchurian colonization program aimed to solve those
problems through the resettlement of 5 million poor tenant farmers in the rural
hinterlands of the new puppet state of Manchukuo. Before the program was in-
terrupted by Japan's defeat in 1945, more than 300,000 people made the voyage
physically, and unmeasurable numbers traveled to the new frontier in journeys of
their imagination.[1] The success of the movement depended in large part on the
construction of a heroic narrative of colonization.

With the exception of Hokkaido, mass colonization was a departure from Japanese colonial practice, but as the program got underway, appeals to support the
Manchurian project increasingly sought to represent it as part of a long-standing
historical tradition of colonization. Propagandists created the illusion of tradition in
a number of ways. They constructed an orthodox historical narrative and built a heroes gallery. In the process, they created an imperial tradition that blended in equal
measure ingredients from the colonization movement at home with those from the
settlements themselves, reinforcing the ties that bound empire to metropolis.

THE MANCHURIAN COLONIZATION MOVEMENT

The Manchurian colonization campaign of the 1930s emerged out of the synthesis
of two social movements that traced their roots to before the turn of the century.

1. The material in this essay draws heavily from chapters 7 and 8 of my book, *Japan's Total Empire:
Manchuria and the Culture of Wartime Imperialism* (Berkeley and Los Angeles: University of California
Press, 1997).

For both the agrarianist and the emigration movements, this joining represented a striking departure from precedent. Prior to 1932, these movements had developed their institutional vehicles and organizational ideology largely in isolation from each other. Advocates of emigration talked about the empire, agrarianists about the rural economy, and neither group shared the other's concerns.

Promoted by landlord associations, the Ministry of Agriculture and Commerce, agricultural colleges, and local training centers, the early agrarian movement sought to protect the rural sector from the socioeconomic transformations brought about by economic development and the integration of Japan into a world economy.[2] Their spokesmen envisioned the village community in utopian terms, imagining a harmony of community interests against the reality of mounting class tensions and trusting that village self-help and self-reliance could buffer farmers from the destabilizing effects of integration into an international market. At a time when taxation and other national government policies were increasingly shaping the realities of the village economy, agrarianists talked about the importance of local autonomy and village self-government. And while the real sociology of Japanese villages revealed a complex hierarchy of landowning and tenant classes, agrarianists conceived the village in terms of a collection of independent owner-cultivators. The exhortations and prescriptions of agrarianists rejected the socioeconomic reality that capitalism was producing in Japan's farm villages: theirs was a vision of an alternate modernity.

While agrarianists were searching for utopian villages in Japan, a movement to promote the interests of an expanding Japanese empire through the establishment of overseas communities of Japanese farmers was forming its own institutions and ideology. The emigration movement began in the 1870s when the northern island of Hokkaido became the first target of mass-colonization schemes as part of the nation-building project of the new Meiji government. Inhabited almost exclusively by the ethnically distinct Ainu population, settlement by ethnic Japanese was regarded as a prerequisite to the political and economic incorporation of the territory into the fabric of the new nation-state.

From its birth in the colonization of Hokkaido, the emigration movement expanded its purview to the European settlement societies of the Americas and the Pacific. With emigration legalized in 1884, Japanese were encouraged by government officials and private organizations to move to Hawaii, the west coast of the United States and Canada, South America, and briefly, to Australia and New Zealand. And when Japanese emigrants began to encounter the hostility of nativist movements in the neo-Europes of the Americas and the Pacific, ending discrimination against Japanese nationals became an object of Japanese diplomacy.

2. For early agrarianism, see Carol Gluck, *Japan's Modern Myths: Ideology in the Late Meiji Period* (Princeton: Princeton University Press, 1985), 178–86; R. P. Dore, *Land Reform in Japan* (New York: Schocken Books, 1985), 56–107; Thomas R. H. Havens, *Farm and Nation in Modern Japan: Agrarian Nationalism, 1870–1940* (Princeton: Princeton University Press, 1974), chaps. 3–4.

Although this failed to avert exclusionary policies in New Zealand, Australia, and the United States, emigration advocates continued to assert the right to the "honorary white" status they felt was due the citizens of an imperial power.

Just as doors were beginning to close against Japanese immigrants in these societies, a new frontier of settlement opened up in Japan's expanding colonial empire. From the turn of the century, the emigration movement expanded its energies to include schemes for mass settlement of Japanese farmers in Taiwan, Korea, and South Manchuria, where settlers were being regarded as a tool in the economic development of colonial resources and the social control of the native population.[3]

In contrast to the colonization of Hokkaido, which was quite successful, the idea of settlement in the more foreign lands across the ocean and in the Japanese colonies seemed more popular in the abstract than in reality. The vast majority of its promoters had no intention of moving themselves, but they thought it imperative that others did. From the early Meiji period a clamorous assembly of bureaucrats, businessmen, and intellectuals lectured each other and a largely unresponsive populace on the benefits of colonization. Institutionally composed of the semi-government colonization companies that subsidized land acquisition and resettlement, and the host of colonization societies that advertised opportunities for emigration, the emigration movement was fueled by the energy of promoters rather than migrants; it was emigration preached from above by a welfare-minded elite, not pushed from below by land-hungry farmers. Moreover, from its beginnings in Hokkaido colonization, emigration advocates viewed the growth of overseas communities of compatriots as a means to enrich the nation and expand Japanese territory. In this sense emigration was tied to Japan's expansion as an imperial power and regarded as a measure of imperial prestige.

Before 1931 the emigration movement maintained only tenuous ideological and institutional ties to Japanese agrarianism: its mission was to build the empire, not to save Japanese agriculture. This would change after 1931, when a combination of social pressures engendered by the depression and opportunities opened up by the Japanese military occupation of Manchuria drove the two movements together. Intensification of the agrarian social crisis in Japan led the emigration and agrarianist movements to join forces in the Manchurian colonization campaign, made possible by the creation in 1932 of the Japanese puppet state of Manchukuo and the extension of control over Manchurian lands.

Already weakened by a decade of crisis, the global reverberations of the Wall Street crash of 1929 dealt the rural economy a stunning blow. The wave of urban factory closings drove displaced workers back to their ancestral homes in the villages. Agricultural prices fell further and came back more slowly than those of manufacturing goods. This sense of relative deprivation heightened the urgency

3. For a discussion of plans for the Japanese settlement of Korea, see Karl Moskowitz, "The Creation of the Oriental Development Company: Japanese Illusions Meet Korean Reality," *Occasional Papers on Korea*, no. 2 (March 1974).

of the appeals for help that bombarded the government in 1931 and 1932, finally inducing the government to convoke a special "save agriculture" session of the Diet from August 22 to September 4, 1932.

It was more than just the specter of human misery that convinced the government of the importance of addressing the rural crisis. The protracted agricultural crisis intensified social conflict in the villages and gave rise to a new wave of tenancy disputes centered in northern Japan.[4] The sharp rise in disputes over eviction in the 1930s focused attention on the issue of land shortage. One bureaucrat from the Ministry of Agriculture and Forestry summarized:

> The deadlock in the rural economy is decidedly not caused by irrationality in the economic structure of the farm community, the need for more organization, a lack of planning, or even, as some argue, the feudal character of the farmers. The basic problem always comes back to the inability to adjust population to land resources.[5]

To many observers at the time, it seemed that the "problem of the villages" boiled down to too many farmers competing for too little land.

Against this backdrop, support gathered for funding the resettlement of this excess population on the reputedly limitless Manchurian frontier. Groups proposing that rural poverty could be solved by Manchurian emigration mushroomed in farm villages throughout the country. Already by September 1932 more than eighty-four local organizations had drawn up emigration plans.[6] But the government had adopted its own program for rural relief, based on debt relief, public works, and what was known as "rehabilitation through self-help." The effect of the reform measures of this program were modest at best, and to some, including a spokesman for the program, it "only deepened the class divisions in the villages."[7] Casting about for new policies, rural elites began to entertain the more radical solution of exporting the problem. Thus, in 1937, with encouragement from local communities and farm organizations, the Agriculture and Forestry Ministry adopted a program to help finance group emigration from villages that wished to participate. Embracing the overall goal of exporting nearly one-fifth of the domestic farm population, the ministry made mass emigration the new cornerstone of its revamped rural rehabilitation policy.

The impact of this policy was dramatic. From the experimental settlements of 1932 through 1936, to the peak of "emigration fever" in the late 1930s and into the years of the Pacific War, 321,882 emigrants were mobilized to participate in the Manchurian project. The Manchurian emigrants came disproportionately from specific regions of Japan. Nagano and Yamagata prefectures sent by far the great-

4. Ann Waswo, *Japanese Landlords: The Decline of a Rural Elite* (Berkeley and Los Angeles: University of California Press, 1977), 127–34.

5. Sugino Tadao, *Nōson kōsei undō to bunson keikaku* (Tokyo: Nōson Kōsei Kyōkai, 1938), 3.

6. Manshū Kaitakushi Kankōkai, *Manshū kaitakushi* (Manshū Kaitakushi Kankōkai, 1966), 33.

7. Sugino, *Nōson kōsei undō*, 5.

est numbers, together accounting for 17 percent of the total.[8] When nearby Fukushima, Niigata, Miyagi, and Gifu are added in, it becomes clear that one-third of the Manchurian colonists came from a small number of prefectures in east central and northeast Japan.

Although overpopulation was the ostensible reason for promoting emigration, the regional clustering of the Manchurian colonization movement emerged from a combination of two factors. First, the agricultural crisis was felt unevenly. The impact of the drop in rice prices affected agriculture as a whole, but the fall in the value of silk and the crop failures of 1933 and 1934 were more localized disasters. The most active prefecture in the colonization movement was Nagano—also the nation's number one silk producer. Adverse weather conditions caused a precipitous drop in rice production in the six prefectures of northeast Japan. Such conditions led both to the disintegration of village finances and to an intensification of social conflict. During the 1930s tenancy disputes were most prevalent in emigration centers of the Tōhoku and Chūbu regions, and in the Tōhoku this represented a 606 percent rise in disputes from the previous decade. Moreover, in contrast to regions such as the Kinki, a high proportion of the Tōhoku disputes concerned eviction.[9] Landlords in the Tōhoku thus had a greater incentive for supporting the resettlement of their tenants overseas.

However, heightened economic hardship and intensified social conflict did not of itself generate the emergence of a Manchurian colonization movement. The second factor explaining participation was the existence of local institutions already active in promoting emigration. Nagano, again, provides an excellent example. The prefectural Board of Education had assiduously promoted emigration since 1888, the date of its first publication on the subject. Numerous local emigration associations formed after the Russo-Japanese War, including Nagano's Overseas Settlement Council. The latter steadily extended the scope of its activities and sponsored a mass emigration plan in the 1920s to establish a Nagano Village in Brazil.[10]

The Manchurian colonization movement of the 1930s was built upon this sturdy institutional base, enabling prefectures like Nagano to get their movements off the ground with astonishing speed. By 1932 local organizations in Nagano had drafted five separate emigration plans, including a ten-year scheme drawn up by the Nagano Overseas Settlement Council to send four hundred households each year in order to build a colony it called the Manchurian Patriotic Nagano Village.

The key to the success of the movement in all of these areas was the organizational and ideological fusion of the agrarian movement, which aimed to save the

8. Nagano-ken Kaitaku Jikōkai Manshū Kaitakushi Kankōkai, *Nagano-ken Manshū kaitakushi*, vol. 1 (Nagano: Nagano-ken Kaitaku Jikōkai Manshū Kaitakushi Kankōkai, 1984), 309.

9. Waswo, *Japanese Landlords*, 97, 102.

10. *Nagano-ken Manshū kaitakushi* 1:1–70, 101–20.

domestic farm villages, with the emigration movement, which aimed to promote the empire. Wedding agriculture to empire, the Manchurian colonization movement hoped to strengthen both.

The rise of a significant constituency of support from among the rural community convinced the government to turn the modest trial emigration project of 1932–35 into the prodigious "Millions to Manchuria" program of 1936. Once mobilized, the central government lent extraordinary financial and institutional backing to the enterprise. Domestically, the Millions to Manchuria policy spurred the emergence of a dense network of institutions and programs to push emigration. At the national level, the machinery to propel migration became the work of two government bureaucracies, the Colonial Ministry and the Agriculture and Forestry Ministry. Both ministries were awarded large budgets to carry out their tasks; in 1937 alone the Colonial Ministry earmarked ¥9 million to promote the emigration of six thousand households while Agriculture and Forestry designated ¥5 million for aid to participating communities.[11]

Manchurian colonists were mobilized through two key programs: the Community Emigration Program and the Patriotic Youth Brigade. The first program mobilized households and dominated Manchurian colonization in the 1936–38 period. The Youth Brigade was inaugurated in 1938. Targeting young men between fourteen and twenty-one, it aimed to keep the colonization movement going in spite of declining interest in emigration among adults.

Most Japanese adults who emigrated did so through the Community Emigration Program.[12] This system involved the participating village or district as an entire community. Everybody, from the mayor to the third sons of tenant farmers, got drawn into a collective effort to remake the social, political, and economic structure of the village. At the village level the mobilization began with the decision to develop countermeasures to alleviate the economic crisis. Sometimes this decision came after pressure from a local emigration movement, sometimes after lobbying from prefectural authorities. In either case, such a decision reflected a consensus among the village elites. Next, an office was set up within the town hall with direct connections to the mayor and vice mayor. This office administered several departments that linked up with local voluntary organizations such as reservists, youth groups, and farm cooperatives. After surveying the village lands to determine an ideal ratio of population to land, the emigration office drew up a plan to resettle "excess" village population in Manchuria. Then an intense recruitment campaign began, concentrating on the village poor, to mobilize volunteers for the creation of a branch village in Manchuria.

The Patriotic Youth Brigade, accounting for more than a third of the Manchurian emigrants, used Colonial Training Courses as a strategy of mobilization.

---

11. *Manshū kaitakushi*, 203, 807.

12. A total of 422 *imindan* (immigration groups) of between 200 and 300 people each were sent to Manchuria, of which 319 were recruited as town or village units. *Manshū kaitakushi*, 332.

The graduating classes of higher primary schools, the equivalent of eighth grade, were encouraged to take part in a week's retreat at one of the prefectural training camps run, typically, by the County Board of Education.[13] The participants from each school would form into ten-boy groups, which became the basic units in the paramilitary organization maintained during the week's training. Commanding the troops in the program of military, spiritual, and physical training were their teachers, youth association leaders, prefectural bureaucrats, and officers from the local regiment and reservist association.[14] Most prefectures held a number of training courses per year at several different locations. Okayama, for example, held twenty training sessions in 1940 attended by a total of 1,121 students.[15] Nationwide, the Manchurian Settlement Yearbook of 1941 recorded 20,000 schoolboys taking part in these courses during the same year.[16]

Together the Community Emigration Program and the Patriotic Youth Brigade mobilized Japanese farm villages in ways unprecedented in both the history of the empire and the history of state interventions in rural society. This feat was made possible by the synthesis of the agrarianist and emigration movements, and their combined ability to mobilize the resources of the state for Manchurian colonization.

THE MISSION TO COLONIZE

Both the Youth Brigade and the Community Emigration Program were essentially recruitment programs. In order to mobilize volunteers, movement organizers devoted a considerable amount of time and energy to the creation and dissemination of emigration propaganda. This they conceived in terms of a mission to colonize that articulated the combined goals of the agrarian and emigration movements. In addition to being an effective rallying cry, the mission was designed to justify the new and large-scale bureaucratic involvement of the Japanese government in colonization. The movement communicated this mission through a staggering volume of propaganda and recruitment literature produced by local committees, prefectural bureaucracies, the Manchurian Emigration Council, and the Ministry of Agriculture and Forestry. In both the production and the dissemination phases, emigration propaganda involved not only the new state institutions

13. Beginning in 1896 the Japanese educational system mandated eight years of education. After 1908 these were divided between six years of regular primary school (*jinjō shōgakkō*) and two years of higher primary school (*kōtō shōgakkō*). In the wartime educational reform of 1941, these became amalgamated into a single school (*kokumin gakkō*), but the division between a lower course of six years (*shotōka*) and an upper course of two years (*kōtōka*) remained unchanged.

14. Sakuramoto Tomio, *Manmō kaitaku seishōnen giyūgun* (Tokyo: Aoki Shoten, 1987), 154–92.

15. Okayama Kenshi Hensan Iinkai, ed., *Okayama kenshi*, vol. 12: *Kindai*, pt. 3 (Okayama: San'yō Shinbunsha, 1989), 364.

16. Manshūkoku Tsūshinsha, ed., *Manshū kaitaku nenkan* (Xinjing: Manshūkoku Tsūshinsha, 1941), 445.

created for that purpose, but also private institutions of the mass media, countless artists, writers, and performers—and finally colonists themselves.

The outlines of what became the orthodox narrative of Manchurian migration began to appear in 1937, as the Millions to Manchuria policy entered its first year. At this juncture it was important to put to rest the doubts and suspicions raised by several years of bad press on the fortunes of the first experimental settlements. Thus when Japanese read pamphlets or articles about Manchurian migration, they were treated to a historical account of the project that focused exclusively on these early years of trial, making heroes of the participants and celebrating the transition of the colonization project from a past era of hardship into a present period of bounty.

Previously emigration promoters had simply tried to minimize reports of unremitting Chinese "bandit attacks" and other hardships. In 1935 a Colonial Ministry official insisted: the bandits that "people at home were so worried about" were "not as numerous as the sensationalistic press accounts would have us believe." The president of an emigration society also dismissed the significance of a "bandit problem," exclaiming, "Why, the true character of these bandits is no different from the household burglars you read about every day in the Japanese papers."[17]

The historical accounts of migration drawn up after 1937 abandoned this line, glorifying instead the dangers of banditry and the corresponding heroism of the settlers. For example, a Mantetsu pamphlet entitled *Manchuria: The Settler's Paradise* focused, as became the pattern, on the adventures of the first and second settlements in Iyasaka and Chiburi, which had suffered more than any subsequent groups from armed attack, poor production, and high desertion rates. As *The Settler's Paradise* described their plight:

> With banditry still rampant . . . the settlers had to arm themselves . . . with a hoe in one hand and a gun in the other. . . . The first and second settlements got drawn into a struggle for their lives even as they struggled to open the land. . . . In May 1934 the first and second settlements were completely surrounded by a group of several thousand bandits. However, they fought bravely and refused to yield even one step to the enemy. On the contrary they drove the bandit forces to retreat.

But the incident took its toll, the authors noted grimly, with twenty-four dead and many others wounded. Forty percent of the colonists withdrew in frustration, making this the low point of Manchurian settlement.

The pamphlet followed this gloomy picture with a stirring speech given by the colonists who decided to stick it out:

> We are the apostles who descended to Manchuria from the holy land of Japan. Just as in the ancient age of the gods the children of heaven descended to the home of the gods, now we will build a new home of the gods in a corner of North Manchuria.

17. Yoshizaki Senshū, "Manshū imin no senku dantai no kūshin," *Ie no hikari* (April 1935): 124; "Yowatari annai," *Ie no hikari* (February 1935): 146.

With these words the story shifted and the fate of the colonists suddenly changed. Brides arrived from Japan, children were born, and the colony began to flourish. Explaining the "joy of ending a desperate fight," *The Settler's Paradise* concluded its historical summary with the happy news that "in thirty skirmishes over five years the colonists demonstrated their bold fighting spirit, and the large and small bandit groups in the area no longer dared to touch them."[18]

Such stories, circulated in the late 1930s, made Iyasaka and Chiburi settlements household names by the early 1940s. As a Colonial Ministry researcher boasted, in 1934 "no one had heard" of Iyasaka and Chiburi, but in 1942 there was "not a soul who do not know their names." Thus, in the space of a few years, an orthodox history of Manchurian colonization had been etched into public memory.[19]

In the course of repetition certain details of this narrative became writ in stone. Even in abridged versions, found in such locations as the Japan Tourist Bureau's *Travel Guide to Manchuria*, it was "five years" and "thirty engagements" before the colonists triumphed over the bandits; and no one failed to mention the arrival of the women and the "baby rush." The settlers were invariably designated the "desperate trial colonists," and the account always ended with the "fear of the colonists" planted in the minds of the bandits.[20]

As a result of the dissemination of this heroic tale, Iyasaka and Chiburi were usually at the top of the sightseer's agenda. Both colonies built hotels to accommodate the crowds that converged on their communities.[21] Calling them the "mecca of settlements," one travel diary noted that tourists "taking a quick trip usually stop only at the first and second settlements." The deluge of visitors was such that many settlers were reportedly forced to give up farming altogether in order to devote full time to "showing people around."[22]

Explaining the popularity of this "immigration showcase," the same travel diary related the excitement of "seeing the scars left by the trials of their early experiences" and realizing how far Japanese colonists had come since then. The Iyasaka and Chiburi colonists were "living testimony to the pain and struggle" of settlement; they demonstrated the perseverance required "to build the flourishing settlements you see today." Chiburi, it was noted, "even has a department store"—the ultimate proof of success.[23] By flocking to the site of the "bandit" attacks, sightseers reinforced the imperial legend of the settlers' heroics and helped it to grow. In this way bureaucrats, journalists, and simple tourists collectively constructed a history of emigration that dispelled popular fears aroused by the hardships of the early settlers.

18. *Manshū wa imin no rakudo* (Dalian: Minami Manshū Tetsudō Kabushiki Gaisha, 1937), 1–7.

19. "Kaitaku jūnen no kaiko," *Ie no hikari* (December 1942): 74.

20. Japan Tsūrisuto Byūrō, ed., *Manshū ryokō nenkan 16 nen* (Tokyo: Hakubunkan, 1941), 164.

21. Ibid., 174.

22. Tōa Mondai Chōsakai, ed., *Manshū imin* (Tokyo: Asahi Shinbunsha, 1939), 24–25.

23. Ibid., 24–25.

Out of this historical narrative two figures emerged to become the twin heroes of Manchurian settlement, Tomiya Kaneo and Katō Kanji. Christened the "fathers of colonization," both were symbolically necessary: Tomiya as spiritual forefather of the colonial pioneers, and Katō as patriarch of the homeside emigration movement. Descriptions of the two men stressed their similarities, from the identical "shaggy goatees" they sported to their kindred spirits and their shared trials. Possessed by the same dream, the two men had "overcome a thousand obstacles" to bring that dream to reality. And like the narratives of the "trial immigrants," their stories were told in a manner intended to disarm negative images. Popular biographers celebrated the fact that Tomiya and Katō were "once laughed at as the 'immigration maniacs,'" contrasting this derogatory nickname with its more flattering replacement: "the immigration gods."[24] In this way their stories communicated the same message as the retold tale of the pioneer immigrants: success follows great suffering and hardship.

The images of Tomiya disseminated in songs like Shiratori Seigo's "Colonel Tomiya—Father of Colonization," and in the obituaries following his death in battle against China in the fall of 1937, were of a man who embodied the spirit of the continental adventurer. With Tomiya, "one glance at his wild beard and fearless countenance" revealed a "fierce warrior." His reputation was such that "bandit chiefs had only to hear his name to start quaking in their boots."[25]

In addition to "god" and "father" of immigration, Tomiya was crowned with numerous popular sobriquets: "sentimental warrior" because of his reputation as a poet, and "the ballast stone of continental expansion" from a line in one of his own poems. He was known also as the "fisherman of Sankiang," referring to his military adventuring in North Manchuria, and (his personal favorite) *hokushin*, or "strike north," the slogan embraced by advocates of war with the USSR. As his various nicknames attest, depictions of Tomiya as explorer, warrior, firebrand, and patriot drew on stock images of the continental wanderer to set standards for manly virtue to which settlement pioneers could aspire.[26]

In the meantime, as the inspiration for the homeside movement, Katō Kanji was carefully styled in the image of the philosopher laureate of imperial agrarianism. One admiring account likened Katō to two of the most celebrated historical figures of the agrarian movement—Ninomiya Sontoku and Tanaka Shōzō. Inheriting their mantle, Katō reportedly embodied "the spirit of the soil and the spirits of the departed." Like them, Katō appeared to answer the "need for such men in this day and age" and to lead the quest to "overcome the trials of the age." Such rapturous descriptions made Katō sound like a charismatic quasi-religious

24. Hata Kennosuke, "Imin no chichi Tōmiya taisa," *Ie no hikari* (June 1938): 60–62.
25. Ibid., 63.
26. Kami Shōichirō, *Manmō kaitaku seishōnen giyūgun* (Tokyo: Chūō Kōronsha, 1973), 14–15; "Tairiku hatten no suteishi," *Ie no hikari* (June 1938): 23; Sakuramoto, *Manmō*, 107; Hata, "Imin no chichi," 62.

leader and a sage. Thus Katō, the "idealist" and the "man of spirit," comple-
mented Tomiya, the "man of action."[27]

With the first two portraits hung in the heroes gallery and the outline of the
emigration narrative sketched in, the fabrication of cultural monuments to the
colonization movement completed the process of tradition making. The symbols
that emerged to represent the Millions to Manchuria program were specifically
drawn not from the settlement experience in Manchuria, but from the mobilization experience at home. Literature on the village-colonization movement always
included examples of the "three models of village colonization": Miyagi Prefecture's Nangō Village, Yamagata Prefecture's Shōnai District, and Nagano Prefecture's Ōhinata Village.[28] Of the three, the story of Ōhinata became by far the
most famous. One of the first villages to participate in the Ministry of Agriculture's Village Colonization Program, Ōhinata was carefully developed as a test
case and model.

To this end, large groups of Ministry of Agriculture and Forestry officials made
several visits to the village. Kodaira Ken'ichi, head of the Rural Rehabilitation
Division in charge of the program, made a personal appearance. Kodaira's wife
recalls that her husband stayed up all night in order to convince villagers to support the scheme, demonstrating the importance the ministry attached to its success with Ōhinata. In particular, ministry officials felt that the appearance of
unanimous village support for emigration was critical. Moreover, the village received a generous government grant for its participation, even before any official
subsidy program was established. And although a number of settlers were recruited from neighboring villages to fill the targets for Ōhinata, this fact was hidden to cultivate a myth that all settlers in the colony came from the same native
place. Such efforts were aimed to guarantee not only that Ōhinata was a success,
but also that it set an appropriate model to follow.[29]

The popularizing of the Ōhinata myth took place largely after 1939, when the
initial surge of enthusiasm for village colonization was fading and recruitment
began to fall off sharply. Partly because of the encouragement of emigration officials, movie companies, playhouses, record companies, and publishers created a
boom in Ōhinata Village productions. Tokyo theaters sent troops of actors to visit
the village and prepare themselves for their roles. The Rural Rehabilitation Council invited leaders of the local movement to advise a Shinbashi playhouse on how
to dramatize their story. In a Tōhō Pictures film, and in novels, short stories, photo

27. Havens, *Farm and Nation*, chap. 7; Katō Takeo, "Manshū kaitaku no chichi Katō Kanjishi o
kataru," *Ie no hikari* (November 1941): 38–40.

28. Miura Etsurō, ed., *Manshū ijū dokuhon* (Tokyo: Kaizōsha, 1939), 95–96; Nōrinshō Keizai
Kōseibu, *Shin nōson no kensetsu: Tairiku no bunson daiidō* (Tokyo: Asahi Shinbunsha, 1939).

29. Yamada Shōji, "Furikaeru Nihon no mirai: kaisetsu Manshū imin no sekai," in Yamada Shōji,
ed., *Kindai minshū no kiroku*, vol. 6: *Manshū imin* (Tokyo: Shinjinbutsu Ōraisha, 1978), 29–30, 36.

essays, and songs, the moving story of Ōhinata's struggles to better the conditions of the community became an advertisement for the Village Colonization movement. As one actor playing the settlement leader issued this invitation to the audience at the close of the play: "You must follow us in great multitudes and build two, three, many Ōhinata Villages!"[30]

The cultural monument to the Ōhinata village colonization movement was Wada Tsutō's classic novel: *Ōhinatamura,* upon which the other movies and plays were based. A prominent member of the anti-urban anti-Marxist "rural literature movement," Wada joined with Minister of Agriculture Arima Yoriyasu in 1938 to form the first "national policy" literature organization, the Rural Literature Association. Under the auspices of this organization, Wada spent time with the villagers in Ōhinata, interviewing them and collecting information for a documentary novel, and then took a paid, one-month tour of the colony in Manchuria. The product of these efforts was published in mid-1939 by the *Asahi* newspaper and again in 1941 as one volume in the *Asahi's* Colonial Literature Series.[31]

Wada's narrative focused almost exclusively on the efforts of the leaders of the Village Colonization movement in Ōhinata, newly appointed village head Asakawa Takemaro and Sangyō Kumiai organizer Horikawa Kiyomi, to mobilize their community. As the story opens, the two men despair at the intractable poverty of their village, the villagers' debt peonage to a rapacious local merchant, and the bleak future of the young people. Hearing how Horikawa's attempts in the past to use the village industrial cooperative (*sangyō kumiai*) to oppose the financial grip of the merchant had failed, Asakawa is suddenly struck with inspiration: Manchuria is the solution.

Before Asakawa can bring his dream to reality, he must convince the poor villagers, defuse the plots of the villainous merchant, and secure government aid to finance the project. After great struggles and the suicide of a tubercular villager to release her family and fiancé to make the trip to the new land, the movement finally triumphs. Everyone in the village—anxious parents, reluctant landlords, even the evil merchant—fall into the group spirit and join the fanfare as the story closes with a joyous send-off ceremony.

The Ōhinata story was entirely home-based. The empire was central to the plot, but it was not the theater of action. This was significant, for it underscored the message that the empire was transforming Japan for the better, not just the other way round. Moreover, by making the mother village into the symbol of imperial emigration, colonization was domesticated and made less fearsome. There were not any bandits, and the hardships were all too familiar.

---

30. "Shibai monogatari Ōhinata-mura," *Ie no hikari* (January 1940): 104–9; Yamada, "Furikaeru Nihon," 36–38.

31. Wada Tsutō, "Ōhinata-mura," in Shōwa Sensō Bungaku Zenshū Henshū Iinkai, ed., *Shōwa sensō bungaku zenshū,* vol. 1: *Senka Manshū ni agaru* (Tokyo: Shūeisha, 1964), 115–71, 494; Kawamura Minato, *Ikyō no Shōwa bungaku: "Manshū" to kindai Nihon* (Tokyo: Iwanami Shoten, 1990), 28–33.

Like the Village Colonization movement, the symbol for the Patriotic Youth Brigade emerged from the domestic landscape. Although extensive press coverage of the Youth Brigade's precursor offered excellent candidates for a brigade hallmark, these were bypassed in favor of the gigantic domestic training complex in Ibaraki Prefecture where the youths went for their initial months of training. Uchiwara Training Center consisted of fields, an enormous parade ground, and about five hundred distinctively shaped, round barracks. It was these curious "sun-shaped barracks"—*nichirin heisha*—that became the popular symbol for the Youth Brigade.

Nichirin heisha rolled off the tongue much more easily than the long official title for the Youth Brigade or even its abbreviated form, Manmō Kaitaku Giyūgun. As in Ōhinata, writers and artists played a large role in popularizing the new imperial symbol. Fukuda Kiyohito, one of the main figures along with Wada Tsutō in the rural literary movement and founder of the Continental Colonization Literary Association, titled his popular novel on the Youth Brigade *Nichirin heisha* in 1939.[32] Tatsumi Seika, the celebrated children's poet, published a collection entitled *Nichirin heisha no asa* (Morning in the sun-shaped barracks).

Like many of the songs about Uchiwara, Tatsumi's poems described what he imagined to be the excitement of the boys who were answering the call to empire. For the new recruits, the camp purportedly fulfilled a "long cherished dream, these barracks that imitate the sun." To this fabled retreat with its exotic "Mongolian" flavor, boys came to play at empire.

Through the dew-drenched leaves
You can see the sun-shaped barracks.
Those sun-shaped barracks
Looking like conical Mongolian hats.
Those perfectly round roofs
Thatched with cedar.
Inside them young men
Silently reading, writing,
Earnestly preparing themselves.
These boys of tender years
Gathered from throughout the nation,
Wishing to give to their country,
Burning with the bold and valiant
Colonial spirit![33]

Uchiwara was designed to imitate empire. The huge parade ground and the camp shrine were both named after the first of the trial settlements—Iyasaka. Katō Kanji had borrowed the idea of the round barracks from a design used by

---

32. Fukuda Kiyohito, *Nichirin heisha* (Tokyo: Asahi Shinbunsha, 1939).
33. Sakuramoto, *Manmō*, 71–72, 78–79.

the Kwantung Army for maximum protection against armed attack. Originally the invention of architect and longtime China resident Koga Hirome, these were not drawn from any indigenous Manchurian model, but out of Japan's imperial tradition.[34]

Yet when they gazed at Uchiwara, Japanese thought they were seeing something that represented Manchurian folk tradition. In a work entitled *Stalwart Uchiwara* one observer wrote:

> You could see several roofs like conical Mongolian hats and barracks shaped rather like upside-down kettles. They call them *nichirin heisha*, but basically they are put together on the outside with split pine logs and on the inside wood slabs. Perhaps five hundred of these sun-shaped barracks are nestled among 40 *chō* (98 acres) of pine woods that stretch between an expanse of hills and fields. When your eye confronts the specter of these alien buildings, you feel for an instant that you are nowhere near Tokyo, indeed, that you have been transported to a corner of Mongolia in the far reaches of Manchuria.[35]

Intrigued by Uchiwara's exotic imperial feel, Japanese chose its distinctive round barracks as the symbol for the Youth Brigade. It was a symbol well suited to the aspirations for a new intimacy between empire and metropolis. Planting a piece of Manchuria in Japan, Uchiwara domesticated empire even as the settlement project was Japanizing Manchuria.

With the construction and popularization of a tradition of Manchurian settlement, agrarian imperialism of the 1930s assimilated new ideas into the mythology of Japanese colonialism. The incorporation of the farm community into the imperial project brought new groups into the process of expansion. As Manchukuo became a land of rural opportunity for poor farmers, villages became symbolic beneficiaries of empire. Before, imperial mythology had reserved the heroes gallery for soldiers and opportunities for the colonial elite. Now the stalwart farmer-colonists partook of the heady success and the glorious heroism of empire building. And all of rural Japan could take vicarious pride in their accomplishments. Agrarian imperialism brought empire home in other ways as well. Representations of Manchurian settlement added to the stock of imperial symbols bucolic images of garden plots and farmhouses, and of the homespun farm family—complete with women, children, and dogs. These pictures of empire as rural daily life took away some of the "otherness" of Manchuria and made it seem more and more like Japan. At the same time, in joining a veneration of the "Japanese village" to the ideas of the colonial enterprise as a manifestation of Japan's successful modernization and "catch-up" with the West, agrarian imperialism imbued empire with the ideological weight of agrarian tradition.

---

34. Ibid., 69–70.
35. Itō Kinjirō, *Takumashiki Uchiwara* (1938), cited in ibid., 69.

The inventing of a colonizing tradition in Manchuria reveals the process of imperial myth making in the late 1930s. Mass colonization represented a bold departure in the strategies of Japanese empire building. And as history was being made on the continent, it was ideologized at home. Events were assimilated into a heroic narrative that transformed the brutality and privation of the settlement experience into a story of community harmony and flourishing success. The massive export of population to Manchuria magically remade the villages into harmonious communities of self-sufficient owner-farmers. A central element in the mythmaking process was the assimilation of the two separate traditions of agrarianism and emigration. Before the 1930s these had separate histories. Manchurian settlement brought them together, weaving agrarianism into the imperial narratives of emigration, and empire into the narratives of agrarianism.

Why this occurred in the 1930s and not before remains a crucial question. The answer lies in part within the multidimensional crisis atmosphere of the era and the radical proposals for change that this produced. Agrarian activists called for revolutionary solutions to the socioeconomic dilemmas of an agricultural sector embattled by industrial and commercial development. Such radicalism was echoed in demands for change in a Manchurian empire imperiled by the rising tide of Chinese nationalism. Propelled together by crisis, the wedding of agriculture to empire led to a government program for rural social welfare unprecedented in Japanese history and a government-subsidized program on a scale unmatched in the history of twentieth-century imperialism.

EIGHT

It Takes a Village

Internationalization and Nostalgia in Postwar Japan

Jennifer Robertson

The sensation of the newest, the most modern, is in fact just as much a dream form of events as the eternal return of the same.

WALTER BENJAMIN

Kokusaika (internationalization) and *furusato* (native place) are perhaps the two most compelling and ubiquitous catchwords used in Japan today.[1] On the surface, they appear to represent opposite trajectories: a centrifugal movement in the case of internationalization, and a centripetal movement in the case of native place-making. The former is popularly associated with open borders, open-mindedness, and in the context of capitalism, open markets; the latter, with parochialism, nostalgia, and protectionism. The one is often cited as the raison d'être of the other, and several scholars have noted the tenacious connection between internationalization and native place-making. The Japanese sociologist Isamu Kurita, for example, has argued that

> the very international-ness of the life-style makes the traditional Japanese arts appear quite alien and exotic. We look at our tradition the way a foreigner does, and

Preliminary, abridged, and revised versions of this article have been presented over the past two years at the University Public Lecture Series, "Japan at the End of the Twentieth Century," Freie Universität Berlin, Berlin (June 13, 1995) and the Public Lecture Series, Copenhagen Business School, Copenhagen, Denmark (December 12, 1995). Grateful thanks to my colleagues at these conferences for their helpful and instructive feedback. Special thanks are due to Stephen Vlastos, the generous and conscientious editor of this volume, and to Celeste Brusati for her insightful reading. All translations from Japanese to English are my own unless otherwise indicated.

1. Although, as Marilyn Ivy notes, "home," "hometown," and "old homeplace" are somewhat warmer and more affectively charged colloquial American English translations of *furusato*, I prefer to use "native place" because of the sense of rightful (by birth) belonging to a place connoted by "native." Whereas "home" is a multivalent term referring to a place of residence or familiarity or domestic attention, "native" more specifically refers to a genealogical claim on and to a particular place, be it imaginary or actual, a condition that informs the homologous relationship between the local and national in *furusato* rhetoric; Ivy, *Discourses of the Vanishing: Modernity, Phantasm, Japan* (Chicago: University of Chicago Press, 1995), 103n.8. *Furusato-zukuri* (native place-making) is the expression used to verbalize *furusato*.

we are beginning to love it. It is the product of a search for something more "advanced" and more modish than what we have found in our century-long quest for a new culture."[2]

Kurita is accurate in emphasizing the dialectical relationship between internationalization and *furusato*. Where I differ is in my treatment of "culture." Kurita alludes to "Japanese culture" and "Japanese tradition" as self-contained, self-evident wholes that perdure unchanged over time and space, history and geography. According to this thesis, Japanese culture and tradition are somehow separate from or immune to the same social transformations that have severed *the Japanese* from their cultural and traditional roots. Obviously, on a very general level, there is something distinctive—collective but not unitary—about the contexts within which Japanese people give meanings to their actions and experiences, and make sense of their lives. While there is no "true" definition of the term "culture," we can understand it as a space-time manifold "in which human beings construct and represent themselves and others, and hence their societies and histories."[3]

Culture, then, is every bit as much an ongoing production as it is a constantly transforming product. Tradition is a relationship of prior to present representations, which is symbolically mediated and not naturally given. Similarly, "traditional" is not a descriptive but an interpretive term: an "arbitrary symbolic designation," an "assigned meaning rather than an objective quality."[4]

The adjective is often used to imbue ideas, things, and practices with the appearance of historicity and thereby legitimate them as authentic and right. By the same token, neither Japanese culture nor Japanese tradition constitutes an autonomous, congealed essence except as a historically specific, dominant expression of Japaneseness, in which case each becomes synonymous with *national culture*.[5]

The contents of both culture and tradition shift continuously with the passage of time:

> What we take to be "our culture" at any time will be a kind of totalisation of cultural memory up to that point. (Moreover), "our culture" . . . is never purely "local produce," but always contains the traces of previous cultural borrowings or influence, which have been part of this "totalising" and have become, as it were, "naturalised."[6]

Because the practices identified with it are represented as embodying an invariant past, tradition is often used, erroneously, as interchangeable with history.

2. Isamu Kurita, "Revival of the Japanese Tradition," *Journal of Popular Culture* 17, no. 1 (1983): 131.

3. John Comaroff and Jean Comaroff, *Ethnography and the Historical Imagination* (Boulder: Westview Press, 1992), 27.

4. Richard Handler and Joyce Linnekin, "Tradition, Genuine or Spurious," *Journal of American Folklore* 97 (1984): 273, 285–86.

5. See the astute analysis of the concept of national culture in John Tomlinson, *Cultural Imperialism* (Baltimore: Johns Hopkins University Press, 1991), 68–101.

6. Ibid., 90–91.

HOMOLOGIES AND ERASURES

I shall argue that internationalization and native place-making exist cotermi-nously as refractive processes and products, and that together they index the am-biguity of Japanese national identity and its tense relationship with cultural iden-tity (or identities). Since at least the 1980s and into the 1990s, internationalization has signified not only the relationship between Japan and the rest of the world, but also the relationship between Tokyo and the rest of Japan, and between cen-tral Tokyo and the cities, towns, and villages in Tokyo Metropolitan Prefecture. These two basic relationships are homologous. Moreover, the Tokyo versus rest-of-Japan relationship is so totalizing, discursively speaking, that it renders redun-dant an equally evolved relationship between Japan and the rest of the world in order to dramatize and allegorize cultural distinction and national difference.

The increasing concentration of the functions of "information capitalism" in central Tokyo has quickened the rediscovery and exoticization of the countryside (*inaka*) as both a desirable, Japanese-style *Lebensraum* and a landscape of nostalgia.[7] This development in turn has exacerbated the asymmetrical relationship between Tokyo, the dominant metropole, and the rest of Japan.[8] Although native place-making is the rubric under which state-sponsored development programs are un-dertaken in specific localities, it also describes a process that upholds the hierar-chical distinction between Tokyo and the provinces, where *furusato* can be discovered in all its living-historical and culturally authentic materiality. Native place-making projects within specific villages, towns, or cities outside Tokyo effec-tively highlight and articulate local differences between "newcomer" and "native" categories of resident. These intra-local differences are homologous to those be-tween central Tokyo and the provinces (including the villages, towns, and cities in Tokyo Metropolitan Prefecture) and to those between Japan and the rest of the world.[9] The relationship between internationalization and native place-making, in short, is characterized by layers of articulated homologies.

Internationalization denotes essentially the same process as native place-making but from the vantage point of the provinces or the periphery. "Internationaliza-tion" qualifies the hierarchical relations mediating specific localities and central

7. See Tessa Morris-Suzuki, *Beyond Computopia: Information, Automation and Democracy in Japan* (Lon-don: Kegan Paul International, 1988). "Rediscovery" for, as I have noted, "although the imagination of *furusato* is not constrained by the necessity of a physically present rural landscape, its current reification is shaped by a history of discourse about the countryside." Jennifer Robertson, *Native and Newcomer: Making and Remaking a Japanese City* (Berkeley and Los Angeles: University of California Press, [1991] 1994), 17. See also Carol Gluck, *Japan's Modern Myths: Ideology in the Late Meiji Period* (Princeton: Prince-ton University Press, 1985), 178–204.

8. See Sam Steffensen, "Regional Development Issues, Localism, and the Emergence of New So-cial Dynamics in Contemporary Japan: An Inquiry into the 'Era of Localities'" (Ph.D. diss., University of Copenhagen, 1994), 88–89, 95–96.

9. See Robertson, *Native and Newcomer*, especially chaps. 1, 2, and 6.

Tokyo, a "world city." The catchword has less to do with the non-Japanese world, and more to do with a discourse within Japan on nationness, in which case "international" serves as a trope for, among other things, the substance of the multipolar, center-periphery relations promoted in regional development projects.[10] A third and related term, globalization (*gurōbarizeshon*) tends to be used to describe socioeconomic diplomacy and trade carried out between foreign states and Japanese corporations and regional cities. Whereas "internationalization" is used most often to convey the self-conscious pursuit of "soft" or affective social relations within Japan, "globalization" refers more to "hard" economic and political linkages between Japan and other nation-states, which may include an affective veneer.[11]

The ambivalent locus of internationalization is indicative of both the metaphoric use of the term and the tense relationship between Japanese national identity and cultural identity (or identities).[12] The integrity and stability of Japanese national identity are commonly attributed to an assumed protean ability to assimilate difference and absorb otherness.[13] Morisaki Kazue, a present-day Japanese litterateur, critic, and human rights activist, suggests that the assimilation of "aliens" and minorities reveals the majority's inability to deal with differences. By insisting on assimilation, or the outward invisibility of otherness, she argues, dominant Japanese thereby avoid having to deal with the social-historical structures and legacies of Japanese colonial and racist practices.[14]

10. See Steffensen, "Regional Development." Compare the use of internationalization as a "counterdiscourse" in post-revolution China. Like Japanese internationalization, it is not about "the rest of the world," but a precise manifestation of the order of things at home. Cf. Chen Xiaomei, "Occidentalism as Counterdiscourse: 'He Shang' in Post-Mao China," *Critical Inquiry* 18, no. 4 (1992): 688, 613, 710.

11. Cf. the interchangeability of internationalization and globalization in Mike Featherstone, Scott Lash, and Roland Robertson, eds., *Global Modernities* (Thousand Oaks, Calif.: SAGE Publications, 1995), and also Tomlinson, *Cultural Imperialism.*

12. Similarly, in his article on educational reform in Japan, Mark Lincicome observes that "the real significance of the internationalization movement lies in its very ambiguity"; "Nationalism, Internationalization, and the Dilemma of Educational Reform in Japan," *Comparative Education Review* 37, no. 2 (1993): 123. See also Ross Mouer and Yoshio Sugimoto, "Internationalization as an Ideology in Japanese Society," in Hiroshi Mannari and Harumi Befu, eds., *The Challenge of Japan's Internationalization: Organization and Culture* (Tokyo: Kwansei Gakuin University and Kodansha International, 1983). John Tomlinson, in a trenchant deconstruction of cultural imperialism, points out the conceptual difficulties in articulating cultural identity and the tendency to elide cultural with national identity: "'The nation' *appears* to be a more concrete, 'identifiable' entity than 'a culture' and there is often a commonsense assumption that nations and cultures more or less go together"; *Cultural Imperialism,* 73.

13. Cf. Kazue Morisaki, "Two Languages, Two Souls," *Concerned Theater Japan* 2, no. 3/4 (1973), and Toshiya Ueno, "Tasha to kikai / The Other and the Machine," in Yukio Fukushima and Marcus Nornes, eds., *Media Wars: Then and Now* (Yamagata International Documentary Film Festival '91; Tokyo: Sōjinsha, 1991).

14. Morisaki, "Two Languages." See also Jennifer Robertson, "Mon Japon: The Revue Theater as a Technology of Japanese Imperialism," *American Ethnologist* 22, no. 4 (1995).

The international theme parks and resorts multiplying throughout the Japanese countryside similarly erase as they reinvent the difference posed by places, artifacts, and peoples not Japanese. The operative logic seems to revolve around the equation Tokyo: Japan:: the rest of Japan: the rest of the world, where Tokyo is a "world city" and the rest of Japan consists of either newly designated native places and/or metonymic simulations of the non-Japanese world. A case in point is Nagasaki Holland Village Huis Ten Bosch (not to be confused with the older Holland Village [Oranda-*mura*] nearby), constructed and paved with bricks imported from the Netherlands—enough to make the Netherlands "the world's No. 1 brick exporter for a year."[15] The "village," completed in 1992 at a cost of ¥225 billion, boasts full-scale replicas of Palace Huis Ten Bosch, the royal residence; Domtoren, the tallest cathedral tower in Utrecht; Nijenrode Castle in the province of Utrecht; the town hall in Gouda; and the world-famous Hotel de l'Europe in Amsterdam, among other structures (see fig. 4). Holland Village contains a similar array of replicas.

The public relations magazine for Huis Ten Bosch dismisses the notion that the canaled complex is a leisure resort or theme park, and stresses that it is an ideal model of a living space where Japanese can enjoy active, enriched lives.[16] Significantly, the complex includes Wassenaar, an island named after an upscale coastal suburb of The Hague, consisting of 120 single-family dwellings modeled after seventeenth- to nineteenth-century Dutch houses available for purchase. The irony of this arrangement has been lost on the planners: from the seventeenth through the nineteenth centuries Dutch traders in Nagasaki were confined to the artificial island of Deshima, in part as a strategy to contain their potentially disruptive difference, and today Japanese citizens are provided with Dutch-style homes constructed on an artificial island designed to transport the visitor/resident "away from modern Japan to a more gracious time and place."[17]

There are many other such international complexes erected throughout the archipelago, including Tokyo Disneyland, although Huis Ten Bosch is among the few that double as residential zones.[18] In fact, Kamichika Yoshikuni, the founder and president of Huis Ten Bosch, and his corporate backers plan to invest ¥322 billion to create a new city around the "exotic" resort that will serve as a model for Asian urban planners.[19] These theme parks were planned for the benefit of Japa-

15. Cameron Hay, "Dutch Resort Has No Trouble Staying Afloat in Recession," *Japan Times* (May 17, 1994): 4.

16. *Haustenbosu* (Tokyo: Shōbunsho, 1994), 160.

17. Hay, "Dutch Resort," 4.

18. For information on other international enclaves in Japan, see *'94–'95 Kansai omoshiro asobirando* (Tokyo: J[apan] T[ravel] B[ureau], 1994), 52–53, 58–61, 66–69); and also Ellen Schattschneider, "The Labor of Mountains," *Positions: East Asia Cultures Critique* 4, no. 1 (1996).

19. Hay, "Dutch Resort," 4. Perhaps, in this context, Tokyo Disneyland could be regarded as the new center of Tokyo, the expansive "world city."

nese citizens and domestic tourists for whom the complexities of different cultural and national histories are simplified and essentialized. Rimmer also suggests that international theme parks are "sanitised alternatives to popular overseas tourist centres," and tourists from Asian countries also make use of the facilities. In 1990 alone, sixty new theme parks worth ¥1.3 trillion were planned throughout Japan.[20] Their presence has not precluded millions of Japanese from traveling abroad each year—11 million travelers in 1990, increasing to nearly 12 million in 1993. Survey research suggests that domestic and international tourism augment rather than compete with each other.[21] In short, the assimilation and containment of multicultural differences and the incorporation of global phenomena into local place-making projects are central to the ongoing processes of sociopsychological security, national cultural-identity formation, and capitalist market development in Japan.

FURUSATO-ZUKURI AS AN OXYMORON

Furusato is one of the most compelling Japanese tropes for cultural, social, and economic self-sufficiency in the face of vexatious domestic problems, such as the dearth of adequate housing and national anxieties associated with transnational "free" trade. Although *furusato* literally means "old village," the word is used most often in an affective capacity to signify not a particular place—that is, an actual old village—but rather the generalized nature of such a place and the nostalgic feelings aroused by its mention. "Furusato Japan" thus imbues the state with a warm, fuzzy, familial, and ultimately maternal aura. Native place-making is the process by which *furusato* is evoked into existence as a political project through which experiences and memories are shaped and socially reproduced. The ubiquity of *furusato* derives from the manifold contexts in which it is appropriated, from the gustatorial (e.g., advertisements extolling the "flavor of *furusato*") to the political-economic (e.g., the domestic policy of the Liberal Democratic Party [LDP] introduced in 1984 as the *Proposal for Furusato Japan*). The LDP, currently trying to resurrect itself after its virtual disintegration over the past several years, has recognized and exploited the metaphoric potential of *furusato* as the image of a new "cultural state" (*bunka kokka*) in tandem with a "new Japanese-style welfare nation-state" (*nihonsei no atarashii fukushi kokka*).

The recent instability of party politics has not affected the state's appropriation of native place-making as an efficacious way of addressing, under a single rubric, troublesome political, social, and environmental issues. The establishment of the

20. P. J. Rimmer, "Japan's 'Resort Archipelago': Creating Regions of Fun, Pleasure, Relaxation, and Recreation," *Environment and Planning A* 24 (1992): 1623.

21. Henning Gödecke, "Japanese Overseas Tourism" (paper delivered at the international conference "The Culture of Japan as Seen Through Its Leisure," University of Vienna, Austria, Institute for Japanese Studies, March 22–24, 1995).

Furusato Information Center in 1985 under the auspices of the Ministry of Agriculture, Forestry, and Fisheries is illustrative.[22] The center was charged with facilitating the rehabilitation of depopulated and depopulating rural communities through the creation of city-country networks. The center's annual operating budget averages around $4 million, part of which is spent computer networking with more than 2,500 cities, towns, and villages; sponsoring symposia; installing a *furusato* information "hot line"; distributing slick public relations pamphlets, newsletters, and guidebooks; and conducting annual surveys on popular *furusato* images. In 1991 these networking activities were categorized under the affective and overdetermined rubric Furusato Family (*furusato famirī*). The metaphor of "family" is used here in reference to the imagined and relational community of the nation, which is constructed in part of localities linked together through domestic tourism.

References to the Japanese nation as "family" (*kazoku*) were made by oligarchs and industrialists in the late nineteenth century to rationalize class and sex/gender inequalities: "The family was the archetypical 'organic' entity, whose inner relationships were inequitable but in theory complementary and harmonious."[23] In the wartime period (1931–45), the "family system" was formally adopted as the dominant domestic ideology delineating the proper place of all Japanese; by 1940 the family metaphor had been extended to the global sphere, where all nations would assume their proper place under a paternalistic Japan.[24] It appears that the patriarchal ideology of the family-system state (*kazoku kokka*) elaborated during the wartime period persists in the *furusato* paradigm of nation-making, a point to which I return in a later section on gender and nostalgia.

The interpellative power and efficacy of *furusato* resides in the image of "traditional culture" conjured up by the word and in its perception as something broadly "Japanese." In this connection, *furusato* connotes a desirable lifestyle aesthetic summed up by the term *soboku*, or artlessness and rustic simplicity, and its quintessential landscape features include forested mountains, fields cut by a meandering river, and a cluster of thatched-roof farmhouses. The postwar revaluation of local practices was promoted from the early 1950s by localists and "antigovernment" forces, although the favored expression then for "authentic" community was not native place but *kyōdōtai*.[25] Today *furusato* is evoked both by the

---

22. See Robertson, *Native and Newcomer*, esp. chap. 1.

23. John Dower, *War Without Mercy: Race and Power in the Pacific War* (New York: Pantheon, 1986), 279; Gluck, *Japan's Modern Myths*, 187–88.

24. Dower, *War Without Mercy*, 279–81.

25. *Kyōdōtai*, literally "common body," is used most commonly in reference to, and conjures up the image of, wet-rice agriculture, the complicated irrigation and labor-intensive cultivation of which allegedly occasioned a special form of rural social organization. As a popular term, *kyōdōtai* is fetishistic, for it is invoked, often nostalgically, as the "authentic" Japanese rural community, the implication being that farm villages are inherently cooperative; Robertson, *Native and Newcomer*, 89. See also the conflicting interpretations of *kyōdōtai* in Masao Maruyama, *Thought and Behavior in Modern Japanese Poli-*

state, for whom the term is the functional and affective equivalent of American "family values" (as suggested by the expression *furusato famirī*), and by local environmentalist groups, which are opposed to the intensive use of chemical fertilizers and pesticides, and the topographical deformation of the country accompanying golf course and resort development projects.[26] *Furusato* is also a compelling catchword and image utilized by a broad spectrum of advertisers. *Furusato*, to paraphrase W. J. T. Mitchell on landscapes, is both a represented and a presented space, both a signifier and a signified, both a frame and what a frame contains—both a package and the commodity inside the package.[27]

The boundaries of native place are experiential and sentimental, and mark concentric circles of interiority: for some Tokyo residents, *furusato* is a provincial town, while for Japanese residing abroad, *furusato* signifies Japan. The particular meaning and significance of interiority or insideness is realized from without, as in the event of exile, migration, expatriatism, estrangement, alienation, or other precipitating factors. In other words, a person marked self-consciously as exterior and foreign (re)possesses a place as *furusato* by reclaiming it mnemonically, thus rendering distance intimate and interiorized. The "reality" of native place lies in paradox and antithesis—that is, the recognition of a place as *furusato* is possible only once that place is, or is imagined as, distant, inaccessible, lost, forsaken, or disappearing.[28] By the same token, *furusato* names a place that exists in contrast with, and therefore amplifies the aimlessness and malaise of, the present moment:[29] the future is foreclosed but the past is open-ended. The temporal dimension of *furusato*, represented by the word *furu(i)*, signifies pastness, historicity, age, quaintness, and the patina of familiarity and naturalness that cultural artifacts and human relationships acquire with age, use, and interaction. These characteristics too, paradoxically, come into mnemonic focus as their concrete referents are erased or become attenuated and disappear from the realm of everyday experience and future possibility.

Native place-making is an ironic euphemism for development projects that actually facilitate the disappearance of the quintessential *furusato* landscape. The

---

tics, trans. Mikiso Hane (reprint of 1963 ed.; London: Oxford University Press, 1969), 25–83; and Daikichi Irokawa, "Japan's Grass-Roots Tradition: Current Issues in the Mirror of History," *Japan Quarterly* 20, no. 1 (1973), and *The Culture of the Meiji Period*, trans. edited by Marius B. Jansen (Princeton: Princeton University Press, 1985), 273–87. Although *furusato* has been appropriated for political ends, as an expression it, more than *kyōdōtai*, prioritizes ambience and affect over specific modes of social structure and organization. Cf. the discussion of *kyōdōtai* in Irwin Scheiner, "The Japanese Village: Imagined, Real, Contested," in this volume.

26. These positions are represented by the magazine *Furusato-mura*.

27. W. J. T. Mitchell, "Imperial Landscape," in W. J. T. Mitchell, ed., *Landscape and Power* (Chicago: University of Chicago Press, 1994), 5.

28. Sakai Tadaichi, *Shi to kokyō* (Tokyo: Ōfūsha, 1971), 13.

29. Yamazaki Masakazu, "Bessekai to no rakusa ga sōzai: 'Furusato' kie 'kokusaika' tōjō," *Asahi shinbun* (Tokyo eve. ed., September 25, 1984): 7.

projects pursued under this rubric, such as international theme parks, touristified farm villages, and the "mini-nations" discussed below, are responsible for and symptomatic of the loss of cultural artifacts and practices identified retrospectively as constituting the essence of *furusato*. Reconstructed or reinvented under the auspices of *furusato-zukuri* programs, these artifacts and practices, such as thatched-roof farmhouses and festivals (*matsuri*), can always only approximate actual historical forms, while the lifestyle associated with them is reified as timelessly and authentically "Japanese." Native place-making programs thus facilitate loss even as they compensate for the ontological anxiety of loss.

Nostalgia is a barometer of present moods. It figures as a distinctive way of relating the past to the present and future, and does this by juxtaposing the "uncertainties and anxieties of the present with presumed verities and comforts of the . . . past."[30] Nostalgia is not a product of the past, for what occasions it resides in the present, regardless of the sustenance provided by memories of the past. The cogency of nostalgia increases in proportion to, among other things, a sense of homelessness. Some Japanese social scientists have suggested that with the rapid urbanization of certain rural areas since the postwar period, the Japanese "can't go home again." And, by extension, since there is no particular place to go home to, there is no particular place to feel nostalgic toward.[31] This notion of an antidotal nostalgia for the experience of nostalgia is a compelling one in the context of social and topographical transformations, although I would argue that a sense of homelessness per se neither is limited to the postwar period nor arises automatically with the destruction through urbanization of the countryside. Rather, the distance and differentiation between rural and urban, then and now, origin and trace, must first be recognized, acknowledged, and bridged; this has certainly been the case since the 1970s.[32] Tourism (whether passive or active) is one important agent of authentication and double nostalgia, drawing popular attention to the countryside as a desirable site of interiorizing practices.

Commercial ventures pursued under the affective rubric of *furusato*-making work to insure that nostalgia becomes a natural(ized) frame of mind shaping desires and motivating patterns of consumption. The ideal, constantly consuming citizen is someone who has been interpellated into a nostalgic frame of mind by ubiquitous media hooks (or bridges) such as the television programs "Provincial Travelogue," "In Praise of Hometowns," and "Furusato Ambassadors," not to mention the "*furusato* report" opening the 7:00 P.M. news on NHK, the public television channel; the "Series Nippon" ode to *furusato* in *VIA*, the "Quarterly Onboard Magazine of the [Narita] Airport Limousine"; the post office's *furusato* par-

---

30. Fred Davis, *Yearning for Yesterday: A Sociology of Nostalgia* (New York: Free Press, 1979), 10.

31. Cf. Minami Hiroshi, "Nihon no ryūkōka," in Kata K. and Tsukuda S., eds., *Ryūkōka no himitsu* (Tokyo: Bunwa, 1980), 146.

32. See Robertson, *Native and Newcomer*, chap. 1; cf. John Frow, *Cultural Studies and Cultural Value* (New York: Oxford University Press, 1991), 145.

cel post service; public relations for the annual Furusato Tokyo Festival in March and its counterparts in regional cities throughout Japan; the weekly "*furusato* information" columns in the three national dailies; savings bond advertisements that eulogize native place; and countless other recent and current commercial and "info-taining" deployments of *furusato*. In addition, the creation of touristic "native villages," to which I now turn, has helped to overdetermine nostalgia as a catalyst for the steady consumption and interiorization of existentially displaced times and places.

THE LANDSCAPE OF NOSTALGIA

The creation of *furusato-mura*, or "old-village villages," as tourist destinations for urbanites in search of an agricultural (read, traditional) experience, has been a primary feature of state-sanctioned native place-making programs. The villages provide an apt example of how a national heritage—namely, Furusato Japan—is created from a diverse collection of localities linked together by tourism. *Furusato* villages are usefully characterized as *in situ* tourist installations whose featured farmers represent a more pristine, authentic, and Japanese lifestyle. As Dean MacCannell has perceptively noted, tourism makes a place for all the "unattached individuals in modern society." Organized sightseeing helps existentially homeless people construct totalities from their disparate experiences by linking one tourist attraction to another and/or to the nation. "Even if only a single linkage is grasped . . . this solitary link is the starting point for an endless . . . system of connections," which constitutes the imagined community of the nation, in this case, in the guise of Furusato Japan.[33]

Generally speaking, the term *furusato-mura* designates economically and demographically unstable villages seeking to attract honorary villagers. Honorary villagers are short- and long-term tourists from the city who can enjoy picking mushrooms, slopping hogs, and transplanting rice seedlings without having to actually depend on agriculture for a living. Neither do the resident villagers, since tourism is regarded as a more lucrative and desirable enterprise. Most of the so-called traditional activities performed in *furusato* villages are either recently invented or newly revived as recreation for domestic tourists. Among them are festivals, *kagura* Shinto music and dancing, folk kabuki, storytelling and folk singing sessions, handicrafts exhibitions, nature hikes, and rice-pounding contests.

Since the 1970s Japan National Railways (privatized in 1987 as Japan Railways) has recognized its potential to transport homeless urbanites back to the countryside and to a nostalgic frame of mind. Those who are unable to travel can take

---

33. Dean MacCannell, *The Tourist: A New Theory of the Leisure Class* (New York: Macmillan, 1976), 15, 56; M. Bommes and P. Wright, " 'Charms of Residence': The Public and the Past," in R. Johnson, G. McLennan, B. Schwarz, and D. Sutton, eds., *Making Histories: Studies in History-Writing and Politics* (London: Hutchinson, 1982), 26.

advantage of the post office's "*furusato* parcel post" service inaugurated in 1985 and in full swing today. Customers choose from a variety of regional foodstuffs and handicrafts, colorfully advertised in "*furusato* parcel post" catalogues, which are then mailed directly to their city addresses by local craftspeople and farmers. Since November 1995 Tokyoites have been able to buy regional goods and produce directly from regional representatives stationed at the newly opened Furusato Plaza in the chic Harajuku district (see fig. 5). According to the public relations literature for the plaza, which also boasts a replica of a 1930s shopping street, "the Japanese countryside is currently back in vogue."[34]

Audiences somehow not reached by these various *furusato*-making strategies can still be captured by the ubiquitous (and touristic) television quiz and game programs, and "Discovery Channel" sorts of shows that regularly feature rice paddies and farmers as representative of *the* traditional Japanese lifestyle. And the magazine *Furusato-Mura Jōhō* combines domestic tourism with rural real estate sales and pragmatic solutions to environmental pollution. Issue no. 9 (1987), for example, carried articles on the use of human feces as fertilizer, medicinal herbs, and the legal definition of farmland, and included an illustrated catalogue of farmland and farmhouses for sale throughout Japan. Like the *furusato* parcel post system, the magazine promotes both a vicarious and a firsthand appreciation and acquisition of the proverbial countryside. Railway companies, the post office, developers of *furusato* villages, publishers, and managers of the new Furusato Plaza all recognize that the tourist industry today constitutes, in part, an anodyne realm in which gratification is offered in compensation for the disturbing consequences of postwar industrial growth and urban sprawl, including environmental pollution, a dearth of decent affordable housing, and the increasing visibility of foreign guestworkers.

The planners of *furusato* villages and international resorts, where the historical artifacts and practices of Japan and other cultures are reinterpreted and represented, appear to subscribe to or exploit a notion of history as entropy; that is, a perception of historical time as a movement toward sociopolitical disarticulation and economic uncertainty. The entropic view of history, like the experience of nostalgia, is accompanied by a sense that the future is foreclosed and will be colored with the same vexation and insecurity that plagues the present. M. Bommes and P. Wright suggest that "under the entropic view of history . . . 'the past' is revalued and reconstructed as an irreplaceable heritage—a trust which is bestowed upon the present and must be serviced and passed on to posterity."[35] At

34. Helene Thian-Sugasawa, "A Touch of Green Acres Comes to Trendy Harajuku," *Asahi Evening News* (February 24, 1996). The plaza, which has attracted more than 70,000 people per month, also represents a clever marketing strategy bypassing the "notorious middlemen of Japan's distribution system, while limited production and high quality affords protection against recession and trade liberalization."

35. Bommes and Wright, "Charms of Residence," 291.

the same time, the role of commercial interests in revaluing and remaking different "pasts" cannot be ignored. As David Lowenthal has observed, "If the past is a foreign country, nostalgia has made it 'the foreign country with the healthiest tourist trade of all'."[36] And the residents of designated *furusato* villages, along with the many honorary villagers, have been transformed through tourism into custodians of the landscape of nostalgia. (See fig. 6.)

INTERNATIONALIZATION AS "INTER-NATION"-MAKING

In 1983 a forty-one-nation summit was held in the city of Nihonmatsu, Fukushima Prefecture. It was an unprecedented conference, attended by heads of state, yet it went unreported in both the national and the international media. The agenda of the summit focused on national survival in the face of negative population growth and economic stagnation.

The summit was hosted by the newly formed Smiling Republic (Nikoniko Kyōwakoku), and included the equally new Humor Republic (Yūmoa Kyōwakoku), Alcohol Republic (Arukōru Kyōwakoku), Republic of Cassette Boy (Kasettobōi Kyōwakoku), Republic of Laugh Mania (Rafumania Kyōwakoku), Nation of Jipangu (Jipangukoku), and Spin Nation (Kirikirikuni).[37]

These republics are among the "independent mini-nations" (*mini dokuritsu koku*) that have been founded throughout Japan since the late 1970s for a variety of overlapping objectives, including attracting tourists both to increase revenues and to counter the adverse effects of the out-migration of young adults. The protection of the environment is another motive, and the mini-nation movement also uses parody to critique dominant Japanese cultural practices, conspicuous consumption, and capitalist excesses. Although the little republics are contemporary with and similar in function to *furusato* villages, they do not enjoy the patronage of the state via the Furusato Information Center. They tend to consist of localities, neighborhoods, or groups of people who have been left behind, overlooked, or disfranchised in the course of social, economic, and cultural transformations. Peripheral to the dominant discourse of cultural nostalgia, these mini-nations parody that discourse, create an enabling place for their "citizens," and market themselves as an enticing place for tourists by posturing as "other" to normative Japanese surroundings. The importance of parody as a political strategy cannot be dismissed as frivolous or ineffectual. In the context of native place-making, the parodic stance of the mini-nations at once employs, exposes, and displaces the conventions associated with the willful nostalgia of *furusato* programs so that the relationship between the global

36. David Lowenthal, *The Past Is a Foreign Country* (Cambridge: Cambridge University Press, 1985), 4.

37. *Jipangu* is the Japanese version of the medieval Italian *Cipangu* and is often evoked today in the mass media as a trendy, exotic name for the country. *Kirikirikuni* is named after the novel *Kirikirijin*, published by Inoue Hisashi in 1981.

capitalist market and Japanese national and cultural identity formation is laid bare.[38]

Collectively, the mini-nations constitute a pastiche of national and international political structures; many of those founded in the late 1970s endure, and new republics continue to be founded. They are headed by kings and queens (*kokuō*), sovereigns (*genshū*), presidents (*daitōryō*), governors (*sōsai*), and daimyo. (No emperors, however. Doubtless the presence of an emperor among the heads of state would be construed as casting aspersions on the unassailable integrity of the imperial household.) The little republics have various combinations of the following offices: information bureaus (*hōdōkan*), foreign ministries (*gaimushō*), finance ministries (*zaimushō*), construction ministries (*kensetsushō*), performing arts ministries (*geinōshō*), women's liberation bureaus (*fujin kaihōkyoku*), and so forth, headed and staffed by members of the local shopkeepers' association, utilities, fire station, and professional sector, and by local, even national, celebrities.[39]

A mini-nation is distinguished from the nation of Japan by borders and checkpoints patrolled by uniformed "immigration officers." Most of the new republics have their own flag, constitution, currency—for example, the *kosumo* of Smiling Republic, equal in value to the yen—and passport, which, together with citizenship, can be purchased by "nonresident aliens." These symbolic artifacts help the mini-nations maintain their appearance as independent, and, more importantly, as different from Japan. So does the practice of renaming and thereby defamiliarizing and exoticizing local and municipal institutions.

Gas stations in Smiling Republic, for example, were renamed Federation of Key Arab Nations, the tourist association was renamed National Diet, and the bus terminal, International Transportation Bureau. In keeping with the parodic spirit of mini-nation-building, these new names capitalize on the conjunction of national and international forces, playing on Japan's dependence on OPEC for oil; the "Discover Japan" and "Exotic Japan" railway tourism campaigns of the 1970s and 1980s; and the increasing popularity of foreign travel. These renaming exercises catalyze the creation through nomenclature of a new "inter-nation,"[40] at once "Japanese" and "foreign," and primed for an invasion by Japanese tourists. The landscape of nostalgia cultivated by the mini-nation movement is not part of

38. Cf. Chuck Kleinhans, "Taking Out the Trash: Camp and the Politics of Parody," in Moe Meyer, ed., *The Politics of Camp* (New York: Routledge, 1994), 194–99; Patricia Waugh, *Metafiction: The Theory and Practice of Self-Conscious Fiction* (New York: Methuen, 1984), 78.

39. Yamami Eijū and Yoshiike Ikuo, "Okuni-buri. Ima tasai," *Asahi Shinbun* (Tokyo eve. ed., December 21, 1983): 3. Most of the information on the mini-nation movement presented here is from this article unless noted otherwise. With its various ministries and professed autonomy, Aum Shinrikyō, the religious cult charged with the 1995 sarin gas attack in the Tokyo subway, represents a very different conception of a mini-nation.

40. My neologism.

a revalorized agrarian lifestyle; rather, it represents a parodic reawakening of a sense of national cultural integrity.[41]

What coincidental eruption and convergence of forces occasioned the emergence of the mini-nations? As the president of Smiling Republic explained, the idea of founding a nation grew out of a "sense of crisis" (*kikikan*) fostered by the termination of express rail service to Nihonmatsu with the completion of the northeast extension of the "bullet train." City officials were desperate for a ploy that would bring tourists back to the local hot springs despite the now-inconvenient transportation situation. The idea of employing parody as a hook appealed to them, and thus Smiling Republic was among the nations that emerged in the early 1980s as caricaturistic antitheses of Japan. Of course, the mini-nations remain completely dependent on Japan for everything from their originating rationale and antithetical, parodic "other" image, to their future solvency (or co-prosperity). Like the colonial strategy of Japanization deployed in the early twentieth century and the *furusato*-making project today, Smiling Republic-ization is an attempt to transform a place into a spectacle—a commodity—visibly different from its prior state and thus eminently more spectacular and consumable.[42]

One shared topos of both Japanese imperialism and postwar native place-making is the securing of *Lebensraum*.[43] Developer and consumer demands alike for the creation of new regional living spaces stimulated thousands of tourist-oriented housing and resort projects initiated under the auspices of the 1977 and 1987 Comprehensive Development Plans.[44] The archipelago as a whole has become the site of and target for radical remodeling, as boldly if wrongly conceived by the late former Prime Minister Tanaka Kakuei in his 1973 book, *Proposal for Remodeling Japan*. However, the metropole itself, and central Tokyo in particular, is no longer the privileged site for the transformation of living space, nor is it the exclusive site of a transformed and transforming living space, as it was perceived in the Taishō and early Shōwa periods. Today, reinvented farm villages, mini-nations, and other resort projects[45] are competing against Tokyo and against each other as

41. See Gluck, *Japan's Modern Myths*, for discussions of the competing definitions and symbols of nation in the Meiji period, which are echoed in the mini-nation movement.

42. In terms of political strategy, the "Smiling Republic-ization" of Nihonmatsu City is not new and is reminiscent of the "Japanization" of Japanese colonies in the first half of this century. The first stage of Japanese imperial policy, designed to secure Japan's cultural hegemony in the Greater East Asia Co-Prosperity Sphere, was the complete nomenclatural, iconographic, and narrative transformation of a given colony; see Robertson, "Mon Japon"; and M. A. Aziz, *Japan's Colonialism and Indonesia* (The Hague: Martinus Nijhoff, 1955), 174–75.

43. See Louise Young, "Colonizing Manchuria: The Making of an Imperial Myth," in this volume.

44. See Rimmer, "Japan's 'Resort Archipelago'"; and Steffensen, "Regional Development."

45. Cf. Miriam Silverberg, "Constructing a New Cultural History of Prewar Japan," in M. Miyoshi and H. Harootunian, eds., *Japan in the World* (Durham: Duke University Press, 1993); Henry D. Smith, II, "Tokyo as an Idea: An Exploration of Japanese Urban Thought Until 1945," *Journal of Japanese Studies* 4, no. 1 (1978).

desirable tourist destinations, as enticing living spaces, and, as I note in the next section, as enclaves of empowerment, however contained and ambivalent the power and authority claimed.

GENDER AND NOSTALGIA

Whether right, left, or centrist; urban, suburban, or rural; commercial or non-profit; the groups employing the *furusato* image in their campaigns invariably link that concept with "mother." The association of mother and *furusato* is so tenacious that some Japanese social critics have insisted that the two words are synonymous. A typical string of associations in this regard is found in the public relations book-let for the 1983 movie *Furusato*, in which the director comments: "*Furusato* is the ancestral land [*sokoku*]. My/our [*waga*] ancestral land is Japan, it is Gifu prefec-ture, it is Saigō village, it is the village's subsection [*aza*] . . . , it is [my] household, it is mother." The director's comment also illustrates the spatial configuration of *furusato* as concentric circles of interiority.

The tenacious equation of mother and *furusato* is related to the patriarchal ide-ology underlying the process of native place-making. "Mother" names a gender role, a semantic construct unconstrained by the experiences (parturient or other-wise) of actual females, who, moreover, are not all female in the same way. The imagination of *furusato* as mother, and vice versa, is independent of the actual ex-istence of either; both constructs gain cogency from the process of privileging pa-triarchy and nostalgia over complex and contradictory experiential and historical realities. *Furusato*-making, in this context, might productively be recognized as a technology "with power to control the field of social meaning and thus produce, promote, and 'implant' representations of gender."[46]

Native place-making projects are premised on a nostalgia for an authentic community symbolized, especially for men, by *ofukuro*, one of the most affective expressions for "mother," used almost exclusively by males. *Ofukuro* literally means "bag lady" and, consequently, refers connotatively to the notion of females as repositories, in this case, of traditional values deposited for safekeeping by the (male) engineers of *furusato*-making programs. This term is a throwback to the his-torical reference to women as *ohara*, or "womb ladies," indicative of a belief in procreation as a monogenetic phenomenon—that is, the belief that the male role is the generative and creative one, and that the male alone is responsible for the identity and subjectivity of a child.[47] Female bodies, literally and figuratively, are the containers for male-identified "babies," from human infants to things such as values and ideologies. In this context, native place-making is a "recuperative proj-

46. Teresa de Lauretis, *Technologies of Gender: Essays on Theory, Film, and Fiction* (Bloomington: Indi-ana University Press, 1987), 18.

47. Cf. Carol Delaney, "The Meaning of Paternity and the Virgin Birth Debate," *Man*, n.s., vol. 21 (1986).

ect":[48] a paternalistic attempt to reconstruct an authentic, ontologically secure past in which is prefigured the shape of the future. The present is but a staging ground for these willfully nostalgic operations. Nostalgia, after all, is not just a sentiment provoked by the perception of fragmentation and loss; it is also a rhetorical practice by which to recuperate wholeness, spontaneity, energy, and community. As both a mnemonic and a rhetorical practice, nostalgia retrieves from the past an authentic, original, and stable referent around which to reconstitute an unstable present. But, of course, the particular configuration of this particular past is itself a product of mnemonic and textual strategies;[49] a composite of selective memories and practices separated out from their messy milieux.

The invention of local traditions is, among other things, a gendered event that points to the instability of patriarchal categories. Although the same "traditions"—a system of mutual culpability, familistic ties, and bounded, homogeneous communities—were eschewed in the immediate postwar period as backward, cumbersome, nationalistic, and undemocratic, they are now being implanted into the landscape of nostalgia, the isomorph of which is the female body qua "mother," where they can be cultivated (gestated) and harvested (delivered). An ideology of sexual difference and gender role segregation informs the image of a "back-to-the-future" Furusato Japan.[50] By collapsing native place and mother, nostalgic men—from state bureaucrats to movie directors—can proclaim the inclusion of precisely what they exclude from the process of nation-making today, namely, female-identified subjectivity and self-representation. Such men are both nostalgic for the Good Old Days and responsible for the vexaciousness of the present.

The tenacious equation of females and native place is also evident in the Miss Furusato contests inaugurated over the past decade in the Tokyo suburbs and in many of the provincial cities, towns, and villages comprising the Furusato Information Center's "*furusato* family" network.[51] It is as potential mothers that the Miss Furusato contestants are celebrated collectively as the ideal Japanese wife. The equation of native place and mother imparts a compelling Japaneseness to the gender role of mother. According to dominant conventions, it is not only unfeminine (and even abnormal) but also un-Japanese for a female to eschew marriage and motherhood, upon which both social maturity and a normative national and

48. Mary Poovey, "Feminism and Deconstruction," *Feminist Studies* 14 (1988): 60.

49. Janice Doane and Devon Hodges, *Nostalgia and Sexual Difference: The Resistance to Contemporary Feminism* (New York: Methuen, 1987), 8.

50. Similarly, as Sharon Sievers notes, the Meiji state sought to maintain women as "repositories of the past, rather than pioneers, with men, of some unknown future"; *Flowers in Salt: The Beginnings of Feminist Consciousness in Modern Japan* (Stanford: Stanford University Press, 1983), 15.

51. "Miss" contests per se date to 1908 and have flourished since the 1950s—nearly 3,400 contests were registered in 1989—although feminist groups have begun to protest their sexist rationale; see *Misu kontesuto non!* (Sakai-shi: Sakai-shi Josei Dantai Renraku Kyōgikai, 1989).

cultural identity are contingent. In short, the thousands of Miss Furusato represent collectively a type of femininity, in the service of both nostalgic males and the dominant gender ideology, summed up by the expression "good wife, wise mother" (*ryōsai kenbo*), coined in the Meiji period.

Ginnankoku (Ginkgo Nut Nation) in Hachiōji City, Tokyo Metropolitan Prefecture, represents a contradictory blend of a type of gynocentrism and complicity in the gender status quo. The founder and queen, Sugita Fusako, is a novelist who created the new republic as a means of involving women in local politics and events. She had observed that women—and female college students in particular, who represented a quarter of the resident student population—did not participate in the city's *furusato*-making efforts, symbolized by the annual Ginkgo Tree Festival (*ichō matsuri*).[52] Aware of the mini-nation movement, Sugita came up with the idea of founding a nation of "women whose power could be asserted explosively" (*ūmanpawā o bakuhatsu saseru*) in areas where women have not been welcome, from high political office to foreign diplomacy. Consequently, only women are permitted to hold cabinet posts in her mini-nation, although men and even nonresidents may become "citizens" simply by purchasing a Ginkgo Nut passport for ¥500.[53]

Sugita reclaimed the locally salient ginkgo tree image for her purposes by using a variant reading, *ginnan*, of the characters for *ichō*. This act of semiotic poaching underscored Sugita's aim to pose a subversive alternative to the male-dominated construction of tradition and native place in Hachiōji, although her own sex-and-gender politics are thoroughly mainstream. She has utilized the annual Ichō Festival as an important venue for Ginkgo Nut nationalist activism. For example, since buckwheat noodles are a local specialty, the purchase of a passport comes with a guide to the city's most authentic *soba* restaurants. New citizens thereby support Ginkgo Nut Nation and enjoy the "flavor of *furusato*."[54]

The queen regards her nation as only nominally contained by Hachiōji City; conceptually, she maintains, Ginkgo Nut Nation represents all of Japan. Sugita also claims that her "frequent travels outside Japan will facilitate the emergence of the new republic as a nexus for sister-city relations between Hachiōji and its European counterparts."[55] Ginkgo Nut Nation poses a parodic difference from Hachiōji and Japan even as the new republic is completely dependent on both places

52. Sugita Fusako, "Mini dokuritsukoku (ginnankoku) kenkoku ni tsuite," in Nōringyogyō Taiken Kyōkai, ed., *Furusato saihakken* (Tokyo: Nōrin Tōkei Kyōkai, 1986), 98.

53. Sugita, "Mini dokuritsukoku," 102–3, 100–101.

54. Also influencing Sugita's appropriation of the ginkgo tree symbol was perhaps its symbolic equation with motherhood, and especially lactation. The ginkgo tree, with its bilobed leaves, is worshiped as the "nurse/nursing" tree; D. C. Holtom, "Some Notes on Japanese Tree Worship," *Transactions of the Asiatic Society of Japan*, 2d series, vol. 8 (December 1931): 14. The montage of "the new" and "the traditional" recalls the slogan of the pamphlet *Nostalgia of Kobe* (no. 95; Kobe: Kobe-shi Keizai Kyoku Bōeki Kankyoka, 1983): Future society is the flavor of *furusato* (*Mirai shakai wa furusato no aji*).

55. Sugita, "Mini dokuritsukoku," 102–3.

for its symbolic significance and financial solvency. The new nation illustrates vividly the coterminous construction of *furusato*-making and internationalization; the one is simultaneously the condition for and a refraction of the other.

The seemingly progressive gender politics behind Sugita's frequent evocation of "woman power" and the assignment of women to cabinet positions in Ginkgo Nut Nation are actually well within the conservative mainstream represented by nostalgic native place-making programs and Miss Furusato contests. Sugita's interest in recruiting female college students and unmarried women to the new republic actually stems from her desire to use Ginkgo Nut nationalism to promote a social engineering (*ningen-zukuri*) program reminiscent of the wartime family-state ideology.[56] Unmarried women, she declares, need training if they are to become good wives, wise mothers:

> On my travels in various countries of the world, I realize again and again that the most stable nations are those in which mothers are stouthearted and secure [*shikkari shiteiru*]—nations where mothers promptly and properly discipline their children; this is exceedingly desirable. . . . The well-being of a nation is premised on an orderly household.[57]

Sugita envisions Ginkgo Nut Nation as a proving ground for the creation of good wives, wise mothers, through the incorporation of potentially maverick female students and other unmarried women into the nostalgic *furusato*-making project. The parodic otherness of Ginkgo Nut Nation provides a discursive space within which "mother" and conventional gender roles are revalorized as if they were something new and different and female-identified. Parody, in this case, is used less as an adaptive defense mechanism (as in the case of Smiling Republic) and more as an objective means of containing the potentially disruptive force of either female indifference or a (radical) feminist consciousness.[58]

CONCLUDING REMARKS: RUPTURE AND RECUPERATION

As fanciful and inconsequential as these native place-making projects and internationalization efforts may appear from outside Japan, they constitute collectively a major clearinghouse for capitalist ventures and social engineering schemes alike. Touristified farm villages, international and Japanese historical theme parks, Dutch-style residences, and idiosyncratic mini-nations are all sites where both "pure" and hybrid forms of Japanese culture are inventoried, reified, transformed,

56. Cf. Yoshiko Miyake, "Doubling Expectations: Motherhood and Women's Factory Work Under State Management in Japan in the 1930s and 1940s," in Gail Bernstein, ed., *Recreating Japanese Women, 1600–1945* (Berkeley and Los Angeles: University of California Press, 1991), 267–95.

57. Sugita, "Mini dokuritsukoku," 107.

58. Regarding the history of the state's suppression of feminism in Japan, see Sievers, *Flowers in Salt*; and Mikiso Hane, *Reflections on the Way to the Gallows: Rebel Women in Prewar Japan* (Berkeley and Los Angeles: University of California Press, 1988).

contested, commercialized, and reproduced. From one vantage point, culture production is perceived in the affective and familiar terms of *furusato*-making; from another, in the cosmopolitan terms of internationalization. Both projects and processes work conjointly to, simultaneously, even out and exacerbate inequities of economic growth, sex and gender, and state formation that have grown since the "miracle 1960s." The mini-nation movement, including Ginkgo Nut Nation, also underscores the related dynamic of *glocalization*, for the new republics represent the adaptation of a global outlook to local conditions even as their "independence" is but a condition of their dependence on Japan—a domestic homologue of world-systemic capitalism.[59]

Internationalization is not antithetical to "Japanese culture"; rather, it is both a product of and central to the ongoing (since the Meiji period) formation of a *Japanese national cultural identity*. The more stereotypic images of Japan associated with *furusato* have deflected attention from the refractive nature of the relationship between internationalization and native place-making. Kurita's insistence on the "international-ness" of the Japanese lifestyle, which had the effect of making Japanese "cultural traditions" appear "alien and exotic," was premised on his arbitrary separation and ahistorical classification of the traces and artifacts of a long history of cultural encounters, borrowings, and influences into two discrete categories, namely, "international" and "Japanese." His perspective epitomizes the shared and willfully nostalgic rationale underpinning the rhetoric of both native place-making and internationalization. Through the dominant discourse of a paternalistic nostalgia refracted as a progressive internationalization, and vice versa, both Japanese and foreign historical, social, and cultural formations—from architectural spectacles to "Miss" contests and "traditional" festivals—are made available as an anodyne realm: a realm in which the status quo is reproduced, gratification offered, and profits made possible to compensate for various social, economic, and political disparities.

Furusato-making and internationalization are two mutually constitutive modalities of modernity: the "old" and the "new" recuperate each other and converge in the latest contemporized version of postwar modernity. Although Kurita has suggested that "traditional" and "international" pull in opposite directions and thereby compromise the historical integrity of Japanese culture (and Japaneseness), I have argued that the conception of eternal recurrence ("tradition") and the belief in progress ("internationalization") are complementary if refractive.[60] Appeals to tradition underscore what Japanese culture has become (where "tradition" serves as a stable benchmark from which to measure the progress of modernity), while the rhetoric of internationalization emphasizes what it was (where the

---

59. *Glocalization*, a blend of *global* and *local*. See *Oxford Dictionary of New Words* (Oxford: Oxford University Press, 1991), 134; cited in Roland Robertson, "Glocalization," in Featherstone, Lash, and Robertson, *Global Modernities*, 28.

60. Cf. Walter Benjamin, in Susan Buck-Morss, *Dialectics of Seeing*, 108–9.

"international-ness of the lifestyle" is invoked to highlight and reify cultural practices and formations forfeited to the progress of modernity).

Writing in the 1930s, Walter Benjamin observed that the "dialectical interpenetration of generational and collective history is a specifically modern phenomenon: 'This inexorable confrontation of the most recent past with the present is something historically new.' "[61] Today, through agencies such as tourism, this "inexorable confrontation" is even more temporally and spatially immediate, relentless, and efficacious. Any given reinvented "traditional" village or "international" theme park constitutes an intersection and synthesis of *apparently*—and only apparently—contradictory trajectories.

61. Buck-Morss, *Dialectics of Seeing*, 278.

Figure 1. New Year's greeting card: an office group of a mid-sized bank (1968). The spatial configuration reveals the postwar interpretation of *wa* as "peace and harmony" among equals. Nevertheless, hierarchy is preserved in the arrangement of the staff in concentric circles. Thomas Rohlen, *For Harmony and Strength* (Berkeley and Los Angeles: University of California Press, 1974).

橘孝三郎主宰

農村研究

一月号

第一巻
第一號

愛郷會

Figure 2. The cover of the inaugural issue of *Nōson kenkyū*, the journal of the Ibaraki Aikyōkai, January 1931. Note the pose of quiet heroism. Mito City Historical Section, Ibaraki Prefecture.

言　頭　卷

協同組合精神（或は）
共に生きんとするの心

神により、惡魔と戰ひつゝ、
ブルをたゝきふせ、プロをふみこゑ
て、

共に生きんとすればこそ生きてゆけ
るのだ。

共に生きておればこそ生きておられ
るのだ。

おゝら六千萬の解放のために、
おゝらが日本の改造のために、
人類の明日のために、

共に生きておればこそ生きておられ
るのだ。

共に生きんとすればこそ生きてゆけ
るのだ。

共に生きんとするの心――協同組
合精神!!

Figure 3. A manifesto of the Ibaraki Aikyōkai, entitled "The Spirit of the [Rural] Cooperative." The first line reads: "Living together is indeed the way to live." Published in the inaugural issue of *Nōson kenkyū* (January 1931). Mito City Historical Section, Ibaraki Prefecture.

Figure 4.   A tourist map of Huis Ten Bosch, a foreign (Holland) theme park and an adjacent upscale residential community in Nagasaki. *Haustenbosu* (Tokyo: Shōbunsho, 1994). Courtesy of Huis Ten Bosch Corporation.

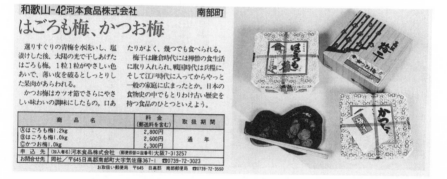

Figure 5.   Part of a page from the *furusato* mail-order catalogue for Wakayama Prefecture advertising the regional specialty, sour plums. *Furusato no tokusanhin: Wakayama-ken* (Tokyo: Chiiki Kaseika Sentā, 1987).

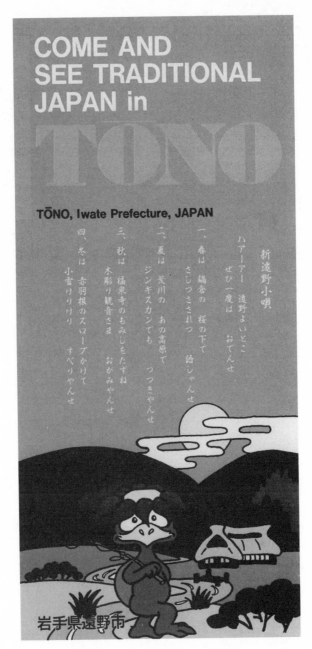

Figure 6. Travel brochure for the Tōno region. Courtesy of the Mayor of Tōno City.

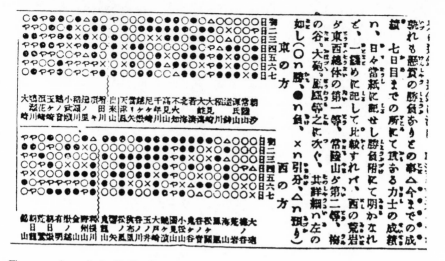

Figure 7. An early *hoshitorihyō* from the *Yorozu shinbun* of May 25, 1900. Notice the symbols designating outcomes other than victory or defeat.

初場所星取表　国技館

（◎勝ち越し　●負け越し　□不戦勝　■不戦敗　や休み）

【東】	1	2	3	4	5	6	7	8	9	10	11		【西】	1	2	3	4	5	6	7	8	9	10	11
◎貴乃花	●武双	○大善	○智花	○琴若	○琴稲	○久島	○浜嶋	●魁皇	○寺尾	○霧島	舞海	横綱	◎曙	○琴若	○安芸	○剣晃	○琴錦	○舞海	○魁皇	○寺尾	●貴闘	○浜嶋	○久島	栃和
◎貴ノ浪	○大善	○智花	○琴稲	○久島	○武双	○浜嶋	●栃和	○舞海	□琴錦	○寺尾	魁皇	大関	◎武蔵丸	○久島	○剣晃	●安芸	○舞海	○琴錦	○寺尾	○魁皇	○琴若	○栃和	○若花	浜嶋
◎若乃花	○智花	○琴稲	○大善	○浜嶋	○久島	●琴錦	○舞海	○寺尾	○霧島	●武丸	剣晃	大関												
魁皇	●剣晃	○舞海	●武双	●安芸	○栃和	●曙	●武丸	○貴花	○久島	○琴稲	貴浪	関脇	琴錦	●舞海	○久島	○浜嶋	●曙	●武丸	○若花	○安芸	●栃和	■貴浪	や	や
安芸島	●琴稲	●曙	○武丸	○魁皇	○剣晃	○舞海	●琴錦	○浜嶋	●智花	○栃和	寺尾	小結	武双山	○貴花	○浜嶋	○魁皇	○剣晃	●貴浪	●貴闘	■琴若	や	や	や	や
琴の若	●曙	●浪花	○久島	●貴花	●霧島	○剣晃	□武双	●武丸	●舞海	○大善	智花	前1	貴闘力	○浜嶋	●霧島	○北関	○大善	●智花	○武双	●琴稲	○曙	●小錦	○舞海	久島
栃和歌	●寺尾	●北関	●浪花	○霧島	●魁皇	○大善	○貴浪	○琴錦	●武丸	●安芸	曙	同2	寺尾	○栃和	●三里	○小錦	●浪花	○春富	●武丸	●曙	●若花	●貴花	●貴浪	安芸
⊗浜ノ嶋	●貴闘	●武双	●琴錦	●若花	○大善	●貴浪	●貴花	●安芸	●曙	●剣晃	武丸	同3	⊗舞の海	○琴錦	●魁皇	●琴別	●武丸	●曙	●安芸	●若花	●貴浪	○琴若	●貴闘	貴花
剣晃	○魁皇	●武丸	●曙	●武双	●安芸	●琴若	●大善	○智花	●城錦	○浜嶋	若花	同4	⊗久島海	●武丸	●琴錦	●琴若	●貴浪	●若花	●貴花	○春富	●大善	●魁皇	●曙	貴闘
琴稲妻	○安芸	●若花	●貴浪	○春富	●貴花	●三里	○貴闘	●小錦	●北関	●魁皇	大善	同5	智ノ花	●若花	●貴浪	●貴花	●朝若	○貴闘	●鬼雷	○北関	●剣晃	○安芸	●大至	琴若
⊗大善	●貴浪	●貴花	●若花	●貴闘	●浜嶋	●栃和	○剣晃	○久島	●大至	●琴若	琴稲	同6	霧島	●北関	○貴闘	●大至	●栃和	○琴若	○城錦	●旭道	○鬼雷	●若花	●貴花	浪花
浪乃花	●小錦	○琴若	○栃和	○寺尾	●大至	○水戸	●肥後	●大鳳	○旭道	●春富	霧島	同7	北勝関	○霧島	○栃和	●貴闘	●琴別	●肥後	○朝若	●智花	●旭道	○琴稲	●城錦	三里
三杉里	○春富	○寺尾	●水戸	●大鳳	●時洋	○琴稲	○鬼雷	●湊富	●琴別	○琴梅	北関	同8	小錦	○浪花	●旭道	●寺尾	○鬼雷	●城錦	●肥後	○湊富	○琴稲	○貴闘	○大鳳	琴別
春日富	●三里	○肥後	○湊富	●琴稲	●寺尾	○時洋	●久島	●若翔	●隆三	○浪花	琴梅	同9	琴別府	○大至	○水戸	○舞海	○北関	●大鳳	○隆三	●朝若	●肥後	○三里	○時洋	小錦
大至	●琴別	○時洋	○霧島	●水戸	○浪花	●旭道	●大鳳	●隆三	○大善	○智花	城錦	同10	朝乃若	●鬼雷	●湊富	○若翔	○智花	○旭道	●北関	○琴別	○水戸	●大鳳	○肥後	隆三
鬼雷砲	○朝若	●隆三	●時洋	●小錦	○若翔	○智花	●三里	●霧島	○琴梅	○湊富	旭道	同11	◎大翔鳳	○旭道	○若翔	○隆三	○三里	○琴別	●湊富	○大至	○浪花	○朝若	●小錦	肥後
旭道山	●大鳳	○小錦	●琴梅	○時洋	●朝若	○大至	○霧島	○北関	●浪花	○隆三	鬼雷	同12	小城錦	●水戸	○琴梅	●肥後	●隆三	○小錦	●霧島	●若翔	○時洋	○剣晃	○北関	大至
水戸泉	○城錦	●琴別	○三里	○大至	○琴梅	●浪花	●隆三	●朝若	●肥後	●若翔	時洋	同13	肥後海	○湊富	●春富	○城錦	●若翔	○北関	○小錦	○浪花	○琴別	○水戸	●朝若	大鳳
湊富士	●肥後	○朝若	●春富	○琴梅	●隆三	○大鳳	●小錦	○三里	●時洋	●鬼雷	若翔	同14	時津洋	○若翔	●大至	○鬼雷	●旭道	○三里	●春富	○琴梅	●城錦	○湊富	●琴別	水戸
若翔洋	●時洋	●大鳳	●朝若	○肥後	●鬼雷	●琴梅	○城錦	○春富	○旭豊	○水戸	湊富	同15	隆三杉	○琴梅	○鬼雷	●大鳳	○城錦	○湊富	●琴別	●水戸	○大至	○春富	●旭道	朝若
⊗琴ケ梅	●隆三	●城錦	○旭道	●湊富	●水戸	○若翔	●時洋	●旭豊	●鬼雷	●三里	春富	同16												

Figure 8. A contemporary *hoshitorihyō* from the *Asahi shinbun* of January 18, 1995. Courtesy of Asahi shinbunsha.

Figure 9. "The Home and the Dining Table": Three generations eating at a common table. The gathering is being conducted in a room without a *tokonoma* alcove or other marks of status. The wife serves from the rice bucket to her left, and there are no servants in the room. Miwada Masako, *Shin katei kun* (Tokyo: Hakubunkan, 1907).

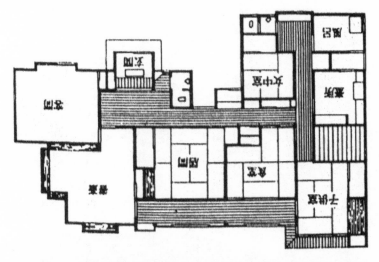

Figure 10. Architect Endō Arata's model house plan for the Home Exposition of 1915. Guidelines for the design specified that the house should be "family-centered" and accommodate chairs and tables. Uchida Seizō, *Nihon no kindai jūtaku* (Tokyo: Kajima Shuppansha, 1992).

Figure 11. The mezzanine of the Ginza Cafe, 1930: a top-class cafe. "Ranpo no jidai: Shōwa no ero-guro-nansensu," *Bessatsu Taiyō*, no. 88. Courtesy of Heibonsha Limited, Publishers.

PART THREE

Folk

NINE

Chihō

Yanagita Kunio's "Japan"

Hashimoto Mitsuru

IN THE BEGINNING . . .

Yanagita Kunio, the renowned Japanese ethnologist, begins one heart-breaking account of a rural family by saying, "This lives in no one's memory but mine today."[1] He continues, "In a year of economic depression, a man around fifty years old, barely surviving by making charcoal in the West Mino area, slaughtered his two children with a broadax." The man's wife had died, and he was raising a thirteen-year-old son as well as an adopted daughter of the same age. He could not sell enough charcoal to feed the family. The two children, polishing the big broadax that he used for his work, said to him, "Father, kill us with this," and laid themselves on their backs. He chopped off their heads. Yanagita concludes his story with the words, "I have had but one chance to read this document. This great story of human suffering must be lying worm-eaten and rotten at the bottom of a wooden chest somewhere."[2]

The time of the tale that "lives in no one's memory but mine" coincided with the ruin of the Matsuoka family, into which Yanagita was born. The experiences of his family reflected the social upheavals of the Meiji period, which disrupted long-established patterns of life in rural areas. It was also the starting point for the school of folklore studies he founded. The goal of Yanagita's school was to excavate the common history of the Japanese people, but its foundation lay in his desire to retell forgotten stories like this one.

Yanagita's construction of the "Japanese people" was imbued with human sympathy. He saw that wrenching changes in the Japanese economy had precipitated

---

1. Yanagita Kunio, *Yama no jinsei* (1926; reprinted in *Yanagita Kunio zenshū*, vol. 4 [Tokyo: Chikuma Shobō, 1989]), 81.
2. Ibid., 82.

an unprecedented depression during the Meiji period. The charcoal maker, for example, who had previously been able to provide for his needs from the natural bounty of the mountains he inhabited, discovered that his livelihood had become inextricably intertwined with the modern system of capitalism engulfing Japan. Even though he found it hard to feed his son, he was trying to take care of an abandoned girl as well. But the straitened times ground down the efforts of the poor to help each other survive.

Where the Matsuoka family resided, people had a history of recognizing others' sorrow and helping each other through hard times. Even so, the Matsuoka family suffered great privations. This family, better educated than the charcoal maker's but also very poor, left Fukuyama, a small town in the mountains of Hyōgo Prefecture, and traveled to Tokyo for economic assistance. All of Yanagita's brothers but one married into wealthy families and abandoned their family name. But life in Tokyo turned out to be as tragic as it had been in West Mino.[3]

Yanagita's description of the scene in which the charcoal maker killed his two children—"the sunset illuminated the entrance of the hut. It was late autumn"—contrasts the beauty and sorrow of nature with the brutality of an unnatural modernity.[4] As the sun disappeared, Yanagita seems to say, so did the Japanese spirit. Believing that only he could know the true meaning of "that great story of human suffering,"[5] Yanagita made it not only the goal of his folklore studies but also his personal mission to pass on this record to the next generation.

ESTABLISHING THE CENTER

Yanagita Kunio was born after the Meiji Restoration. By the time he became conscious of Japan, the new central government had already set out to construct a modern nation-state. Rural communities had become mired in poverty as profound as that of the charcoal maker's family.[6] When the Matsuoka family left its hometown, the "Japan" that Yanagita sought throughout the rest of his life had already perished.

3. In an unpublished conversation with Maruyama Masao, Miyata Noboru told the tragic history of Yanagita's brother and his wife. I had access to this story courtesy of Katsumata Mitsumasa, an editor at Shin'yōsha.

4. Yanagita, *Yama no jinsei*, 82.

5. Ibid.

6. Noro Eitarō describes the drastic changes that Japan went through as capitalist society developed during the decade of the Sino-Japanese War (1894–95) and the Russo-Japanese War (1904–5); *Nihon shihonshugi hattatsu shi* (Tokyo: Iwanami Shoten, 1983). Yanagita entered Tokyo Imperial University in 1897, just as the leftist Shakai Mondai Kenkyūkai (Social Problem Research Group) was organized, and began his career as a bureaucrat at the Ministry of Agriculture and Commerce in 1901, the date of the establishment, and immediate banning, of the Social Democratic Party, the first socialist party in Japan.

Yanagita graduated from Tokyo Imperial University and became a ranking official in the Ministry of Agriculture and Commerce. His urgent concern was rural poverty, which he sought to alleviate through agricultural reforms. But his proposals ran counter to the government's plans for development.[7] He resigned from the Ministry of Agriculture and Commerce and became chief secretary of the House of Peers, only to resign this position as well. From this point he abandoned all hope of saving Japan by setting economic policy within the modern bureaucratic system.

Having failed to provide political relief through bureaucratic channels, Yanagita traveled to rural Tōno in search of authentic Japan, a place (*chihō*) where true Japaneseness still lived, even though fragmented, in the customs and habits of rural life.[8] He believed that the centralized government was incapable of fashioning a new Japan according to its own fundamental cultural patterns. If modern Japan could not maintain the rural essence that was the source of its true identity, he argued, then neither could it establish true modernity in its metropolitan center. And in his view, only he, who knew at first hand the misery of the rural poor, possessed the vision capable of bringing authentic Japan back to life.

MOUNTAIN PEOPLE—THE ORIGINAL JAPANESE

Feeling that the true Japan was not accessible through standard written histories, Yanagita sought it in stories about the lives of mountain people. He assumed that authentic Japanese, the true bearers of Japanese culture, would live in areas even more remote than Tōno. Without their support, Yanagita reasoned, how could the center, and even the emperor system, hold its place?

In 1915 the enthronement ceremony of the Taishō emperor was held in Kyoto. Attending the ceremony as a high government official, Yanagita described how the *sanka* (mountain people) came to celebrate this event: "Looking to the slopes of Mount Nyakōji, I saw a few streams of white smoke going up in the pine forest. Aha, the *sanka* are talking."[9] To Yanagita the mountain people's recognition of the enthronement was more significant than that of the dignitaries who had come to Kyoto from all over the country for the official celebration.

The *sanka* had been erased from "history" by a modernity that privileged written records. Yanagita believed that modernity had destroyed the true spirit of the common Japanese people, and that only those who had taken refuge deep in the

7. Yanagita outlined his ideas for reform in *Jidai to nōsei* (1910; reprinted in *Yanagita Kunio zenshū*, vol. 29 (Tokyo: Chikuma Shobō, 1989).

8. Tōno is a small town in southern Iwate Prefecture. A local historian showed Yanagita his collection of local folk stories and legends, which Yanagita rewrote and published as the monumental book of his folklore studies, *Tōno monogatari* (1910; reprinted in *Yanagita Kunio zenshū*, vol. 4 (Tokyo: Chikuma Shobō, 1989).

9. Yanagita, *Yama no jinsei*, 86.

mountains could keep this spirit alive. In order to revive the true Japanese world on the sacred day (*hare no hi*) of the enthronement, Yanagita believed, the ceremony had to be acknowledged by those people who had preserved Japanese culture in its pristine form. The emperor, in whose person were preserved the powers of the ancients and Japan's unifying national identity, ascended the throne under the watchful eyes of the *sanka*. Only Yanagita, however, knew the meaning of the smoke rising in the sky that day.

The *sanka* represented a forgotten world that could still be discovered in unwritten legends, which had been kept alive in the minds of the ordinary people from generation to generation. Therefore, Yanagita began his folklore studies by collecting those stories.[10] From them, he attempted to reconstruct an archaic Japanese life that only survived deep in the "worm-eaten and rotten" fragmentary memories of ordinary people.[11] Although he insisted that "legends passed on in each family stand as explanations complete in themselves,"[12] he also recognized that "in the attempt to write down those legends, people interpret them according to their own ideas."[13] He assumed that he could bring these vanished or distorted worlds back to life.

Yanagita argued that Japanese people had two kinds of beliefs. One was systematically propagated when "shrines such as Munakata, Kamo, Hachiman, Kumano, Kasuga, Sumiyoshi, Suwa, Hakusan, Kashima, and Katori sent organized missions throughout the country to establish new shrines." The other was local and unofficial, consisting of "the ancient communal beliefs that local people held firmly in their hearts."[14] Since most feudal lords shared blood ties and ways of thinking with city elites, they reinforced the influence of the central government, so that Japanese had become "inclined to patronize large central shrines that were supported by Buddhism." Gradually, "the ancient shrines registered in the *Engishiki* lost their names" as they joined the organization of these central shrines.[15] But often, Yanagita explained, the peasants in their conservatism "simply added the rituals and festivals of the new shrines to those of their old one." Thus, the two kinds of beliefs created a "double-layered" structure in the peasants' consciousness: people "often demonstrated their sincere faith in the old local deities" by recognizing them as their family and village gods, in addition to acknowledging the

10. Yanagita Kunio, *Minkan denshō ron* (1934; reprinted in *Yanagita Kunio zenshū*, vol. 28 [Tokyo: Chikuma Shobō, 1989]). This is the first and only theoretical book that Yanagita wrote on folklore studies. Here Yanagita defined the fields and methods of his folklore studies, which he compared with anthropology and ethnology. It contains the only discussion of the key methodological concept *jūshutsu-risshō-hō*, which holds that the past can be found preserved in remote areas.

11. Yanagita, *Yama no jinsei*, 82.

12. Yanagita Kunio, *Densetsu* (1940; reprinted in *Yanagita Kunio zenshū*, vol. 4 [Tokyo: Chikuma Shobō, 1989]), 44.

13. Ibid., 39.

14. Yanagita, *Yama no jinsei*, 232.

15. Ibid., 233.

national deities supported by the state.[16] This explains the uniqueness of Japanese syncretism, which laid a new, universal religion on top of local folk practices and beliefs.

Yanagita thought that traditional folk beliefs flowed "silently from family to family, and from mother to daughter. . . . As long as no sign of interruption is evident, the older beliefs can be assumed to have survived."[17] He argued that these beliefs were "based on the natural demands of everyday life. . . . At every season, and in the mornings and the evenings, people pray for ordinary happiness in their lives. . . . They worship gods of the mountains and the wild fields, and gods of the sea and the river. The ancient past we love has continued to the present in a naive form, undamaged by the intervention of learned people."[18]

Yanagita claimed that the original form of this ancient faith, which was not knowable by modern Japanese, was based on the continuous observation of natural phenomena and could therefore still be found in families and villages of remote rural areas. Here, he was rereading the geographical distinction between center and periphery as a temporal distinction between modern and ancient. Because the peripheral/ancient sphere preserved Japanese beliefs in their purest form, it was only by using it as a base that the "true" Japan could be recuperated in the modern sphere. Yanagita, in a searing critique of modernity, juxtaposed the beliefs he found there with the consciousness of contemporary Japanese, who took distorted modern life for granted and accepted the modern as the best of all possible worlds: "In even more remote places than Tōno, there must be countless legends of mountain gods and mountain people. I tell these legends to strike fear in the hearts of the lowland people."[19]

THE PATH ON THE SEA

Yanagita sought to locate the "mountain people" even though he realized that their world could not exist except as a "phenomenon of the mind" (shin'i genshō). His position elicited a devastating criticism from Minakata Kumagusu, an anthropologist trained as a botanist, who had just returned to Japan from studies in England. Minakata labeled Yanagita's methodology "positivistic" and excoriated his attempt to document the beliefs of "real" mountain people.[20]

16. Ibid.

17. Ibid.

18. Ibid., 233–34.

19. Yanagita, Tōno monogatari, 9.

20. Yanagita wrote to Minakata, requesting his help in locating "mountain people" living in the Kishū mountains near where Minakata made his home. Minakata did not respond to this or subsequent letters, perhaps because he felt he was being used. Later Minakata harshly criticized Yanagita's folklore studies as pseudo-scientific; an ethnologist, in Minakata's view, should not take such a positivistic approach. See Minakata's letter to Yanagita dated December 23, 1916, in Iikura Shōhei, ed., Yanagita Kunio Minakata Kumagusu ōfuku shokan shū (Tokyo: Heibonsha, 1994), 2:345–48.

Yanagita subsequently abandoned the mountain people. He shifted his quest for the ancient past to Okinawa and the knowledge that had been preserved in the daily experiences of seafaring people. This year-by-year accretion of knowledge had sustained them in their life on the sea: "Only people who have lived for years on the sea have the experiential wisdom to understand how much the wind in different seasons and the tide at different times can help, hinder, or constrain navigation."[21] Land-dwellers had ignored this kind of practical wisdom. It was on the verge of disappearing, "remembered only in simple proverbs that survive in remote corners of the country."[22]

Because of Okinawa's location, far from the center of Japan, Yanagita believed that the wisdom people on the mainland had forgotten still remained alive there. He assumed that the distant ancestors of the Japanese people, who had migrated from the south, had left behind the wisdom that had guided their lives on the islands. Their insights must have been preserved, undistorted by modernity, at Japan's outer limits. Again, Yanagita was reading a synchronic geographical difference as diachronic difference.

JŌMIN: THE ORIGINAL JAPANESE, EVERYWHERE AND NOWHERE

Jōmin (abiding folk) is Yanagita's most famous concept. Yanagita thought that *jōmin* resided everywhere in Japan, yet at the same time they existed nowhere. It was precisely because they were invisible that they truly existed.[23] Especially in modern times, it was difficult to discern that they existed in the invisible world. Despite living in the center, Yanagita thought he could see this invisible world because he, unlike other people, identified with the periphery. What the diachronic changes of modernity had rendered unrecognizable would become revealed by the synchronic turn of his mind to the periphery. Yanagita believed that when folklore employed this method, it could establish a "new nativism" (*shin-kokugaku*) to represent the authentic Japan.

No concept has troubled Japanese social sciences more than *jōmin*. Even the field of folklore studies that Yanagita established has found his real intent hard to comprehend. Initially, for Yanagita, *jōmin* was a descriptive category of the everyday life of the common people living in the "villages" (*kyōdo*) of Japan. It became an imaginative reconstruction of essential Japanese life. *Jōmin* were both the key to

21. Yanagita Kunio, *Kaijō no michi* (1961; reprinted in *Yanagita Kunio zenshū*, vol. 1 [Tokyo: Chikuma Shobō, 1989]), 43. After resigning as chief secretary of the House of Peers, Yanagita made his one and only trip to Okinawa, a two-month visit beginning in late 1920. In 1925 he wrote *Kainan shoki* (Tokyo: Ōokayama Shoten, 1939), on which he based *Kaijō no michi*.

22. Ibid.

23. The contrast between things seen and unseen is central to the epistemology of Japanese nativism (*kokugaku*). See H. D. Harootunian, *Things Seen and Unseen: Discourse and Ideology in Tokugawa Nativism* (Chicago: University of Chicago Press, 1988).

Yanagita's historical reading of the common people of Japan and the model of a common mode of life, which he believed was held deep in the heart of every Japanese.

Yanagita claimed that what passes for the history of Japan "has no history of the ordinary people; . . . [it] has treated the records of ordinary people with little respect." Ordinary people are "rank-and-file soldiers." They are represented not as human figures but as countless short, bent lines resembling the phonetic character for *he* in illustrated scrolls. These foot soldiers "returned to their villages as brave warriors; their descendants became village headmen, pursued learning, and assisted their communities." In the Meiji era many Diet members and prefectural assembly representatives came from these families. "Many scions of these families became local notables, but they have been 'coldly treated' in history."[24] These people, Yanagita postulated, functioned historically as the spiritual backbone of Japan.

But "*jōmin*" did not refer only to village notables (*omodachi*), who "occupied the central positions of power in villages until the middle of the Tokugawa era." It also meant people who did not engage in agriculture, who "belonged to a lower status, and whose traces, however faint, exist even today." Among them were people who were not "ordinary peasants but craftsmen engaged in miscellaneous trades: mendicant monks, blacksmiths, and coopers who would live for a while in one village and then drift on to another." Between these strata were "the very ordinary peasants." This is not a definition.[25]

At the time Yanagita was writing, *jōmin* were no longer to be found in the villages. *Jōmin* who had moved to cities and were not living as farmers could not, of course, be called "ordinary peasants." They took on an existence that could not be spatially located. Documented as faint historical traces of people dispersed throughout strata of villagers and rural social drifters, *jōmin* could only be reconstructed by Yanagita in his mind. After being rendered invisible by history, their true existence—once revealed—was precious.

Yanagita's high regard for the emperor is evident in this frequently quoted reference to the imperial family: "With all due respect, I would say the imperial family shares much with *jōmin*."[26] He insisted that *jōmin* lived on in the imperial family, as evidenced by the *sanka*'s celebration of the imperial enthronement ceremony. This was a very different face from the one worn by the emperor who had been

---

24. Yanagita Kunio, *Kyōdo shi ron* (1914; reprinted in *Yanagita Kunio zenshū*, vol. 27 [Tokyo: Chikuma Shobō, 1989]), 16–77.

25. Yanagita Kunio, *Kyōdo seikatsu no kenkyū hōhō* (1935; reprinted in *Yanagita Kunio zenshū*, vol. 28 [Tokyo: Chikuma Shobō, 1989]), 150.

26. Conversation between Yanagita and Miyata Noboru in 1957. See "Nihon bunka no dentō ni tsuite," cited in Kajiki Gō, ed., *Yanagita Kunio no shisō* (Tokyo: Keiso Shobō, 1989). In *Densetsu*, 349, Yanagita had already suggested similiarities between the customs of the imperial family and those of the *jōmin*.

institutionalized in the Meiji era at the center of the modern nationalistic state. Through the *jōmin* this emperor embodied the whole of Japanese culture.

As an institution of the nation-state, the emperor reigned at the center of Japan. But for Yanagita, the emperor was first recognized as fully enthroned only when he participated in the ceremony of eating with the ancestor gods the crops that the *jōmin* offered up. An emperor who did not celebrate the rite of *ōname-sai* was only a half-emperor, for he could not truly ascend the throne unless *jōmin* celebrated his enthronement. In the same way that *jōmin* were "everywhere and nowhere," Yanagita thought, to be the true guardian of Japan, the emperor must not only reign at the center but also be omnipresent throughout the country.

YANAGITA'S INVENTION OF "ONE JAPAN"

For Yanagita, Japan had existed as a single entity without interruption since ancient times. The center of this entity was the emperor, and the *jōmin* unified Japan through their practices of everyday life. But historical development had undermined Japan's original purity. "One Japan" was sundered by modernization. In the modern era, and especially in the cities, Yanagita asserted, it had become virtually impossible to see this continuity. Even the periphery was not immune to the influences emanating from the center. Only in the fragments of people's memories did the true Japan endure, barely living on in the form of legends; only through the concept of *jōmin* could it be revived as a phenomenon of the mind. And only in Okinawa, southern islands that history had passed by, did this pure Japan continue to exist into present times.

Yanagita believed that on certain occasions the *jōmin* revived this ancient memory. At festivals *jōmin* shared food and drink and common dress, rejoicing in their togetherness. The experience did not last long, however. Their togetherness lived only briefly in the limen between the sacred (*hare*) and the profane (*ke*). A symbolic world created in collective activity, this communal world was the spiritual home of the Japanese people (*yamatogokoro*) that Motoori Norinaga discovered in the ancient poems of the *Kojiki*. It was also the source of Hirata Atsutane's expanded conception of rites as the basis of an ideal ruling system.

In the present historical era, Yanagita believed, the world Motoori and Hirata endeavored to create could not be established at the center. Japan had lost its unity precisely because the center had been occupied by the modern political state. Just as railroads cut through villages, the modern nation-state severed Japan's unity. In this context Yanagita saw *jōmin* as the central concept in a social discourse capable of reviving the communal ideal. As an official in the Department of Agriculture and Commerce, he had failed in his efforts to save the impoverished peasants. The materialistic political revolution of the Meiji Restoration, he believed, had impoverished Japan and destroyed its unity; only a cultural revolution could rescue it. To this end, he sought the "true Japan," a phenomenon of the mind that could be recovered in the sacred world created when ordinary people gathered to reactivate their fragmented memories.

Later, during the Pacific War, the devastation of the air raids recalled for Yanagita the destruction of rural Japan in the Meiji era, when massive forces of change destroyed the rural families and natural communities that had sustained the lives of the *jōmin*. He thought it was his duty to revive the true Japan, to reconstruct its ideals and preserve them for future generations. In this conception of historical continuity, the emperor was essential.

To rule as heir to the continuous cultural tradition of the true Japan, the emperor, as the center of Japan, must be celebrated in the sacred sphere created by the *jōmin*. Unless he too was of the *jōmin*, the emperor could not symbolically represent the whole of Japan. With the Meiji Restoration, the emperor moved into the palace of the Tokugawa shogun, the former ruler, to establish a new political center. But for Yanagita, this was not enough. For the emperor to embody the true Japan, he had to be the preserver of Japanese culture. He must put himself at the center of the center.

In the Meiji period, to herald the beginning of modern Japan, a new modern center—Tokyo Station—was built facing the Imperial Palace. Thus, the old city of Edo was pierced by a new axis running through the palace and the station. Communal Edo was remade into a site where traditional and modern Japan were integrated. But the focus of the new unification seemed to be located not in the palace but in the station at the opposite end of the axis. Tokyo Station stood at the center of railroad lines radiating out to local areas and, at the same time, connecting the center with the forgotten world of the local rural areas where *jōmin* lived. No matter that the geographical distance from Tokyo Station to local areas varied. The distance along the spatial axis of center-periphery was reinterpreted in the simple temporal antinomy of modern and premodern.

As the only "terminal station," Tokyo Station connected every locale to the center; at the same time, the Imperial Palace presided as the sole center of Japan, surrounded by the modern city and counterpoised to Tokyo Station. When people from the countryside arrived at Tokyo Station, they saw in front of them the Imperial Palace, "the true Japan," transcending modern Japan and integrating the whole. This was the point where all time and space in Japan was concentrated. And here Yanagita's problematizing of time and space in Japan—that is, the identification of history and locality—coalesced.

INVENTING THE PERIPHERY

Yanagita attempted to reconstruct the "true Japan" in the "present Japan" through the spirit of the *jōmin*. The "true Japan" had no tangible or visible existence. Orikuchi Shinobu, a leading disciple and close friend of Yanagita, searched for the true Japan in the religion of the ancient Japanese, and in the arts and literature that had developed around religious life.[27] Orikuchi theorized that the true Japan, which had existed in ancient times but disappeared in the present, could be recovered by going back in history. A traditionalist to the end, he believed that Shinto, as the living religion of the ancient Japanese, continued to live in the depths of the Japanese mind.

For Yanagita, the spiritual life of the *jōmin* could appear only when folklore studies reconstituted it in the present. *Jōmin*, existing "everywhere and nowhere," were the latent potential of all Japanese and therefore not limited to historical, geographical, or social specificity. For Orikuchi, however, the way Japanese people actually lived in ancient times—the true way of Japanese life—could be grasped by a proper reading of history. Orikuchi argued that it was obvious that ancient Japan had organized itself as one unified religious community. To Yanagita, the world Orikuchi assumed to be self-evident was an imaginary one, which could only be made to appear through the mental images of the *jōmin*. But even Yanagita sought fragments of an earlier "reality," in a quest that took him from Tōno to the faraway Okinawa Islands. For Yanagita, "Japan" could not be apprehended as a cultural unity. It was a "reality" lacking in form, whose core could only exist as it was continuously reconstituted as a mental image.

Yanagita used the rhetoric of center-periphery to locate Japan in the world. He reasoned that since the "*jōmin* mind" lived everywhere and nowhere, it was unique to Japan, making possible a "nation-specific folklore studies" (*ikkoku minzokugaku*).[28] By identifying phenomena "peculiar" to Japan, Yanagita's folklore studies could reactivate the "true Japan" in the present. This was not possible in contemporary European countries whose modern societies were disconnected from their tradition. According to Yanagita, the renowned Scottish anthropologist James George Frazer could not analyze European folklore in *The Golden Bough* without referring to the primitive areas beyond its borders. In contrast, Yanagita believed that Japan was a treasure-house of folklore studies because the *jōmin* had preserved Japan's indigenous culture from ancient times: though latent, it was ubiquitous.[29]

Yanagita assigned Japanese folklore studies a privileged position, arguing that among modern countries only in Japan had tradition been well maintained, so that "modern Japan" was merely a thin veneer overlaying traditional culture. In Yanagita's eyes, modernity had extinguished the characteristic "indigenous culture" of other countries: their modernity had indeed developed from their own culture

27. See, for example, Orikuchi Shinobu, *Kodai seikatsu no kenkyū: Tokoyo no kuni* (1925; reprinted in *Orikuchi Shinobu zenshū*, vol. 2 [Tokyo: Chūō Kōronsha, 1975]). Orikuchi believed the true Japanese soul lived in ancient times, or in the Okinawa Islands, constituting the "eternal world" (*tokoyo*). For Yanagita's critical response, see Miyata Noboru, ed., *Yanagita Kunio taidanshū* (Tokyo: Chikuma Shobō, 1992).

28. Yanagita Kunio, *Densetsu*, 268. Yanagita declared that development of national folklore studies logically came first.

29. See Yanagita, *Kyōdo seikatsu*, 30–31, and *Densetsu*, 276, 288, 294.

but only by denying that culture. Japan, on the other hand, had imported modernity; however much Japan modernized its center and however well it dressed itself in modern clothes, it still maintained indigenous characteristics deep in its core.

In this view, Japan itself was the periphery (*chihō*) of the global modern world. The distinctive indigenous culture that the "foreign countries" had lost was preserved intact in Japan. Yet even among "foreign countries," late-modernizing nations such as Germany had succeeded in producing folklore studies—for example, the work of the Grimm brothers. Because Japan was more of a latecomer than Germany, Yanagita reasoned, it must be a treasure-house of folklore studies.

Yanagita shared with modernization theory two basic notions: the geographical metaphor that the Western countries are the center of modernity and Japan stands at the periphery, and the idea of a developmental historiography. But Yanagita differed from modernization theorists because he never accepted "foreign countries" as the model of modernization. Rather, he embraced Japan's uniqueness. Recognizing Yanagita's passionate concern for Japanese tradition, some critics have even regarded him as a major opponent of modernism. But Yanagita's great concern was Japan's cultural uniqueness; the "Japan" that endured through time and space. Even in modern Japan's spatial hierarchy, where all local areas were arranged around Tokyo Station, the terminal station itself found meaning by facing toward the Imperial Palace. And this true center, whose essence pointed backward in time, found its meaning in the present in the encompassing modernity.

Yanagita's basic theme was Japan as a unified whole. Yet the very act of questioning Japan's modern identity produced a modern social-scientific way of thinking about society. To ask what a culture was like was to conceive of it as a dimension distinct from the nation-state; culture took on the function of social integration. Since Yanagita claimed that culture acted as a diachronic continuum on a historical time series, he had to assume that something made unseen by modernity was a cultural phenomenon, a tradition that had been active in the past. Furthermore, by projecting the diachronic dimension onto the synchronic metaphor of center and periphery, he could argue that things unseen in fact lived on, in the spatial margins he called *chihō*. This method of Yanagita's folklore studies reconstituted the invisible as a tradition that had survived into the present; the past that had been rendered invisible by the modern world actually occupied the center. Thus *jōmin*, found everywhere and nowhere, were the bearers of Japanese indigenous culture, because only through them did the unseen culture reveal itself. The Japan that had been "distorted" by modernity could be restored to its "real" shape only through *jōmin*. By juxtaposing the periphery with modernity and discovering the true Japan in the periphery, Yanagita used his invented tradition of *chihō* to prescribe the direction Japan should follow in the present.

TEN

Figuring the Folk

History, Poetics, and Representation

H. D. Harootunian

The rapid pace of Japan's capitalist modernization in the twentieth century, and especially in the interwar period, prompted a widespread effort among intellectuals, writers, thinkers, scholars, and activists to discover a fixed identity in relation to origin in the pre-capitalist past and to establish a poetics of historical repetition that could supply an alternative to the rhythms of linear narrative, which proclaimed successive and ceaseless change. This quest, which the novelist Yokomitsu Riichi named "the lonely journey," and others the "return to Japan," inflected a broader modernist discourse that was being formulated to solve the problem of social indeterminacy produced by the introduction of continuing social and technological change, new patterns of consumption, and the constant revolutionizing of received social relationships. Hence, an earlier preoccupation with recovering Japan's lost origin, epically pronounced by the Meiji Restoration, was now mapped onto a new attempt to regain the ground of an authentic, unchanging, and originary presence. It frequently salvaged memories *of* rather than *from* another time for protection against the dizzying experience of shock, speed, and sensation generated by capitalist modernization.

In response to their loss of access to experience unmediated by capitalism (with the advent of social abstraction and the disappearance of the referent), Japanese thinkers appealed to practices that they believed were created prior to the modern period and thus exempt from the corrosions inflicted by exchange value. In other words, the distrust of mere representation under capitalism and the certain changeability of all things led to an attempt to get outside it in order to think the concrete. The project of native ethnology (*minzokugaku*) formulated by Yanagita Kunio (1875–1962), Orikuchi Shinobu (1887–1953), and their followers, involved a turn toward constructing an imaginary folk, complete, coherent and unchanging, continuously living everyday life under the sign of immutable custom. The folk provided the prospect of realizing a repetitive history, with its rhythmic cycle of a socionatural order, which was capable of challenging the presumption of an evo-lutionary, progressive schema. The folk also provided a grant of immunity from abstraction and the instabilities caused by constant change because they claimed to be outside history.

In the writings of Yanagita, especially, and Orikuchi, we have the construction of an epic narrative of an essential folk that successfully remained unaffected by the ravages of capitalist change. It must be read alongside Shimazaki Tōson's epic novel *Yoakemae* (1935), which sought to chronicle the history of loss and unfulfilled expectation experienced by nativism and the folk they spoke for in the early Meiji period. My essay seeks to show how creating an image of the folk furnished both a reservoir of authentic meaning in an environment where it was always in danger of vanishing and resources for attacking an everydayness that was always escaping because it lacked a true subject that could ground it. Native ethnologists, and oth-ers, sought to redefine daily life and give it form and lasting meaning in order to define an indeterminate public space—the streets of the great metropolitan cen-ters—where alienations, fetishisms and reifications were producing their effects.

Even though enduring essentials were figured in the discourse of native ethnol-ogists simply as constructions to ward off problems fostered by capitalist modern-ization, it should not be supposed that their deployment aimed either at contest-ing the state or advocating the overthrow of capitalism. Despite an original antipathy toward the state, practitioners of native ethnology usually supported it and imagined a communal realm compatible with capitalism. It should be re-membered that the state made available the space of the nation the folk occupied once they were constructed. The state therefore preceded both the nation and the folk; it constituted the *referent* for whatever was designated as the sign of an endur-ing and ineluctable national existence that lay below the surface of contemporary life, waiting to be recalled. In the writings of Yanagita, the folk became simply an epistemic subject rather than a subject of practice, whose existence was realized in discourse, in the very act of representation he had disclaimed. As for capitalism, Japanese theorists merely affirmed Marx's observations about the supposed com-patibility of capitalism and romanticism: he explained in *Grundrisse* that "it is as ridiculous to yearn for a return to the original fullness as it is to believe that with this complete emptiness history has come to a standstill. The bourgeois viewpoint has never advanced beyond this antithesis between itself and this romantic view-point, and therefore the latter [the 'childish world of antiquity'] will accompany it as legitimate antithesis up to its blessed end."[1]

While Yanagita Kunio's program stemmed originally from the community studies movement started by people like Nitobe Inazō before World War I and was devoted to supplying relief to the rural poor, he shifted his attention away from relief to re-presenting the image of a timeless, essential communal order

---

1. Karl Marx, *Grundrisse* (London: Penguin, 1973), 162.

marking the place of the folk and their everyday life—what he described as "returning to the community in the community." As early as 1910, in *Jidai to nōsei*, he confessed that he had been mistaken in his earlier support for "agricultural management" and the role played by the state. Years later, with the publication in 1929 of *Toshi to nōson*, he called for a "communal management of the land" and advocated the implementation of a program that would lead to the "public production of a previous age." Faced by the enormous unevenness between city and countryside, which this text documents, Yanagita promoted not a new rural policy designed to improve the lot of Japan's farming classes but rather a return to older precedents and spiritual exemplars. In addition, he began to emphasize practices and beliefs derived from the ancient past that were capable, because of their survival, of binding together a group in collective solidarity. By 1935, when he published his major text on the methodology of the native place, his commitment had solidified into a resolution to concentrate not on community as such, but rather on what he identified as "certain aspects of the life of the community," those practices and beliefs that constituted the enduring life of the folk.

After 1935 Yanagita moved to a strategy aimed at representing folk life rather than engaging it as an ongoing practice, as in his earlier agricultural writings. This involved a conception of subjectivity that identified the people with the "folk" and society with nature. It also revealed the immense risk of upholding an imaginary in which the subject/agent reproduced social relationships and customs in a timeless productive order. To realize this program Yanagita turned to traveling and collecting tales and stories produced by the folk over many generations.

Collecting tales, Yanagita believed, preserved the voice of the folk and, presumably, allowed them to speak for themselves. Presenting stories in an authentic voice avoided ethnographic reporting, which, for him, risked falling into representation. But Yanagita was never able to sufficiently differentiate the native place from the boundaries fixed by the state; his communitarian discourse was never able to articulate a sufficiently different narrative rising from that other place—from the outside—that might lastingly challenge the state's capacity to appropriate whatever version it wished to project as its own. Place was where one lived, produced custom, and repeated timeless practices that constituted cyclical and unchanging daily life. Place was also where a person became a resident ancestor after death. This conception of enduring folk life functioned as an invisible realm that co-existed with the visible world of power and change, recalling the earlier nativist division of labor between things seen and unseen. What differed in modern Japan were the temporalities; two realms—a double structure—occupied the same place.

The discipline of native ethnology could only seek to compensate for the loss experienced in modern life by recalling the memory of a prior form of existence whose traces, presumably, remained available in the countryside. The immediate impulse for this new discipline, which served to inflect the broader modernist project, was the perception of unevenness Yanagita recognized early and shared with others. He thereby challenged the claims of capitalism that modernization inevitably led to evenness and a universal ground. For Yanagita, unevenness was principally expressed in the observable political and economic disparity between city and countryside and the co-existence of differing temporalities and modes of production within capitalism.

In time, unevenness on the political-economic level was recoded in things and objects on the spatial and cultural level to produce the image of different temporalities. At the spatio-cultural level, where historical differences are lived and observed in everyday life, differing rhythms produced noncontemporaneous and nonsynchronous contrasts. Within sight of the immense commercial and political power of metropolitan Tokyo—the spectacle of modernity—was a vast population of depleted human beings who lived within its widening shadow. Materially, there were sharp contrasts between the newer metropolitan centers and the countryside, where center and periphery met to form temporal and spatial boundaries and where the contradictions of capitalism were often greatest. Yet behind this figure of unevenness was a lived experience of unequal development manifested in the relationship between colonizer and colonized.

The spectacle of contrasts, so vividly portrayed by Yanagita and systematically analyzed by sociologists like Takata Yasuma, threw into question the relationship between representation and experience. This explains why early on Yanagita discounted literary naturalism and its program of privileging surface description—what was called *shaseibun*, "sketching from nature," or direct description. In time he abandoned direct description, which pretended to a photographic recording of reality, because it failed to account for a vast diversity of experience. In its place he installed what we might call depth hermeneutics (Orikuchi called it *jikkan*): despite his well-documented penchant for positivism and science, he chose a method that posited an inside and an outside, a surface and a depth, whose operation he first revealed in 1910 in *Tōno no monogatari*.

In *Tōno no monogatari*, Yanagita's inaugural collection of folktales, he moved beyond merely retelling the stories recounted to him by Sasaki Kyoseki and beyond ethnographic reporting to the more complex operation of penetrating the essence of experiences and then giving it expression. During his encounter with the teller of the tales, Yanagita noted that Kyoseki was "sincere and honest, even though he was not skilled in recounting the stories. I added no word or sentence [to these tales] and wrote [them] down as I *felt* them" (italics added).[2] Yanagita placed himself in the position of the traveler, not the teller of tales but a patient listener, in order to act as a witness to the self-presence and timelessness of the folk experience. (He even made a trip to Tōno to give further authority to the role of witness and the effect of presence.) He "prayed" that by relaying the tales he would make plain people "shudder," adding that it was his desire to "present this book to all

2. "Kanjitaru mama o kakitaru," in *Teihon Yanagita Kunio zenshū* (Tokyo: Chikuma Shobō, 1968–71), 4:5. Hereafter *TYKz*.

people who live in foreign lands." This self-conscious preamble attesting to his innocence and his intention to familiarize the strange in the midst of Japanese society shows that from the beginning he was not interested in simply describing but
rather in expressing things as they moved him. Understanding meant getting inside, beneath the surface. For this reason, he and his followers dismissed ethnography: because it consisted of reporting from the perspective of an outsider, it
could never hope to reach the interior of folk experience, which derived from an
inaugural moment that could only be ascertained in memory and trace, in "vestiges" and "survivals."[3] The importance of Yanagita's program was its capacity to
replace capitalism as the source of all activity with the seemingly concrete but historically indeterminate agency of the unchanging life of the folk in their native
place, and thus to substitute a fixed and static cultural space for the changes in
temporality wrought by the political economy.

This theme was expressed first in earlier works like *Jidai to nōsei*, where he reported that the "splendor" of the cities was outpacing the "glory of the villages,"
which were being sacrificed to the development of the former.[4] Owing to the massive migration from the farmlands to the cities, the rural population was being
emptied out from the countryside and the demographic shift was creating an uneven distribution everywhere between capital and labor.[5] Depleting the countryside of resources for the sake of modernization in the cities meant also that the
farm population was paying for Japanese colonialism. "The savings from the agricultural sector," he wrote, "are gathered by the center; before capital accumulation becomes substantial, the center uses it up for enterprises in Korea and
Manchuria." Two decades later, he submitted the subject of unevenness to a thorough analysis in *Toshi to nōson*, where he sought to account for the deepening disparities between city and countryside and the "loneliness it caused by separating
people from production on the land, making them suddenly sensitive and un-
easy."[6] Convinced that before long continued unevenness would inflict incalcula-
ble damage on the country, he worried about the alienation caused by a process
that removed people from the land, where they had for so long produced their
own food, clothing and shelter by hand, and where stable social relations had
defined daily life.[7] Over the previous sixty years, he declared in 1929, the cities of
Japan, "resembling a waterfall that pushes out the pool of water below in all di-

3. Ibid. 25:355.
4. Ibid. 16:28.
5. Ibid. 31:40. This is as good a description of alienation by an avowed non-Marxist as I have seen.
6. Ibid., 250.

7. Ibid., 241–42. It is interesting to note that at almost the same moment that Yanagita was expressing his fears concerning alienation and the removal of people from the land to the cities, the
writer of *policiers* Edogawa Ranpo was making the subject of many of his stories the loneliness and estrangement people experienced when coming to cities like Tokyo from the countryside, as well as the
difficulties they faced in their new social relationships and sexual roles.

rections," had displaced large numbers of peoples and areas with a constant stream of newcomers.[8] Peasants were starving and the invasion of city capitalism into the countryside had denuded mountains and thus eliminated "spare lands for continued living in forested regions."[9] Publicly owned fields and forests had been "bathed" up to their "shoulders" in the "blessings of capital from the cities." The great symbol of this unevenness was the centralization of culture and an imbalance that had produced a "despotism of the urban arts."[10] "Eternal things" like the village were no more.[11]

Although Yanagita had once believed that it was the task of a proper agricultural economics to resolve the problem of sacrificing the countryside for "the splendors of the city" and its resulting economic and ecological consequences, he found that it was beyond the capacity of prevailing disciplines to either identify the spectacle of cultural unevenness as a problem or to comprehend it. A recognition of a cultural unevenness more complex than the material division between city and countryside prompted Yanagita to move away from the "science" of agricultural economics, with its policies of rural relief. He now sought to formulate a method that might more adequately account for the incidence of unequal development and thus delay the conquest of capital over the surviving forms of received social life. The new discipline would also alter the way he viewed the question of rural relief. As he watched capitalism eliminating all traces of an older form of life in the countryside, he was persuaded that neither the historical method, with its reliance on narrative form, nor the new social sciences like anthropology and sociology could supply guidance in explaining this new phenomenon. Moreover, the task was particularly urgent. When capital accumulated in "every nook and cranny of the country," the struggle for power to sustain the quality of rural life would cease.[12] There was no time to lose: the growth of these vast contradictions had occurred in a scant twelve years, since World War I.

To freeze-dry this moment of cultural unevenness, it was necessary to create an image of a timeless and eternal folk (*jōmin*), which continued to exist in custom and religious observances within the vortex of modernizing changes. In a parallel to the formation of a discipline of popular culture-folklore in the Third French Republic as Michel de Certeau has described it, the Japanese desire for discourse was to stave off death; such a discourse could only be sustained by producing an epistemic subject—the folk—and a narrative of eternality centered on their native place, Japan.[13] Yanagita's new discipline sought to resituate a timeless communal

---

8. Ibid., 253.
9. Ibid., 261.
10. Ibid., 272.
11. Ibid., 264.
12. Ibid., 274.
13. Michel de Certeau, *Heterologies*, trans. Brian Massumi (Minneapolis: University of Minnesota Press, 1986), 119–36.

order that followed the rhythms of a repetitive socionatural process within a linear, evolutionary, and progressive historical schema driven ceaselessly by the laws of capitalist motion. Native ethnology aimed at implanting an image of an unmoving social order at the heart of a society in constant motion, a historyless and classless community within the historical epoch of capitalism, which was dominated by class relationships. The result was gemeinschaft capitalism, a vision of capitalism without the divisive effects of class conflict, a prefiguration of what Alice Kaplan later called the "gathering of fascism."[14] By making this move Yanagita was able to offer his contemporaries a picture of a world that had always existed, one that transcended both class divisions and class conflict at precisely the moment when an industrial work force was being created and mobilized and, equally important, when a consciousness of new gender relationships was being forged and represented in overdetermined figures like the "modern girl," "the kissing girl," and the cafe waitress. Furthermore, he managed to project a conception of regional diversity and marginality at the moment when economic and political power was being centralized in the expanding metropolitan cities. Nevertheless, while Yanagita wanted to challenge the metropolitan interpretation of its own experience as universal, it would be wrong to assume that the new discipline of *minzokugaku* was a critique of capitalism.

In Japan such thinkers as Yanagita, Takata Yasuma, and Suzuki Eitarō understood how, because of capital's propensity for controlling representation and deterritorializing fixed relationships, the metropolitan perspective concealed the reality of unevenness. He was acutely aware of the predominance of imperial metropolitan centers of production, exchange, distribution, and consumption, which had swept immigrants up from the countryside to become internal migrants and exiles in their own land. In response, they tried to articulate a micro-historical experience of the local as a counter-explanation and necessary supplement to the universalizing claims of global capitalism. The reality they wished to disclose—which was invariably excluded in universalizing macro-historical representations like H. G. Wells's *Outline of History* (1921)—was visible primarily at the periphery. The margins, where the modern and its other met along a boundary that was both spatial and temporal, produced "nonsynchronisms" because they contained dissonant forms of being, where people occupied places marked by differing modes of production and temporalities that co-existed uneasily with capitalism in the "Now."

Although Yanagita did not criticize capitalism, he called attention to its problematic status and the way its production of unevenness could become the purpose of a research program. The task of re-presenting this fading world, what Marilyn Ivy has properly called a "discourse of the vanishing,"[15] was clearly epic.

---

14. Alice Yaeger Kaplan, *Reproductions of Banality: Fascism, Literature, and French Intellectual Life* (Minneapolis: University of Minnesota Press, 1986).

15. Marilyn Ivy, *Discourses of the Vanishing: Modernity, Phantasm, Japan* (Chicago: University of Chicago Press, 1995).

In the opening passages of *Yama no jinsei* (1925), for example, it must have required immense personal resources to avoid slipping into a ceaseless condemnation of the very forces causing the lamentable circumstances of the mountain villages he was describing.[16] As a way of preserving endangered life-forms, he hoped to establish a discipline that would make manifest what had hitherto remained hidden.

At the heart of Yanagita's effort to construct a discipline capable of understanding the folk and their life in a modern society was a critique of history and historical representation in narrative form. In fact, the construction of a new "science" of community studies (*kyōdogaku*) was supposed to make up for the deficits of a historical method that suppressed knowledge about the folk and remained silent about the details of their everyday life. Historical narratives, he contended, "obscured the role of the ordinary folk by concentrating on wars and heroes." Even records written in the past that managed to disclose aspects of farming life were invariably written by government and village officials, people who were outside the daily life of the folk. The three-thousand-year genealogy of the folk had not been conveyed in writing.[17] Concentrating only on "great events narrating the story of politicians and military struggles," history was limited to representing the past, rather than accounting for how the past constantly interacted with the present and survived within its precincts. A study of the native place must try to secure a "knowledge of the past of the common folk in order to understand the real-life doubts confronting society today."[18]

History failed principally because it assumed a single, nonrecurring, one-time event instead of taking into consideration the ceaseless rhythms of repetition.[19] "Because many people are resigned to the fact that history is limited to a reality or facts that occur only once rather than over again . . . it is confusing to know that there are so many types of the same tales and legends throughout the country."[20] The availability of a vast hoard of tales testified to the way that historical representation worked to put different and alternative modes of existence "into the shadows," and excluded them from the public record. Even so, their presence illustrated incontrovertibly their capacity to escape concealment and endure down to the present. Since culture was continuous, the daily life of earlier times was contained within the present.[21] The principle of historical repetition, which was suppressed by conventional historiographical practices, constituted the "great strength" of the study of the folk in the native place. The "history to which we

---

16. *TYKz* 4:59–60.

17. Ibid. 25:266. Writing in 1929–30, Yanagita called for a study of custom based on "seeing" and "listening." See Yanagita Kunio, *Meiji Taishō shi sesōhen* (Tokyo: Kōdansha, 1992), 21.

18. Ibid. 25: 264.

19. It is interesting to contrast Yanagita's dismissal of history because it was not repetitive with Kobayashi Hideo's discounting of history a few years later because it seemed to repeat itself.

20. *TYKz* 15:313.

21. Ibid. 25:267.

have become accustomed," Yanagita declared, "is repetitive" and appears as a great unbroken record of everyday life that has been repeated over and again since the beginning of the race. "The footprints of the people's past have never stopped": concrete practices employed to gather and produce food, make shelters and clothing, and perform yearly and seasonal rituals constituted enduring life forms, which were immune to historical change and epochal events. Even practices and material artifacts that originated in a distant past were now acquiring new manifestations as contemporaries embraced them in their everyday lives.[22] Yet this doubling or fold (*repli*) that resulted from repetition compulsion invariably produced a difference that represented an encounter with the realm of the uncanny—the same but yet the not-same, the past that was still present, the modern and its other. Noting that when "repetitive deeds are gathered together and piled on top of each other, we will certainly [find] there the immediacy of national existence," Yanagita continued:

> For us the realities of everyday life narrate the past that existed before the present. We name those things that have been left behind [for future generations] as survivals. In calling these things continuing vestiges, an excessively large amount of archaic custom surrounds and envelops us and lies concealed within us. Even the most cultivated among us finds it impossible to live without being conscious of the past within us. In many circumstances, the act of reflecting [on this] leads to collecting and where an assortment and classification of materials accumulates, there is also comparison. No other country can hope to have such good conditions for consolidating material to understand the past.[23]

Only by directly experiencing cultural unevenness was it possible to grasp it. Yanagita's method entailed travel, spending time on the road, as if he were continually returning to a home he would reach only in the last, lonely instance, in order to collect tales and legends of ancestral life forms. Yanagita contrasted this procedure with the practices of the "white man" who stood at a distance to observe and judge the life histories of the natives. Relying on ethnographic reporting of field observers resembled the act of looking at photographs, if not taking them, because both operations placed the viewer outside the picture or scene.[24] Such a method, Yanagita explained, produced only ethnographic reports, inseparable from representations and interpretations, which could only scratch the surface of a culture. Returning home and collecting what the folk had produced was a far more accurate method than recording observations.

Yanagita's dismissal of photographic realism echoed his earlier rejection of *shaseibun* (direct description), the technique favored by naturalist writers. The discipline of native ethnology put the investigator inside the scene of investigation to

22. Ibid.
23. Ibid. 25:355.
24. Ibid., 297–98.

become one with it. The knowledge gathered and collected was about the native place, finding what had been lost, one's home. This conception of native ethnology recuperated the intransitive knowledge of Tokugawa nativism known only by those who lived it; it was a move that anticipated what, later, was to be called *Nihonjinron*, the discourse of Japanese uniqueness. Despite his celebrations of scientific rigor and its implied openness, Yanagita came close to promoting a methodology restricted to those who, like himself, were inside the scene.

Such a strategy put the investigator inside the scene of investigation, the precinct of the uncanny where modern Japan confronted its double, where the present encountered a past that was similar in all respects but now outside time.[25] In modern society this was precisely how an appeal to memory worked against the claims of history. For Yanagita, however, this ethnographic method was not capable of engaging the cultural unevenness that signified the historical watermark of this uncanny experience and which now marked the native place.

> Among scholars of Europe and the United States, there are many who believe that old and new customs exist separately from each other, like fresh and salt water. Even people like Levy-Bruhl, the renowned author of *The Primitive Mind*, believes this to be true. But if one looks at the conditions of Japan as they are today, he will see that they seem more to resemble the ebb and flow of the tide of a river. If one is a scholar of conscience, he will not be too greatly attached to the presumption [that there are separate spheres of existence]. Civilizational hybridity [*ainoko bunmei*] exists not only in Japan but in the harbors and ports throughout East Asia. In mixed cultures, there are no fixed forms. Even if one [cultural form] is not rejected, another may still find a place for itself. In situations where ways of thinking or modes of deportment that do not seem to harmonize with the general currents of the times, one [cultural form] is favoring one side or the other, advancing or retreating. When such circumstances are regarded with a cold eye from an external perspective [i.e., ethnographically], they will be deemed contradictory; in the reality of daily life, however, people live [*kurashite ikeru*] in these circumstances all the time without any concern whatsoever. The countryside exists in the capital; all kinds of archaisms enter into and mix with the modern.[26]

Yanagita named this experience of unevenness "the treasure island of scholarship." He was convinced that it was Japan's good fortune and his happy destiny to have witnessed and lived it. Foreigners, he charged, were always constrained by "laughable" and "appalling" circumstances of research and were compelled to speculate on and embellish whatever "gleanings" they could skim off secondary reports rather than relying on first-hand experience. Understanding the folk required

25. I am indebted to Marilyn Ivy's powerful meditation on Yanagita and the operation of the uncanny for this formulation. See, by all means, Ivy, *Discourses*, 84–85.

26. *TYKz* 25:279–80. I am also indebted to Neil Larsen, *Modernity and Hegemony* (Minneapolis: University of Minnesota Press, 1990), for formulating the relationship between uneven development and "'peripheral' modernisms." See xxii–xlvi, and especially xxxiii–xlvi.

not interpretation but empathy. The study of native ethnology meant probing beneath the surface to locate those deeply embedded unconscious habits of mind that ceaselessly regulated the repetitive rhythms of everyday life. The investigator had to be in a position to recognize what constituted the fund of spiritual beliefs that the folk took as second nature, which would remain forever beyond the powers of the outsider to grasp. "It is difficult to understand what is behind an interlocutor's words without possessing considerable skill," he warned, and the investigator must make every effort to avoid a "regrettable imitation" that "chases after the footprints stamped by the white man."[27] In *Minkan denshō* (1937), he argued that the final step in a research agenda, and clearly the most important, was collecting materials relating to the heart and consciousness of everyday life—that is to say, the "essentials," which most foreigners are "excluded" from reaching.[28]

In England, Yanagita noted, the old style of daily life derived from a remote age that had become indistinct. Because of its disappearance a community studies program dedicated to examining the native place was not possible. Scholars who usually congregated in London, he continued, resorted to collecting materials by going outside the country.[29] In other words, they collected materials from abroad to speak about an everyday life in England that no longer was accessible to them, even in traces. Their procedure reinforced an even greater specular distance by establishing a division between people who investigated and those who were investigated. A perspective that posited an outside to investigation was already mediated and forever prevented the investigator from gaining direct access to the object of inquiry. Ethnography could have no surety that the information it was collecting from abroad had any direct relevance to daily life at home. Unlike folk ethnology it was simply an encounter with the strange and unfamiliar, not a confrontation with the uncanny, the recognizable repetition of the same with difference, the return of the repressed in the collective experience of the native place and one's home.

Yanagita insisted that custom constructed referents for the scene under examination, which had meaning only for those who lived within them and belonged to the cultural configuration in which they were produced. In this restricted sense he, like Tokugawa nativists, saw folk studies as a discipline (*gakumon*) committed to revealing self-knowledge and understanding.[30] In order to avoid a slavish dependence on faulty foreign methods of investigation, he reclassified the levels of research to demonstrate how differing objects of inquiry corresponded to deeper layers of experience: at the first level lay travelers' collections of reports obtained by observation, which described external forms of daily life; at the next were collections and reports that commented on daily life and required a knowledge of the

27. *TTKz* 25:355.

28. Ibid., 337. Not too many years ago, in a workshop held at the University of Chicago, I heard the historian Irokawa Daikichi claim the same exceptionalism.

29. *TTKz* 25:292.

30. Ibid., 325–28.

language; finally, there were collections that revealed "essential" information about the spirit and everyday consciousness of the folk.[31] The third level was the most important and "excluded foreigners, with few exceptions." But the first and second ultimately depended on the operation of the third; they served as stages of an itinerary that led from the surface to the heart of things, promising to disclose "the inner secrets of the heart of the native [*kyōjin*], which can never be realized [by] viewing and listening from the outside." As he had explained in the earlier *Meiji Taishō shi sesohen*, listening and viewing had to be carried out from an interior perspective. "Our collecting," he claimed, "is *also* [italics added], at the same time, a consideration of the inner life of the native."[32] It supplied the means to "return to the community within the community." With this move Yanagita supplied native ethnology (and also, perhaps, the modern Japanese consciousness) with a structure of desire for an origin that could never be reached and opened the way for a nostalgia driven by irretrievable loss.

Yanagita's apparent slippage into exceptionalism, a gesture shared by most of his contemporaries in the 1930s, was linked to the conviction that the purpose of inquiry was to attain self-knowledge that might yield "good fortune" in the future.[33] This argument had already been articulated by Orikuchi Shinobu in the theory that national literature derived from the chanters of yearly rituals in archaic times as they asked the deities to continue abundance and good fortune for the community. Never entirely abandoning his first interest in rural relief, Yanagita believed by the 1930s that relief meant identifying the principles and collective experiences that guaranteed social solidarity. Knowledge of the inner, spiritual life of the native and social utility converged to constitute what he called a "new nativism" in the early 1930s.

The new nativism was reinforced by Yanagita's "discovery of Okinawa" after making his first trip there in 1921, which he later described as an "epoch-making event in our studies." He was persuaded to believe that Okinawa offered a treasure trove of unchanging religious beliefs and practices, which were fundamental to the figure of an enduring Japanese daily life. Yanagita viewed Okinawa as a surviving reminder of what Japanese life must have looked like in archaic times. In an act of misrecognition noted by Orikuchi, Okinawa appeared to Yanagita as a vast, living replica or even a laboratory of seventh-century Japan in the present. Ironically, Yanagita had come close to committing the very same misrecognition he had condemned foreign ethnography for making. But this easy and seemingly unproblematic assimilation of Okinawa and its own claims to difference, a move that was being tried in Korea at the same time with far less success, constituted the sign of a colonial unconscious that stalked the cultural sciences in Japan during the interwar period. It was shared by others as diverse as Orikuchi, who saw in the

31. Ibid., 336–37.
32. Ibid., 270.
33. Ibid.

island ancient Nara; Miki Kiyoshi, whose formulation of "cooperativism" based on communal brotherhood easily overlooked differences among East Asian peoples; and Watsuji Tetsurō's philosophical anthropology, which authorized assimilative concepts like "relationality" (*aidagara*), the determination of Being by spatiality rather than temporality, and Heideggerian "historicality."[34]

Yanagita rhapsodized Okinawa as a singularly important source. He thought that it was capable of providing inexhaustible possibilities for the continuing study of the folk because of the antiquity of life still existing there, which he attributed to the relative isolation of the island from foreign contact.[35] Even the presence and influence of Buddhism was negligible and had failed to affect deeper-rooted and more remote native beliefs and practices. If Okinawa did not provide a complete template for understanding the authentic and unchanging Japan, it nevertheless offered an important interpretative target of opportunity. "Today," he wrote, [Okinawa] preserves unconscious archaic customs that cannot be seen and compared [elsewhere]" and "imparts a key to understanding our own doubts."[36] The restoration of the fundamental beliefs that could still be observed in Okinawa, which once configured the organization of the ancient Japanese collectivity, would serve the present in its search for principles of social determinacy and the appropriate forms for binding the folk into a socially cohesive unit.

Yanagita came around to believing that an explanation of rural distress and a policy of reconstruction aimed at preserving families on the land, so much in the air in the 1920s, could not rely exclusively, if at all, on an appeal to material factors. The solution, he was persuaded, was not political and economic but rather cultural, specifically religious and spiritual. The problem of rural distress derived, in great measure, from the weakening of religious consciousness in the countryside and, by extension, in the nation as a whole. The task of the new nativism was, therefore, to restore archaic religious practices to the center of national life. And this could not be accomplished without acknowledging the existence of "remnants" of ancient beliefs existing within the depths of contemporary rural "agitation" and "suffering"—without, in fact, recognizing the presence of the repressed real of religious consciousness. To fully grasp the crisis, he proposed, and to "know the processes we have passed through, we cannot set aside the problem of ancient beliefs."[37] Folk studies therefore became "useful" by recognizing the importance of religion and its function in the modern society.

---

34. See Naoki Sakai, "Return to the West / Return to the East: Watsuji Tetsurō's Anthropology and Discussion of Authenticity," *Boundary 2* 18, no. 3 (1991), for an assessment of the dangers created by Watsuji's anthropology.

35. The Okinawa ruling house was contemporary with the Kamakura Bakufu (1192–1333). Yanagita made virtually the same arguments after World War II when urging the reversion of Okinawa to Japan.

36. *TYKz* 25:317.

37. Ibid., 327.

Yet an equally compelling argument for utility lay in the conviction that the study of the folk must contribute to "self-understanding" and thereby to "relieving the people." Yanagita saw the contemporary crisis, signified by continuing un-evenness, as one caused by capitalism, which undermined all settled relationships and fixed beliefs. It was especially manifest in unemployment and the chronic distress experienced by the farming classes. The movement for social reconstruction announced in the 1920s was a response to a "beehive of problems."[38] Although there was observable widespread unemployment throughout the country as well as a large number of people committed to finding solutions, much of their activity was simply talk. Many proposals advanced were "unsuitable to the current of the times."[39] By employing a meaning-laden term of an earlier era, *jisei*, which referred to any solution that was produced by human labor and thus counted as natural, he suggested that the various proposals for reconstruction enthusiastically promoted in his day went against nature.

With this move Yanagita was plainly pointing to the left-wing political ideologies and programs that had been imported to Japan. By returning to his earlier commitment to a program that would lead to practice and useful knowledge, he refracted the modernist assault on abstraction and its search for the concrete. "If slipping into a theory of abstraction is avoided," he advised, "people will be firmly rooted at the source, where they will be able to extract from the state of affairs those things that need to be reformed; they will come to the necessity of seeing and carefully scrutinizing the causes of the distress that need to be discarded."[40] Knowledge of the native place taught him that rural distress and the necessity to preserve families on the land could not, in the end, rely on material-economic solutions.[41] Although willing to acknowledge the existence of widespread rural poverty, Yanagita refused to support any scheme that failed to account for the way things were before the present crisis. If contemporaries refused to recognize the existence of archaic beliefs, he warned, there would be no chance for reconstructing the everyday life of the folk. They had to plumb the depths of folk consciousness for archaic religious beliefs that had been forgotten and bring them to the surface of life in the present. People had to work for a reunion with their true self, even though it appeared uncannily other and strange to them. In this inflection Yanagita came close to aping the moralistic palliatives that were being peddled by contemporary agrarianists. But he differed from the strident rural fascists in his deep concern for resituating religious beliefs at the heart of the modernizing society as the surest way to ward off the even greater threats of Marxism and rural class conflict, which could disrupt the bonds of social cohesion and tear society apart. The new nativism he imagined in this historical juncture also promised to answer his "prayer that man will understand himself."

38. Ibid., 326.
39. Ibid.
40. Ibid.
41. Ibid., 327.

At this point, Yanagita's construction of the folk converged with the ideologization that was taking place in the 1930s by social thinkers like Takata Yasuma, who called for a transformation of "anthropologism" to "folkism"; Suzuki Eitarō, who celebrated the communalism signified by the "folk spirit"; and Ariga Kizaemon, who located hierarchical relationships like *oyakata/kokata* in the folk substrate of the extended family (*dōzoku*). This ideologization, named "folkism" and condemned as "archaism," eventually employed the figure of the folk and their unchanging social order as a stand-in for the state itself. Yet it was also in this historical juncture that thinkers like Hani Gorō and Tōsaka Jun were questioning whether the fields of native ethnology and community studies, with their representation of the folk as a fantasy and their longing for a lost origin that never existed, were based on a technique of oppression and social control. In a searing critique of community studies—"Nine in ten people no longer live in a community," he roared—Hani called for a new subject of action. Not the epistemic subject embraced by folklorists, which was captured in and controlled by representation, but rather a subject of praxis, capable of making history by liberating the community for the masses instead of the folk. Although Hani never acknowledged the immense consequences of unevenness, even between the city and the countryside, he was nevertheless committed to establishing a proper community science, which would "emancipate the people from illusions and deceptions." When Tosaka Jun discounted as a fiction the lavish claims of "Japanists" upholding the family system as continuous since antiquity, he too was trying to liberate the Japanese from a longing for what was lost and the nostalgia it produced.

The program of Yanagita, Orikuchi, and others devoted to figuring a folk imaginary was principally concerned with demonstrating how the "natural community" worked to produce its own essence in the customs of everyday life. In their hands, the image of community acquired a preeminently immanentist representation, appearing as an organized, living totality that was always present. The fashioning of the folk was produced by an interpretative framework that emphasized orality; spatiality, the synchronic picture of a system with no history; and alterity, especially the difference signified by a cultural break. It also promoted unconsciousness—the blending of collective phenomena and the averaging of elements that were believed to have permeated the ordinary life of the people—as against concepts like writing and temporality, which signified the succession of historical moments marked by events, identity, and consciousness. This appeal to a "natural, organic community" and its timeless folk was deployed to displace the threat of social dispersion and the agency of historical classes. By the end of the 1930s folkic Japan had become the basis for a larger, more encompassing identity called the East Asian folk, providing ideological support to a variety of imperial and colonial policies that were demanding regional integration and incorporation.

The discourse devoted to figuring the folk and their natural community often slid under a larger discourse on culture, just as earlier discussions of community were assimilated to considerations of culture. The implications of this triumph of the epistemic subject for the practices of social science and thought in Japan are difficult to gauge, although we can detect its ghostly presence in all those shrill discussions of what differentiates "we Japanese" from the outside world (Heidegger's distinction between authenticity and inauthenticity, played in yet another register). We can say that, as a discourse, it ultimately authorized the formation of a discipline called Japanology, which made folk, community, and culture (a synonym for race) interchangeable subjects of knowledge representing a completed history and an immutable essence.

PART FOUR

Sports

ELEVEN

The Invention of the Martial Arts

Kanō Jigorō and Kōdōkan Judo

Inoue Shun

Although *bugei* and *bujutsu* have a long history, the Japanese martial arts known today as *budō* are a modern invention.[1] This is not to say that the word *budō* was not used before the modern era. As can be seen in Ihara Saikaku's *Budō denraiki* and Daidōji Yūzan's *Budō shoshinshū*, however, in the Tokugawa era *budō* meant *bushidō*, "the way of the warrior," signifying the code of conduct and ethos of the samurai class. Today *budō* refers to Japanese martial arts such as judo, kendo, aikido and *kyūdō*.[2] According to Nakabayashi Shinji, however, this usage of *budō* dates from the last decade of the nineteenth century.[3]

This essay explores the modern invention, and subsequent reinvention, of the Japanese martial arts by an examination of Kōdōkan judo. Founded by Kanō Jigorō in the late nineteenth century, Kōdōkan judo is the earliest example of the invention of *budō*; specifically, the transformation of jujutsu, a Tokugawa-era

---

1. Translator's note: *Bugei* is an ancient word that appears in very early chronicles, referring to actual combat or training for combat. The only concessions made in practice were the substitution of dummy for real weapons, and the use of *kata* (set forms) in sparring. The "great peace" of the Tokugawa era (1600–1867) led to the practice of martial arts for their own sake rather than as a form of combat training, with much more emphasis on *kata* for safety. The various arts of *bugei* bear the suffix-*jutsu* (technique), as in *kenjutsu* and *jujutsu*, hence the collective noun, *bujutsu*. There are some instances in Tokugawa-era literature, however, when the suffix *dō* (way) was used instead of *jutsu*, implying that the ancient *bugei* skills were being studied for their own sake rather than as training for combat. The modern usage of *budō* is different: it assumes that the martial arts are far removed from an actual combat situation. Modern *budō* may be performed in a competitive or a sporting context, but this is by no means universal. There is often a reduced emphasis on *kata*, and safety is achieved by modifying the weapons used, the protection worn, or the moves performed. See Stephen Turnbull, *The Lone Samurai and the Martial Arts* (London: Arms and Armour, 1990).

2. Judo, karate, and aikido have become international sports; others such as kendo (a form of fencing) and *kyūdō* (Japanese-style archery) are not widely practiced outside Japan.

3. Nakabayashi Shinji, "Budō," *Heibonsha daihyakkajiten* (Tokyo: Heibonsha, 1985), 12:1274.

martial art into a "national sport" (*kokugi*) and body culture, which came to sym-bolize Japan's modern national identity. *Budō*, of which Kōdōkan judo was the prototype, was originally conceived as a hybrid cultural form produced by mod-ernizing "traditional" practice. With the rise of militarism and ultranationalism, however, *budō* was reinvented as a counter to Western values and to infuse Japan's modern sports culture with "Japanese spirit."

FROM JUJUTSU TO JUDO

In May 1882 Kanō Jigorō established the Kōdōkan as an "academy for the teach-ing of judo," by converting a study at the Eishōji temple in the Shimoya Ki-tainarichō district of Tokyo into a dojo.[4] When Kanō opened the Kōdōkan, judo was not yet fundamentally different from jujutsu in terms of technique; nor had Kanō fully developed the organizational and theoretical principles that enabled judo to overwhelm competing schools.[5] The great success of Kōdōkan judo, I will show, was due to Kanō's embrace of the scientific method and institutional inno-vations that enhanced its appeal and secured a mass clientele.

Kanō was only twenty-three years old and still a graduate student in the Liter-ature Faculty of Tokyo Imperial University when he opened the Kōdōkan.[6] As a teenager he had been at the top of his class academically but weak physically. Often bullied and belittled by classmates, he was the loser of many student brawls. The late 1870s, during the high tide of enthusiasm for Western civilization, the Japanese martial arts were in decline. But persecuted by his classmates, the young Jigorō was determined to learn jujutsu to compensate for his frail constitution. In 1877 he became the pupil of Fukuda Hachinosuke, a practitioner of the Tenjin Shin'yō school of jujutsu. When Fukuda died just two years later, Kanō took over the dojo at the family's request. He continued his study of jujutsu, first under Iso Masatomo, Fukuda's teacher, and next under Iikubo Tsunetoshi, a former sho-gunal military instructor and a master of the Kitō school of jujutsu. In October 1883, one year after the Kōdōkan's inauguration, Kanō was initiated into the Kitō school and became a licensed teacher.

From the beginning of the Kōdōkan, rather than wedding himself to any one school, Kanō created a new, "scientific" martial art by selecting the best tech-niques of the established schools of jujutsu. Initially, he combined wrestling moves

4. Kanō Jigorō, *Kanō Jigorō taikei* (Tokyo: Honnotomosha, 1988), 10:23. Hereafter, *Taikei*.

5. Translator's note: Jujutsu, also rendered as jujitsu in English, is a term that first came into gen-eral use during the Tokugawa period for the grappling art based on the principle of *jū*, "pliancy" or "flexibility." Commonly assumed to be a "weaponless" martial art, in fact weapons were sometimes used in jujutsu training. See Turnbull, *Lone Samurai*.

6. Kanō Jigorō graduated from the Department of Political Science and Finance at Tokyo Impe-rial University in July 1881 but later became a special student of the Ethics Department. He completed his studies in July 1882.

and techniques of delivering blows to vital points of the body emphasized in the Tenjin Shin'yō school with throwing techniques that were the mainstay of the Kitō school. But Kanō did not limit his research to the techniques of these two schools. Owing to the declining popularity of *bujutsu*, he was able to purchase at used bookstores previously closely guarded martial arts instructional manuals.

Kanō assiduously collected and studied all the material he could lay his hands on.[7] Applying principles of dynamics and human physiology, Kanō systematized and classified the techniques he adopted from the various schools of jujutsu. In promoting Kōdōkan judo, he emphasized the role of innovation and rigorous empiricism and lauded its modern character. In a lecture in 1889, for example, Kanō began by remarking that "the word 'judo' might sound new"; he reassured the audience that "following scientific principles, I have selected the best elements of established schools of jujutsu and discarded the rest, thereby creating a new school, which is best suited to today's world."[8]

In addition to utilizing scientific principles, Kanō pioneered a new mode of instruction and a new relationship between teacher and student. The teaching of jujutsu was firmly rooted in the hermetic tradition, on the assumption that knowledge of the martial arts could only be learned directly from experience. Thus, students observed the master in action and practiced set forms (*kata*) under his watchful gaze. Cognitive learning was slighted. Kanō, however, stressed the importance of verbal communication and rational explanation. Students at the Kōdōkan attended lectures, and question-and-answer sessions followed demonstrations and practice sessions.

Kanō, a rationalist, believed in the power of science and wanted Kōdōkan judo to be grounded in scientific thought. As he remarked toward the end of his life, in an interview in 1935:

> Of course it was not possible to thoroughly investigate every technique of Kōdōkan judo on a scientific basis. But on the whole, because they were fashioned in accord with science, their superiority to older schools was readily apparent. As a result, trainees all over the country began to study Kōdōkan judo.[9]

Kanō makes it sound as if the development and diffusion of Kōdōkan judo were a "victory of science"; but of course it was not that simple. Many factors contributed to the overwhelming success of Kōdōkan judo.

---

7. *Taikei* 10:2–5.

8. *Taikei* 2:102. The phrase "following scientific principles" refers to principles of dynamics and physiology.

9. *Taikei* 1:55. Tadano Hideo argues that in concept and convention, jujutsu in the Tokugawa period already possessed the characteristics of modern sports and criticizes the popular view of jujutsu as reflecting "the point of view from the Kōdōkan side." This important critique applies to this paper as well, though at this point I have not determined the full implications. See Tadano Hideo, "Seido toshite no jūdō no henyō katei," a paper presented at the first Japan Sports Sociology Symposium, Nara Women's University, March 30, 1992.

GROWTH OF THE KŌDŌKAN

When the Kōdōkan opened in 1882, there were only nine students, though they included Kanō's stellar pupils Tomita Tsunejirō and Saigō Shirō. Only ten students were enrolled two years later. Beginning in 1885, however, the number of students started to increase dramatically, and by 1887 the total number of students enrolled reached almost five hundred. Five years later, in 1892, 434 students enrolled within the year, bringing the total membership to 2,755 students. What accounted for the sudden surge?

The initial success of the Kōdōkan followed highly publicized victories of Kanō's pupils over practitioners of jujutsu in competitions sponsored by the Tokyo Metropolitan Police Bureau. In 1883, when policemen were ordered to learn jujutsu, masters of the leading schools were placed in charge of training. In 1885, however, the new police superintendent, Mishima Michitsune, hosted an open competition pitting Kōdōkan judo against jujutsu. While it is difficult to distinguish fact from legend, there is no doubt that from the first encounter, the members of the Kōdōkan team overpowered their opponents.[10] Some years later Kanō gave the following account of the triumph of his pupils over students of the renowned Totsuka-Yōshin school of jujutsu:

> In 1887 and 1888, as the Kōdōkan's fame spread, whenever the Police Bureau hosted big competitions, the Totsuka school and the Kōdōkan competed. At one contest in 1888, each sent fourteen or fifteen contestants. Four or five Kōdōkan students were matched against other jujutsu teams, but about ten had matches with members of the Totsuka team, which included Terushima Tarō, a great technician, and Nishimura Tadasuke, renowned for his great strength. Terushima was pitted against Yamashita Yoshitsugu, and Nishimura against Satō Hōken. Surprisingly, two or three matches ended in a tie, with the Kōdōkan winning all the rest. Kōdōkan pupils had greatly improved, but I never dreamed their skills had progressed to the point that they could achieve such results. I think they won primarily because of their spirit.[11]

Once he had established the Kōdōkan, Kanō himself never had a match with anyone from another school, formally or informally; he always sent his pupils. Tomita Tsunejirō, Saigō Shirō, Yamashita Yoshitsugu, and Yokoyama Sakujirō—known as the "four kings" of Kōdōkan judo—carried the banner in the pioneer days of the Kōdōkan. Tomita Tsunejirō was the father of the novelist Tomita Tsuneo, who later wrote the best-seller *Sugata Sanshiro* (1942), modeled on Saigō Shirō's life. Although slight of frame, Saigō was a master technician.[12] Yamashita Yoshitsugu, whom Kanō sent to America with his wife in 1903–7, was instrumental in the internationalization of judo. In contrast to Saigō, Yokoyama Sakujirō

---

10. See Togawa Yukio, *Shōsetsu Kanō Jigorō* (Tokyo: Yomiuri Shinbunsha, 1992), 170–248.
11. *Taikei* 10:63–64.
12. Concerning Saigō Shirō, see Makino Noboru, *Shiden Saigō Shirō* (Tokyo: Shimazu Shobō, 1983).

was a very large man with a formidable presence. People were so afraid of him that he was dubbed "Oni [demon] Yokoyama!" He was never known to lose a match.

Following the stunning success of Kōdōkan judo, the Metropolitan Police Department began to hire Kanō's students as martial arts instructors. Kanō also used his position as a prominent educator to promote Kōdōkan judo. In April 1883 Kanō, then a professor at Gakushūin University, established a practice hall on the campus and offered instruction in judo to students of the university. In 1887, when the Naval Academy adopted Kōdōkan judo, Kanō sent his star students, Yamashita Yoshitsugu and Satō Hōken, to serve as instructors. Shortly afterward, when the Naval Academy moved to Edajima, a splendid judo hall was constructed.

The connection with the Naval Academy allowed Kōdōkan judo to penetrate the military. Both Hirose Takeo, the great war hero who died at Port Arthur during the Russo-Japanese War, and Takarabe Takeshi, who went on to become secretary of the navy, became initiates of Kōdōkan judo at the Naval Academy.[13]

Tokyo Imperial University and Keiō University, respectively Japan's premier public and private universities, followed the Naval Academy in instituting Kōdōkan judo; soon other institutions of higher learning followed suit. During his tenure as principal of Kumamoto Fifth Higher School, Tokyo First Higher School, and Tokyo Higher Normal School, Kanō personally strove to promote Kōdōkan judo, instructing students himself. The match in 1898 between the First Higher School of Tokyo and the Second Higher School of Sendai was the beginning of interscholastic competition in Japan. The flourishing of judo in the prewar educational system laid the foundation for its enduring success.[14]

Keenly aware of the need not only to attract but to retain students, Kanō created a new system of ranks to reward students' progress. Subsequently adopted by the other Japanese martial arts, the *dan-kyū* (rank-step) system proved to be a successful marketing strategy. Previously, ranks denoting mastery varied depending on the school but basically consisted of only three stages: *mokuroku*, mastery of a set of techniques; *menkyo*, license to teach; and *kaiden*, initiation in all the secrets. Kanō believed that the great distance between ranks caused students to become discouraged. He therefore created a *dan* system composed of ten ascending steps. For trainees not yet ranked in the *dan* system, he devised a subsystem of *kyū*, eventually with six steps.

Kanō created the *dan-kyū* system to heighten students' motivation. The same logic led him to make *randori*, free-form sparring, the main component of judo training. Traditional training in *bujutsu* placed great emphasis on practice of *kata*,

13. Hirose Takeo was admitted on November 15, 1887; Takarabe Takeshi on March 20, 1888.

14. Iizuka Ichiyō, *Jūdō o tsukutta otokotachi* (Tokyo: Bungei Shunjū, 1991), 85–92. See also Ōtaki Tadao, "Gakusei jūdō no genryū," in Zen Nihon Gakusei Jūdō Renmei, ed., *Gakusei jūdō sanjūnen no ayumi* (Tokyo: Mainichi Shinbunsha, 1981), 13.

set forms. Kanō compared the former to grammar and the later to composition, arguing that while a solid grounding in grammar was indispensable, a mastery of grammar did not in itself produce fluid composition. Learning to cope with unexpected moves, as in *randori*, was both vital to success in competitions and more interesting to students than the repetition of *kata*.

Kanō's approach was to treat those who came to study judo as clients, even as consumers. This was something new, something "modern," that he brought to the teacher-pupil relationship in martial arts.

JUDO AND JAPANESE CULTURE

The word 'judo', Kanō was fond of saying, "is no longer merely a martial art but names a principle applicable to all aspects of human existence."[15] Accordingly, in publicizing Kōdōkan judo, Kanō stressed its character-building aspect. The ultimate goal of judo training, he maintained, was to "perfect oneself and contribute something to the world."[16] Thus, judo had an educational role to play, producing a new type of talented and capable citizen who, through self-improvement, made a positive contribution to society and the nation. In the later stages of the development of Kōdōkan judo, Kanō increasingly emphasized judo's role in building character, and in 1922 he established the Kōdōkan Cultural Association (Kōdōkan Bunkakai). According to the prospectus, the purpose of the association was to contribute to society by promoting three basic principles: (1) The most efficient use of energy is the secret of self-perfection; (2) Self-perfection is accomplished by helping others [to achieve] perfection; and (3) Mutual self-perfection is the foundation of the mutual prosperity of humankind.[17]

Kanō believed the "most efficient use of energy" to be the fundamental principle of judo. "Energy" included "both mental and physical power," and "most efficient use" entailed both not wasting energy and promoting goodness. "Goodness," as conceived by Kanō, "is something that promotes the continuing development of collective and social life."[18] Kanō frequently stressed in his writings that spiritual cultivation was as important as physical mastery of technique.

Kanō seized every opportunity to expound on the cultural significance of Kōdōkan judo. I have already discussed how Kanō revolutionized the use of language in martial arts instruction. The discursive turn was not, however, limited to instruction. Kanō made the whole system of Kōdōkan judo "accountable," including its theory, principles, and purposes. He was a persuasive spokesman who, in countless lectures and essays now collected in fourteen volumes, seized every opportunity to publicize, justify, and promote judo. He began publishing the first

15. *Taikei* 2:250.
16. *Taikei* 3:124.
17. *Taikei* 12:14.
18. *Taikei* 1:70–72.

Kōdōkan magazine, *Kano juku dōsōkai zasshi*, in 1894. Devoting much of his energy to publicizing judo and its philosophy through the print media, Kanō also brought out *Kokushi* (1898–1903), *Jūdō* (1914–18), *Yūkō no katsudō* (1919–22), *Taisei* (1922), *Sakkō* (1924–38), and *Jūdō* (Kōdōkan Bunkakai, 1930–38).

Thus, we see that Kanō was much more than the founder of a new and improved school of jujutsu. He was a man of letters who successfully incorporated judo into the discursive space of modern Japan and established its raison d'être in a society that no longer possessed *bushi*, feudal warriors. In this sense, the prosperity and growth of Kōdōkan judo can be understood to represent the triumph of the word over the sword; of the literary (*bun*) arts of the samurai over the martial (*bu*) arts.

CONTINUITY AND DISCONTINUITY WITH TRADITION

Through his speaking and publishing activities, Kanō propagated a new conception of the martial arts. In modernizing jujutsu, he had frequently stressed that judo not only differed from jujutsu but was better suited to the modern world. At the same time he was mindful of judo's connection to the older tradition of *bujutsu*. The two sides of Kōdōkan judo are evident in the various reasons Kanō offered for choosing the name "judo." First, there were practical considerations behind the new name. When Kanō founded the Kōdōkan, the traditional martial arts were in decline and the popular image of jujutsu was rather unsavory. Therefore, he thought that "at least the name should be new in order to draw in pupils."[19] Second, since the word *jutsu* denotes practical application, he substituted *dō* (way), which signifies underlying principle, thereby implying that Kōdōkan judo embodied the fundamental way while jujutsu was merely one application.

But why *dō*? The third factor in the choice of judo was that Kanō "didn't want the old masters' contributions to be forgotten."[20] The word "judo" had been used by some schools of jujutsu. The Kitō school of jujutsu, which Kanō himself had studied, was sometimes called *Kitō jūdō*, and the diploma Iikubo Tsunetoshi awarded Kanō in 1883 read *Nihonden* [Japanese tradition] *Kitō jūdō*. Kanō followed suit in adopting the name "Nihonden Kōdōkan Judo."

With these resonances of "tradition," judo, which began as a new type of the martial arts made suitable to the modern world, developed into a "body culture" associated with Japanese national identity, something unchanged in the midst of the changing times. Here we see a form of what Eric Hobsbawm has called the "invention of tradition."[21]

19. *Taikei* 3:123–24.
20. *Taikei* 2:103.
21. Eric J. Hobsbawm and Terence O. Ranger, eds., *The Invention of Tradition* (Cambridge: Cambridge University Press, 1983).

The association with "tradition" facilitated the development of Kōdōkan judo and benefited Kanō in a variety of ways. For example, Kanō, whose own views were quite moderate, enjoyed the patronage of influential politicians of the conservative-nationalist camp such as Mishima Michitsune, Tani Kanjō, and Shinagawa Yajirō. In 1910 the International Olympic Committee appointed Kanō as the first Japanese member. Kanō was, of course, a prominent educator, but the fact that he was a master of a "traditional" Japanese martial art undoubtedly played a role in the appointment.

THE OLYMPICS AND THE MODERNIZATION OF JAPAN'S SPORTS

Kanō was not a narrow cultural nationalist. While he vigorously promoted a revitalized martial arts tradition, he also made persistent efforts to foster Western-style sports. The development of these sports was greatly advanced by Japan's participation in the Olympic games. Here Kanō played an instrumental role. He established the Japan Amateur Sports Association (Dai Nihon Taiiku Kyōkai) in 1911 as the central body for selecting athletes and sending them to the Olympic games. As a result of the first qualifying competitions, Kanaguri Shizō from Tokyo Higher Normal School, who was later called "the father of Japan's marathon," and sprinter Mishima Yahiko of Tokyo Imperial University were selected. Kanō accompanied them to Stockholm in 1912 to participate in the Fifth Olympic Games, the first Olympiad that Japan participated in.

Fifteen athletes were sent to the next Olympic games in Antwerp in 1920; two silver medals came home. In the Amsterdam games in 1928, forty-three athletes participated: Oda Mikio in the triple jump and Tsuruta Yoshiyuki in the 200-meter breast stroke both won gold medals. This was the first time that athletes from East Asia won Olympic gold medals. Japan's sports were thus rapidly modernized. The Japan Amateur Sports Association quickly broadened its role and became the governing body for all amateur sports.

The association of Kōdōkan judo with Japanese tradition proved beneficial to Kanō in his role as kingpin of the Japan Amateur Sports Association. The image of traditional *budō* that Kanō cultivated lent a patina of orthodoxy, which enabled him to gain broad support. This is one example of how the "invention of tradition" can be linked to the promotion of modernization.

In his later years Kanō made great efforts to host the Olympics in Japan. At the 1936 International Olympic Committee convention in Berlin, he succeeded in attracting the Twelfth Olympic Games to Tokyo. Even though the Sino-Japanese War broke out the next year, the committee confirmed its decision at the March meeting in Cairo to award the games to Japan and officially announced the 1940 Tokyo Olympics. Kanō, who attended the Cairo meeting as the chief of the Japanese delegation, contracted pneumonia on the return voyage and died on May 4, 1938, at the age of 79. He died believing that two years later the Olympics would be held in Tokyo, but his dream was not realized. In July 1938, as the clouds of war gathered, the Japanese government decided to decline the invitation to host the 1940 Olympics.

IDEOLOGIZING BUDŌ

Kōdōkan judo was instrumental in the formation of *budō*. The modern form of Japanese martial arts, of which judo served as prototype, had a two-sided character. On the one hand, *budō* incorporated such modern elements as the scientific investigation of technique, the *dan-kyū* ranking system, verbal instruction, and emphasis on character building. On the other hand, *budō* built upon practices of the old martial arts to which it was linked discursively.

Kanō's conception of *budō* was neither narrowly nationalistic nor socially conservative. Kanō both promoted the development of Western sports in Japan and sent one of his star students to introduce judo to America. He also opened the Kōdōkan to women who wished to study judo. As time passed, however, *budō* was appropriated by strident nationalists, who propagated an essentialist conception of Japan's martial arts.

The Dai Nihon Butokukai (Japan martial virtue association) played an important role in the institutional and ideological development of *budō*. The Butokukai was established in 1895 in Kyoto to commemorate the 1,100th anniversary of the founding of the old imperial capital, Heian-kyō (Kyoto) by Emperor Kanmu. According to the prospectus, the purpose of the association was to use Japanese martial arts to promote the "martial spirit" of Emperor Kanmu, which formed the basis of *wakon*, or pure Japanese spirit. Judo, kendo and *kyūdō* exemplified "Japan's unique culture of physical education and the essential spirit of the Japanese people."[22] In 1899 the association built the Butokuden (martial virtue hall) adjoining Kyoto's Heian Shrine and organized branches throughout the country. Every May the Butokukai convened a "martial virtue" festival attended by instructors of all Japanese martial arts from every corner of the country. In 1905 it opened a training institute for martial arts teachers, which became a college in 1912 and in 1919 was renamed the Budō Senmon Gakkō.

In the 1920s and the 1930s *budō* experienced a remarkable growth. The Kōdōkan, among others, continued to prosper. By 1926 approximately two thousand new students were enrolling each year, and the total enrollment in that year reached almost 37,000.[23] In the process, however, *budō* was steadily drawn into closer association with Japanese militarism. As the war escalated from the Manchurian Incident of 1931 to full-scale war with China beginning in 1937 and the Pacific War in 1941–45, *budō* became ever more closely associated with ultranationalism and emperor-centered thought. The martial arts were raised to the

---

22. Hayashi Takatoshi, "Dai Nihon Butokukai no seikaku to tokuchō ni tsuite," in *Taiiku supōtsu shakaigaku kenkyū* (Tokyo: Dōwa Shoin, 1982), 1:59.

23. *Taikei* 2:31.

status of *kokugi* (national sport) and became part of the ideological apparatus of mobilization for total war. Under these circumstances, the Butokukai was reorganized in 1941 and placed directly under government control.

During this period martial arts training was incorporated into the state education curriculum. With the advent of *gakko* (school) *budō*, the state formally authorized the moral and educational value of *budō*. As promoted by the state, however, the goal of *budō* training diverged sharply from Kanō's goals of pursuing self-perfection and improving society. Now *budō* was encouraged as a means of fostering the spirit of "self-abandonment" and "devotion to the nation-state."

In addition to state education, such best-selling novels as Yoshikawa Eiji's *Miyamoto Musashi* and Tomita Tsuneo's *Sugata Sanshirō* played an important part in spreading the ideologies of *budō*. *Miyamoto Musashi* appeared serially in the *Asahi* newspaper from 1935 to 1939 and was published in eight volumes in 1939–40. *Sugata Sanshirō*, published in 1942, was brought to the screen by Kurosawa Akira one year later. In 1944 Tomita brought out a widely read sequel, which was also made into a movie by Kurosawa.

BUDŌ VERSUS SPORTS

In the 1930s and 1940s, Western-style sports were discouraged and the state vigorously promoted a nationalistic and essentialist conception of *budō*. *Budō*, it increasingly stressed, had an ancient history and embodied *wakon*. The emphasis on modernity and a discontinuity with tradition, which was so central to Kanō's conception of *budō*, disappeared. "Modernity" came to be regarded as a characteristic of "imported sports," undesirable and something to be denied.

In the rhetoric of the day, "imported sports" were contrasted with "traditional" *budō*. Because the former were based on Western individualism and liberalism, ideologues argued, they should be "Japanized" through *budō*, which embodied Japanese spiritual values. Noguchi Genzaburō exemplifies this ideological current. To Noguchi, Japan's national sports were "cultural treasures whose value extended from the front lines and to the home front of the national defense."[24] While acknowledging that Western sports, like all imported culture, had certain strong points, Noguchi and other critics warned against the spirit of individualism and selfishness that lay at the heart of the Western conception of sportsmanship. By promoting such doctrines as *Nihon taiiku dō* (the way of Japanese physical culture) they attempted, in short, to replace the Western spirit in sports with the Japanese spirit of *budō*. In this sense what developed was an ultranationalistic version of the *wakon yōsai* (Japanese spirit, Western technology) conception of Japanese modernization. *Budō*, originally a modern hybrid typical of late Meiji culture, was redefined as "timeless" and utilized to infuse Western-type sports with "pure" Japanese spirit.

24. Irie Katsumi, *Nihon fashizumu-ka no taiiku shisō* (Tokyo: Fumaidō Shuppan, 1986), 201.

The relationship between *budō* and sports was reversed after Japan's defeat in 1945. Because of its close association with Japanese militarism and ultranationalism, *budō* was prohibited by GHQ, the American occupation authority, and the Butokukai was ordered to disband in 1946. The GHQ was especially hostile to kendo, while judo was treated a little more leniently. In 1948 the Kōdōkan was allowed to resume the All-Japan Judo Championships founded by Kanō in 1930. Nevertheless, the teaching of judo and kendo in schools was still prohibited.

Facing a difficult situation, interested parties made every effort to "democratize" *budō*; that is, to re-create *budō* as a sport. In contrast to the "*budō*-ization" of sports in the 1930s, *budō* had to be "sports-ified" to survive in the political climate of the occupation, which insisted on democratization. For example, *shinai kyōgi*, a new martial art using bamboo swords, was invented as a "sport" version of kendo acceptable to the occupation authorities.

The revival of *budō* began around 1950. The All-Japan Judo Federation and the Japan *Kyūdō* Federation were organized in 1949; following the end of the occupation in 1952, the All-Japan Kendo Federation was established. School *budō* was also revived: judo in 1950, *shinai kyōgi* in 1952, and kendo in 1957. In 1956 the first World Judo Championships were held in Tokyo. In 1964, when Tokyo hosted the Olympic Games, judo was adopted as an official Olympic sport. Judo as an invented tradition had come full circle.

TWELVE

The Invention of the *Yokozuna* and the Championship System, Or, Futahaguro's Revenge

Lee A. Thompson

On December 27, 1987, the young *yokozuna* Futahaguro stormed out of his stable after an argument with his stable master, shouting that he wasn't coming back. A few days later he resigned from the Sumo Association,[1] putting an end to his career at the age of 24. The director of the association, Kasugano—a former *yokozuna* himself—was quoted as saying: "I've been involved with sumo for fifty years, one-fortieth of its 2,000-year history, and I've never heard of such a thing as a *yokozuna* running away."[2]

Kasugano's comment assumes not only the antiquity of sumo, but also its continuity. He implies that the *yokozuna* as we know it dates back to the supposedly ancient origins of the sport. Because of its roots in the Edo period and the ritual trappings surrounding it, the rank of *yokozuna* is commonly thought to be a venerable tradition. On inspection, it turns out to be largely modern.

The sport of sumo is a prominent example of Japanese tradition. In rhetoric as well as appearance, it claims a long and continuous history, as is apparent even in scholarly works in both Japanese and English. P. L. Cuyler writes: "Sumo . . . is much more than a sport alone. It is a ritual of timeless dignity and classical form. It is a glimpse of ages past, of the history of Japan. Repeated interaction with Shinto religious belief and practice from the early centuries of the Christian era

---

1. The Sumo Association is the organization that operates professional sumo. It is a foundation registered with the Ministry of Education. There are more than one hundred shares in the association, all held by former sumo wrestlers. Headed by a ten-man executive board, the association traces its origin to the organization of retired sumo wrestlers who ran sumo in Edo (Tokyo) during the Tokugawa period (1600–1867). Originally there were parallel organizations in other cities, but in 1926 the Osaka group, the last independent organization, merged with the Tokyo group, creating the present nationwide organization.

2. *Sumō* (February 1988): 158.

left a profound and indelible mark on the sport."[3] Richard Mandell writes in the same vein: "The modern sport retains the ceremony and refinements . . . of ancient Sumo."[4]

Japanese scholars of sumo also emphasize continuity with the past, even to mythical antiquity. The basic story told is the same: in *Sumō ima mukashi* the historian Wakamori Tarō, for example, cites myths in the early eighth-century chronicles *Kojiki* and *Nihonshoki*, speculates on the ancient practice of sumo as an agricultural rite, and then moves on to *sechie* sumo, performed at one of the main court banquets of the Heian period.[5] The essay on historical sumo in an authoritative twenty-volume encyclopedia of sport and physical education quotes Wakamori extensively in locating the origins of sumo in Japan's ancient myths.[6]

The very same writers, however, are well aware that most of what we know as sumo today is of much more recent origin. Cuyler admits: "The present form of sumo is of relatively recent evolution, for most of the ceremonial traditions as performed today . . . date back no earlier than the late seventeenth century."[7] Indeed, the stories of fights in the ancient chronicles that are incorporated into the history of sumo in no way resemble the sport as we know it today, and are not referred to as sumo in the texts. Where the term does appear, the activity it refers to is not described.

Sechie sumo was quite different from modern sumo. The most obvious difference is that it was not performed within a ring, thereby precluding the means of victory most common today—delivering your opponent out of the ring. Wrestlers won by throwing their opponents to the ground, much as in judo today. Indeed, judo also claims *sechie* sumo in its own history.[8] What has become two sports began to differentiate only in the middle of the Edo period, when the wrestlers were separated from spectators by a boundary, which eventually developed into the ring. Sumo as we know it today developed during the Edo period as a spectator sport, while the elements that emphasized the martial arts were later refashioned into judo by Kanō Jigorō.

This essay will focus on one aspect of invented tradition in sumo that is at the heart of sumo performance today. It is the question of how supremacy is recognized. Today there are two separate but related institutions that recognize dominant performance in sumo: the tournament championship and the rank of *yokozuna*. This essay traces the development of both and the relationship between them.

3. P. L. Cuyler, *Sumo: From Rite to Sport* (New York and Tokyo: Weatherhill, 1985), 13.
4. Richard D. Mandell, *Sport: A Cultural History* (New York: Columbia University Press, 1984), 101.
5. Wakamori Tarō, *Sumō ima mukashi* (Tokyo: Kawade Shobō Shinsha, 1963), 13–30.
6. Fujikawa Seikatsu, "Sumō no gaiyō," in *Gendai taiiku supōtsu taikei* (Tokyo: Kōdansha, 1984), 20:14–18.
7. Cuyler, *Sumo*, 14.
8. See Kishino Yūzō, ed., *Saishin supōtsu daijiten* (Tokyo: Taishūkan Shoten, 1987), 419.

THE *YOKOZUNA*

The conventional genealogy of *yokozuna* begins with Akashi Shiganosuke in the early seventeenth century. However, there is no record that such a wrestler even existed, much less that he was awarded the *yokozuna* license. Instead, the origins of the *yokozuna* system can be dated to November 1789, when two wrestlers, Tanikaze Kajinosuke and Onokawa Kisaburō, were each allowed to perform an individual ring-entering ceremony wearing a white rope around the waist. The term *yokozuna* originally referred to this rope, which is commonly associated with *shimenawa*, the ropes on the gables of Shinto shrines. The ceremony was the inspiration of Yoshida Zenzaemon, a referee who was in the process of successfully arranging for sumo to be performed before the eleventh shogun, Tokugawa Ienari, in 1791. The invention of the *yokozuna*, and indeed much of the lore surrounding sumo today, originated with Yoshida's efforts to elevate sumo's status. He introduced many of the rituals. He also created a great deal of spurious history going back to the ninth century, history that asserts his family's intimate involvement with the sport. Much of this pseudo-history is still widely accepted.[9]

Yoshida introduced the individual ring-entering ceremony with the white rope for a specific occasion, and no further licenses to perform the ceremony were issued for almost forty years. The license was revived in 1828, but by the end of the Edo period only nine had been awarded. By comparison, fifty-three have been awarded since the beginning of the Meiji period.[10]

The invention of the *yokozuna* system involved a series of innovations dating from the late nineteenth century, which led to the emergence of the *yokozuna* as the highest rank in sumo. Even after Tanikaze and Onokawa, the highest rank was *ōzeki*, while *yokozuna* merely referred to the rope worn by the wrestler licensed to perform the ring-entering ceremony by himself. Tanikaze was a *sekiwake* in the tournament where he was awarded the *yokozuna* license. Shiranui Dakuemon, awarded the license in 1840, was subsequently demoted to *sekiwake* for a tournament.

The first *banzuke*—table of rankings printed before each tournament—to include the word *yokozuna* appeared for the May tournament of 1890. The motive, ironically, was to placate rather than to reward, and the consequences were en-

---

9. The most widely referenced standard history of sumo is Sasaki Tadamasa, *Nippon sumō shi*, 2 vols. (Tokyo: Bêsubōru Magajinsha, 1956, 1964). For a reliable history, see also Ikeda Masao, *Sumō no rekishi* (Tokyo: Heibonsha, 1977). For the recent history of sumo, see Nippon Sumō Kyōkai Hakubutsukan Un'ei Iin, ed., *Kinsei Nihon sumō shi* (Tokyo: Bêsubōru Magajinsha, 1975–81), 5 vols. In English, see Harold Bolitho, "Sumō and Popular Culture: The Tokugawa Period," in Gavan McCormack and Yoshio Sugimoto, eds., *The Japanese Trajectory: Modernization and Beyond* (Cambridge: Cambridge University Press, 1988).

10. According to the conventional list, Tanikaze and Onokawa were the fourth and fifth *yokozuna*. However, since the two wrestlers following the legendary Akashi Shiganosuke also predate the innovation of the *yokozuna* license, I discount the first three.

tirely unintended. These were the circumstances. Two new *ōzeki* had just been promoted, but the two reigning *ōzeki* were left in place. For the first time there were more than two *ōzeki* on the *banzuke*, four in all. This unprecedented situation was dealt with by appending the extra two on tabs (*haridashi*) protruding from the top sides of the printed *banzuke*. The *ōzeki* with the worst record in the previous tournament, Nishinoumi, was one of those listed as *haridashi*. Nishinoumi, however, had also just been awarded a *yokozuna* license, and he complained to the Sumo Association that a wrestler so honored deserved better treatment. To pacify him, the association put the characters for *yokozuna* next to his name. Once the precedent was established, it became the custom to write *yokozuna* alongside the names of *ōzeki* with the license.

Shortly after the term *yokozuna* entered the *banzuke* rankings, a private campaign was started to distinguish *ōzeki* with the *yokozuna* license from those without. Jinmaku Kyūgorō had received a license, the ninth issued, in 1867, and in 1895 he started a campaign to erect a monument, the *yokozuna rikishi hi*, to wrestlers who had been honored with the license. The monument was erected in 1900 independently of both the Sumo Association and the Yoshida family, which still awarded the license.[11]

The Sumo Association finally recognized *yokozuna* as a rank in 1909 and wrote it into the rules. However, the Yoshida family continued to award the license and did not accept the association's interpretation of *yokozuna* as a rank. Only in 1951 did the Yoshida family finally agree that the *yokozuna* could be a rank.[12]

From all this we can conclude that the late director Kasugano, quoted at the beginning of this essay, was far too modest. His involvement with sumo encompasses a much greater share of the history of the *yokozuna* than he acknowledges. His fifty-year connection represents one-fourth of the two hundred years since the first licenses were awarded, and half of the hundred years since the term *yokozuna* first appeared on the *banzuke*. Kasugano joined sumo when the thirtieth *yokozuna* was still active, and so experienced firsthand the careers of half the *yokozuna* to date. He joined twelve years before the Yoshida family agreed that *yokozuna* was a rank, and he was the fourth *yokozuna* promoted after that agreement. The *yokozuna* emerged as a rank only in the last hundred years, well into the modern period. Yet, as Kasugano implied in his rebuke to Futahaguro, the *yokozuna* rank now symbolizes sumo's "traditional" status and is subsumed within sumo's alleged "2,000-year" history.

The emergence of the *yokozuna* as a rank was only one of a number of changes in sumo ritual and practice in the early twentieth century that reinforced its "traditional" status. In 1909, for example, referees began to wear new costumes for the main tournaments. From the Edo period referees were bare-headed and wore

---

11. Ikeda, *Sumō*, 126.
12. Nippon Sumō Kyōkai Hakubutsukan Un'ei Iin, ed., *Kinsei Nihon sumō shi* 3:18.

kamishimo, but now they dressed in the more picturesque garb of the *suō* and *eboshi*. In the same year the Sumo Association staked out its claim to being Japan's "national sport." In 1909 the association completed construction of a large indoor stadium, named the Kokugikan (national sport hall), so that tournaments could be held free from the vagaries of the weather. With the opening of the new arena, wrestlers were required to attend the tournaments wearing *haori* and *hakama*, formal dress of the Edo period. Until then, they had walked the streets in casual dress. Indeed, wrestlers themselves had not been quite respectable, being associated in the public's mind with gamblers and other disreputable elements.[13]

Further changes that emphasized sumo's claim to being Japan's "national sport" included the redesign of the roof suspended over the wrestling ring. Formerly constructed in the *irimoyazukuri* style (seen most often these days on farmhouses), in 1931 it was rebuilt in the *shinmeizukuri* style of many Shinto shrines, including the Ise Shrine, the shrine of the Sun Goddess Amaterasu and the ancestral shrine of Japan's Imperial family.

The new emphasis on tradition was an integral part of a more fundamental process of the modernization of sumo as a spectator sport. Indeed, the invention of the *yokozuna* system developed in tandem with the introduction of a championship system based on the distinctly modern principle of achievement.

THE CHAMPIONSHIP SYSTEM

From around the middle of the Meiji period, individual wrestlers began to be singled out for their performance over the course of a tournament. This practice evolved into the championship system, in which an individual wrestler is declared the champion at the end of each tournament. The champion is simply the wrestler with the best record during a tournament. Champions are now determined for each of the divisions, while the tournament champion is the winner of the upper division, the *makunouchi*.

Today it is hard to imagine sumo without the championship system, since who will win each tournament is the focus of fan and media interest. Many people are surprised, therefore, to learn that the tournament championship is a relatively recent innovation. It did not exist at all until well into the modern period.

Champions were regularly designated starting from 1909, and the Sumo Association officially recognized the individual champion from 1926. However, the championship system grew out of antecedents, and continued to develop in tandem with a change in the focus of interest of the fans. The development of the championship system can be seen as an aspect of the modernization of sumo.

In the Edo period fans used to throw money or articles of clothing into the ring after particularly exciting matches. The winning wrestler would pocket the cash

13. Wakamori, *Sumō*, 79, 86.

and sell or pawn the other items. In the Meiji period new practices of appreciation and reward appeared, which developed into the championship system of today. Wrestlers began to be rewarded with trophies and other prizes for performance over the course of a whole tournament, rather than a single match.

The awards were sponsored by private groups, which makes the precise origins of the practice difficult to document. Often newspapers sponsored awards, and business rivalries may explain why the sponsor of an award is sometimes omitted from an article, or the awarding of a trophy is sometimes mentioned in one newspaper but not others.

There is even ambiguity concerning the vital question of exactly what was being rewarded. Initially, trophies were awarded to wrestlers who were undefeated. Undefeated records were not necessarily identical, however, since there were two different kinds of draws and absences were not recorded as losses. More than one wrestler could finish the tournament without a defeat, in which case each received a trophy. For example, after a tournament in January 1889, Konishiki (a talented small wrestler, unlike his namesake of a century later) was awarded a trophy by the Tokyo newspaper *Jiji shinpō*. However, he did not win all of his matches, only seven, with one tie and one match in which there was no decision. Two lower-division wrestlers were also awarded trophies for being undefeated after wrestling to a draw on the last day of the tournament. But if no wrestler went undefeated, no trophy was awarded.

A shift in the criteria used in awarding trophies occurred in 1900, producing a tournament champion we would recognize today. In January of that year the *Ōsaka mainichi shinbun* announced it would award a decorated apron (*keshōmawashi*) to an undefeated wrestler in the *makunouchi* division; and if no wrestler was undefeated, the apron would be awarded to the wrestler with the fewest losses. If two or more wrestlers tied for the fewest losses, the one who defeated the greater number of higher-ranked opponents won the apron.[14] The new criteria provided for a single champion and resolved certain ambiguities in the determination of "the best" tournament record.

Interest in the best record over an entire tournament was reflected in and greatly stimulated by the modern print media. Most sumo fans rarely, if ever, have the opportunity to attend a tournament. Before the advent of radio and television, fans depended on newspapers, which early on devoted considerable coverage to the sport.

Today newspapers print a daily *hoshitorihyō*, a table containing the names of the wrestlers on one axis and the days of the tournament on the other and recording the results of each wrestler's match on each day. From this table, one can tell at a glance each wrestler's standing and which wrestlers are still in contention for the tournament championship. The first *hoshitorihyō* appeared in 1884. However, it was

---

14. *Ōsaka mainichi shinbun,* January 21, 1900.

published after the last day of the tournament and only summed up the results. An indication that at this time accumulated record was not the main focus of interest can be found in the fact that daily coverage of tournaments did not summarize individual wrestlers' records.

The first publication of a *hoshitorihyō* while the tournament was still in progress was in May 1900 in the *Yorozu chōhō* newspaper (see fig. 7). The superscription makes its purpose clear:

> Results to date: The records of the main wrestlers as of the seventh day can be gleaned from this paper's daily coverage of individual matches. To summarize, Araiwa of the East is leading both sides, Hitachiyama is second, followed by Umenotani, Ōzutsu, Hōō, etc. The details are as follows.[15]

The daily *hoshitorihyō* made it possible to tell at a glance who was in the lead. The appearance of *hoshitorihyō* both reflected and further stimulated interest in recognizing an individual tournament champion.

Although individual wrestlers with the best records were singled out before 1909, it was in that year that an ongoing designation of champions was established. The newspaper *Jiji Shinpō* began to award a trophy regularly to the individual wrestler with the best record and to provide a large portrait to be hung in the Kokugikan. However, the individual championship was not officially recognized by the Tokyo Sumo Association until 1926. And, at least until then, the crowning of the champion was often ignored by other newspapers. Moreover, in 1909, with the opening of the Kokugikan, the Sumo Association institutionalized competition between the two sides, East and West.[16] Wrestlers from one side met only opponents from the other side, and at the end of the tournament, the side with the most wins was declared the victor. The winning side was awarded the victory flag, and the wrestler from the victorious side with the best record below the rank of *ōzeki* was chosen to carry the flag in a victory parade around the city. Coverage of sumo in the press often emphasized the winning side over the individual champion, and the flag-bearer often overshadowed the individual champion.

Competition between the sides was eliminated in 1947 because of a desire to strengthen the individual championship. Competition between sides weakened the legitimacy of the individual champion, since wrestlers from the same side did not face each other. Competition became even more open in 1965, when for the first time wrestlers from the same family of stables were matched against each other. To this day, however, wrestlers from the same stable do not wrestle each other, which creates problems when one stable dominates the upper division and upper ranks. In March 1993 the Futagoyama stable had ten wrestlers out of the forty in the upper division. By 1994 three out of the top five ranking wrestlers were

15. *Yorozu chōhō*, May 25, 1900.
16. The division is arbitrary and void of symbolic significance.

from the Futagoyama stable. The dominance of Futagoyama stable wrestlers was aided by the fact that they did not have to wrestle each other.

When the championship system was officially adopted by the Sumo Association in 1926, certain changes were made in the rules to eliminate ambiguity in determining the champion. Previously, not all matches resulted in clear-cut victories and defeats. When the judges could not agree after an objection (*monoii*) to the decision of the referee, the match was declared "no decision" (*azukari*). If a match appeared stalemated, it could be halted and declared a draw (*hikiwake*). When one wrestler failed to appear, the match was recorded as an absence (*yasumi*) on both wrestlers' records. Such outcomes were not at all rare. For example, according to the *hoshitorihyō* of May 25, 1900, about one-third of the matches were draws, no-decisions, or absences. These ambiguous outcomes complicated the comparison of records necessary to determine a tournament champion. Which record is better: nine wins and one loss; or eight wins, one draw, and one no-decision?

Azukari and *hikiwake* were eliminated beginning with the January tournament of 1926. Matches with disputed outcomes were replayed immediately. Matches ending in draws were rescheduled, to be replayed two matches later or at a later date. It is now unthinkable for a match to be left undecided. If the judges cannot agree, the match is replayed until a clear victor emerges. In May 1988 a *makunouchi* match was replayed three times.[17] Finally, beginning in March 1928, "no shows" were declared forfeitures. A wrestler who withdraws from a scheduled match is now given an "uncontested loss," and his opponent an "uncontested win."

The abolition of these three outcomes meant that each match now ends in a clear-cut decision: a win for one wrestler, and a loss for his opponent (see fig. 8). The wrestler with the most wins (and the fewest losses) can be declared the undisputed tournament champion. Since the tournament is not an elimination (or even round-robin) tournament, however, two or more wrestlers may tie for the best record. Following the adoption of the championship system by the Sumo Association in 1926, in the event two wrestlers ended with the same record, the cup was awarded to the higher-ranked wrestler, who presumably faced tougher competition. In 1947 a play-off was instituted, adding drama and removing final vestiges of ambiguity in determining the tournament winner.

The motivation for these changes was to ensure sumo's popularity and to maintain its base of paying customers. The same motivation is demonstrated by another significant change instituted in 1928, two years after official adoption of the tournament champion system. A time limit was put on the *shikiri*, the long buildup (to what often proved to be very short bouts), during which the wrestlers

---

17. Draws were somewhat more difficult to eliminate, since the will to win cannot be legislated. As we have seen, there may have been some incentive to avoid a loss by settling for a draw. Although greatly reduced in number after 1926, draws still sometimes occurred, even into the postwar period. There have been no draws for at least fifteen years, however, with the exception of draws resulting from injuries, a minor category I am not treating here.

repeatedly face off in a crouch, then return to their corners for another handful of salt to throw into the ring. Formerly the *shikiri* was allowed to continue indefinitely, until both wrestlers were prepared to commence. With the beginning of radio broadcasts of sumo tournaments in 1928, the *shikiri* was limited to ten minutes. In the era of television broadcasts, it is four minutes for *makunouchi*. Time limits were instituted to insure that the day's matches would finish within the time allocated for the broadcast.[18]

THE TOURNAMENT CHAMPION AND THE *YOKOZUNA*

It is often said that Japan has preserved or maintained its traditions while undergoing modernization. In the case of the *yokozuna*, however, it has been shown that "tradition" was largely a modern invention. This finding raises the question of the relationship between tradition and modernization. I will argue that the two concepts are interdependent: awareness of modernity is impossible without awareness of tradition, and vice versa. The simultaneous development of the "traditional" *yokozuna* alongside the "modern" championship system demonstrates the complexity of the relationship.

The *yokozuna* and the championship system are two ways of recognizing supremacy in the performance of sumo. The championship system is the "modern" way, to the extent that the determination is based on "objective" data. The champion trophy passes through many hands. The *yokozuna*, on the other hand, is expected to be strong and to win consistently. There is an essentially ascriptive expectation placed on the *yokozuna*, reflecting its role as a representation of "tradition." However, the image of the strongest of the strong became harder to uphold under the statistical scrutiny and pressure of the championship system.

The *yokozuna* and the tournament champion system are basically in tension. The *yokozuna* will not, of course, win every tournament, although they are expected to do so. Quantitative evaluation of performance, the basis of the championship system, thus reveals their vulnerability. At the same time, however, the *yokozuna* institution is dependent on the championship system. This tension between the expectations arising from the ascriptive aspect of rank and actual achievement in the ring is an important source of excitement in sumo, as can be seen from the uproar when a lower-ranking wrestler scores an upset. However, when a *yokozuna* cannot vindicate his rank with a superior record, he and the institution of sumo are open to criticism.

At the fall tournament in Osaka in 1949, for example, the *yokozuna* Maedayama won his first match but dropped the next five. After the fifth defeat he withdrew from the tournament, ostensibly with colitis, and returned to Tokyo. However, the

---

18. The wrestlers had difficulty adjusting to the new rules, and the final matches of the day were often not broadcast, giving rise to a comic verse about how the *yokozuna* Tsunenohana never wrestled on the radio: *Rajio de wa / Sumō wo toranu / Tsunenohana.*

very next day he showed up at an exhibition baseball game between the Yomiuri Giants and the San Francisco Seals. His appearance got into the newspapers, and a great fuss ensued. The enraged executive board of the Sumo Association forced him to retire.[19]

At the time sumo's popularity was in a slump, and baseball's was on the rise. The symbolic significance of a *yokozuna* abandoning his duties in the ring to watch a baseball game was potentially devastating. The incident also shows, though, how expectations surrounding *yokozuna* had changed with the development of the tournament champion system. Hitachiyama, a great *yokozuna* of late Meiji, skipped a number of matches, practically all of those of his last two years, without harm to his reputation.

All three reigning *yokozuna* dropped out early in the January tournament of 1950 after suffering defeats. The executive board of the Sumo Association went so far as to vote to demote *ōzeki* and *yokozuna* with losing records. However, some of the members objected on the grounds that the prestige of the *yokozuna* goes back three hundred years to (the legendary) Akashi Shiganosuke. After further discussion, they decided to form a Yokozuna Review Board, consisting of representatives from outside the association, to recommend and evaluate *yokozuna*. The committee was formed in May 1950 and consists of scholars, businessmen, and politicians.

The *ōzeki* Chiyonoyama won the January 1950 tournament, and having also won the previous tournament, he could have expected to be promoted to *yokozuna*. However, because of the furor over the poor performances of the three current *yokozuna*, he was passed over. He was promoted that summer after his third tournament victory.

Chiyonoyama got off to a bad start in the March tournament of 1953. He was 1–4 after five days and faced a difficult battle to achieve a winning record. On the sixth day he petitioned the director of the association to be allowed to give up the rank of *yokozuna* and start over from *ōzeki*. This request was leaked to the media. Pressed for an explanation, the director retorted that for a *yokozuna* to give up his position would make the association and the Yokozuna Review Board look like fools. If Chiyonoyama had doubts about his ability to perform as a *yokozuna*, the director admonished, he should have declined the appointment. Chiyonoyama struggled on to a winning record.

On January 6, 1958, the Yokozuna Review Board announced the following by-laws for recommending the promotion and retirement of *yokozuna*:

1. Candidates for *yokozuna* shall be of outstanding character and ability.
2. In principle, future candidates for *yokozuna* recommended by the Yokozuna Review Board shall have two consecutive tournament championships at the rank of *ōzeki*.

---

19. Maedayama was *nimai kansatsu*, which meant that he already ran his own stable, and he continued to run it after his retirement as an active wrestler.

3. A unanimous vote is required to recommend a wrestler with a record equivalent [but not equal] to the criteria of Article 2. [Subsequently changed to "a two-thirds vote."]

4. Under the following conditions, the Yokozuna Review Board may conduct an investigation of a *yokozuna* and, by a vote of two-thirds of its members, take such action as issuing a warning or recommending retirement:

   a. He has numerous absences. However, when extended absence is due to injury or illness, the possibility of recovery can be taken into consideration and a sufficient treatment period be granted.

   b. He dishonors the rank of *yokozuna*.

   c. He has an extremely poor record for a *yokozuna*, one judged not deserving of the rank.[20]

During the January tournament of 1958, the first tournament after the announcement of these bylaws, the two *yokozuna* Yoshibayama and Kagamisato both announced their retirement. It was the first time two *yokozuna* had retired during the same tournament. That September Kashiwado and Taihō were chosen for promotion to *yokozuna*. Messengers were sent to their respective stables, where they both accepted the honor, pledging to strive to do their utmost not to defile the rank of *yokozuna*: "I will do the best that I can as *yokozuna*, so as not to disgrace the rank."[21]

The bylaws of the Yokozuna Review Board clearly base promotion on winning championships. But even though clear criteria for promotion are provided in Article 2, a huge loophole is created in Article 3. The phrase translated here as "equivalent," *junzuru*, carries the nuance of "next best." In the past this has been interpreted to mean that a wrestler can be promoted after being runner-up in a tournament before or after winning a championship. But other factors enter in. Kasugano himself once admitted that promotion is easier when few wrestlers hold the rank. Table 1 shows the records of *yokozuna*, beginning with Chiyonoyama, in the three tournaments prior to their promotion. As can be seen, until quite recently very few were promoted after fulfilling the condition of Article 2. Indeed, many do not even seem to fulfill the usual interpretation of Article 3. Promotion to *yokozuna*, then, while in principle based on clear, objective criteria, is far less clear-cut in practice. And once promoted, tension between ascription and achievement continues to cause problems—no more dramatically than in the incident involving Futahaguro narrated at the beginning of this essay.

Futahaguro had been promoted in July 1986 without having won any tournaments. Although he finished a close second several times, failure to clinch the trophy led to criticism of his behavior and attitude. This was the cause of the argument that precipitated his departure from sumo.

---

20. Nippon Sumō Kyōkai Hakubutsukan Un'ei Iin, ed., *Kinsei Nihon sumō shi* 4:18.

21. Ibid. 5:12. This is the first reference this official history of modern sumo makes to messengers being sent to the stables and to the reply of the new *yokozuna*, which is the standard format today.

TABLE I   Records in three tournaments
prior to promotion to *yokozuna*

Name	3d tourney	2d tourney	Prior tourney
Chiyonoyama	11–4	8–7	C14–1
Kagamisato	11–4	R12–3	C14–1
Yoshibayama	R14–1	11–4	C15–0
Tochinishiki	9–6	C14–1	C14–1
Wakanohana I	11–4	R12–3	C13–2
Asashio	C14–1	R11–4	R13–2
Kashiwado	10–5	11–4	T12–3
Taihō	R11–4	C13–2	C12–3
Tochinoumi	11–4	C14–1	13–2
Sadanoyama	R13–2	R13–2	C13–2
Tamanoumi	C13–2	10–5	T13–2
Kitanofuji	R12–3	C13–2	C13–2
Kotozakura	9–6	C14–1	C14–1
Wajima	R11–4	R13–2	C15–0
Kitanoumi	10–5	C13–2	T13–2
Wakanohana II	R13–2	T13–2	T14–1
Mienoumi	10–5	R13–2	T14–1
Chiyonofuji	R11–4	R13–2	C14–1
Takanosato	R12–3	R13–2	C14–1
Futahaguro	10–5	R12–3	T14–1
Hokutoumi	11–4	C12–3	R13–2
Ōnokuni	C15–0	R12–3	R13–2
Asahifuji	8–7	C14–1	C14–1
Akebono	9–6	C14–1	C13–2
Takanohana	11–4	C15–0	C15–0

Passed over for promotion (some examples)			
Wakanohana I	R13–2	T12–3	C12–3
Asahifuji (1988)	11–4	C14–1	R12–3
Konishiki (1992)	C13–2	12–3	C13–2
Takanohana (1993)	R11–4	C14–1	T13–2
Takanohana (1994)	C14–1	11–4	C15–0

(C = Champion; T = Tied for championship but lost play-off; R = Runner-up)

A year later Ōnokuni was promoted with a questionable record. Ōnokuni also failed to live up to expectations. It was unthinkable for a *yokozuna* to have a losing record in a tournament, yet Ōnokuni finished a tournament at 7–8. He sat out six of the next ten tournaments and retired in 1991 at the early age of 28.

In 1987 Hokutoumi was also promoted with a less-than-sterling record. He acquitted himself better than his immediate predecessors had, but their early departure forced him to linger on as the only *yokozuna*. In the only tournament he finished in his last year, his record, 9 wins and 6 losses, was far from outstanding.

Behind these premature promotions and postponed retirements in the late 1980s lurked the foreign threat. Futahaguro, Hokutoumi, and Ōnokuni may have been promoted prematurely to "fill up" the *yokozuna* rank to make it more difficult for the rapidly rising Hawaiian-born Konishiki to achieve the highest honor in Japan's "national sport."[22] Whether the Sumo Association had intended to stack the rank or not, when the three *yokozuna* did not live up to expectations the chairman announced that the criteria for promotion would henceforth be more strictly applied. The association, he said, wanted a strong *yokozuna*. Again, this worked to keep Konishiki out.

By March 1992 Konishiki had compiled a record that arguably warranted his promotion, since he had won two out of the previous three tournaments. Although he had not won two in succession, wrestlers in the past had been promoted to *yokozuna* with lesser records. The only remaining *yokozuna*, Hokutoumi, was on his last legs, but Konishiki was passed over. Soon after, he passed his peak performance and his record has declined ever since.

The lame duck *yokozuna*, Hokutoumi, retired in May, and the *banzuke* was without a *yokozuna* for the first time in sixty years. This situation lasted for six months, until Akebono, from Hawaii, won two consecutive tournaments and was promoted in January 1993 to become the first *yokozuna* who was also obviously a foreigner.[23]

With the promotion of Akebono, many sumo fans and officials desperately wanted a native-born *yokozuna*. For several years, however, the Sumo Association had insisted on a strict application of the criteria for promotion. Suddenly relaxing the standards to allow the promotion of a native Japanese wrestler would support the charges of discrimination that followed Konishiki's career.

The strongest candidate for promotion was Takanohana, of the famous Hanada family of wrestlers. His uncle is a former *yokozuna*, who succeeded Kasugano as chairman of the association, and his father, a former *ōzeki*, runs the Futagoyama stable to which Takanohana and his brother, also an *ōzeki*, belong. Takanohana was performing extremely well in the tournaments in Tokyo, where he grew up, but not in the alternating tournaments that take place outside of the capital. In 1994 he won all three Tokyo tournaments, in January, May, and September. During the September tournament, the director of the association, Dewanoumi, the successor to Takanohana's uncle, announced that he would like the

22. While the leaders of the Sumo Association maintained that national origin was no obstacle to promotion and Konishiki enjoyed considerable popular support, many fans were against a foreigner holding the highest rank in Japan's "traditional" sport. A member of the Yokozuna Review Board went so far as to publish an article in a leading journal saying that it would be difficult for a foreigner to meet the criteria of Article 1, because a foreigner wouldn't understand the meaning of character. The term *hinkaku* (character) enjoyed a brief popularity in the American press and was even discussed at length by Mike Royko. *Japan Times*, April 10, 1992.

23. What constitutes a "foreigner" in Japan is beyond the scope of this paper. There have been other *yokozuna* who could be said to have been foreign by certain criteria.

Yokozuna Review Board to review its criteria for promotion, to take a longer period into account. When Takanohana won the September tournament with an undefeated record, the association nominated him for *yokozuna*, even though his record in the previous tournament had only been the fourth best, 11–4.

To use a metaphor from another sport, the ball was in the Review Board's court. Since the Review Board had not vetoed a nomination of the Sumo Association in twenty-five years, nomination by the association was considered tantamount to promotion. The *Asahi* newspaper even announced on the front page: "Takanohana Clinches Yokozuna."

The newspaper, however, had committed *isamiashi*, a sumo term that has entered everyday speech, used to describe rash errors. The Review Board met on the day the headline appeared. The bylaws required a two-thirds majority for promotion. After two hours of discussion, the matter was put to a vote. Takanohana's promotion was rejected when only six of the eleven members voted in favor, two less than the eight required. Back in the ring, Takanohana went on to win the November tournament in Fukuoka, again going undefeated, and, with two consecutive undefeated tournaments, was promoted with the best record on our chart.[24]

CONCLUSION

As one commentator wrote at the height of the controversy over Takanohana's promotion: "The *yokozuna* is an illogical sort of thing. And that's what gives it the essence of a uniquely Japanese traditional performing art."[25] Quite aside from the ironies of invoking "tradition" in this context, we see that the tensions between the achievement-oriented championship system and the ascriptive aspect of the *yokozuna* make the rank inherently problematic. While the development of the championship system can be easily explained as part of the modernization of the sport, the *yokozuna* is popularly perceived as a traditional institution. But as we have seen, rather than the *yokozuna* system being older and the championship system newer, they arose together, and, if anything, the "traditional" *yokozuna* system is in large measure a product of the championship system. The image of the omnipotent *yokozuna* represents security and assurance in the face of the indifferent objectivity of statistically measured achievement.[26] Together, they illustrate the complex relationship between tradition and modernity.

24. This takes us up to the time of writing, but the saga of the *yokozuna* continues. The latest issues of sumo magazines have carried articles calling for the revision of the way *yokozuna* are selected. Some advocate changes in the Yokozuna Review Board's bylaws along the lines proposed by the director of the association in September 1994, taking a greater period of time into account. Others call for the abolition of the Yokozuna Review Board altogether. But whatever changes are introduced (if any are at all), as long as *yokozuna* are promoted and judged based on performance, the controversy surrounding the status will continue.

25. Kosaka Shūji, "Sumō tankyū 80," *Ōzumo* (November 1994): 61.

26. This is not to say that records are always impartially achieved. Collusion between the wrestlers may in some cases manipulate records. The ideals of modernity are not necessarily perfectly realized.

PART FIVE

Gender

THIRTEEN

At Home in the Meiji Period

Inventing Japanese Domesticity

Jordan Sand

The English word "home" is a curious conflation, embodying elements of both place and affect. A historical narrative plotting the gradual union of these elements and the growing importance of "the home" in modern Western societies is now familiar to many readers. This history typically describes the intensification of emotional ties within the nuclear family group, and the nineteenth-century development of what has been called a "cult of domesticity," accompanying the proverbial "separation of work and home" and the retreat of the middle class from the industrial city to the suburbs.[1]

Like many short, evocative English words, "home" has entered the Japanese lexicon. The modern history of domestic life in Japan, however, has not been described in terms analogous with the West. Until recently, to speak of the prewar Japanese family was to speak of the distinctly Japanese institution identified by the term *ie*, a word implying house, family, or lineage. Phrases such as "*ie* system" and "*ie* society" have served as all-purpose explanatory devices in both the social sciences and popular discourse. In relation to domestic life, *ie* evokes the image of an absolute and often arbitrarily exercised patriarchal authority. Postwar democracy is regarded as the source of both family "nuclearization" and more enlightened domestic behavior, although, by most accounts, democratic reform in the years after the war failed to eradicate completely the evils of the *ie*. Discussions of domestic life in modern Japan have thus positioned their object along an axis between two political poles of family relations, asking in effect, "how authoritarian, how democratic?"

---

1. Lawrence Stone, *The Family, Sex, and Marriage in England, 1500–1800* (London: Weidenfeld and Nicholson, 1977), places the origin of the "closed domesticated nuclear family" in the late seventeenth century. The seminal text on the cult of domesticity is Barbara Welter, "The Cult of True Womanhood, 1820–1860," *American Quarterly* 18 (1966): 151–74.

Yet, irrespective of the answers to such questions, the importance of home life generally for Japanese has been viewed as a constant. Tightly knit cohabitant families, the valuation of family privacy, and the devotion of married women to housekeeping and the care of their children have often been treated as stable elements of Japanese life.[2]

In fact, much of the tradition of the Japanese home is a creation of late nineteenth-century intellectuals. Nineteenth-century households were varied and fluid in composition, among the wealthy often including numerous servants, apprentices, and lodgers, in addition to extended family. Parents of all classes commonly sent their children away at a young age (to wet nurses and foster parents in infancy, to boarding schools and apprenticeships thereafter). The social and physical boundaries of the household were porous and often submerged in a net of intersecting relations of obligation with the village community, occupational association, or vassal group. Most of all, before the end of the century, no one in government, religion, or the world of letters identified the site of family life as a locus of moral meaning.

In Anglo-American texts, and in the exhortations of missionaries, Meiji-period social reformers encountered the rich Victorian language of domesticity, something without parallel in Japan. Persuaded of the importance of the institutions of home to the bourgeois nations of the West, these reformers responded by inventing new domestic discourses and norms of practice suited to their own circumstances. In time, these were manifested in new architectural forms. The West, represented particularly by England and the United States, provided ideas and images to be adopted, interpreted, and recontextualized. Yet at the same time, Japanese reformers were compelled to invent a great deal, as there was little available in Japan corresponding to either the physical forms or the moral norms of the Victorian "middle-class home."

The polarity of two family types pictured today is a rhetorical invention of the 1880s. The terms *ie sei* (family system or family authority) and *hōmu* (home) were, in effect, products of the same historical moment, since they both emerged during the debates around the drafting of the Meiji Civil Code. *Ie sei* was championed by legal scholar Hozumi Yatsuka in his defense of the customs of patriarchal authority common among samurai.[3] The word *hōmu* was introduced by Protestant social reformers and began its career as a weapon against *ie sei*, or against conservative mores generally. In the first period of their formulation, the two concepts, *ie* and *hōmu*, thus appeared to be antitheses—indigenous and foreign, feudal and modern. But they were not, in fact, mutually exclusive. While the central axis of the legal *ie* was heredity, a temporal concept, "home" posited a space, with definite boundaries. In the subsequent decades, both terms proved malleable enough to

---

2. A reiteration of this modern Japanese self-perception may be found, for example, in Ezra F. Vogel, *Japan's New Middle Class*, 2d ed. (Berkeley and Los Angeles: University of California Press, 1971), 208–29, 279.

3. Kano Masanao, *Senzen "ie" no shisō* (Tokyo: Sōbunsha, 1983), 51.

coexist without conflict. "Home," in particular, shed its polemical connotations as it was manipulated and transformed to become part of a Japanese discourse on women, family, and dwelling.[4]

The discourse of domesticity did not take place only on the plane of language. Normalizing the home in Japan required redrawing the contours of domestic space and reappointing its interior. Two fundamental spatial problems had to be solved in the invention of Japanese domesticity. First, to bind family and place, and give the bond normative significance, families had to be persuaded not merely to cohabit, but to exhibit family solidarity in some concrete form. Devising and encouraging such manifestations became the concern of progressive journalists and educators in the 1890s. Second, to articulate the priority of family over other social groups, a house design was needed that would segregate the cohabitant family from non-kin and the outside world. Here architects had a role to play.

The members of the small progressive vanguard instrumental in promoting domesticity at the turn of the century were anxious first to assert their own social place before turning to reforming others' homes. In its Meiji construction, the Japanese domestic ideal was vehemently "middle class," representing the segment of society in which the journalists, educators, and architects doing the writing, speaking and designing located themselves and their audience. New gender roles and new moral meanings imbued in material life and daily practice were invented to provide substance to the middle-class image. Thus, in defining home, the framers of Japanese domesticity were also defining themselves.

AN AUDIENCE FOR HOME

The first reformers to address the habits of Japanese domestic life were Protestants, whose points of reference, dictated by the source of their conversion, were inevitably Anglo-American. In describing the Anglo-American alternative, they looked less to religious or political philosophy than to tangible characteristics— the kind of households, and the activities and behavior of family members, as they had seen them in the West, encountered them among missionary acquaintances, or read about them in moral literature.

Iwamoto Yoshiharu, principal of the Meiji School for Women and editor of *Jogaku zasshi*, Japan's first major women's magazine (established 1885), was the premier spokesman of the Protestant home ideal, and proud claimant to the English words "discovery" and popularization. Iwamoto attributed a lack of harmony and joy in Japanese families to the practice of adoption, and to the presence in the house of parents-in-law, other in-laws, concubines, and lodgers, all of whom inhibited conjugal happiness and provided a poor environment for children. Japan would have no "*hōmu*," he professed, until adoption was ended and

---

4. On the dual emergence of the *ie* and the modern home, see Nishikawa Yūko, "The Changing Form of Dwellings and the Establishment of the *Katei* (Home) in Modern Japan," *Nichibei josei jānaru* [U.S.-Japan Women's Journal] English Supplement, no. 8 (1995): 3–36.

these interlopers were removed.[5] Echoing Iwamoto, Ueki Emori called for physical separation of the older and younger generations.[6] The fundamental domestic problem for these men was one of composing Japanese households of the proper members.

Addressing a Women's Temperance Union meeting in Tokyo, Uchimura Kanzō described the Christian home as characterized most of all by efficient management. His observations were drawn from a visit to the United States, yet, he explained, "this home [*hōmu*]" was not something that could be understood through "the constitution or civilization of a country"; one had to enter it and "breathe its air." In the home, there was a fixed order to each day, marked by bells the servants rang. The housewife led her daughters in a strict cleaning routine. Meals were taken with all the family together and followed by music or conversation. The interior was always dust-free and frugally appointed. Child rearing was the family's highest priority. For the education of small children, there were generally "ten or fifteen of the implements used in nursery school." In contrast, houses in Japan were unconducive to accomplishing things efficiently, and people "kept too many servants."[7]

In the 1880s, talk of "*hōmu*" in Japan was still confined to a small circle of Christian social reformers and their audience. But Iwamoto, Ueki, and Uchimura had adumbrated an idea that would persist, with modifications, in other contexts. The first step in its diffusion was linguistic naturalization. Although proponents often uttered the caveat that the English "home" was untranslatable into any language (Uchimura attributed this observation to Bismarck), the Japanese neologism "*katei*" came increasingly to stand in for the English term. Combining the characters for "house" and "garden," *katei* literally designated a space. It also served as a modifier, in expressions such as *katei kyōiku* (home education) and *katei eisei* (home hygiene), each of which gave a special valence to the second term beyond simply locating it in the domicile. It implied half of an equation in which new public institutions and the nascent public space of society formed the other half. With the assistance of such expressions, the word entered common parlance during the 1880s.[8]

Like the Victorian home, the *katei* bore powerful gender connotations. The curriculum of Meiji girls' education was an important source of *katei* rhetoric, cre-

---

5. "Shasetsu: Nihon no kazoku, dai 1: Ikka no waraku danran," *Jogaku zasshi* 96 (February 11, 1888): 1–4; "Nihon no kazoku, dai 2: Nihon ni kōfuku naru kazoku sukunashi," *Jogaku zasshi* 97 (February 18, 1888): 1–4.

6. Ueki Emori, "Shifu wa kyūko to bekkyo subeshi," *Kokumin no tomo* 33 (November 2, 1888). Reprinted in Sotozaki Mitsuhiro, ed., *Ueki Emori katei kaikaku, fujinron* (Tokyo: Heibunsha, 1971), 367–79.

7. Uchimura Kanzō, "Kurisuchan hōmu," *Jogaku zasshi* 125 (September 1, 1888): 4–8.

8. *Katei*, strictly speaking, was only a quasi-neologism, since the combination of characters had occasionally been used before. It appeared in the titles of a few Tokugawa morals texts. In addition, between 1876 and 1877, Fukuzawa Yukichi published a magazine called *Katei sōdan*. Although this magazine's title may have been influential in spreading use of the term among Meiji intellectuals, *katei* seldom appeared elsewhere in this magazine, and the word's meaning was not discussed. *Katei* does not appear as an entry in dictionaries until the turn of the century. See Muta Kazue, "Images of the Fam-

ating a field of reference around the *katei* while teaching the rules of modern housewifery. From 1872, when the first government-sponsored schools for girls were created, a diversity of texts in *kaji* (literally, "domestic matters") were published by the Ministry of Education and by private publishers following ministry guidelines. These included translations of English works such as Catharine Beecher's *The American Woman's Home or Principles of Domestic Science,*[9] as well as texts written by Japanese authors.

By the 1890s members of a second generation of pedagogues at the girls' higher schools were writing new textbooks, which placed more emphasis on the unique suitability of women to domestic responsibilities. Several of these authors were women. In classroom lectures as well as in popular-press writings, they aggrandized the importance of the duties of home with metaphors borrowed from the Anglo-American literature of domesticity, relating housewives to counterparts in a male world outside. The housewife was the "prime minister" of the household, or a soldier whose "battlefield" was the home.[10] Texts from this period also began to introduce a range of instructions about household finances, nutrition, childcare, scientific hygiene, and house design, building "domestic matters" into a comprehensive body of technical knowledge sufficient to create for the educated housewife a specialization comparable to the male professions. *Ie* and *katei* were often used interchangeably in these texts, both of them to refer to a domain of female labor and family refuge. The newer term, however, was increasingly preferred.

If the nuance of *katei* was feminine, the word's popularity in print represented journalism's discovery of the growing market of literate women. Tokutomi Sohō was the first publisher to exploit the term as a device to open this market, introducing the magazine *Katei zasshi* in 1892 as a companion to *Kokumin no tomo.*[11] *Taiyō* magazine began a column titled *Katei* in 1896, expanding it under the editorship of Iwamoto Yoshiharu the following year. In 1898, the *Ōsaka mainichi shinbun* was the first major newspaper to run a regular *katei* column, followed by the *Yomiuri* in

---

ily in Meiji Periodicals: The Paradox Underlying the Emergence of the 'Home,'" *U.S.-Japan Women's Journal* (English Supplement) no. 7 (1994): 53–71; Nakazawa Yōko, "Katei, uchi, kanai, hōmu," in Satō Kiyoji, ed., *Kōza Nihongo no goi,* vol. 9: *Goshi,* pt. 1 (Tokyo: Meiji Shoin, 1983), 222–27.

9. Catharine E. Beecher and Harriet Beecher Stowe, *The American Woman's Home, or Principles of Domestic Science* (New York: J. B. Ford and Co., 1869), translated as *Kaji yōhō* (Tokyo: Monbushō Henshūkyoku, 1881).

10. For example, Sakata Shizu and Gokan Kikuno, *Kaji kyōkasho* (1898), reprinted in Tanaka Chitako, Tanaka Hatsuo, eds., *Kaseigaku bunken shūsei zokuhen: Meiji ki 8* (Tokyo: Watanabe Shoten, 1976), 4.

11. The first issue contained columns on household management, cooking, and prices of daily necessities, as well as an article on trends in women's education and a biography of Garibaldi's wife. In contrast to *Katei zasshi, Jogaku zasshi* was as much about women as for them. Despite its central role in framing the Japanese home idea, its pages were dominated until the mid-1890s by fiction and Christian homilies rather than practical information or advice specifically targeted at women. A review of the field in the second issue of *Katei zasshi* classified *Jogaku zasshi* as a magazine for "woman-like men" (*joseiteki danshi*). Cited in Nagahara Kazuko, "Heiminshugi no fujinron: 'Kokumin no tomo' to 'Katei zasshi' ni tsuite," *Rekishi hyōron* 311 (March, 1976): 63.

1900. By the first years of the twentieth century, there were at least five magazines on the market with *katei* in their titles.

Normalization of the *katei* was made possible by shifts of connotation that accompanied the idea's propagation in journalism, easing the way to mass acceptance. First, it lost its Christian tone. Iwamoto's preaching had considerable influence on the content of Tokutomi Sohō's *Katei zasshi*, but religion was not an explicit topic in the magazine. Also largely absent from the pages of *Katei zasshi*, and from the *katei* landscape generally as it developed in the magazines that followed Iwamoto's *Jogaku zasshi*, was Iwamoto's emphasis on the romantic bond between husband and wife and the need to purify the domestic environment of anything that might vitiate it. Frequently, this was supplanted by a solitary focus on the wife/mother. At the same time, parents-in-law crept back into many of the magazines' depictions of home life—although significantly, concubines and adopted children did not.

An explicit class definition also entered characterizations of the *katei*. Whatever their social position, *katei* writers from Tokutomi on overwhelmingly proclaimed themselves to be addressing the "middle ranks of society" (*chūtō shakai*). *Katei zasshi* devoted pages in almost every issue to preaching an ethos for the middle ranks. In place of Christianity, Tokutomi offered the "common man's faith" of *heiminshugi*. Although Tokutomi sometimes held up the urban poor as a moral example, his common man's home was ideally that of a "country gentleman," reflecting the publisher's own rural samurai origins. The image also reflected the important distinction between the social middle conceived by Tokutomi's Minyūsha and the traditional urban bourgeoisie. The model families of late Meiji-period *katei* literature were with few exceptions headed by the company directors, elite bureaucrats, university professors, military officers, and other professionals who laid claim to the middle primarily by virtue of not belonging to the aristocracy of former daimyo and courtiers. These people were notably products of the modern educational system; while likely to share Tokutomi's rural gentry roots, they were, also like Tokutomi, now permanent city-dwellers, literally without the baggage of the old house. Their families bore special privilege in determining the norms of taste and enlightened behavior in progressive society.

The magazines frequently included portraits of particular households, detailing everything from the appointments of their interiors and daily life within them to the particulars of the family budget. For readers, these portraits could provide checklists of the goods and conduct that marked class membership. A variety of examples appeared in a special issue of the magazine *Jogaku sekai* in 1904, titled "One Hundred Walks of Life" ("Shakai hyaku seikatsu"), which situated the "middle-class" home model within a spectrum of social types. The issue contained descriptions of twenty-two households. A diagram of class structure was included, showing Japan to be among the "healthy societies" (along with England and Germany) with 65 percent of its population in the middle class. An accompanying list of the attributes of upper, middle, and lower classes showed all virtues accruing to the middle, which was described as the "producing class," while the upper class was "unproductive" and the lower class "low in productivity."[12]

Individual portraits in the issue elaborated this claim and added a moral dimension to the distinction between the new professional and old merchant middle classes. "The Home of an Osaka Merchant" ("Ōsaka shōka no katei") presented a largely denigrating stereotype that stressed the divergence of Osaka families from recognized contemporary norms. Education was not valued, boys in the house were taught feminine manners, family members shared little affection and anyway had little to talk to one another about.[13] Articles describing professionals' households introduced particular families through interviews with the housewife or accounts of a visit to the house. The portrait titled "Life of a Naval Officer" ("Kaigun shikan no seikatsu"), for example, opened with an enumeration of each piece of furnishing in the family's reception room, from the arabesque-patterned carpet and leather-covered chairs to the pair of Kano-school scrolls, the Kutani vase, lion-shaped incense burner, and jade cannons in the *tokonoma* alcove. The other six rooms in the house were also described and a dinnertime conversation recorded, along with a month's menus and the husband's salary.[14]

These minutiae of family possessions and practices advertised a lifestyle that was at least in some measure a product of choice. The naval officer's house was rented, not inherited from his father. The furniture in the reception room would probably have been purchased after marriage. Other stories of model households in "One Hundred Walks of Life" and elsewhere in turn-of-the-century women's magazines described second or third sons and their wives starting married life without house or belongings, and having to shop for them. Ueki Emori had perceived in 1888 that a greater number of "convenient and complete" rental houses would have to be made available in order for progressive young couples to live apart from their conservative parents.[15] For youths who were free of the obligations of inheritance, this market was already growing. *Kashiya fuda*, Tokyo's first specialty publication advertising houses for rent, began in September 1890.

FAMILY PERFORMANCE

New social forms required new rituals for their expression. The ritual most commonly promoted in the Meiji home was a periodic gathering of its members. This simple act might not seem to warrant the term ritual, yet champions of the *katei* provided specific protocols for its enactment and invested it with a symbolic significance suggesting its ceremonial character. The ideal they sought to manifest in

12. "Jogaku sekai shūki zōkan: Shakai hyaku seikatsu," *Jogaku sekai* 4, no. 12 (September 15, 1904): 144.

13. Kishimoto Ryūko, "Ōsaka shōka no katei," ibid., 65–72.

14. "Kaigun shikan no seikatsu," ibid., 85–96.

15. Ueki, "Shifu," 378.

the gathering was known as *ikka danran*, or *kazoku danran*, phrases that, like *katei*, became ubiquitous after the 1880s through propagation in the language of domestic reform. *Danran* implies a circle or group; together with "household" or "family" it meant something like "the family circle."

A chorus of texts incanting the same phrases, calling the *katei* life's "sanctuary" (*rakuen*), and the family circle "life's greatest pleasure" (*jinsei no saidai kōfuku*), also stressed the moral influence (*kankaryoku*) of the gathering, placing it at the center of "home education." *Katei no waraku*, the first volume in a series of pocket-size home manuals published by Minyūsha concurrent with *Katei zasshi*, devoted a chapter to pastimes suited to the family circle, encouraging music in particular. "But since the true essence of domestic entertainment," the book's discussion concluded,

> is for everyone in the house, old and young, man and wife, master and servant, to come together and enjoy themselves, one should choose common, simple, and inexpensive pastimes that anyone can appreciate. This is not so difficult to do. Institute a conversation or [tea] gathering at home every evening for an hour or two after supper, bring the family together, and console one another with mutual love and kindness after the day's labors. Tell one another amusing anecdotes of things you have seen and heard during the day, tell old tales of educational value, or read light and interesting passages from a newspaper or magazine; gaze at the baby's endearing face and smile together, or listen to the innocent voices of the children recounting the subjects they studied or the moral lessons they learned at school.[16]

The text was accompanied by an illustration labeled "the family tea party" (*ikka danran no sawakai*). Its emphasis on the instructive value of the event appears to have found sympathetic ears at the Education Ministry, since the entire passage reappeared almost to the word (including even the neologism *sawakai*) in state-compiled morals texts for the higher elementary school nine years later.[17]

Elsewhere, the prescription was for a weekly rather than nightly household meeting. These were sometimes prescribed with great care, and with the clear intention to objectify in ritual a strict household hierarchy under patriarchal authority. A drama whose not-so-distant origins lay in a progressive ideal of conjugal family intimacy could thus become a ritual embodiment of the very patriarchal ideal then being legally and conceptually framed by conservatives.[18]

EATING TOGETHER

The most usual prescription, however, better suited to the occupants of small households but equally addressed to readers of all classes, regarded the most basic

16. Minyūsha, ed., *Katei no waraku* (Tokyo: Minyūsha, 1894), 98–101.

17. Manpuku Naokiyo, *Kokutei kyōkasho ni mietaru kaji kyōju shiryō* (Tokyo: Hōbunkan, 1906), 77–78.

18. Additional examples of texts promoting ritualizations of the family circle may be found in Jordan Sand, "House and Home in Modern Japan, 1880s–1920s," Ph.D. diss., Columbia University, 1995.

of human rituals: the taking of a common meal. Establishing a fixed practice of family dining meant synchronizing mealtimes and sharing an eating place, practices that required a fundamental change of habit for many households. Descriptions abound of the strictness with which barriers of status within nineteenth-century households were enforced by temporal and spatial distinctions, particularly of eating time and place. In some households children, apprentices, and servants were grouped apart from the master and mistress and allowed to eat only after they had finished their meal, while in others the room in which the husband dined was off limits to his wife.[19]

But it was not enough simply to assemble the family in one place for meals. To make the gathering *danran*, "life's greatest pleasure," also required introducing one central prop—families did not enjoy dining together, reformers argued, because they did not have dining tables. Sakai Toshihiko, who later became a founding member of the Japan Socialist Party, began his social activism as a vigorous proponent of reform in the middle-class home, founding a *Katei zasshi* of his own in 1903. In *Katei ni shinfūmi* (A new taste for the home), written in 1901, Sakai couched his faith in simple terms:

> A family meeting is held at mealtime. Scenes of the "family circle" occur most often at mealtime. In light of this, meals absolutely must be taken at the same time and the same dining table. When I say dining table, I mean one large surface, whether round or square—you can call it a *tēburu* or a *shippokudai*. In any event, I believe we should abandon the old trays [*zen*].[20]

Meals in most Japanese houses at this time were taken on individual trays, one tray and set of utensils possessed by each member of the household.[21] Sakai believed that sharing one table would also entail everyone in the house eating the same food, thus putting an end to the feudal habits of husbands who behaved like "little lords" and impeded the development of a "beautiful common-man's home" (*heiminshugi no utsukushii katei*).[22] Recent scholars have regarded the use of separate trays in a similar light, as a manifestation of feudalism. In Japan's status society, it has been argued, each individual stood in a position of either inferiority or

19. Examples from personal memoirs may be found in Yoshida Noboru, "Jiden ni yoru katei kyōiku no kenkyū," *Noma kyōiku kenkyūjo kiyō dai 10 shū: Katei kankyō no kyōiku ni oyobosu eikyō* (Tokyo: Kōdansha, 1953), 256–57.

20. Sakai Toshihiko, "Katei ni shinfūmi" (Tokyo: Naigai Shuppan Kyōkai, 1901), reprinted in *Sakai Toshihiko zenshū*, vol. 3 (Tokyo: Hōritsu Bunkasha, 1971), 51. Sakai's *Katei zasshi* and other writings of this period are discussed more closely in relation to issues of class identity in David Ambaras, "Social Knowledge, Cultural Capital, and the New Middle Class in Japan, 1895–1912" (unpublished manuscript).

21. This practice appears to have been general among all classes in dwellings of the Tokugawa period. The *shippokudai*, a Chinese-based novelty popular for banquets in Nagasaki, was exotic to Tokugawa Japanese because it offered a single surface from which several people could eat at once.

22. Sakai, "Katei no shin fūmi," 51.

superiority to others, making it an impropriety for two people to eat from the same surface.[23]

In urban households at the time that Sakai wrote, the frequent custom of the "little lords" whom he censured was to have a separate meal delivered from the local restaurant in the evening for private consumption in the master's room, usually one of the finest rooms in the house. In such households, the women of the house, often both mistress and servants, would take supper together in a room near the kitchen. The maid in Sakai's household reportedly joined master, wife, and children at the dinner table—a practice that many bourgeois families would resist.

Liberals like Sakai were not the only ones to promote the family dining table. A compilation of moral instruction and advice on household management published in 1907 under the title *Ie* began with a discussion of the house as foundation of the state and chapters on ancestor worship and the authority of the patriarch, but elsewhere instructed that "houses of the middle rank of society [*chūtō shakai*] should make a custom whenever possible of gathering the whole family for meals." Meals should be taken in the most pleasant place in the house, conversation should be encouraged, and "to the degree possible, trays should be abandoned for a dining-table structure [*shokutaku soshiki*]." Assembling for meals provided a time for the household head to hear the progress of the day's work and to give instructions.[24] The word *katei* was conspicuously absent from *Ie*, as was the romantic vocabulary of domestic bliss. But both Sakai's proto-socialist *katei* and this author's vision of the ideal house made the common table a device for imposing a regime on the household's time, and bringing about, at least in appearance, a convivial domestic group governed by egalitarian rules (see fig. 9).

Written and illustrated depictions of the "family circle" in most domestic management texts represented an assembly of children, parents, and sometimes grandparents, omitting other household members, with the occasional exception of a maid, who waited on the family but did not join them at the table. In actual practice, meals and other gatherings in large households were governed by protocols for sitting position and eating utensils that maintained status distinctions. But

---

23. For example, Koizumi Kazuko, *Kagu to shitsunai ishō no bunka shi* (Tokyo: Hōsei Daigaku Shuppan, 1979), 318. The modern shift from individual trays to a common table is intriguing from the perspective of comparative ethnology, since it appears to be a reverse of the process that occurred in Europe and the United States, where the refinement of table manners and increased variety of household goods engendered the replacement of a common pot with individual dishes. See Richard Bushman, *The Refinement of America: Persons, Houses, Cities* (New York: Knopf, 1992), 74–75. Pollution taboos and strict rules of distribution are possible reasons for the widespread use of separate utensils by each household member in Japan before the twentieth century. Shared one-pot dishes such as *sukiyaki* and *yosenabe* were therefore a new phenomenon when women's magazines began to promote them in the Taishō period. See Kumakura Isao, "Enkyo toshite no shokutaku," in Umesao Tadao, ed., *Gendai Nihon bunka ni okeru dentō to henyō*, vol. 9: *Shōwa no sesō shi* (Tokyo: Domesu Shuppan, 1993), 29–46.

24. Zushi Shōichirō, *Ie* (Tokyo: Keieisha, 1907), 289–92.

lacking any physical delimitation, such assemblies were centrifugally configured and spatially open-ended. A small dining table, on the other hand, created a focus of limited size for a closed and intimate family circle, delineating inside from out at the same time that it implied internal egalitarianism. Peripheral household members, particularly servants, were usually located on the outside.[25]

By the 1920s, taking meals at a single table was the norm in urban areas. In some parts of the country, however, individual trays survived in daily use until the 1960s. A complex web of social factors were involved in the switch of the mass of households from meals on individual trays to common tables, including increases in the housewife's role in kitchen labor and meal service, the spread of hygiene ideas, and changes in diet. From the 1890s, the "family circle," the central embodiment of the *katei* in practice, was woven through all of these strands of social change.

A LAND OF DUTIES AND A LAND OF BEAUTY

Despite the growing movement for domestic reform at the turn of the century, in the male profession of architecture, the home as refuge had yet to receive clear articulation. Certainly, change had taken place in elite domestic architecture, but there was little discussion in the academy of redesigning houses to meet the values of the age. The first men to raise the issue of proper architectural forms for the modern Japanese family were men of letters.

In an essay entitled "Kaoku" (Houses) published in October 1897, Kōda Rohan called for a reform of "the relationship between people and houses," to bring houses in step with the progress of the nation. After outlining the history of Japanese houses, Rohan concluded that the houses developed under pacific Tokugawa rule were "comfortable like armchairs, but prone to encourage indolence" (*anraku isu no gotoku yukai naredomo daki o fukumeru*). They may have been adequate for the people of Tokugawa, but in a fiercely competitive world, the people of Meiji needed separate "specialized houses" (*senmonteki kaoku*) for work and for rest. Not only could one not expect Japanese to work efficiently in houses that did not distinguish the two; one could not teach them the pleasures of the home. There were some men of property, Rohan noted, who had already built themselves two houses and accomplished the separation. The rest of society would have to follow suit. The house for work would be a "land of duties" (*gi no kuni*) and the second, for rest, a "land of beauty" (*bi no kuni*).[26]

A series of articles in *Jiji shinpō* in 1898 enumerated the shortcomings of Japanese houses in greater detail. The author pronounced Japanese houses to be primitive,

25. The three-member household depicted in Natsume Sōseki's *Mon* provides one such example. Husband and wife eat together at a small table while the maid has a separate tray and utensils.

26. Kōda Rohan, "Kaoku," in *Rohan zenshū*, vol. 29: *Zuihitsu*, pt. 1 (Tokyo: Iwanami Shoten, 1954), 89–94.

unsanitary, and ill-suited to work. But advocating such an appalling extravagance as the maintenance of two separate houses was of no utility to the middle ranks. The solution would have to be in one structure. One serious obstacle in existing houses was their interior layout. Rooms were not designated for specific functions and lacked proper partitions. Family members should have their own bedrooms, and one room should be set aside for dining.[27]

This polemic was probably the first public utterance to be quoted and discussed in the pages of both *Jogaku zasshi*, still the premier organ of women's education at the time, and *Kenchiku zasshi*, the official journal of the Society of Architects (Kenchiku Gakkai). Both praised the author, but *Kenchiku zasshi* noted that the articles had offered more criticism than solutions. This put the ball in the architects' court. Everyone had long been aware that Japanese houses were "imperfect" (*fukanzen*), but the solutions, after all, were the responsibility of "our nation's only Society of Architects."[28]

In 1903 and 1904, three of the society's leading architects discussed the problem of domestic reform in the pages of *Kenchiku zasshi*, reiterating many of the arguments that had been made earlier in *Jiji shinpō*, particularly about the ill-suitedness of *tatami* mats for work and the lack of proper interior partitions. The latter problem was described with the English words "privacy" and "secrecy"— neither of which was in common parlance, as the writers' proposals of Japanese translations (*inmitsu, himitsu*) indicate.[29] The use of rooms opening directly to one another, it was observed, put Japan 450 years behind the West, where they had had corridors since the Renaissance. Voices carried easily through paper sliding doors, often causing unpleasantness to visitors and embarrassment to the household. Private space for individual family members, however, was not discussed in these articles. Privacy was presented as a matter of the contact among three groups: the family, servants, and outsiders. The household was posed against its neighbors and guests, and the family against servants.[30]

These architects did not offer concrete plans to answer the challenge for architectural reform. One-half of the architectural profession's solution had already been given, in the addition to Japanese houses of a small wing with chairs and tables. A few houses of this type, termed "eclectic-style" (*wayō setchū*), could already be found in Tokyo, and designs for a somewhat refined version by Kitada Kyūichi,

27. Tsuchiya Gensaku, *Kaoku kairyōdan* (Tokyo: Jiji Shinpōsha, 1898), 2, 90–125.

28. T.A., "Nihon kaoku kairyōdan ni tsuite," *Kenchiku zasshi* 142 (October 1898): 321.

29. The word "privacy" had actually appeared once previously in *Kenchiku zasshi*, intriguingly translated *okumaritaru tokoro*, "a deeply recessed place." Uchida Seizō, "Meiji ki no jūtaku kairyō ni mirareru puraibashii no ishiki ni tsuite," *Nihon kenchiku gakkai taikai gakujutsu kōen kōgaishū* (Kantō), no. 8088 (October 1975): 1565–66.

30. Shiga Jūretsu, "Jūka (Kairyō no hōshin ni tsuite)," *Kenchiku zasshi*, nos. 194 (February 1903), 196 (April 1903), 199 (July 1903), 201 (September 1903), 202 (October 1903); Tsukamoto Yasushi, "Jūka no hanashi," *Kenchiku zasshi*, no. 199 (July 1903); Yahashi Kenkichi, "Honpō ni okeru kaoku kairyōdan," *Kenchiku zasshi*, no. 203 (November 1903).

a little-known member of the society, had appeared in *Kenchiku zasshi* in 1898, right on the heels of the *Jiji shinpō* articles.[31] The eclectic-style house sequestered reception and the household head's study at a position to one side of the entry vestibule, creating a zone with no *tatami* and ensuring the separation of household and guests. This space was viewed to be necessary for maintaining a gentleman's proper relations with society. It had to be in Western style, since "society"—the world of duties and work—wore Western trousers and shoes, and sat on chairs. Architects often observed that no one sat on the floor in government and company offices.

Since the remaining problem in house plans was an unpartitioned interior, the other half of the solution was naturally to put corridors between rooms. Architect Tanabe Junkichi introduced the West Australian bungalow to members of the society in 1908 as a model for improving the Japanese dwelling by reorganizing rooms around a central corridor. Tanabe's treatise was the earliest expression of what is known among architectural historians as the "interior corridor" (*nakarōka gata*) plan, which appeared with increasing frequency in pattern books and magazines subsequently. It is impossible to say whether Tanabe's study had a direct influence on the building trade at large, but surviving buildings from the 1910s and after reveal that more interior space was being devoted to corridors, with reception, kitchen, and servants' room situated on one side, and family living quarters on the other.[32]

ARCHITECTURE AND MANNERS

The process of fashioning a space primarily for the male household head's contact with the outside world and segregating other zones within the house purified the *tatami* portion of the house into a place to segregate the family from society. Domestic reformers more interested in the woman's side of the home ideal than in men's professional responsibilities sought to articulate further the dwelling as a family space by calling for a layout in which guest rooms were placed to the north and family rooms given the healthy southern exposure. Domestic management and reform texts often referred to this in shorthand as the "family-center approach" (*kazoku chūshin setsu*) or the "family-oriented house" (*kazoku hon'i no jūtaku*). Most detached houses still had a *tatami* "best room" (*kyakuma* or *zashiki*) for formal meals and overnight guests. This became the reformers' target. It was a fine thing to honor guests, they argued, but the most pleasant room in the house ought not to be set aside for nonfamily use. Opinions on the proper solution differed, and

31. Kitada Kyūichi, "Wayō setchū jūka," *Kenchiku zasshi*, no. 144 (December 1898): 377–80.

32. Tanabe Junkichi, "Nishi Gōshū no jūka," *Kenchiku zasshi*, no. 253 (January 1908): 23–33. The *nakarōka* plan was first defined as a type in Kimura Norikuni, "Nihon kindai toshi dokuritsu jūtaku yōshiki no seiritsu to tenkai ni kansuru shiteki kenkyū," Ph.D. diss., Tokyo University, 1959. There has been debate about whether its origins are foreign or indigenous.

not all floor plans, either in reality or in the prescriptive literature, demoted the "guest room" to an inferior position.[33] Since a range of actual living arrangements was possible within any layout, the particular solution offered by each text is less significant than the fact that most addressed the issue in the same terms, using a vocabulary that reflected the normative role of the family in dwelling design.

In the girls' schools and the women's magazines at the same time, educators were seeking a broader reform of the customs of guest reception. Texts discouraged unscheduled visits and service of anything more than tea and confections to unscheduled visitors. Conversation at these times, they urged, should be limited to business as much as possible. A chapter titled "The Housewife and Social Exchange" ("Shufu to kōsai") in a domestic manual began by observing the "very unfortunate" fact that unlike the West, Japan had no custom of fixed visiting times. Things may have been different in "the extreme leisure" of the feudal era, the writer allowed, but in the twentieth century every minute was money.[34] "Fifteen to thirty minutes" were the polite limits, according to another text.[35]

Anterooms linked to the guest room, associated with elaborate feudal practices of reception, were counted unnecessary and omitted from reformed house plans. Since the main *tatami*-matted areas in the houses of samurai, as well as propertied merchants and peasants, had originally been designed to accommodate extended family gatherings and community rituals, and in most cases were still required to perform these functions, the restriction of reception time and space entailed a change not merely in leisure habits, but also in the relations between the household and the traditional institutions surrounding it.[36]

It is easy to interpret these admonishments and alterations of practice as signifying a general reduction of formal etiquette. Viewed broadly, the reverse is probably true. The rules of etiquette taught to samurai by the Ogasawara school since the medieval period filled textbooks for girls' instruction in the modern period. Even the most progressive of educators treated the dictates of the Ogasawara school as the essential canon of manners. Magazines and other media transmitted the same ideas to a wider audience. The traditional etiquette masters themselves published texts and manuals for popular consumption, aimed particularly at the female reading public. These texts often stated that less formality was required

---

33. Actual practice varied, too. Despite the implication in this criticism that people were sacrificing comfort to preserve their "best rooms," some families used the room as a bedroom on ordinary nights. Jukichi Inouye, *Home Life in Tokyo* (London: Routledge and Kegan Paul, 1985), refers to this room as the "parlor" and indicates that families without a separate bedchamber slept in it.

34. *Katei bunko: Fujin no shiori* (Tokyo: Dai Nihon Kasei Gakkai, 1909), 299.

35. Tsukamoto Hamako, *Shinpen kaji kyōhon* (Tokyo: Kinkōdō, 1903), 2:145.

36. Ōkawa Naomi, *Sumai no jinruigaku* (Tokyo: Heibonsha Imēji Rīdingu Sōsho, 1986), discusses in detail the evolution of ritual uses of domestic space in the premodern period. See particularly 117–20, 178–88.

today than in the past, but they assumed their audience to be of a class both capable of maintaining ceremonial forms and aware to some degree of the code of practice. Manners now were looser, one Ogasawara master explained to Hani Motoko, the editor of *Katei jogaku kōgi*, so it was acceptable in "ordinary homes today" to have a servant go to the door in place of the host "unless receiving someone of much higher station."[37]

If the expulsion of casual visitors gave the family more of the house to themselves, it was not given unconditionally. As the universal application of an aristocratic canon of etiquette and the prescriptions for the performance of the "family circle" suggest, women's education and journalism sought to remodel the family for the parlor as much as the parlor for the family. This was true of mealtime gatherings no less than planned weekly family assemblies. The fact that the practice was new in Meiji-period Japan is one reason that it was equally important to reformers addressing this gathering to see that decorum was observed. Proper attire and morally beneficial conversation topics were stressed, with "the West" inevitably held up in contrast to native habits.

The reformers who sought to redesign domestic architecture for a more intimate family had much in common with authors of an earlier literature of domestic reform in the United States.[38] Also comparable was the effort paralleling architectural reform to modify occupants' behavior. Indeed, Japanese reformers were prone to regard as evidence of Western standards the prescriptive writings of Anglo-American reformers who, like themselves, had been compelled to write because of their own dissatisfaction with native conditions.

Unlike the ideal of the domestic haven that developed in England and the United States, however, the vessel for domesticity proffered to the Japanese urban elite retained a small piece of the household head's working world, albeit enclosed in solid walls and kept near the entry in the name of "privacy." Rohan's two types of house were not the suburban residence and office in town that bourgeois men in England and the United States were coming to possess. The exclusive middle-class suburb in Japan still lay two decades ahead. But the fact that the Japanese middle-class model placed the "land of duties" and the "land of beauty" not only on the same lot but under one roof reflected distinctive characteristics of domestic management writing and of the architectural profession in Japan.

The image of home as a haven and the housewife as its spiritual center persisted in *katei* discourse even after overt Christianity had been purged from the literature, but the sacred nature of the conjugal relationship ceased to play a large role in Japanese domesticity. A new perception of childhood whose seeds were evident in

---

37. Ogasawara Seimu interview, "Raikyaku ni tai suru reigi," *Katei jogaku kōgi* 9 (March 10, 1907): 80. *Katei jogaku kōgi* was the precursor of *Fujin no tomo*.

38. In 1857 American architect Calvert Vaux had criticized the custom of setting aside rooms for company, asserting that the most pleasant rooms should go to daily use. Bushman, *Refinement*, 270.

textbooks of the Meiji period would later grow into a cult of the mother-child relationship no less extreme than in the United States. Nevertheless, the ideologues of
the *katei* did not demand either conjugal or feminine hegemony over the entire
house. A gender-specific cloister could be retained under the same roof as the family haven without fundamental contradiction.

EPILOGUE AND CONCLUSION

In 1915, the newspaper *Kokumin shinbun* assembled exhibits of ideas for improving
the home and sponsored an event in Tokyo called the Katei Hakurankai (home
exposition). Model room interiors were presented by several women in the field of
domestic management, including Hani Motoko and a group of students from the
Japan Women's Higher School. The newspaper company published a volume of
essays entitled *Risō no katei* (The ideal home) to accompany the exposition and
offered its own house exhibit, featuring plans for a model middle-class house by
architect Endō Arata (see fig. 10). The house was a neat encapsulation of the late
Meiji-period solution—"family-centered," with good exposure for *tatami* rooms, a
reception room set off to the right of the entry, and a corridor separating family
rooms from servants. Revealing where the designer's primary aesthetic interests
lay, the Western-style reception room and study were the only rooms represented
by interior perspectives.[39]

This exposition was the beginning of a direct collaboration among journalists,
architects, and women's educators for reform of the physical dwelling. Endō
would later design for Hani, while publishing his plans and architectural ideas in
Hani's *Fujin no tomo*. After World War I, the efforts of these reformers in disparate
fields would be organized under the auspices of the Ministry of Education into
the Daily Life Reform League (Seikatsu Kaizen Dōmeikai).

At the same time, the exposition signified the advent of an era in which images
of the dwelling and domestic improvements became market commodities. In the
same year, a similar "Home Exposition" was held in Takarazuka to attract tourists
to the new resort town, and another newspaper, the *Hōchi shinbun*, solicited readers'
entries for the country's first publicly held house-design competition. Model house
expositions at which the houses were actually sold followed a few years later. Identified with the social characteristics of a new urban class, the *katei* was becoming a
nexus between social reform and the emerging consumer culture evident in com-
mercially sponsored expositions. The discourse of home and womanhood that
flourished in print from the time of the Sino-Japanese War had prepared the way
for this relationship by making the social institution of family a material problem,
and by making management of the household a specialization whose canon of
knowledge and claims to legitimacy came from external institutions.

---

39. Kokumin Shinbunsha, ed., *Risō no katei* (Tokyo: Katei Hakurankai, 1915). See also Uchida
Seizō, *Nihon no kindai jūtaku* (Tokyo: Kajima Shuppan, 1992), 76–78.

For all of the talk of family in *Risō no katei* and similar books of this period, their pages seldom contained either praise for or criticism of the "Japanese family system." After the 1898 Civil Code, the *ie* pursued its own course. The *katei*, meanwhile, had made its peace with the older generation, still cohabitant with their children in many cases. The pedagogues and journalists who developed this compromise devalued or ignored the community functions of the dwelling and often regarded non-kin household members as interlopers. In a social environment not conducive to a domestic ideal built upon the romanticization of femininity and conjugal love, they promoted activities that expressed the unity of cohabitant kin in ritual form. Architects and builders spatially rationalized the isolation of the family group with the interior corridor plan, allotting the family the "traditional" *tatami*-mat area of the house and reserving a modern room or suite of rooms in "Western style" for the conduct of men's affairs. *Tatami* and floor-sitting were thus associated with new conceptions of family leisure and of women's roles.

By the end of the Meiji period, Japanese reformers had succeeded in inventing a domestic variety of domesticity, that is, a linguistic and material rhetoric that joined family in a normative way with the space of the house. The objective elements were in some cases quite distinct from those elsewhere (the orientation of rooms, for example, was given particular prominence as a vehicle for the Japanese invention of "family-centered" space), in others ostensibly the same but very different in their local meaning (dining tables could represent Westernism in Japan while possessing a Japanese significance that was without an analogue in the West), but common ground was shared with Western nations at the more general level of the dispositions and expectations of the modern bourgeoisie. The gradual convergence of discourse among a diversity of actors produced a conception of home suited to the identity of this class. By 1915 *katei* rhetoric had been sufficiently digested by the literate public to obviate polemics. Debates concerning the authority of the family versus the individual that had begun in the Meiji period continued in subsequent decades, eventually to be inherited by postwar historians and feminists. Yet family discourse as a whole remained within the invented space of home.

FOURTEEN

The Cafe Waitress Serving Modern Japan

Miriam Silverberg

In a short story by Ozaki Midori, avant-garde woman writer of the 1920s, the solitary heroine seeks solace from her buddy, a *jokyū* (hereafter, cafe waitress) working in a grungy coffee-house. Kimi-chan lights a match for the heroine and explains why she should not be in love with Charlie Chaplin: "Nobody's going to be crazy about a guy who's not an erotic man." Kimi-chan then adds her very own illustration: "Even I stopped going to the flicks after Valentino died."[1] This fictional interaction between women offers one of the historical representations of the cafe waitress, whose image was ubiquitous in the mass media of pre–Pacific War Japan in surveys, fiction, and documentary reportage. Any imagining of the subjectivity and activity of the cafe waitress, Kimi-chan, raises questions about the new traditions created during what the Japanese media termed the "modern years," and a look inside the cafe helps to define how the Japanese lived what they self-consciously termed their *modan seikatsu* (modern life).

The term *seikatsu* was associated with a radically transformed material culture or rationalized lifestyle accompanying new forms of leisure activity, and the cafe, along with the cinema, was the site most often associated with experiences characteristic of the new age, which was defined by a series of "vanguard" gestures that had ostensibly broken away from any traditional framework. During the modern years, aesthetes, salaried corporate workers participating in a new white-collar culture, and literary intellectuals sought refuge in cafes, where they imagined a revolutionary change that would overthrow the stifling imperial order. The

---

1. For my translation of the Ozaki story, see *Manoa* 3, no. 2 (Fall 1991): 187–90. I have cited this encounter as a site of fantasy in "Remembering Pearl Harbor, Forgetting Charlie Chaplin, and the Case of the Disappearing Western Woman: A Picture Story," *Positions: East Asia Cultures Critique* 1, no. 1 (Spring 1993): 29–30.

cafe waitresses, possessing their own modern dreams and, in some cases, intellectual aspirations, were the women serving them.

Within the space of the cafe, the cafe waitress of the 1920s and 1930s made new traditions. This was a very different heroine from the premodern (and also the modern-ized) geisha. My primary concern is to draw attention to the history of her labors and desires, those manufactured in the confines of the cafe and those experienced with heartfelt emotion at a time when women and men knew that because their customs and conversations had been invented, they could also be changed.

THE JAPANESE CAFE WAITRESS AS *MODAN* INVENTION

In the West the notion of a "modernist" culture has been used to encompass art movements, popular culture artifacts, and an avant-garde, bohemian culture in Europe and in the United States that emerged by the late nineteenth century in the context of an active rejection of bourgeois culture. This bourgeois culture encompassed economic and political structures, family relationships, household decoration, and numerous other forms of expressions of social relationship, sensibility, and affect. Such an entrenched bourgeois culture did not exist in Japan in the 1920s or 1930s, but the culture of the West had to be addressed and reworked. Many commentators agreed with Ōya Sōichi's much-quoted essay that the Japanese "modern life" was a superficial expression of petit-bourgeois decadence. I do not. Nor do I think, as Ōya did, that the new customs of the 1920s and 1930s— which encompassed foreign words, consumer items, and most of all, media images, along with the cafe waitress—were a reaction against a feudal society. The transformation of local habits, especially by the mid-1920s, had been too comprehensive to presume that feudal habits were still in place, as even the folklorist Yanagita Kunio recognized by 1930. While Yanagita, no admirer of what was termed "modern," could wax nostalgic about the "important things that had been lost," he was acutely aware that aspects of daily living encompassing such cultural practices as the color of the clothing worn by his countrymen and women, their eating habits, and their dental hygiene had been radically transformed; in some cases he even appeared to conclude that this was all for the good.[2]

To give the reader a frame of reference (one that was not far from the minds of the sophisticated Japanese intellectuals of the "modern years"), it is fair to say that the Japanese term *modan* in one sense approximates the image of modernism put forth by Raymond Williams. Williams placed modernism within the late nineteenth-century history of the "greatest changes ever seen in the media of cultural production." The media he listed, "photography, cinema, radio, television, reproduction and recording"—with the exception of television—are listed in

2. Ōya Sōichi, "Modan sō to modan sō" (*Chūō Kōron*, February 1929), reprinted in *Ōya Sōichi zenshū* 2 (Tokyo: Eiochosha, 1981); Yanagita Kunio, *Meiji Taishō shi sesōhen*, 2 vols. (Tokyo: Kōdansha, 1992).

postwar Japanese-language histories. The Japanese discourse on the modern was characterized by the "innocence" Paul Gilroy has so astutely critiqued in his reference to the "apparently happy social relations that graced post-Enlightenment life in Paris, Berlin, and London." In other words, like their European counterparts, Japanese intellectuals were unconcerned to work relationships of empire into their picture of metropolitan activities. When the Japanese presence in Taiwan and on the Asian continent is mentioned in the discourse on the modern, it emerges only inadvertently.[3] But unlike Williams and Gilroy, Japanese commentators on Japanese modernity were very much aware of the presence of women in the modern picture. The images of the cafe waitress, along with the vibrating presence of the modern girl, were placed front and center.[4]

In the Japanese mass media of the 1920s and 1930s, "modern" was often explained in terms of lexicons. In July 1930, for example, the influential journal of the rural cooperative moment, *Ie no hikari*, offered a skit called "Interpreting Modern Language," starring a male student, a female student, and a teacher, in order to teach new terms commonly appearing in newspapers and magazines. Through this didactic genre, and with the use of puns, the editors encouraged its readership to become acquainted with the modern by listing such Japanese language neologisms (what the French theorist Georges Bataille would have called "tasks") as *rasshuawā* (rush hour), *puchiburu* (petit-bourgeois), *ideorogī* (ideology), *slōgan* (slogan), *nansensu* (nonsense), *fuan* (fan), *modan gāru* (modern girl), and *boikotto* (boycott). The new experience of jazz, defined for the rural readership as "arrhythmic music made popular by Negroes," was commonly associated with Japanese modern times.[5]

---

3. The avant-garde movements listed by Williams also entered Japan during the 1920s and 1930s. Constructivism, Futurism, Surrealism, and Dadaism all found expression in journals produced by Japanese intellectuals who either had personal contact with the "anti-bourgeois" artists in Europe or were emotional kin to these "émigrés." But the borders that most Japanese intellectuals first crossed lay between the provinces or the rural towns and the metropolitan centers of Tokyo or Osaka. (A decade later they would cross into the Asian continent at the behest of the state.) Raymond Williams, *The Politics of Modernism* (London and New York: Verso, 1989), 31–48. Paul Gilroy, *The Black Atlantic: Modernity and Double Consciousness* (Cambridge: Harvard University Press, 1993), 44. The Japanese case can be said to meet two out of three of Perry Anderson's criteria in his discussion of modernism. These are the presence of a "cultural force field 'triangulated' by three decisive coordinates: the emergence of key technologies of telephone, radio, automobile, etc., and the imaginative proximity of social revolution." The third coordinate is "the codification of a highly formalized *academicism* in the visual and other arts within regimes of state and society" dominated by aristocratic landowning classes. Perry Anderson, "Modernity and Revolution," in Cary Nelson and Lawrence Grossberg, eds., *Marxism and the Interpretation of Culture* (Urbana and Chicago: University of Illinois Press, 1988), 324–25.

4. On the Modern Girl, see Miriam Silverberg, "The Modern Girl as Militant," in Gail Lee Bernstein, ed., *Recreating Japanese Women, 1600–1945* (Berkeley and Los Angeles: University of California Press, 1991).

5. "Modango kaishaku," in *Ie no hikari* (July 1930): 153–57. During the 1920s Georges Bataille defined the function of the dictionary as teaching a task, rather than offering meaning (cited by Rosalind Krauss at a talk at the University of California, Irvine, May 1995).

During the pre–Pacific War years modernity was most constantly associated with leisure and centered on the male-coded pleasure of the cafe, as made clear in the essay "Renewed Scrutiny of the Life of Modern Pleasure" published in the January 1932 issue of *Chūō kōron*. The author-commentator claimed that "we are far from giving up the interpretation of the Cafe Era." While cafes might be fully established, they were not passé and no comparable institution was as widely apparent in the metropolitan areas, the medium-sized cities, the smaller cities, or the rural areas. Cafes, he noted, had spread throughout the country even before the telegraph and the telephone.[6] In February 1929, in an article entitled "Cafe Sociology," *Chūō kōron* had already adopted the Marxist language of the media of the era. With irony, the author pointed to the "dialectical union of coffee and liquor" in the cafe as an unprecedented product of the modern Japanese city, which differed from both the coffee shop and the small emporium serving sake. (Socrates had drunk wine at the house of a prostitute, but he knew nothing like a cafe!) Sharing the common and confident notion that Japanese modernity could be compared to the modern experiences of Europe and the United States, the author of "Cafe Sociology" noted that "just as Japanese civilization is united with that of Europe and America in some senses, Japanese cafes are united dialectically by European aspects, American aspects, and Japanese aspects. In this sense, Japanese cafes possess characteristics not seen abroad." What the Japanese cafe possessed, of course, was the cafe waitress, and as the connoisseur concluded, while in Japan one could image the cafe without wine, one could not imagine the cafe without the cafe waitress. Another critic of modern life, who talked of abandoning Ginza for Paris, set the scene: a "corps" of "slave waitresses" catered flirtatiously with their customers, who clashed with the architecture and the interior furnishings of the cafes.[7]

Traditions do not of course spring up ex nihilo; genealogies, if not origins, can be found. Thus the history of the *jokyū* that looks at the process of how she was made to feel and gesture, and the meanings attendant on the invention of this eroticization, calls for comparisons from within Japanese history. While we can say that the *jokyū* was a form of sex worker who provided erotically charged services (usually remunerated only by tips) and that she was not a prostitute because she did not engage in sexual intercourse, we are also obliged to associate her both diachronically and synchronically with other categories of women paid to be erotic. Igarashi Tomio's discussion of the prehistory and of the restrictions on *meshimori onna* of the Edo period, whose ostensible job was to serve food and drink to travelers at designated way-stations and whose labors coincided with the Tokugawa shogun's proscriptions against prostitution at these places of rest and recreation, contributes to a Japan-specific history of the sale of the female (feminized)

6. "Modan raifu no saiginmi," *Chūō kōron* (February 1929): 127–28.

7. "Cafe Shakaigaku," *Chūō kōron* (February 1929): 190, cited in Ōya, "Bunshi yōkō buyōron," in *Ōya Sōichi zenshū* 2:244–245; originally published in *Shinchō*, Sept. 1929.

body by recording the ambiguous position of these women. Sone Hiromi's research on prostitution in the early modern era of Japanese history, which focuses on unregulated, unlicensed prostitutes, forces us to differentiate between—but at the same time to acknowledge—similarities between types of prostitution. Sone makes clear that while the image of the *yūjo* of the pleasure quarters is one of sympathy-inducing beauty, she was as much a product of the "prostitution culture" of her era as the lowest-level prostitute (*inbaita*), who also sold her body through contractual agreement during the emergence of a commercial, cash economy.[8]

The *jokyū* was not a prostitute; her presence in the marketplace of the consumer culture of urban Japan in the 1920s was not aimed at the selling of her body for intercourse, although this did occur. But if we replace Sone's notion of a shared experience of prostitution euphemized by different categories with the concept of the sale of Japanese woman's eroticized services, we can engage in the complex analytical process of comparing her to non-Japanese counterparts, to her predecessors in the medieval and early modern period, and to her contemporaries, including geisha, the serving women known as *shakufu*, and both licensed and unlicensed prostitutes.[9] Most prewar Japanese commentary on the cafe waitresses, which was based on presumptions about the training of the geisha, implied that cafe waitresses were not in possession of *gei* (the arts) and therefore were a very different sort of purveyor of services. But the eroticized interaction between these sex workers and their male customers was informed by many practices and presumptions of the geisha and of other working women who served men. The gendered practice of having women and not men serve the drinks and the food did not come from the French cafe (the ostensible model for the Japanese institution), where men served that function. The serving up of conversation and play (encompassing various forms of performance) by women for hire interacting intimately with male customers was a long-held tradition. Synchronically, it must be argued that the *jokyū* who entered the cafes (along with their sisters in other forms of sex work) had already been shaped by contemporary notions of gender, sexuality, and the erotic.

The Japanese cafe was new; it was not to be confused with the Japanese coffeehouse, the first of which was established as early as 1888. These were followed by the coffeehouses serving classical music, with cafe waitresses as coffee servers to serious intellectuals, and their successors, which offered coffee along with lighter and more indigenous music. The coffeehouse was considered an updated version of the premodern teahouse. The cafe, in contrast, was considered a

---

8. Igarashi Tomio, *Nihon josei bunka shi* (Tokyo: Agatsuma shōkan, 1984), 133–48. Sone Hiromi, "Baitakō—kinsei no baishun," in Josei Shi Sōgō Kenkyūkai, ed., *Nihon josei shi seikatsu shi*, vol. 3: *Kinsei* (Tōkyō Daigaku Shuppankai, 1991).

9. For a rich ethnographic treatment of the hierarchy and the complex practices and relationships of Yoshiwara, see J. E. de Becker's *The Nightless City* (Yokohama: Z. P. Maruya, 1899); on "classes of prostitutes," see p. 44.

"modern" successor to the Taishō-period milk halls. The first cafe, Purantan (Printemps), established in the spring of 1911, was run by the artist Matsuyama Shōzō, a painter in the Western style who served food and wine to go with the graffiti he had painted on the cafe walls. It soon attracted a clientele of artists, literati, and theater people. By August Cafe Lion, also on Ginza, which would become the model for the modern Japanese cafe, had hired beauties to serve food and drink, and by 1930 there were 800 cafes and 10,000 waitresses in Osaka alone. These bar hostesses, considered a modern innovation, like the glamorous movie starlet, numbered 112,000 in 1936 and as many as 90,200 as late as 1939, a year after a massive roundup of students found in cafes. The cafes, which catered mainly to the salaried middle class and intellectuals, numbered 37,000 by 1933; however, as the sources make clear *jokyū* served all classes in varied establishments.[10] (See fig. 11.)

It was the *jokyū*—originally dressed primly in kimono and apron—rather than the food or even the drink, that lured customers into these places, which were more bar than coffeehouse in atmosphere and menu. They served food, poured the drinks and joined in the drinking as they made conversation with their customers. These young women were spectacularized in the print media, in the movies, and in movie song lyrics. Some *jokyū* became celebrities, comparable to screen and stage idols who sold their own form of eroticism. But to see the cafes only as decadent, immoral challenges to or evasions of state authority simplifies the important historical questions surrounding the inventions of the cafe waitress, inventions that are part of the pre–Pacific War history of "erotic-grotesque-nonsense," a catchphrase of the era then and now associated with decadence. All three constitutive parts of this buzz-word had political implications that must be given serious attention. The recognition of the prevalence of the cafe waitress as an actress personifying the erotic is one way to begin to reformulate this cultural history.

THE CREATION OF THE EROTIC

The tension between the specificity of the eroticism commodified within the *jokyū*-customer relationship and the eroticism imposed on all women within what can be termed the "eroticism industry" is best illustrated by the case of Abe Sada, the notorious heroine of 1936, made famous in the West through the Ōshima Nagisa movie "In the Realm of the Senses." The various jobs held by Abe Sada reveal the range of jobs available to an uneducated woman, for Abe Sada survived poverty as a delinquent young girl and moved from a low-class geisha position to the status of prostitute by the time she was seventeen. She was also a higher class of prostitute, a mistress, and a cafe waitress. In all of these positions Abe served male expectations

---

10. Minami Hiroshi, ed., *Shōwa bunka* (Tokyo: Keisō Shobō, 1987), 78, 169, 477–78. The "onna bōi" (woman boy) preceded the *jokyū*. Sheldon Garon cites Ozaki Yukio's discussion of the police action in *Molding Japanese Minds: The State in Everyday Life* (Princeton: Princeton University Press, 1997), 108.

regarding eroticized femininity, yet she lasted only two weeks in her incarnation as cafe waitress. Why? According to Sada's biographers, she saw through the theatrics of the romantic mood created in the cafe, recognizing that what was taking place was merely the "control of romance" wherein even the conversation and exchange of gazes between men and women were controlled. The conclusion of the biographers: Sada must have decided that if she were going to work in a situation where sex was transacted, it would be more "rational" to approach the interaction directly.[11] While it is true that Sada turned next to prostitution for financial reasons, her discomfort with the job of cafe waitress may also have had to do with the expertise of interaction required of the *jokyū*, whose income depended not on a controlled set of moves, as implied by Abe's biographers, but on her own ability to marshal conceptions of the erotic and place them in the context of exchanged conversation, including culturally coded teasing or flirtation, gazes, and other practices of female-male engagement. A more metaphoric, blunt way of posing Abe's move was that she was unable to engage in anything but the most literal of actions when, five years later, she cut off and walked away with her lover's penis, an act that she defended in legal testimony as the most natural of outcomes for any woman so passionately involved with a true *iro otoko* (erotic man).[12]

As the case of Abe Sada so vividly shows, the eroticized behavior that the *jokyū* "did" for money and the "erotic experiences" that they encountered were both similar and different. There was a range of behaviors along a spectrum—from eroticism at play (or "at work" might be more appropriate) to eroticism in earnest. There might be a disjunction between the customer's attraction to the *jokyū* and the commodified mercenary behavior of the sex-worker waitress, leading to an ambiguity in the meanings attached to eroticism, within the social space of the cafe. But the positions of male and female appeared to be safely delineated at a historical moment when there was unease about femininity and masculinity. As the discourse on the "modern girl" makes clear, a new femininity appeared to have usurped the aggressiveness that had been the domain of the male. At this time mass magazines were obsessively defining "manliness" and "womanliness" in such formulations as movie star fantasies about male and female ideals captured in articles like "If I Were Born a Woman, How Would I Treat Men / If I were Born a Man, How Would I Treat Women."[13] In contrast, in the cafe, gender

---

11. Awazu Kiyoshi, Ii Tarō, and Hosaka Kunio, *Shōwa jūichinen no onna: Abe Sada* (Tokyo: Tabata Shoten, 1976), 118–21. According to the authors, high-class unlicensed prostitutes used the telephone and the taxi as tools of the trade and tended to specialize. Some catered only to student lodgings in Kanda, Waseda, and Hongō.

12. In my essay "The Japanese Cafe Waitress Sang the Blues," I associate Abe Sada with the blues. This essay has been published in Japanese as "Nihon no jokyū wa buruusu o utatta," in Wakita Haruko and Susan Hanley, eds., *Jendā no Nihon shi* (Tokyo: Tōkyō Daigaku Shuppankai, 1995), 2:585–607.

13. See, for example, "Watashi ga onna ni umaretara? Dō otoko o gūsuru ka? Watashi ga otoko ni umaretara? Dō onna o gūsuru ka?" *Fujin kōron* (April 1923): 17.

roles were at least clear, even if etiquette was being invented: the males were paying for the females' services. Erotic exchanges had to be negotiated; gender distinctions were clear-cut.[14]

Gender was eroticized through various practices within the cafe, including the manipulation of space organized to encourage a sense of intimacy. Customers interested in the reworking of indigenous tradition could confine themselves to the "Salon Momoyama," whose cafe waitresses sat on brocade chairs and wore their kimono and their hair in appropriate fashion, or they could drink and visit in another area on the same floor that had wicker and wood chairs, potted plants, and waitresses in kimono with their hair wrapped in contemporary but modest buns. Photographs revealing the placement of art deco sofas backed by stylized lamps in the shape of Japanese lanterns in the famous Ginza Cafe Tiger, and the strategically placed shrubbery and the division of space by standing panels and high backs of banquettes in the Star of Gold in Shinjuku, give a sense not only of the cultural syncretism of the era but of how customers were isolated and consolidated among clusters of *jokyū*. There were numerous forms of exoticization. Photographs of chinoiserie decoration and of cafe waitresses in Chinese costume illustrate the eroticization of the colonial experience in what may be termed a reversal of the "mimicry" of the colonizer discussed by Homi Bhabha. The colonial mimic in Bhabha's analysis is the colonial subject who is "not quite / not white." Here of course, the colonizer is passing as colonized. Waitresses also catered to customers who paid for the "Salon Manchuria" space on the second floor of the Ginza Palace, which had advertised for three hundred *jokyū* when it opened.[15] Relations within the cafe were implicated in the constitution of gendered and eroticized relations in other spaces, including the household, during the same historical moment. Within what Nishikawa Yūko has termed the "abstract space" of the prewar (middle-class) "tea-room household," the relationship of the modern married couple was being invented, as foregrounded by the advice columnist and critic Yamada Waka: "Husband-wife problems" were to be resolved

14. On gender fluidity in interwar Japan, see "Advertising Every Body: Images from the Japanese Modern Years," in Susan Foster, ed., *Choreographing History* (Bloomington: Indiana University Press, 1995); Jennifer Robertson, "Gender Bending in Paradise: Doing 'Female' and 'Male' in Japan," *Genders*, no. 5 (Summer 1989); and Don Roden, "Taishō Culture and the Problem of Gender Ambivalence," in J. Thomas Rimer, ed., *Culture and Identity: Japanese Intellectuals During the Interwar Years* (Princeton: Princeton University Press, 1990).

15. My finding of the term *tairikuteki nihonjin* (continental Japanese) indicates that Japanese ethnic identity within the colonial context may have exhibited a fluidity (countering state ideology) not unlike that of the fluctuation in determinations of gender. For a series of richly detailed photos of cafe exteriors and interiors that give a sense of the lush use of art deco conceits, see the section on cafes in Fujimori Terunobu, Hatsuda Tōru, and Fujioka Hiroyasu, eds., *Ushinawareta teito Tōkyō: Taishō Shōwa no machi to sumai* (Tokyo: Kashiwa Shobō, 1991), 76–95. For photographs of chinoiserie decor and of "Salon Manshū" and "Salon Momoyama," see ibid., 83, 92, 93. The gendering and sexualizing of the reverse mimic is most likely crucial to this Japanese phenomenon and bears further study. Another

via the "making of the *seikatsu* of two people into one." The men and women involved in such an undertaking surely took presumptions and expectations from
the household to the cafe and back, as suggested in the article in *Shufu no tomo* instructing the housewife that the eighth out of one hundred ways to avoid a mari-
tal quarrel was to recognize that household discord would send him directly to a
cafe. Three years later, the March 1932 issue of *Shufu no tomo* reassured its female
readership that all was going well in Manchuria because the disposition of the
military and the people of the nation were as one, while indicating at the same
time that things were not as sanguine on the household front. The newlywed who
was concerned that her husband was stopping off at the neighborhood cafe on his
way home from work was told by the experts to recognize that the cafe offered her
husband a "soft, sweet, liberated" atmosphere. She was to create such an ambiance by buying wine and inviting his colleagues to the house but was told not to
behave like a cafe waitress. The articles in *Ie no hikari* tended to represent the cafe
waitress as a threat to family life from another perspective. It was clear from its numerous lamentations—echoing the September 1925 "There Are No Brides in
the Countryside," about country girls who were drawn to the neon lights of the
big city only to be pulled down into the squalor and turpitude represented by the
life of the cafe waitress—that women in the cities were supporting households
through such labor.[16]

The Japanese cafe waitress was like Peter Bailey's Victorian barmaid, a "cultural prototype" expressing "open yet licit sexuality" made possible by "capitalist
cultural managers." She could earn more money than other working-class women
by engaging in "sexualized social encounter" informed by the flow of banter and
alcohol in the context of a "modern sexualized consumerism and of the blurring
of class and gender categories due to the emergence of working women." The
crucial difference was that the British barmaid was behind the bar. According to
Bailey, this simultaneously heightened and contained the sexual attraction of the
barmaid, thus qualifying her as a glamour figure."[17]

---

example of the eroticization of the colonial experience via what may be termed "reverse mimicry" for
the purposes of *naichi* (the "interior" or metropole) consumption is the phenomenon of the popularity
of the ostensibly Chinese movie star Rikōran, who was in fact a Japanese actress. Regarding the "continental Japanese" and the Rikōran phenomenon, see Silverberg, "Remembering Pearl Harbor." For a
discussion of Homi Bhabha's notion of mimicry, developed from Lacan, see Robert Young, *White
Mythologies: Writing History and the West* (London: Routledge, 1990), 147–48.

16. Nishikawa Yūko, "Otoko no ie, onna no ie, seibetsu no nai heya," in Wakita Haruko and
Susan Hanley, eds., *Jendā no Nihon shi* (Tokyo: Tōkyō Daigaku Shuppankai, 1995), 2:609–43. "Fūfu
kenka no yobōhiketsu no hyakkajō," *Shufu no tomo* (June 1929): 48. "Shinfūfu no ninjo sōdankai," *Shufu
no tomo* (March 1932): 126–27. "Nōson ni yome ga nai," *Ie no hikari* (September 1925): 5–7. The warnings
of *Ie no hikari* were not wholly unfounded. Cafes could be fronts for prostitution, drawing in young
women under false pretenses.

17. Peter Bailey, "Parasexuality and Glamour: The Victorian Barmaid as Cultural Prototype,"
Gender and History 2, no. 2 (Summer 1990).

The *jokyū*, seated alongside her customer, was also a glamour figure, who often consciously modeled her looks on the appearance of starlets. By the time of the depression in the late 1920s there appears to have been an increasingly heightened sexualization of the encounters between *jokyū* and customer at some cafes, as contending cafe managers institutionalized such desperate sexual acts as "the underground" or "subway service" (the first Japanese subway began transporting customers to the night life district of inexpensive movie houses and cafes in 1927), wherein the customer's hand could go "underground" from a slit strategically sewn into the *jokyū*'s skirt.[18] T. J. Clarke's analysis of relationships based on both class and gendered "sexual theatricals," wherein the client had to feel he had access to "some mystery," probably "of Woman," appears applicable to an understanding of the subjectivity of the male client in the Japanese modern cafe. Even more applicable is Clarke's insight that even if the barmaid is not for sale, she is believed to be for sale by some of her customers. The self-presentation of the bar girl represents her to the customer as an object for consumption, and the barmaid's work is to "maintain this illusion" within a capitalist nexus of commodities. But the *jokyū* is not an object; she expresses agency (if not independence) and challenges to her commodified relationships with her customers (if not absolute resistance).[19]

THE INVENTIONS OF THE CAFE WAITRESSES

The *jokyū* created an eroticized identity within the context of a working-class culture *at the same time* that she sold a commodified gendered identity within the class-based and class-coded leisure culture inhabited by the cafe, a term denoting both the large establishments on Ginza in Tokyo and the flashier Dōtonbori in Osaka, and smaller drinking establishments. The cafe waitress both sold and experienced desire within her relationships with customers, the cafe management, and other *jokyū*, in the shadow of expanding state control[20] and an expanding Japanese empire that was taken for granted.

Hirotsu Kazuo's novel *Jokyū*, serialized in *Fujin kōron* from August 1930 until March 1932, caused a scandal when man-of-letters Kikuchi Kan recognized himself as one of the predatory patrons. By the same token, *jokyū* practices are herein

18. Abe Sada's biographers trace a trajectory of the degeneration of the cafes into sites of contending "erotic services." Awazu Kiyoshi, Ii Tarō, and Hosaka Kunio, *Abe Sada: Shōwa jūichinen no onna* (Tokyo: Tabata Shoten, 1976), 115–21.

19. T. J. Clarke, *The Painting of Modern Life: Paris in the Art of Manet and His Followers* (Princeton: Princeton University Press, 1984), 109–11; 245–46; 252–55.

20. A more comprehensive history of the *jokyū* must of course include the history of the state crack-downs on cafe and cafe workers and what I term the *tenkō* (political turning) of the *jokyū* as they were incorporated into the reformulated national polity by 1940. See Sheldon Garon, "The World's Oldest Debate?: Prostitution and the State in Imperial Japan, 1868–1945," *American Historical Review* 98, no. 3 (June 1993).

represented as manipulative. Hirotsu documents the machinations of carefully organized groups (ten *jokyū* divided into "red," "blue," and "purple" groups) who initiate "motions" to draw men into their designated spaces within the cafe, and the ensuing flirtatious high-pitched coy banter of persuasion and flattery constituting the "handling of customers." He also suggests a typology of *jokyū*, making sure to point out the "vamp type" and to note how *jokyū* specialized in topics of discussion—there were some who could talk about sports; others specialized in current literary trends. The novelist informs us of the gaudy decorations of the colonial cafe culture and suggests a typology of overseas/colonial Japanese "types" when he refers to those who saved up money in the colonies, and a generosity uncharacteristic of women "brought up in the *naichi* [metropole]" expressed by a woman who had lived in South America.[21] Ultimately however, the book reads like a male fantasy of a series of bathos-ridden crises inflicted upon desperate *jokyū* who survive seduction as virgins, pregnancy, and unnuanced ruminations about love.

Three other documents from the modern era, a classic survey of Osaka *jokyū*, a popular ethnographic account of Ginza night-life, and a hit novel of 1930, offer us a much more textured sense of the *jokyū's* inventions and intentions.

One of many surveys sponsored by government agencies to analyze new forms of leisure and criminality, *Jokyū seikatsu no shinkenkyū* was based on fieldwork conducted between April and June of 1930 by the Ōhara Institute for the Study of Social Problems.[22] Based on responses from 515 establishments where *jokyū* worked for tips as wages, it situated the often déclassé waitresses within a modern capitalist space and hinted at her desires. The introductory section delineated the social space of the *jokyū*; she was present in cafeterias, coffeehouses, bars, restaurants, and cabarets. This study aimed to fix the *jokyū* within a *seikatsu* informed by material, class relationships with family members, employers, and customers. It did not analyze the exact nature of her work (new traditions had already been naturalized?!), yet at the outset her labor was distinguished from that of the professional working woman who was trained, and the laboring woman from the factories and mines. The eroticized dimension to her work was hinted at in the conclusion that the *jokyū* had to relate to "various sorts of human beings," which required "quite a working of the mental faculties" and "actions of the emotions," and that she was not a mechanical server of food and drink within the capitalist system run by "cafe capitalists."[23]

---

21. Hirotsu Kazuo, *Jokyū*, in *Hirotsu Kazuo zenshū* (Tokyo: Chūō Kōronsha, 1988), 5:234.

22. Ōbayashi Munetsugu, *Jokyū seikatsu no shinkenkyū: Ōsaka shi ni okeru kafee jokyū chōsa* (Tokyo: Ganshōdō, 1932). Information was organized under such categories as place of work, status relations of *jokyū*, movement conditions, management methods of owners of establishments, thoughts on management and customers, previous jobs and schooling, income and expenses, and particular attributes and disposition of *jokyū* based on such aspects as hobbies and cultivation.

23. Ōbayashi, *Jokyū seikatsu*, 12–13.

We glimpse a vision of the large Osaka cafes employing more than one hundred *jokyū*, where male desire was magnified through such "modern fixings" as the neon sign, the jazz band, stage dancing, and decorations that changed with the seasons. (According to the survey, the *jokyū* was thus both a new modern fixture and a special category of working woman within a modern site of entertainment, which was eroticized by a "commodification" of "atmosphere" stimulating the sensations and emotions of customers. The study placed the class origin of the *jokyū* within a category that can be termed petit-bourgeois. According to the findings, more than half of the *jokyū* between the ages of 24 and 26 were married, and the majority of the husbands, like the fathers and siblings, were engaged in trade.[24]

Most *jokyū*, the survey tells us, were between the ages of 18 and 21. They had thus just begun to develop blooming womanly beauty, a thick eroticism, and fragrance. We can also infer how the cafe waitresses themselves defined their femininity by the following examples of magazines the survey listed as free time reading: *Fujo kai* (Woman's world), *Shufu no tomo* (Housewife's friend), *Fujin kurabu* (Woman's club), *Shōjo no tomo* (Young girl's friend), and *Fujin no tomo* (Woman's friend).[25]

The survey also hints at the notion of the ideal male when it lists their "favorite people." These included, first of all, Prime Minister Hamaguchi Osachi and General Nogi, the tragic hero of the Russo-Japanese War, who was much celebrated in the popular journalism of the 1930s. One response to the query "List the good things about your work" stated, "I can find out all about men." Unfortunately, there was no elaboration of what this woman discovered.[26] Regarding national, racialized differences and the relationship of the culture of the waitress to the culture of the colonies, the survey mentions "Japanese" born in America and Hawaii who worked as waitresses and the existence of Russian and Chinese *jokyū*. The annexation of Korea had enabled Korean *jokyū* to dress in Korean dress and serve Korean customers while also serving Japanese customers in Japanese.[27]

The waitresses' beliefs also emerge in their answers to a query as to why they had chosen to become *jokyū*. Most listed financial reasons; some were "sick of the

24. Ibid., 28, 40–48, 67. Brothers of the *jokyū* worked predominantly in occupations involving the sale of goods or office work, or were students; older sisters were unemployed (younger sisters were not noted) or worked as *jokyū* themselves. More than 20 percent of fathers worked in commercial endeavors and the majority of these sold goods. More than half of the declassé *jokyū* had not finished elementary school and most worked as maids, in agricultural labor, or as factory girls before becoming *jokyū*.

25. Ibid., 28–29, 131.

26. Ibid., 85–86. The very unprecedented "modernity"—in the Japanese discourse on the *modan*, newness was central—of it all was expressed by the fact that there are no Japanese-language equivalents for *neon sain, jazubando*, and *stēji dansu*. Ibid., 19; 22–23. The "favorite people" were not all male but were predominantly so; see p. 141.

27. The report is exceedingly vague in its discussion of Korean *jokyū* who were born and raised in Korea and their relationship to the waitresses from the metropole (ibid., 53). The discussion of the easy availability of Korean waitresses brings to mind the *ianfu*, or "comfort woman," and connections should be explored.

countryside." Possible similarities to American working girls described by Stansell and Peiss emerge in such statements as "I wanted to wear beautiful clothes" and "It was for revenge on a man."[28] The nature of the revenge is not described, just as work routines are not recorded, but the acting out of relations of domination in the cafe—comparable to T. J. Clarke's set of "sexual theatricals" centered on the act of drinking—are hinted at in the following expressions of *jokyū* attitudes, which are characterized by a patronizing critical distance: (1) *Sake* drinkers are fun; (2) Gentlemen who do not drink are good; (3) I give good service; (4) I satisfy them and treat them with care; (5) They all cheat on you; (6) It's like caring for an invalid; and (7) The youths of today have an air of delinquency about them. The answers express a profound romantic disinterest, an impression strengthened by Obayashi's statement that most of the *jokyū* respondents did not understand the query regarding "experiences of having been seduced." Most likely the cafe waitresses experienced "seduction" in different words, although one woman responded unequivocally: "I do the seducing."[29]

A second text, *Ginza saiken*, written by the art historian Andō Kōsei in 1931, is much more specific about cultural practices that drew men to the *jokyū*, as when he offers images of *jokyū* wearing low clogs and carrying small cloth bundles walking by customers who stand in wait after hours.[30] He also quotes *jokyū* dialect, their own invented version of *satokotoba*, the dialect spoken in the premodern Yoshiwara quarter. At Cafe Printemps "hot sandwich" (*hotto sandoitchi*) was shortened to *torisan*—for chicken sandwich—which was then given the cachet of a French prefix when a *jokyū* took an order for *un torisan*. According to Andō eroticism took on different styles: at some cafes the *jokyū* were vamps, at others they displayed respectable class airs. Customers could seek out cafes where the *jokyū* make-up was thicker and the kimono more garish, and where the waitress who wanted to say the slightest thing brushed her body against customers, drawing in those in search of the more physically erotic.[31]

For Andō there were local variations on what was conceptualized as a modern, industrial model: "The Osaka *jokyū* is a skilled worker in an erotics factory" (eroticism was being mass-marketed). In a stunning reference to the connections

28. Ibid., 80–81. Cf. Christine Stansell, *City of Women: Sex and Class in New York City, 1789–1860* (New York: Knopf, 1986), 186–87; and Kathy Peiss, *Cheap Amusements: Working Women and Leisure in Turn-of-the-Century New York* (Philadelphia: Temple University Press, 1985), 5.

29. Ōbayashi, *Jokyū seikatsu*, 93–94.

30. Andō Kōsei, *Ginza saiken* (Tokyo: Chūō Kōronsha, 1977), 68–69. Maeda Ichi described the *jokyū* carrying a small basket containing cosmetics and a change of clothes in *Shokugyō fujin monogatari* (Tokyo: Tōyō Keizai Shuppanbu, 1929), 192.

31. Andō, *Ginza saiken*, 80–83, 88. Such a discussion of style (relating it to sexuality, taste, and by implication, class) compares with Peiss's notion of "putting on style," which she associates with dress as "a particularly potent way to display and play with notions of respectability, allure, independence, and status and to assert a distinctive identity and presence" (p. 63) and her notion of prostitutes as a cultural model (pp. 56–67), or to Clarke's relating of appearance to the ostensible denial of class.

among forms of commodified mass-oriented leisure, Andō remarks that all were welcome—to enter an Osaka cafe was like entering the Shirokiya department store; upon crossing the threshold of a cafe, the Osaka customer yelled out a lusty "So-and-So, I'm here!" to his *jokyū* of choice. But Andō's waitresses also possessed a sense of agency both passively aggressive and aggressively manipulative: The *jokyū* knowingly took money meant to buy her love or her body in silence. Conspiracy among *jokyū* is also catalogued. For example, the social practice of labeling a man "so-and-so's customer"—thus granting one of the women proprietary rights—had been institutionalized by 1931. (Part of the training process for the *jokyū* entailed learning how to assign, maintain, and steal customers.) There was a code of behavior among the women whose sense of community was forged at work and during off hours at such places as the public bath—the Cafe Lion group habituated one, the Cafe Tiger *jokyū* used another in the Ginza neighborhood. There they used rough language among themselves in a gender inversion that served as another form of self-empowerment. Not only did customers follow *jokyū* from cafe to cafe; waitresses moved to be with former co-workers who had found work elsewhere.[32]

There were other off-duty routines. In addition to buying magazines and kimono from dealers who entered the cafe, *jokyū* learned to respond to eager customers who sought their company at the sweet bean restaurants and noodle shops where they congregated after hours. Andō reveals that within these relations of power, the *jokyū* had *their own* techniques of responding to attempts at seduction. There was, for example, the story of the *jokyū* who wrote her address on the back of a ticket for one eager customer, who said he would visit her on her day off. In addition to giving her a big tip he offered to bring her a treat of her choice, to which she replied (in terms, it should be noted, that were marked as innocently feminine), "Well, I do like cod roe." The gallant would-be seducer spent the following afternoon in a taxi, driving around one neighborhood, pungent offering in hand, searching for an address that did not exist.[33]

It is neither surprising nor essentializing to recognize that in her novel *Hōrōki* Hayashi Fumiko takes us further than these male writers into the consumer subculture of the cafe waitress as it relates to erotic desires for food, objects, and physical intimacy.[34] This culture is made up of the routines of the *nagaya* (the elongated narrow dwelling of Japanese working-class families of the era), the "barracks" of the cafe waitress's room, and the limited choices available to women without skills in dire economic straits. Hayashi treats cafe relationships as defined by economic and gender domination. The account of a customer who has absconded without paying is but the most immediate cause of her declaration, "It was after all nothing

32. Andō, *Ginza saiken*, 116–18, 131–34, 136.
33. Ibid., 141, 159–60.
34. Hayashi Fumiko, *Hōrōki* (Tokyo: Shinchōsha, 1974).

but a one-on-one battle between customer and *jokyū*. (I'm sick of it all when I think of the ruses of the cafe.)"[35] When one *jokyū* likens the customers to Jews (exhibiting an anti-Semitism that emerges in various texts of the era), she is corrected by Hayashi, who makes clear that all relationships in Japanese society are marked by greed. *Hōrōki* traces the process of becoming a *jokyū* within this system. When the heroine talks about having "fully become a *jokyū*," she is not merely referring to the acquisition of skills, as implied by Ōbayashi or Andō; she refers to a process of eroticization that takes into account her own erotic desires as much as the needs of the men she serves.

The heroine of Hayashi's novel has been aware of the gendering of women in society since the age of 12, when she found it necessary to gender her desire for wealth in claiming the desire to become a "woman nouveau-riche," and she plays with other fantasies embodying womanhood, imagining herself at various times as Kachūsha (the heroine of the play based on Tolstoy's *Resurrection*, popularized throughout Japan in stage and song by 1914), a drunkard woman, a woman thief, a woman gambler, and a "mess of a woman." When she gains work as a journalist, it is as a "newly rising lady reporter." Clearly Hayashi is aware of popular conventions of womanliness and how such glamour is conveyed; her ideal of beauty is the actress Matsui Sumako (for whom the "Song of Kachūsha" was written), "as seen in a photo." Hayashi's narrative links conceptions of femininity with the history of the cafe waitress when she claims that "in such a cafe, all you have to do is be a woman."[36]

And to be a woman means to recognize that male-female relationships inside and outside the cafe are governed by domination. When Hayashi fantasizes, "Maybe I'll just go home to my province and go be a bride," she knows that this will not satisfy her desires for erotic connection, food, or such material goods as the shawl she covets—for the power implied by the phrase "going to be a bride" implies fitting into a family and meeting the demands of an institutionalized kinship system. The heroine is also brutally honest about erotic domination, which takes the form of violence made possible by obsession. Because of an obsession with one man, she goes from cafe to cafe, and because of men, she is forced to "retreat back into the cafes." She curses and mourns for the departed man who has abused her and her poverty forces her to borrow money from another man, who treats her as though he is coming home to a mistress.[37]

But Hayashi's *jokyū* also resists her fate in love, in part because, as the heroine says (echoing one response in Ōbayashi's survey), illusions regarding men disappear when one works at cafes. One example of a defiant response accompanying humiliation, reminiscent of the powerful denouement of the short story "Drau-

35. Ibid., 242.
36. Ibid., 106, 131, 132, 23, 284, 303, 261.
37. Ibid., 265, 283.

padi" by Mahasweta Devi,[38] takes place after a customer bets that she cannot drink ten shots of whiskey. All those nearby in the cafe laugh, and the cafe proprietor is delighted when she takes on the bet:

> I swear that I resent all and every one of the bastards. Ahh, I am but a woman with no chastity. Shall I present you with one naked dance. All you fine personages. . . . When I think of having to have a man provide for board, I have to work one hundred times harder, don't I?[39]

A more direct example of *jokyū* challenges to domination is a trick related by Hayashi implying both that this was but one of many "fads" and that the effect of such a challenge to the authority of the men who paid for their services was transitory:

> Around that time, it was a fad among the *jokyū* to promise a number of customers to be with them on one's day off, to gather them in one place, and then to stand them up. Resistance is fruitless but the *jokyū* must keep on resisting: "Of all of women's 'I've got to do something about this'—of all such things, there is not a worthwhile one. All one can do in front of such a fine, upstanding man is to open wide and be gobbling away. Cracking a hard-boiled egg on the edge of the table, I eat with Oyusan."

The heroine's determination to resist takes an alternative form of theatrics when she gets drunk, because she refuses to collude in erotic pretense: "I think I'll show them how I can act like a ghost. That's because no matter how honest a face he's got, the man at the liquor joint is more fleeting than draft beer." Ultimately the cafe waitress is a woman without a man, like a friend whose apartment she visits: "When I opened the closet, I breathed in the sharp smell of a woman living alone."[40]

IN CONCLUSION: THE REINVENTION OF THE *JOKYŪ*

As Gayle Rubin has noted, there are "historical periods in which sexuality is more sharply contested and more overtly politicized. In such periods, the domain of erotic life, is in effect, renegotiated."[41] Such was the case during the Japanese modern years. Hayashi Fumiko gave voice to the experiences of the impoverished *jokyū* during this era when the erotic may have been "grotesque" at times but was hardly "nonsense." Her words illuminate the history of the *jokyū* in relationship to men, at her workplace in the cafe and in the small, dimly lit *tatami* rooms of the

---

38. See Mahasweta Devi, "Draupadi," trans. and with a foreword by Gayatri Chakravorty Spivak, in Gayatri Chakravorty Spivak, *In Other Worlds: Essays in Cultural Politics* (New York and London: Methuen, 1987).

39. Hayashi, *Hōrōki*, 103.

40. Ibid., 260, 259, 265.

41. Gayle Rubin, "Thinking Sex," in Ann Snitow, Christine Stansell, and Sharon Thompson, eds., *Powers of Desire: The Politics of Sexuality* (New York: Monthly Review Press, 1983), 267.

cheap lodgings of "modern" Japan where women and men struggled toward and against each other, within structures of domination and resistance we have barely begun to know.

New social traditions within the cafe were being overtly negotiated during the "modern" era in Japanese history. The "modern girl" was largely a media construct, but the cafe waitress, free in her highly restricted way to "move up to Ginza" in response to want ads or to descend down into the back alleys where prostitutes hid behind false store-fronts, embodied capitalist tensions through the commodification of her services in ways that the geisha who was both owned and trained could never do. These traditions were displaced first by wartime regulation and scarcity, then by a postwar corporate culture that appears on the surface to continue the tradition of the *jokyū* in the form of the bar hostess on Ginza and her less glamorous sisters in myriad small bars and "snack bars." But the bar hostess of postwar Japan who displaced the Ginza *jokyū*, especially since the 1960s, is enmeshed in a web of corporate and family relationships defined by the corporation and its strict division of labor between the sphere of the salaryman, who labors at both office and hostess club, and the domestic sphere of mother and child. As Anne Allison has shown, the successor to the cafe is a homosocial site wherein the serving woman facilitates the business between men.[42] If this can be called erotic (and here heterosexual eroticism can be separated out from homoerotic and homosocial attraction), it is a very different form of erotic play from its prewar predecessor, just as the poverty, desperation, and middle-class economic roller coaster ride of the modern years—when salaryman culture was in the process of formation—are in marked contrast to the vaunted years of economic miracle in Japan which saw the rise of the postwar bar hostess.[43] Women working at other levels of the "eroticism industry" hierarchy must be studied in relation to seduction, resistance, and social incorporation. Of course the sense of an overexpanding economic miracle and its attendant night-life traditions could not remain stable, as indicated by a newspaper article of the early 1990s that explained why the sale of bean paste and rice had gone up considerably. The reason was simple: the white-collar worker was now returning home to dinner instead of going out "to play" after hours. Tradition was being reformulated just as it had been reshaped earlier, when the cafe provided a new spectacle in the modern Japanese landscape of the cities, the provinces, and the colonies.

In the cafes of modern Japan, seduction moved both ways between men and women in an era when woman's articulation of erotic desire was explicit. Male

---

42. Anne Allison, *Nightwork: Sexuality, Pleasure, and Corporate Masculinity in a Tokyo Hostess Club* (Chicago: University of Chicago Press, 1994).

43. Laura Jackson points out that the postwar bar hostess tends to choose her work over other white-collar options, whereas the *jokyū* held blue-collar jobs before turning to waitressing. See Laura Jackson, "Bar Hostesses," in Joyce Lebra, Joy Paulson, and Elizabeth Powers, eds., *Women in Changing Japan* (Stanford: Stanford University Press, 1976), 139.

customers seduced women who were forced to seduce them, especially because each interaction was a new negotiation determining payment arbitrarily fixed by the consumer. The cultural consequence for both male and female during the modern years was an awareness of the power of the erotic. The consequence of forgetting the complexity of Japanese "modern" culture in the postwar years has been its dismissal as "erotic-grotesque-nonsense." The legacy of this denial is graphically evident, for it thrives in the disembodied violent representations of dominated women in the canonized comic books and other forms of visual culture half a century later, in a society that has repressed memories of the inventions of the cafe waitress along with memories of the empire within which she lost her innocence.

PART SIX

History

FIFTEEN

Constructing Shinano

The Invention of a Neo-Traditional Region

Kären Wigen

Shinano regional identity might appear to be a classic example of an invented tradition. Once located high in the mountains of central Japan, the province of Shinano (also known as Shinshū) has not existed at all since 1871; it was not a meaningful political entity for hundreds of years before that; and it has never marked off an unambiguously united social world. On the contrary, Shinano straddled the biggest single cultural boundary in Japan, that dividing Honshū into eastern and western cultural spheres. Yet present-day residents of Nagano Prefecture—the political entity that has replaced Shinano on the modern Japanese map—regularly refer to themselves as *Shinshūjin*, or "Shinano people," and the existence of both a "Shinshū personality" and a unified Shinshū tradition is widely accepted.

The term "Shinano people" calls to mind a specific social stereotype that is presumed to have deep historical roots. Nagano natives are famous throughout Japan for their penchant for argument, their passion for education, and a stubborn, self-sufficient quality that Americans might identify as rugged individualism. Tsukada Masatomo offers a typical elaboration on these themes:

> The people of Nagano Prefecture, having been raised in this [harsh, mountainous] environment, share a common quality or character that can only be called "the Shinshū personality." This consists of an enterprising spirit that leaps toward anything novel, and an argumentative temperament drawn more to the world of ideas

The research presented here was supported in part by a Graduate School Research Award from the University of Wisconsin, Madison. The author would like to thank Gary Allinson, Laura Hein, David Howell, and Stephen Vlastos for their careful critiques of an earlier version. The analysis has also benefited from the insights of colleagues in the History Department and the Institute for Research in the Humanities at the University of Wisconsin, who raised probing questions about modernity and tradition in response to preliminary presentations of this research. Responsibility for any remaining errors of fact or judgment rests solely with the author.

than to practical concerns. Again, it is marked by single-mindedness, a spurning of compromise, and a proud, independent spirit that considers haughty isolationism to be the essence of manliness. . . . Their charismatic individualism, capacity for logic, and critical spirit, along with a keen sensitivity and creativity, idealism, and sense of mission, has predisposed them to become scholars, educators, journalists, men of religion, and artists.[1]

Although some elements of the stereotype predate the modern period, the full articulation—and internalization—of a putative Shinano identity was accomplished only in the late nineteenth century. Before the advent of modern transport, the mountains that traverse the province raised major barriers between its several basins, giving rise not to a unified Shinano sensibility but rather to a half-dozen or more distinctive subregional identities at the district level. Yet in the late 1800s, this very history of division came to be seen as a valuable component of the region's tradition, responsible for fostering a richly variegated regional culture. Shinano came to be imagined as a community whose mountainous environment was responsible for all three of its most notable features: its "independent spirit," its cultural diversity, and its belated discovery of solidarity in modern times.[2]

In this way, Nagano residents have been able to acknowledge the deep divisions in Shinano's past as well as the belated evolution of "Shinshū consciousness" in the modern era. As a result, if Shinano identity is an invented tradition, it is one whose invention is relatively transparent. What I have attempted in the following pages is therefore something other than exposing a regional myth. Rather, it is my goal here to analyze why it suddenly became important in the late nineteenth century to assert a united Shinano identity, why that identity assumed the form that it did, and what this particular case can tell us about Japanese regionalism more generally.[3]

I begin by reconstructing the contentious context in which Shinshū regionalism was first invoked: namely, a long-running battle over the geography of Nagano Prefecture. The trouble began in 1876, with the merger of two smaller prefectures (Chikuma in the south and the original Nagano in the north) into a new unit of government—one that inherited precisely the same boundaries as the former Shinano Province. Clashes over the shape of the new prefecture began immediately and continued sporadically into the postwar period. But the sharpest confrontations occurred toward the end of the nineteenth century, making the

1. Tsukada Masatomo, *Nagano-ken no rekishi* (Tokyo: Yamakawa Shuppansha, 1974), 6, 8.

2. The notion of an imagined community is from Benedict Anderson, *Imagined Communities* (London: Verso, 1991). For a fuller analysis of the rhetoric of regional identity in present-day Nagano Prefecture, see Kären Wigen, "Politics and Piety in Japanese Native-Place Studies: The Rhetoric of Solidarity in Shinano," *Positions: East Asia Cultures Critique* 4, no. 3 (1996).

3. I should emphasize that my primary concern is to understand how Shinano identity was articulated and promoted within Nagano, rather than to analyze how the region was imagined by outsiders.

1890s a definitive decade for the prefecture's survival. The integration of the sprawling prefecture was finally begun at this time through three related developments: road improvements, a pan-prefectural school system, and a campaign to instill a sense of pride and solidarity in the region. Roads and schools, of course, also contributed in tangible ways to merging Nagano into the modern Japanese state. Yet in a seeming paradox, both became central to the new claims for Shinano's uniqueness, as regional boosters discovered a legacy for each in the region's premodern past.

Having reached this point in exploring the Nagano story, the essay then turns to the national level. Here I suggest that similar political-economic forces were shaping regional formation across Japan at the time, channeling local sentiments everywhere into forms conducive to national goals. More specifically, I contend that the benign character of Meiji regionalism throughout the country was the joint product of a weak but ambitious central government on the one hand, and a canny provincial lobby on the other. Since local elites were anxious both to secure patronage and to participate in Japan's modernization, territorial conflicts erupted less between the prefecture and the state than between counties and even rival cities within the prefecture. It was ultimately for their potency as tools in these highly local contests, I argue, that neo-traditional regions like Shinano were summoned into existence.

FROM CRISIS TO CONSOLIDATION:
THE FORGING OF A PREFECTURE, 1880–1900

In the dark of night on June 16, 1876, a fire in Matsumoto City destroyed the headquarters of a short-lived entity called Chikuma Prefecture.[4] Chikuma had appeared on the Japanese administrative map only half a decade earlier, but its officials had had a busy five years, laying the groundwork for Meiji state building in a sizable portion of central Honshu's mountainous terrain. Responsible for the southern half of the late Shinano Province, and for portions of the former Hida and Mino provinces as well, Chikuma authorities had taken an early lead in implementing Tokyo's reforms. Local guidelines had been established for calculating new land values well before national formulas had been worked out, and the appointed governor, Nagayama Moriteru (a former samurai from Satsuma), had visited village after village to proselytize on behalf of public schools. Thanks in part to his exhortations, Chikuma boasted the highest rates of elementary school enrollment in the country. And Matsumoto City, which housed the Chikuma prefectural offices (and catered to the stream of petitioners and lobbyists who visited

---

4. The following account is based on Fujioka Kenjirō, *Nihon rekishi chiri sōsetsu*, vol. 7: *Kindai hen* (Tokyo: Yoshikawa Kōbunkan, 1977), 173–76; Furukawa Sadao, *Zusetsu Nagano-ken no rekishi* (*Zusetsu Nihon no rekishi*, vol. 20) (Tokyo: Kawade Shobō Shinsha, 1988), 232–35; and Nagano-ken, ed., *Nagano-kensei shi*, vol. 1 (Nagano City: Nagano-ken, 1971), 104–5, 300–307.

them throughout the year), was basking in its newfound prosperity as an important regional capital.

The mid-summer fire of 1876 brought all of this activity to an abrupt halt. A wave of consolidations was reconfiguring the map of local government at the time in any case, and rather than face the expense of rebuilding Chikuma's headquarters, the central government decided to abolish it altogether. Chikuma lands were parceled out to neighboring prefectures, the bulk of its territory going to its northern neighbor, Nagano. From headquarters in the famous temple town of the same name, Nagano officials would henceforward be responsible for an area twice the size of their original turf, subsuming the entirety of the former Shinano Province. The merger made Nagano one of the largest prefectures in Japan and skewed its political center of gravity decidedly to the north—giving inhabitants of the former Chikuma Prefecture, and particularly Matsumoto residents, a grievance that would smolder for nearly a century.

Especially as Tokyo's support for public works dried up after 1880, the new Nagano prefectural assembly became the site of heated north-south competition over coveted funds. Representatives from the seven counties (*gun*) of southern and central Nagano formed a consistent voting block to steer road improvements, bridges, waterworks, and specialized schools into the former Chikuma territory. But their frustrations were many, and when it came time to allocate money for facilities that could only be sited in the prefectural capital (including expanded government offices or a new assembly hall), Matsumoto representatives in particular dug in their heels. Convinced that their northern rivals had deliberately set the fire that destroyed Chikuma's headquarters in the first place, Liberal Party activists from Matsumoto mounted five separate attempts during the Meiji era (in 1880, 1888, 1890, 1905, and 1908) to "restore" the headquarters of the (now-merged) prefecture to their own, more centrally located town. On three other occasions (1882, 1889, and 1899), they raised the ante still higher, calling for the sundering of southern and northern Shinano into separate prefectures altogether. The result was an intense and sometimes militant struggle over the region's political geography.

This struggle reached its highest pitch around the year 1890. By 1888 the Matsumoto faction had secured a slim majority in favor of moving the government offices out of Nagano City.[5] But at a Liberal Party rally shortly before their bill came to a vote, two Matsumoto sympathizers were attacked by Nagano men, sustaining injuries severe enough to hospitalize them and derail the movement. Outraged at this incident—and at the way northern forces took advantage of the situation to maneuver their defeat—representatives from central and southern Nagano immediately began circulating a petition calling for splitting the prefec-

---

5. Technically speaking, Nagano was a town (*chō*) rather than a city (*shi*) at the time. Following English usage, however, I will refer to Nagano City when distinguishing the urban area from the prefecture of the same name.

ture (an action that required Tokyo's blessing). Signed by some 12,000 household heads, the petition was presented to the Home Ministry in 1889, along with a declaration that splitting the prefecture would advance local self-determination (*jichi*) and prosperity, not just for the seven districts of the south but for the whole region. For reasons to be detailed below, the government denied this request, throwing the struggle back into the prefectural assembly and spurring another, more desperate attempt to relocate the capital. But just as it appeared that the Matsumoto faction would prevail, a second violent incident on the eve of a crucial vote cost the movement its majority, and parliamentary maneuvers the next day doomed the measure once again.[6] This time, Matsumoto activists responded by attempting to secede from the prefecture on their own, claiming that the assembly had acted illegally and therefore had no claim on their taxes. In May 1891, in the midst of the short-lived tax-resistance movement, a restore-the-capital rally in Matsumoto brought out 15,000 supporters. By nightfall, the rally had degenerated into a riot; rocks were lobbed at the police station, police officers were assaulted, and an angry mob attacked the house of a prominent local leader who did not support the secessionist cause.

After this futile outburst, however, Nagano's north-south conflict appears to have slowly cooled off. To be sure, over the next fifty years, central and southern representatives tried half a dozen more times either to relocate the prefectural capital or to divide the prefecture.[7] Some of these later efforts, moreover, came surprisingly close to succeeding; in 1948 a majority vote in favor of cleaving the prefecture was prevented only by a clever legerdemain on the floor of the assembly hall.[8] But compared to the open street-fights of the 1890s, these later legislative skirmishes seem positively demure. In some fundamental sense, antagonism between southern and northern Nagano appears to have shifted key in mid-Meiji; while regional resentments continued to smolder, the basic legitimacy of the prefectural map was no longer called into question after 1900.

Contributing to this gradual legitimation of the prefecture were three developments of the 1890s. One was the creation of a modern transport network; another

---

6. With one of their members in the hospital, the southern faction fled Nagano City, denouncing it as unsafe for their representatives, and demanded that the prefectural assembly reconvene on neutral territory. Not only was this request denied, but during the southerners' absence, the northern representatives pushed additional legislation through even though they did not have a quorum. Despite repeated entreaties from the southern representatives to annul the actions of this legislative session, both the governor and the Home Ministry refused to intervene. For further details, see Nagano-ken, *Nagano-ken*, 304.

7. Successive attempts to relocate the prefectural capital or divide the prefecture occurred in 1908, when the prefectural headquarters burned again; in 1926, when the district offices were abolished; in 1933, in the depths of the depression; in 1948, when the prefectural buildings burned yet again; and finally as recently as 1961. See Furukawa, *Zusetsu*, 235.

8. For an explanation of this complicated legislative sleight-of-hand, see Nakamura Katsumi, *Shinshū nanboku sensō* (Saku: Ichii, 1991).

was the organization of school teachers on a prefectural level; and last but not least was a campaign to create a sense of pride in, and loyalty to, the prefecture as a whole. Together, these processes brought the prefecture's disparate subregions together in tangible ways and succeeded in creating a sense of unity (*ittaikan*) as well. A word about how this worked is in order.

The last years of the nineteenth century proved a crucial watershed for both road work and rail construction in the Japanese Alps, witnessing the inauguration of Nagano's so-called Seven Roads Project as well as three major rail lines (the Shin'etsu, Chūō Eastern, and Shinonoi lines). The Seven Roads scheme proved especially important for securing prefectural unity. This ambitious undertaking targeted all the major trunk lines through the prefecture for upgrading, to convert what were often little more than steep, narrow horse tracks into the smooth, wide, gently graded roads needed for wheeled vehicles to penetrate Nagano's intermontane basins. The benefits of roadwork on this scale for facilitating communication between Nagano's capital and its far-flung county seats require no elaboration. Less obvious, however, is the way in which, even before its completion, the Seven Roads project helped hold the prefecture together. Fearful of losing the promised funds before their own stretch of road was improved, representatives from Shimoina, Nagano's southernmost county, joined with northern forces in 1890 to oppose the petition to split the prefecture. This dissension in the southern ranks was cited by the central government in its denial of the secession request.[9]

If modern transport was the first instrument of prefectural integration, education was the second. The consolidation of a truly prefecturewide school system was begun in the 1880s on two levels. First was the founding of a centralized facility for teacher training, the Nagano Gijuku (normal school). Located in Nagano City, the Gijuku recruited from the entire prefecture, exposing many of its students to residents of distant counties for the first time in their lives. Through the formative experience of training together, village teachers were gradually transformed into members of a prefectural corps, broadening the regional consciousness of a singularly influential class of civil servants. Moreover, once in their new posts, these teachers linked arms to create local educational associations, which were brought under the auspices of a prefecturewide group (the Shinano Kyōikukai) after 1886. Each branch association took a keen scholarly interest in its own locale, investigating its history, geography, and folkways, collating archives, transcribing documents, and communicating findings with colleagues across Nagano through the *Shinano kyōikukai zasshi*.[10]

9. Nagano-ken, *Nagano-ken*, 302–3.

10. On the early development of education in Nagano, see Tsukada, *Nagano-ken*, 250–53. For suggestive evidence of how foreign one part of the prefecture could look to a teacher from another district, see Shimazaki Tōson's *Chikuma River Sketches*, trans. William E. Naff (Honolulu: University of Hawaii Press, 1991).

It is thus not surprising to learn that the teaching profession gave rise to the third force for prefectural unity, an ideological campaign to instill a sense of pride and common purpose in the people of the prefecture. The main instrument of this campaign was a carefully crafted song called "Shinano no kuni," or "The Land of Shinano." Its author, a teacher named Asai Retsu,[11] had personal attachments on both sides of the prefectural conflict that raged in the early 1890s. Born in Matsumoto, Asai had moved to Nagano City in 1886, just as the north-south rivalry was coming to a head, to become an instructor of national literature and calligraphy at the Nagano Normal School. When the Shinano Kyōikukai's Elementary Music Committee commissioned a song on the theme of prefectural unity a decade later, he rose to the challenge. In six short thematic verses, Asai managed to praise each of the prefecture's districts, working in the names of thirty-one natural features and four towering historical figures that collectively represented every part of Nagano. Published in 1899 in the association's journal, this paean to the province was promptly adopted as the official song of the Nagano Gijuku, where it was soon drilled into the memories of all alumni. As these normal-school graduates returned to their villages to teach, they in turn taught their school song to children in every corner of the prefecture. In this way, "Shinano no kuni" spread deeply and quickly into the countryside, becoming in time the textual embodiment and veritable liturgy of "Shinshū consciousness"— and a potent refrain for those dedicated to preserving the prefecture in its present form.[12]

THE BIG PICTURE:
REGIONALISM AND NATIONALISM IN MEIJI JAPAN

By any comparative standard, modern Japanese regionalism is undeniably weak. Latter-day local identities on the four main islands are mild, apolitical inflections of a shared national identity. Opposition groups have not made territorial claims; with the important exception of Okinawa, no prefecture within the modern Japanese state has become the subject of a regional autonomy movement.[13] Even

---

11. Asai's personal name is rendered Kiyoshi in some sources.

12. In a famous incident of March 19, 1948, the strains of "Shinano no kuni" resounded through the prefectural assembly as unificationists attempted to put down yet another attempt to split the prefecture. Twenty years later the song was adopted as the official anthem of Nagano Prefecture. For an exhaustive history of this song's origins and career, see Nakamura Sadenji, *Kenka 'Shinano no kuni' o kangaeru* (Nagano-shi: Shinano Kyōikukai, 1976).

13. On Okinawa, see Norma Field, *In the Realm of a Dying Emperor* (New York: Pantheon, 1990), 33–106, and Alan S. Christy, "The Making of Imperial Subjects in Okinawa," *Positions: East Asia Cultures Critique* 1, no. 3 (1993). The Ainu of Hokkaido have been forcibly assimilated and outnumbered for so long that territorial resistance has not been tenable. For an analysis of the shift in the Ainu's position from Tokugawa to Meiji, see David L. Howell, "Ainu Ethnicity and the Boundaries of the Early Modern Japanese State," *Past and Present*, no. 142 (1994).

in strictly cultural terms, the contemporary Japanese landscape could hardly be characterized as one of "tenacious diversities." Linguistic differences from one end of the archipelago to the other had been bridged before Meiji in the crucial sense that literate Japanese everywhere already shared a common written language. Religion, too, was already proto-nationalized by the end of Edo; the dominant clerical institutions had long been organized on a national level, with interpenetrating rather than mutually exclusive territorial structures.[14] In sum, for all the fuss over its local festivals and folk arts, modern Japan lacks the "vigorous particularism of the provinces" still evident across much of Europe.[15]

Yet if the weakness of Japanese regionalism is commonly remarked, it is also not the whole story. The commonalities among Japanese regions may have lent a certain passive support to Tokyo's modern projects in the Meiji era, in the sense that local sentiments did not actively impede central imperatives. But to frame the issue in this way is to miss three equally important aspects of the regional experience in modern Japan. First, by locating the origins of weak regionalism in the premodern period, this formulation underestimates the extent to which that weakness was further exacerbated during Meiji. Second, by conceptualizing the relationship between regional and national identities solely in terms of conflict (or its absence), it overlooks the possibility of complementarity: the potential for regional identities to positively facilitate national integration. Finally, by focusing solely on the region-state dynamic, it fails to analyze tensions within and between regions. The following comments represent an avowedly speculative foray into these three areas, in hopes of elucidating more fully the political context within which regional traditions like Shinano's were invented.

My starting point is the observation that, despite its weakness in comparative terms, localist sentiment posed a non-trivial threat to the Meiji regime. Having come to power in part by fanning centuries-old domainal resentments against Tokugawa rule, the Satsuma and Chōshū samurai who took power in 1868 knew well that parochial loyalties were alive in the countryside and could rise again to threaten their own nascent state. Determined to remove any obstacle that might derail their ambitions for Japan as a whole, these leaders broke radically and swiftly with feudal geography. Their principal weapon was a new administrative map: one whose units were effectively uniform both in size and in status, and whose boundaries were essentially arbitrary with respect to existing regions. The latter point is essential. To the extent that cultural and political differences *were* in-

---

14. Christianity might have heightened a sense of regional distinctiveness in Kyushu had it not been persecuted so effectively in the 1600s. If Kyushu had become a predominantly Christian realm, might its people have suffered routine discrimination as the Irish have in Great Britain—and responded with a similarly territorial rebellion?

15. Fernand Braudel, *The Identity of France*, vol. 1: *History and Environment*, trans. Sian Reynolds (New York: Harper and Row, 1988), 67, 78. In the original, both phrases ("tenacious diversities" and "vigorous particularism") refer to France.

scribed on the early modern landscape, the sentiments they might have called forth were assaulted by the spatial structures of Meiji government. Like the *départements* of the French revolutionaries,[16] Meiji prefectures intentionally violated the previous regime's political geography. While the new units might make use of ancient provincial boundaries (which were derelict anyway), they were always given new names to underscore the break with the past.[17] The result was a political map without historical content, intended to render prefectures blank slates that could more easily be inscribed with the modern state's priorities.

I would argue that this severing of political geography from history was the essential launching point for the invention of modern Japan's "traditional" regions. From Tokyo's point of view, the defensive advantages of breaking up the old objects of local loyalty—or alternatively, of piecing them together into new combinations—was clear. By disrupting the social networks of the former domains, the nation's leaders both simplified the chain of command and made it difficult for opposition to take a territorial form. Because prefectures had no history, opponents of the regime would find in them no ready-made traditions to rally around. Any threat of insubordination was further undermined by the appointment of nonnative governors, whose loyalties lay clearly with the new rulers (many, like the first governor of Chikuma, being drawn from Satsuma and Chōshū). These measures suggest that the relative shallowness of inherited regional differences alone was seen as insufficient for securing the national interest.

But if preventing obstructionist localism was important, it was also merely a beginning. The Meiji regime's crash program for arming and industrializing the nation called for painful sacrifices from the countryside—sacrifices that would be forthcoming only if provincial people identified strongly with the state. And since the effective representative of the state in most instances was local rather than central government, it was essential to begin cultivating loyalty toward the new administrative units. My second point, then, is that diluting domain-based regionalism was not enough. The scope of Tokyo's ambitions set up a dual challenge: not only to defuse inherited identities, but also to reinvent them in a nationalist idiom. An articulation of new loyalties would have to accompany the liquidation of the old.

The political realities that compelled this move are limned by Carol Gluck in *Japan's Modern Myths*:

---

16. On French revolutionary geography, see Braudel, *Identity of France*, 80–81, and J. W. Konvitz, "The Nation-State, Paris, and Cartography in Eighteenth- and Nineteenth-Century France," *Journal of Historical Geography* 16, no. 1 (1990).

17. See, for instance, Fujioka, *Nihon rekishi* 7:176. The new regime evidently felt no need to borrow the prestige of the ancient court by preserving its territorial units, as Philip Brown suggests that the Bakufu did; see Brown, "The Shogun's New Clothes: Image, 'Reality,' and Political Authority of the Tokugawa Bakufu" (paper presented at the Washington and Southeast Region Japan Seminar, American University, April 24, 1992), 15.

Although Japan had virtually no independent regional cultures within its borders, the homogeneity of which we hear so much worked no miracles on the nationalization of sentiment. Even on an institutional level, it is possible to argue that Japan had given a greater appearance of centralization since the 1870s than it in fact possessed. That is, the center had charged the localities with a range of national responsibilities, from electing assemblies and collecting taxes to providing police and teachers and building schools. Since the government decreed, but seldom paid for, many of these requisites of state, seventy to eighty percent of local budgets was devoted to executing national tasks on the local level. That the localities did so may have been one of the most important elements in Japan's nineteenth-century transformation, more important perhaps than the government's measures, which without local compliance would have meant very little indeed.[18]

If a poorly equipped central government needed localities to do its daily work, then local loyalties could not simply be destroyed. On the contrary, identification with these intermediate bodies would have to be encouraged. But it would also have to be managed. In the ideal scenario, contributing to the nation's welfare would somehow become a logical extension of membership in the local community.

In the case of Nagano, this ideal was realized by promoting a version of regional pride that focused on precisely those traits (and traditions) that furthered national goals. Preeminent here was the trinity of roads, schools, and industry. Roads and schools were the main object of prefectural activism—and local sacrifice—in the 1870s and 1880s; the silk industry was a target of massive public and private enterprise throughout the period. Not coincidentally, all three of these modern projects had a counterpart in the Shinano tradition that began to be touted at the turn of the century. In the realm of transport, boosters could point to Shinano's important position in the premodern turnpike network, cultivating pride in the Tōsandō of the classical era as well as the Nakasendō of Edo. (The province's private packhorse network, which later joined the roster of celebrated transport traditions, could be read simultaneously as testimony to an entrepreneurial bent.) Proof of the region's proclivity for education was found in its high concentration of temple schools (terakoya), poetry circles, and nativist study groups. And in the drive to industrialize, attention could be drawn to Shinano's proto-industrial crafts: cotton spinning, paper making, the production of fine lacquerware, and silk reeling itself. All of these legacies could usefully be invoked in the name of modernization.

It may seem paradoxical that the inventors of Shinano identity seized on transport, education, and industrialization: the very processes by which local identities are usually said to be undermined.[19] Indisputably, modern roads, schools, and fac-

---

18. Carol Gluck, *Japan's Modern Myths: Ideology in the Late Meiji Period* (Princeton: Princeton University Press, 1985), 37–38.

19. The classic presentation of this thesis is Eugen Weber's *Peasants into Frenchmen: The Modernization of Rural France, 1870–1914* (Stanford: Stanford University Press, 1976); see esp. chaps. 12 (on roads and industry) and 18 (on schools as agents of national unification).

tories incorporated the people of central Honshu into the nation as never before, eroding dialects and standardizing customs over the long run. But this was also precisely why they worked as instruments of prefectural loyalty at the time, for in the late nineteenth century, most provincial Japanese demonstrably wanted to be connected to the nation and the world.[20] From the perspective of Nagano residents, improved roads, mass education, and industry were the most promising vehicles for enticing national resources into the region—and for bringing the region, in turn, into modernity. Their related role in overcoming the prefecture's fragmentation seems only to have increased the incentive to trace a lineage for each back to the premodern period.

This interaction between local desires and national imperatives was clearly an important determinant of Meiji neo-regionalism. But the invention of Shinano can only be partially understood in terms of center-local relations. In addition, prefectural identities were shaped by three distinct social relationships at lower levels of the spatial hierarchy. The first of these was rivalry between prefectures, a pervasive phenomenon that has been analyzed as an unwanted but inevitable byproduct of the "responsive dependency" elicited by the Meiji state.[21] A second local determinant of regional identities may be located in competition between counties. Tensions between Nagano's districts contributed in crucial ways to the calls for a pan-Shinano identity. Against a larger backdrop of interprefectural rivalry, the need to surmount competition at the district or county level clearly provided another important context in which Nagano politicians found the notion of "Shinano" a useful rhetorical tool. Finally, one must not overlook class conflicts, which regional rhetoric conveniently served to mask. As William Kelly astutely points out, in modern Japan "both family and region are significant not only for what they stand for and reveal, but also for what they stand in front of (or in place of) and thus conceal—the even more striking disparities of gender and class."[22]

What is crucial to understand here is the interplay between traditional county identities and the specific interests of dominant urban elites. As mentioned above, district loyalties were a natural outgrowth of Nagano's historical geography. Like

<hr>

20. The high enrollment rates in the prefecture's new public schools might be cited as evidence of this desire. One wonders whether the long experience of wintertime *dekasegi* migration to Edo might have whetted Nagano residents' appetite for education. As Weber points out, "People went to school not because school was offered or imposed, but because it was useful. . . . [But] it needed personal experience to persuade people of the usefulness of education. Certain migrants had learned this, and we have seen how they and their children recognized at an early date 'the value of instruction and the profit one can derive from it in the great centers.'" Weber, *Peasants into Frenchmen*, 303, 327.

21. Gary Allinson, *Japanese Urbanism: Industry and Politics in Kariya, 1872–1972* (Berkeley and Los Angeles: University of California Press, 1975); see also Gluck, *Japan's Modern Myths*, 191–93.

22. William W. Kelly, "Anatomy of a Swing: Oh Sadaharu and the Spirit of Japanese Baseball" (unpublished manuscript). On the deployment of regional rhetoric in southern Nagano as a cover for class interests, see Kären Wigen, *The Making of a Japanese Periphery, 1750–1920* (Berkeley and Los Angeles: University of California Press, 1995), chap. 6.

the characters in Shimazaki Tōson's *Before the Dawn*, early Meiji men and women throughout the prefecture identified strongly with the valleys and basins (*tani, taira, kobonchi*) in which their ancestors had lived out their lives.[23] Since the contours of these home districts corresponded closely to the county boundaries of the Meiji period, the *gun* emerged as potent units of affiliation in the new regime. The running battle between southern and northern forces in the Nagano prefectural assembly took shape as a series of contests between blocks of counties, as we have seen. Even in their role as leaders of the south-central or north-east faction, the combatants were primarily identified as representatives of one or another *gun*.

But while home-district loyalties help to make sense of the usual voting blocks in the prefectural assembly, they cannot account for the uneven pattern of support for moving the prefectural capital to Matsumoto—an agenda that many southern Nagano residents viewed with contempt.[24] To understand this contempt, one must look within counties to the urban professionals who dominated county politics. For *gun*, like prefectures, were not undifferentiated territorial blocks but spatial networks of power, whose circuits (roads and other communication corridors) channeled goods, people, and information through a central distribution point (the county seat or prefectural headquarters).[25] All of Nagano's major towns had a piece of this action, but the prefectural capital was clearly the one site on the landscape where wealth and power would be most concentrated.[26] Accordingly, while regional strife within Nagano may have played itself out as a contest between blocks of *gun*, the strongest sentiment on both sides came from local notables in the cities of Matsumoto and Nagano, rival claimants for the prefectural headquarters. The struggle over the location of the prefectural capital, like the struggle over boundaries, ultimately boiled down to a contest for the perks of centrality: government offices, special schools, road improvements, and other investments that would funnel prosperity to and through the chosen site.

The official history of Nagano prefectural government, *Nagano-ken sei shi*, shows a partial recognition of the ways in which regional rhetoric sometimes served to

23. Shimazaki Tōson, *Before the Dawn*, trans. William Naff (Honolulu: University of Hawaii Press, 1987). Naff notes that Tōson's people were "rooted in their home districts in a way that is almost beyond the reach of imagination a century later." William Naff, "Shimazaki Tōson's *Before the Dawn:* Historical Fiction as History and as Literature," in James W. White, Michio Umegaki, and Thomas R. H. Havens, eds., *The Ambivalence of Nationalism: Modern Japan Between East and West* (Lanham and New York: University Press of America, 1990), 105.

24. Shimoina Chiiki Shi Kenkyūkai, ed., *Shimoina no hyakunen* (Nagano-shi: Shimoina Chiiki Shi Kenkyūkai, 1982), 36.

25. The concept of societies as composed of sociospatial networks of power is elaborated in the introduction to Michael Mann, *The Sources of Social Power*, vol. 1: *A History of Power from the Beginning to* A.D. *1750* (Cambridge: Cambridge University Press, 1986).

26. The crucial infrastructure included roads, railroads, and telegraphs, of course, but also linked institutions like schools, libraries, and newspaper and postal routes. The latter constituted networks through which ideas were disseminated in print, or what Michael Mann calls "circuits of discursive literacy." *The Sources of Social Power*, vol. 2, *The Rise of Classes and Nation-States, 1760–1914* (Cambridge: Cambridge University Press, 1993), 228–29.

mask material interests. The authors of this weighty, two-volume work interrupt their narrative twice to scold Matsumoto's partisans, questioning the latter's claim that local self-determination (*jichi*) required moving the prefectural capital to the center of the prefecture. Such lofty rhetoric was merely a cynical cover, these historians claim, for a naked attempt to further the economic interests of Matsumoto.[27] Perhaps so; but was Matsumoto the only party to this game? One could well argue that *all* projects advocated in the name of the region—and indeed, every decision made by the prefectural government—had implications for the relative prosperity of one settlement (and its dominant class) over another. As Braudel bluntly points out in regard to early modern Europe, "the town stood, above all, for domination, and what matters most when we try to define or rank it, is its capacity to command and the area it commanded."[28]

Given the stakes involved, perhaps the real question is not why Nagano's geography was so hotly contested, but why (or indeed whether) similar battles did not erupt more often in the Meiji landscape. Prefectures across Japan faced essentially the same internal strains; all were charged with raising and allocating public moneys, a function that could not but mire them in intraregional controversy. Moreover, as new geographical entities, all prefectures were visibly arbitrary pieces of terrain; for at least a generation, their boundaries had no real aura of natural or historical legitimacy. The only external force working to galvanize their constituents was the need to present a united front when going before the center in rivalry with other prefectures. But as the Tokyo trough began to dry up in the 1880s, that particular principle of coherence must have correspondingly weakened. Under Matsukata's retrenchment policies, residents of overlooked localities might well question the benefits of prefectural belonging. What arguments could the pro-unity forces fall back on then? Why did prefectures hang together as well as they did?

If Nagano is any indication, the ultimate answer is that regional rhetoric was backed up by ample patronage. To be sure, other kinds of interventions proved crucial on occasion. Northern Nagano politicians more than once resorted to creative (if not flatly illegal) legislative maneuvering. They also received passive but helpful support from the Home Ministry at times. But the glue that held Nagano together over the long run was pork. In 1882 the appointed prefectural governor managed to quell the first secessionist movement by bribing its leaders with plum appointments as county heads (*gunchō*).[29] Seven years later, leaders in the southern county of Shimoina sided with northern unificationists because they had been promised road funds.[30] And over the succeeding decades, Nagano representatives bought the allegiance of their Matsumoto counterparts by dividing the spoils of the public trough almost evenly between the two cities.

27. Nagano-ken, *Nagano-ken*, 301, 307.
28. Braudel, *Identity of France*, 181.
29. Shimoina Chiiki Shi Kenkyūkai, *Shimoina*, 36.
30. Nagano-ken, *Nagano-ken*, 302.

This succession of horse-trades serves as an important reminder that territorial identities are never purely rhetorical. Exhortations toward identification with the nation or the region are most compelling when they can be backed up with material rewards.[31] Conversely, secessionist sentiment is difficult to sustain in the absence of consistently unfair treatment by those in power. One can do no better than to quote the wistful words of a French Catalan landowner, answering a Spaniard's query about why Catalan nationalism had not spread to his district:

> You all, you can be catalanistes! Your government in Madrid treats you very badly. We cannot be [catalanistes] since our government in Paris treats us very well. We ask for a road, they build it right away. We want a telegraph, they put one in. We ask for a school, they give us one. We cannot be catalanistes, but you all, you can be catalanistes.[32]

In trouble-spots like Matsumoto, I would suggest, the yoking of regionalist sentiment to the new administrative geography of Meiji Japan was accomplished through a similarly material matrix. Like the French state, the Japanese prefecture could if need be "create the ties of loyalty and identity instrumentally, by fulfilling the material needs of its citizens."[33]

In sum, I would argue that regional affiliations played a positive role in the creation of the modern Japanese state. As pressing as Japan's national interests must have seemed in the later nineteenth century, Meiji nationalists could not simply eradicate inherited localisms; rather, they had to reshape and make use of them. There was no other way, for like Germany in the same period, Japan began its modern life as a "nation of provincials."[34] In the process of national formation, however, a crowded field of inherited territorialities had to be narrowed down and made congruent with the new political hierarchy. I have further argued that this process was driven not solely from above but by a potent confluence of interests at the sub- and supra-prefectural levels. On the one hand, an ambitious central regime—having done its best to obliterate the last vestiges of feudal loyalties from the landscape—strove to foster positive identification with the regional representatives of the state, for local government alone could mobilize the resources it needed for modernization. On the other hand, elites in the new centers of local government found economic incentives of their own for rousing the public's pride in the prefecture. It was ultimately this convergence of local and national interests that summoned neotraditional regions like Shinano into existence in turn-of-the-century Japan.

31. On the importance of patronage as an agent of French unification—and on the political context in which it arose—see Weber, *Peasants into Frenchmen*, 209–10, 220.

32. Joaquim Cases Cabró, *Catalunya françesca* (Barcelona, 1934), 30. Quoted in Peter Sahlins, *Boundaries: The Making of France and Spain in the Pyrenees* (Berkeley and Los Angeles: University of California Press, 1989), 291.

33. Sahlins, *Boundaries*, 291.

34. Celia Applegate, *A Nation of Provincials: The German Idea of Heimat* (Berkeley and Los Angeles: University of California Press, 1990).

SIXTEEN

"Doubly Cruel"

Marxism and the Presence of the Past in Japanese Capitalism

Andrew E. Barshay

The subject of this essay is the relation between the process of the invention of tradition and the development of capitalism in Japan, or better, the development of capitalism in Japan as a case of the invention of tradition. I begin with the observation that Japan has developed a *tradition of noncapitalist capitalism*, a capitalism in which non- or precapitalist values and practices are held to remain salient, indeed decisive in shaping institutional as well as personal behavior in the economic sphere. This much, of course, has been said for decades by critics and apologists alike, almost to the point of *tedium ideologicum*. Specifically, I argue that Japanese Marxists, especially those of the Comintern-associated Kōza-ha or "Lectures Faction,"[1] played a crucial role in defining the contours of a Japanese-*type* capitalism. While accepting the well-established critique of capitalism that arraigned it for justifying immorality and exploitation in the name of individual gain, they went beyond this critique to develop a theoretical analysis of Japan's "version." The exploitative mechanisms of Japanese capitalism, they insisted, combined those of the market with a persistent semi-feudalism in the social relations of production; indeed such relations were the *foundation* of "Japanese-type" capitalism. This framework of uneven development and backwardness has been extremely tenacious in Japanese social science.

Despite these analytical achievements, the Kōza-ha perspective, as is often pointed out, ignored issues of ideology, and therefore failed to grasp the real dynamic of Japanese capitalism, indeed of Japan's modernization as a whole. This lay in the invented—and *strategic*—character of the process through which "tradition," or the past, entered the present: via the state's systematic attempt to mobilize

---

1. See below for a discussion of the theoretical positions of the Kōza [lectures] and Rōnō [worker-farmer] schools of Japanese Marxist historiography.

it in its "virtual" war for survival as an imperial power. Kōza-ha Marxism revealed the structural presence of the past, but only at the cost of effacing *past-consciousness*, the ideological medium through which that structural presence took on its meaning. Yet it may well be wondered whether a model of capitalism without ideology can grasp capitalism at all.

THE PRESENCE OF THE PAST IN JAPANESE CAPITALISM

At the risk of perpetuating the *tedium ideologicum* mentioned above, let me fill out briefly the notion of noncapitalist capitalism as it was first developed in the 1890s, and as it stands today. In a sense, of course, all capitalism is self-denying at some level: the "invisible hand" both explains the social productiveness of self-interest and provides a secular theodicy of exploitation. The capitalist unconscious is *everywhere* a condition of the system's success, so that the invisibility of the system, rather than being a problem, is in fact a sign of ideological normalcy. The self-image of original capitalism was that of a force akin to "the Deity working its will to direct human action into socially beneficial paths that men could not discover for themselves."[2] In Japan the disinclination to speak of "capitalism" as a defining element in national identity has a specific valence. There, the invisible hand seems to cut little or no moral ice, either at the individual or collective level. To be sure, some studies of Tokugawa economy and society hint at notions of the social benefits of individual (= family) "selfishness," or the equation by merchant financiers of virtue with rationally calculated profit. But it seems doubtful that these ideas ever met unqualified social acceptance, before or after 1868.[3] Rather, "capitalist" ideology has been understood in Japan as a license for the assertion of self-interest; self-interest has in turn been regarded as the foundation of Western civil society—"a system of desires," as Hegel put it. The ideological "operating system," so to speak, of Japanese capitalism, is different: it denies the productivity of self-interest or the necessity of any link between "civil society" and capitalism. One scholar writes: "Contemporary Japanese capitalism has developed . . . through the association of the supermodern with the premodern, and not with the modern or civil. It is precisely the survival of premodernity itself that has permitted such a rapid development of super modernity in Japan. From which one may conclude, paradoxical though it may seem, that in Japan capitalism has developed thanks to the weakness of civil society."[4]

In place of the social fractiousness and calculated interpersonal coldness of "civil society," and therefore of ideological appeals to the "invisible hand," expla-

---

2. Robert Heilbroner, *The Nature and Logic of Capitalism* (New York: Norton, 1985), 17.

3. See Thomas C. Smith, *Native Sources of Japanese Industrialization* (Berkeley and Los Angeles: University of California Press, 1988), and Tetsuo Najita, *Visions of Virtue: The Kaitokudō Merchant Academy in Tokugawa Japan* (Chicago: University of Chicago Press, 1987).

4. Toshio Yamada, "Les tendances du marxisme japonais contemporain," *Actuel Marx*, no. 2 (1987; special issue: *Le marxisme au Japon*): 40. Yamada's essay summarizes the views of Uchida Yoshihiko.

nations of Japan's noncapitalist capitalism look to a collectivist dynamism that derives from Tokugawa "prehistory," one associated with the *ie*, or household, and village, and with familial corporatism in agricultural, artisanal, and commercial enterprises that is the supposed origin—along with *bushidō* redux—of today's corporate ethos of group competitiveness, individual self-sacrifice, and loyalty to the firm. Not surprisingly, "many Japanese are not aware of the fact that Japan is a capitalist country": as long as capitalism is associated with the selfishly motivated pursuit of profit, and civil society regarded as a system committed to underwriting such selfishness, how could Japan possibly be capitalist?[5] Indeed, to discuss capitalism hinted (and continues to hint) at disapproval; capitalism should be invisible. Growth, on the other hand, was unambiguously good.

If we may take the issue of capitalism beyond the current *habitus* of Japanese firms and project it along a historical plane at the national level, what we see is not "the business of Japan is business," but "the business of business is Japan": a Listian notion of economy as a national project, one aspect of which was the creation of economic instruments that operate in a "capitalist" mode.[6] In Japan's modern history, this project is most closely associated with the Meiji-era slogan of "Rich Country, Strong Army" (*fukoku kyōhei*), albeit with a later admixture of *Sozialpolitik*.

Slogan, yes, but also a project realized. In terms of the development of productive forces that became the (self-imposed) yardstick for measuring progress along the road to Western-style modernity, Japan on the eve of the Meiji Restoration was a woefully backward place. This backwardness, and the military and economic vulnerability to the Great Powers that came with it, was a matter of common-sense observation. It was also intellectually and psychologically oppressive, and had somehow to be overcome. Here was a political and "values" problem of the first order. Capitalism as a system, however, was never seen as a goal to be attained, nor was it a prescription ever offered as such by the intellectual agents of the West to Japan. Even if it had been, could the potent but centrifugally tending values of the invisible hand be trusted to direct popular energies to the manifestly political goals of winning Western "respect" and building a strong and independent state? A liberal such as Fukuzawa Yukichi might say yes; but his high profile notwithstanding, the goals of industry and empire were understood to require the state to weld Japan's best and brightest into a self-described moral force. By the beginning of the twentieth century, this most visible hand had done its work: Japan could boast of a dedicated bureaucracy with a fearsome esprit de corps, emergent heavy industry, and an empire.

---

5. That is, while the ideologues of "original" capitalism denied that it was exploitative, Japanese thinkers admitted that it was but denied that Japan was "really" capitalist. The quotation comes from a statement in graduate seminar by a Tokyo University graduate and Ph.D. student (at the University of California, Berkeley) in Central European history.

6. I owe these formulations to William Johnston, Wesleyan University.

"Overcoming backwardness," then, was the national project of Japan, enunci-
ated in the Charter Oath, captured in the "Rich Country, Strong Army" imperative, and realized, to the amazement and discomfort of the West, by late Meiji.
Accompanying these organizational triumphs, and integral to them was the "neo-
traditional" turn of that era. "The past" returned, both to validate the present—
modernity placed under the discipline of tradition—and to constrain the future.
The timing of this return can hardly have been fortuitous. The institutional completion of the modern order had generated real social traumas, and real anxieties,
in Japan. For elites, as for masses, appeal to a rearticulated tradition (albeit differently defined) was one response to the modern (dis)order. For present purposes,
the version advanced in 1909 by Itō Hirobumi is illuminating, in the sense that he
points both to the hoped-for stabilizing effects, and to the political risks, of the traditionalizing strategy.

Itō begins with a critical evocation of the "feudal legacy" of the Tokugawa period. Prior, perhaps, even to feudalism, Japan was "homogeneous in race, language, religion, and sentiments"; and then, long seclusion and "the centuries-long
traditions and inertia of the feudal system" did their work. Under the Tokugawa,
"family and quasi-family ties permeated and formed the essence of every social
organization . . . with such moral and religious tenets as laid *undue stress* on duties
of fraternal aid and mutual succor." We had, Itō declares, "unconsciously become
a vast village community where cold intellect and calculation of public events
were always restrained and even often hindered by warm emotions between man
and man." This legacy, for Itō, brought with it both strengths and dangers. In a
village community, he observes, "feelings and emotions hold a higher place than
intellect, free discussion is apt to be smothered," and the "attainment and trans-
ference of power" tends to become "a family question of a powerful oligarchy."
His prescription: Japan's elite should strive not to eliminate completely, but to manipulate, feudal tendencies. On the one hand, he recognizes, "Passions and emotions have to be stopped for the sake of cool calculations of national welfare, and
even the best of friends have often to be sacrificed if the best abilities and highest
intellects are to guide the helm." On the other, the "feudal" legacy, if handled correctly, may represent an enormous, unrepeatable historical opportunity. "In industry," Itō notes, "in spite of the recent enormous development of manufactures
in our country, our laborers have *not yet* degenerated into spiritless machines and
toiling beasts. There *still survives* the bond of patron and *protégé* between them and
the capitalist employers. It is this moral and emotional factor which will, in the future, form a healthy barrier against the threatening advance of socialistic ideas."[7]

Successful because village-type social hierarchy could be brought to bear in
effecting labor discipline and constraining political conflict between tenants,

7. Hirobumi Itō, "Some Reminiscences of the Grant of the New Constitution," in Shigenobu
Ōkuma, ed., *Fifty Years of New Japan* (New York: Dutton, 1909), 1:128–29.

smallholders, and workers on the one hand and large landlords and employers on the other; the reliance on *junpū bizoku* (warm manners and beautiful customs) in fact constituted a wager on backwardness and its sustaining values. The wager held that the rapid development of heavy industry, with its immense requirements of capital and labor, could be achieved initially on the basis of surpluses extracted from agriculture and rural-based industry and obedient workers. The same extractive process would also support the establishment of the empire, which, along with heavy industry itself, would eventually begin, at least psychologically, to repay the effort. In this way, the security, independence, and historical standing of Japan and the Japanese would be assured.

Such, at least, was the wager. But did it pay off? Was the traditionalizing strategy successful? The historiography of the abolition of backwardness—of Japan's capitalist development—is divided on this point. Itō's qualified optimism was negated by the Kōza-ha assault on backwardness, which in turn defined a historiographical tradition of its own that has extended far beyond Marxist circles. From this point of view, the Meiji achievement of a "rich country and strong army," far from overcoming backwardness, actually ramified it. Evoking the "three differences"—between city and country, industry and agriculture, brain work and manual work—that were the target of rage in China's Cultural Revolution, the economist Michio Morishima observes: "The policies adopted by the Japanese government after the Meiji Revolution . . . [were] pushed ahead so as to make ever greater the . . . 'three differences.' "[8] That is, decades-long landlord dominance, smallholder weakness, and widespread—if not universal—tenant penury made for debilitating inefficiency and class resentment, but they were necessary elements of a "Japanese-type" capitalism that used backwardness in one area to overcome it in another. T. C. Smith saw things similarly a generation ago: "The peasant had to be relentlessly exploited for the modernization of the nonagricultural sector of the economy. Since this condemned the peasant to poverty and backwardness, it did much to produce the profound gulf between urban and rural worlds that is so obvious and characteristic a feature of modern Japan."[9] It is beyond my purpose here to discuss how, when, and to what extent this gulf was redressed.[10] But I would emphasize, first, that the wager on backwardness *was* made, and second, that the relation between agriculture and modern industry,

8. Michio Morishima, *Why Has Japan "Succeeded"?* (Cambridge: Cambridge University Press, 1982), 199–200.

9. Thomas C. Smith, *Political Change and Industrial Development in Japan: Government Enterprise, 1868–1880* (Stanford: Stanford University Press, 1965), 85.

10. Nor do I have the space to address recent scholarship by Richard Smethurst and Penelope Francks that has stressed the internal differentiation of the tenant population and the economic benefits of tenancy in certain circumstances. The issue of tenancy remains controversial, however; witness the extended critique of Smethurst by Nishida Yoshiaki (and Smethurst's countercritique) in *Journal of Japanese Studies* 15, no. 2 (Summer 1989).

and between industrial strata themselves, implied in that wager *did* largely define Japan's particularistic mode of development, perhaps through the 1960s.

I do not mean to suggest that liberalism—in both an economic and a political sense—played no significant role in the development of Japanese capitalism. Of course it did. But it did so, over the long run, as an *adjunct* to a particularist ideology in which capitalism served as an *invisible* means to the end of overcoming the country's backwardness. No one "saw" it, in part because it was morally dubious, if not ugly. And in part because appeals to the invisible hand were difficult or impossible to disengage from liberal political notions that did not sit well with Meiji's oligarchic elites. Nevertheless, to some degree all Japanese experienced the effects of capitalism. Some were thrilled by it, seeing in its ceaseless activity part of a "struggle for existence"—national existence—that was thought desirable to wage.[11] Others, such as the youthful Kawakami Hajime, saw it as a moral disaster. But it took the combined effects of the Russian Revolution and the post–World War I bust to bring the Marxist advocates of "scientific socialism" to the forefront of social science and criticism: not until then did anyone *theorize* Japanese capitalism in its specificity.

Thus far we have spoken of a "commonsensical," pre-theoretical, but in a political sense highly charged project of "overcoming backwardness." Marxists, whether of the "feudalist" or "bourgeois" (Kōza or Rōnō) schools, took that project as a central object of their critique but did not abandon the goal: they sought rather to revolutionize both the means of overcoming backwardness and the goal itself. But when Japanese Marxists looked at Japan's capitalism, what did they see?

YAMADA MORITARŌ AND THE *ANALYSIS OF JAPANESE CAPITALISM*

> *Its militaristic, semi-feudal character configured the prototype of Japanese capitalism, one formed by superimposing, on the "barbarous cruelty of . . . serfdom," the "civilized horrors of over-work."*
>
> YAMADA MORITARŌ

As a vehicle of inquiry into this question I have chosen Yamada Moritarō's 1934 *Nihon shihonshugi bunseki* (Analysis of Japanese capitalism; hereafter rendered as *Analysis*).[12] Widely regarded as the highest theoretical achievement of prewar Kōza-ha Marxism, Yamada's text was influential far beyond Marxist circles and remained a point of departure for discussions of Japanese capitalism well into the postwar period. Although met with forceful criticisms from the moment of its first

---

11. See Akira Nagazumi, "The Diffusion of the Idea of Social Darwinism in East and Southeast Asia," *Historia Scientiarum* 24 (1983).

12. Yamada Moritarō, *Nihon shihonshugi bunseki* (Tokyo: Iwanami Shoten, 1934), hereafter *Bunseki*; the quotation in the epigraph is drawn from *Yamada Moritarō chosakushū* (Tokyo: Iwanami Shoten, 1983), 2:150, hereafter *YMCS*. The internal quotes in the epigraph are from *Capital*, vol. 1, chap. 10, sec. 2 (Penguin/NLB ed., p. 345; Iwanami Bunko ed., 2:100–101).

appearance, no other text in the history of Japanese social science (or Japanese capitalism) came as close as Yamada's to exposing the specificities of industrial capitalism in Japan in its prewar form, to defining, as he put it, Japanese capitalism as a *type* among types, including British, French, German, Russian, and American variants. This typicality, as the citation from the *Analysis* given above suggests, has to do with the powerful presence of the past in shaping the social relations, and therefore (for a Marxist) the consciousness, of Japanese living under this particular regime of capital. Whether despite or because of its method of analysis and theoretical point of departure—an issue I address in the final section of this essay—Yamada's case for the past-in-the-present as the salient feature of Japanese capitalism was not successfully refuted on theoretical or empirical grounds by Marxist critics.[13]

It *was* refuted, as far as its prognostications are concerned, by developments within capitalism itself. Contrary to Yamada's expectations, Japanese capitalism survived the devastation of the country's agrarian (textile)-based export sector after 1929. Against a backdrop of stepped-up state planning, a campaign of light industrial exports provided capital for intensified heavy industrialization, which was in turn spurred on by and channeled into military expenditure and continental expansion. Clearly Yamada had missed something; he made no mention of these forces, already at work in the industrial economy, and this not so much by oversight as by systematic exclusion from analysis. Instead he continued to emphasize, correctly enough, the enormous burden of agrarian tenancy and, implicitly, the gap between the industrial strata that made up Japan's "dual structure." The specificity and ineradicable weakness of Japanese capitalism lay, for Yamada, in the indispensability of "semi-feudal" social relations to its entire process of development, and their depressing, distortive effects on that development. Yamada was concerned, first and last, with inherited backwardness. The presence of the past, as embodied in specific social relations and institutions, was his problem.

Yamada's Project in Context

Along with Hirano Yoshitarō's *Nihon shihonshugi shakai no kikō* (1934), Yamada's *Analysis* is generally recognized as the foremost product of its enunciative moment: the debate among Japanese Marxists, beginning in the late 1920s, over the mode of capitalist development in Japan. As is well known, the controversies between the Comintern-associated Kōza (Lectures) and dissident Rōnō (Worker-Farmer) factions developed respectively along particularist/universalist lines. Adherents of the Kōza-ha focused their analyses on the entrenched and powerful "feudal" forces that controlled the absolutist imperial state. Japanese capitalism was "special," a kind of hybrid; bourgeois political institutions were immature or

13. See Yamazaki Ryūzō, "*Nihon shihonshugi bunseki* no hōhō to sono hihanshi," in Yamazaki, *Kindai Nihon keizaishi no kihon mondai* (Kyoto: Mineruva Shobō, 1989), 173, 225–31.

malformed, and a retrograde consciousness persisted among the peasantry. There was backwardness everywhere. The political task at hand, therefore, was to complete the democratic revolution as the necessary first step in a two-stage drive toward socialism. The Rōnō faction, in dissent, argued that with the Meiji Restoration, Japan had achieved its bourgeois revolution. The task of the present, therefore, lay in making the single-stage leap to socialism; "vestiges" of feudalism were incidental and would be swept away as a matter of course. Rōnō faction analyses tended to be economistic in character, and though lacking a cultural theory per se, tended generally to stress the universal character of Japan as one of a number of imperialist finance capitalisms; domestically, Japan was becoming a commoditized "bourgeois society."

Yamada's perspective, as should already be clear, was unambiguously particularist. What distinguished his approach from more narrative-centered work, by Noro Eitarō or Hattori Shisō for example, was its concern to analyze Japan's capitalist development within an explicit and rigorously elaborated framework of Marxian economic theory. As we shall see, he not only adopted a broad materialist narrative but abstracted it, raised (or reduced) it to a mechanistic, equilibrium-oriented analysis of components and functions within a "type." But it is clear that as with Noro, the perspective of *backwardness and its abolition* was "ground into the lenses" with which Yamada looked at Japan.[14]

Yamada carried out this task under highly unfavorable conditions that profoundly colored his perspective. Japan was in the midst of the world depression; the specter of class conflict had raised elite fears of a bolshevizing revolution promoted by the external agency of the USSR and the Comintern. To the considerable extent that Comintern theses set the keynote for Japanese Marxist attempts to explicate the structure and tendencies of capitalism, Yamada was engaged in highly political work. This would have made his task difficult enough had those theses been self-consistent. But they were not. Comintern policy toward Japan was tied to the vagaries of its China strategy—not an area of notable success. The 1927 and 1932 Theses resemble each other more than they do the 1931 Draft Political Theses; their existence at all is hardly comprehensible without considering the revolutionary situation in China, particularly the shifts from the rural-oriented efforts of the Autumn Harvest and other uprisings of 1927–29 to the attempt at urban insurrection under the Li Lisan line, then back to a rural-centered approach after 1931. The Comintern's Japan policy replicated these shifts in miniature. Common to them both is the contradiction between the inviolable, professedly scientific authority of the Theses and the fractiousness of the Comintern as an organization.[15] For those

14. The quote is from Heilbroner, *Nature and Logic*, 117.

15. Nakamura Takafusa, "Nihon shihonshugi ronsō ni tsuite," *Shisō*, no. 624 (June 1976): esp. 187–90.

like Yamada, whose perspective was informed by the Comintern's Theses, especially those of 1932, theory was more than science; it was also war.[16]

Yamada was directly affected by the repression of the left that had mounted steadily since 1928. In a pattern quite common among leftist scholars of his era, Yamada was arrested and imprisoned (twice—in 1930 and 1936), and compelled to resign his position as assistant professor of economics at Tokyo Imperial University; he returned to his post in 1945. Yamada's frequent invocations in the *Analysis* of "rationality" and the need for a "rational grasp" of Japanese capitalism testify to his belief in the link, in however disguised a form, between theoretical analysis and political practice.[17] Indeed, under the conditions of the 1930s, making capitalism visible through a text was itself a form of political practice.

Yamada's Text

What sort of text is the *Analysis*? Its prose is infamous: repetitive and systematic in the extreme, it strings together interminable relative clauses in and among sentence fragments, and is studded with abstract, frequently neologistic terminology. Its repeated verbatim references to the "militaristic, semi-serflike character of Japanese-type capitalism," and to "large industry, with its sub-Indian labor wages and flesh-grinding labor conditions," have an almost incantatory quality.[18] Indeed, the *Analysis* is a work of obvious moral passion, of cold anger at a system that exploited and exhausted those who worked under it, the victims not only of modern selfishness but of semi-feudal cruelty. It bears the psychological scars of backwardness: time and again Yamada decries the "inverted," "deformed," "withered," and "barbaric" character of "Japanese-type" capitalism (*Nihongata shihonshugi*). It is the skill with which this anger is sublimated into theory that has made the *Analysis* a classic of Japanese social science.

Yamada opens with a typology of capitalist development in historical sequence (England, France, Germany, Russia, with the United States as a special case), and then identifies the Japanese variant in the following terms:[19]

16. On the various Theses issued between 1927 and 1932, see George Beckmann and Genji Okubo, *The Japanese Communist Party, 1922–1945* (Stanford: Stanford University Press, 1969), and Germaine Hoston, *Marxism and the Crisis of Development in Prewar Japan* (Princeton: Princeton University Press, 1986).

17. The words *tennō* (emperor) and *tennōsei zettaishugi* (imperial absolutism) appear nowhere in his text.

18. Yamada's characterization of Japanese factory wages as "sub-Indian" was based on a misreading of statistics, which "concerned not wages but the wage cost per unit of output." See Yasukichi Yasuba, "Anatomy of the Debate on Japanese Capitalism," *Journal of Japanese Studies* 2, no. 1 (Autumn 1975): 64–65 and note. Yasuba is citing Sakisaka Itsurō's 1935 critique of Yamada as reprinted in *Nihon shihonshugi no shomondai* (Tokyo: Shiseidō, 1958), chap. 1.

19. *Bunseki*, preface, 3–5.

The characteristics of Japan's special, inverted capitalism stemming from its low position in world history—those characteristics being a semi-serf system of petty agriculture founded on labor servitude / labor rent, the semi-serflike rule of in-kind payment of land taxes, and a general tendency toward debt serfdom—have their basis in the Restoration reforms of 1868; which were undertaken owing to the pressure exerted by the advanced capitalist countries on the despotic Tokugawa system that had been in place since the early seventeenth century, and assumed condensed structural (categorical, organizational) form in the process of defining industrial capitalism. That Japanese capitalism represents a departure, or deviation, from a [generalized] structural grasp should be clear in view of the points just enumerated.[20]

The key feature of "Japanese-type" capitalism was its inversion of the relation between the departments of production (as Marx defines them). Instead of a "classic" capitalist mode emerging as a result of developing the means of consumption in textiles, in Japan the "production of the means of production"—specifically in military and state-dominated heavy industry—formed the "pivot" of a revolution in production. This feature of the system, to which Japan "had been driven by necessity," brought with it the subordination of consumption along with extremes of exploitation, both of industrial labor and of peasant agriculture.[21] Also, and integrally, it brought the rapid—premature—acquisition of colonial holdings, on which capital was to rely for resources and markets.[22]

Backwardness, for Yamada, was not a psychological complex born of the sense of urgency felt by the leadership vis-à-vis the West, but reflected rather the control of the present by the past within Japan's production and social relations. By the mid-nineteenth century, Japan was already *objectively* backward, and only objective social transformation could abolish the condition. Yet it was important that this backwardness was not absolute, but relative. There was a crucial connection between the degree and quality of agricultural development and the capacity of a society to organize itself politically: "Japanese agriculture," he observed elsewhere, "from the point of view of (1) technology and (2) farm-household economy, is in a position superior to that of China and India. Indeed, this fact goes a long way in explaining why, in the face of Western expansion into Asia, the South [*nanpō*] was colonized by, and China subjected to the influence of, the Great Powers; while Japan alone managed to transform itself into a capitalist country."[23]

At the same time, the objective transformations necessary for the abolition of backwardness—that is, the transformation of feudalistic elements within the capitalist structure, to prepare the way for *socialist* revolution—were as yet unrealized and in fact blocked by interests in the state and society whose power rested on

20. Ibid., 4.
21. Ibid., 71.
22. Ibid., 4, 20, 70, 71.
23. "Nihon nōgyō no tokushusei" (November 1945), in *YMCS* 3:172.

their preservation. To this extent, backwardness was a supremely political—and ideological—issue as well as a social fact. Yamada's own treatment of "super-structure," however, is sketchy at best; he was "deaf" to the voices of ideology.[24] To be sure, younger scholars broadly in the Kōza-ha line, such as Maruyama Masao, went beyond Yamada to define the key issue in Japanese-type capitalism not as backwardness per se but as its knowing, strategic perpetuation by elites: those who occupied the "enlightened" side of the coin of a persistent "premod-ern" peasant mentality. To this extent, they foreshadow the "invention of tradi-tion" approach taken here. Even their focus, however, remains on the deforma-tions caused by the continued elaboration of this productive mode—now extended to the realm not just of politics but of ethics and morality. For analysts in this lineage, backwardness was real, had a social foundation, and was powerful enough to "infect" elites themselves.[25]

For Yamada, the "key to the whole process" of clarifying the basic structure—the antagonisms—and prospects of Japanese capitalism lay in explicating the ini-tial formation of *industrial* capitalism, roughly in the period between Japan's two successful wars, that is, between the mid-1890s and mid-1900s.[26] In that formation was subsumed the process of primitive accumulation; the simultaneous, mutually-determining moments of domestic industrial revolution and turn toward imperi-alism; the initial emergence of finance capital (the second, "genuine" appearance came around 1918); and the "necessary" impetus toward the general crisis of the late 1920s—the latter, of course, forming the enunciative moment of the *Analysis* itself. In other words, the dissolution of industrial capitalism in Japan was imma-nent in its own structure and was the condition for the—cataclysmic—general cri-sis that was now not only immanent, but imminent as well.

The text itself has a tripartite structure, each element focusing on a different branch of the economy in analyzing how "the reproduction process in Japanese capitalism was set underway." The first, treating the incorporation of cotton weav-ing and silk reeling (both putting out and manufacture) into the capitalist mode of production, outlines the phase of primitive accumulation, one "complete in its es-sentials" by the late 1890s.[27] Yamada strongly emphasized the "feudalistic" condi-tions of labor, particularly prison and forced labor, and the exploitation of female labor, taking note of protests and strikes by mill workers; similarly he described, but did not analyze, the ideological forms of control—patriotism, patriarchy, religion

---

24. Yamada's handling of ideological issues in the *Analysis* is indirect and implicit: "The force that decimated the armies of China, whose Asiatic despotism had already entered in its final decay; that smashed the armies of Imperial Russia; and liquidated those of Korea was not spiritual but nothing other than weaponry itself." *Bunseki*, 88.

25. For Maruyama, see his statements in Umemoto Katsumi, Satō Noboru, and Maruyama Masao, *Sengo Nihon no kakushin shisō* (Tokyo: Gendai no Rironsha, 1983), 48–49.

26. Marx provides a strong warrant for this position: see *Capital* (Harmondsworth: Penguin, 1992), 2:35–36.

27. Yamada, *Bunseki*, 19–20.

(requiring workers to swear oaths to *kami* [gods])—used by *oyakata* in the crucial mining industry.

The second part locates the "pivot" of the production revolution in the military organization and key industries (railroads, mining, machine works), the "decisive driving force," for Yamada, of Japan's capitalist development. The key indicator of development in this sector, he held, was "the fulfillment of the expectation that instruments of labor can be produced" through both securing raw materials (iron, both Chinese and Manchurian) for processing and "surpassing world levels" in shipbuilding technology, specifically in producing "machines to make machines"—for example, lathes. Pointing to the overwhelming presence of the Yahata works, Yamada sought to demonstrate the dominance of state capital over heavy industry. This was the mode of development that both determined Japan's turn to imperialism in order to secure primary material, fuels, and markets, and promoted in two "jerky" stages the emergence of finance capital. But, Yamada contended, the entire heavy industrial sector, to the extent that it depended on labor drawn from villages and was subject to a semi-feudal labor regime in the factory, would find that its growth was socially constrained; hence the "fragility" of Japan's heavy industry and its industrial "bourgeoisie." Thus, the attempt by heavy industry to resolve the precipitous downturn of the late 1920s via "industrial rationalization"—mass dismissals and intensification of labor—would provoke a general collapse of the semi-feudal form of labor and related conditions.[28] Yamada did not foresee the survival of industrial capitalism, let alone its successful adaptation to a "post–semi-feudal" era.

Part 3, finally, treats "the base"—Japan's system of "semi-feudal land tenure" and "semi-serf system of petty cultivation." It was here that the worst features of the industrial economy had their source: the "sub-Indian labor wages and flesh-grinding labor conditions" of large industry made possible by the "miserably laggard"[29] state of agriculture. As critics consistently and correctly point out, in the long run, Yamada was primarily concerned with the base, as if to echo Marx's own conviction that "the social revolution can only *seriously* begin from the bottom up; that is, with landlordism."[30] Yamada elaborated a typology of landlords: the first being the still "pivotal" Northeastern (Tōhoku) type, marked by "semi-feudal" landlord-tenant relations, whose "reproduction" was carried out within the village, and a combination of concentrated ownership and direct cultivation along with a slow-paced parcelization of tenant holdings. To this was counterpoised the "usurious and parasitical" Home Province (Kinki) type of landlordism, where extensive and accelerating land parcelization was taking place in a relatively commercialized environment: "reproduction" of the landlord-tenant rela-

28. Ibid., 147.

29. Ibid., 175–76.

30. Letter to Kugelmann, April 4, 1868, in Marx, *Political Writings*, vol. 3: *The First International and After* (Harmondsworth: Penguin, 1992), 162.

tion took place via ties to urban markets. Taken together these represented "nothing other than two types that have emerged on the basis of a semi-feudal system of land ownership—and a semi-serflike regime of parcelized cultivation—that has two strata, each with its specific type of subordination [*nisō no jūzoku kitei*]."[31] Yamada did not extend his considerations to landlord entrepreneurship, and certainly saw no evidence from any quarter of their having performed a progressive role in the development of capitalism in Japan. For Yamada, it was only with the transformation of social relations in the countryside, through the reform of the system of land tenure, that the category of smallholder could emerge as the bearer of a home market and "bourgeois" consciousness. Until then, feudalistic relations would always form fetters on production and obstruct the development of a genuinely proportional—healthy—demand in the economy. Japan's *idée napolienne*—the "middling peasant" (*chūnō*)—would remain an ideological mockery of a tenanted mass still subject to "noneconomic coercion." Concretely, this meant that payment in-kind (in rice) of land rent would remain the norm—cash payments, Yamada argued, were no more than a modern mask over a feudal form—and that the village would continue, not as a true community but as a "simple addition of homologous magnitudes," whose units shared no more than "identity of interest" and were devoid of unity or class consciousness.[32]

No matter where he looked, Yamada saw a structurally determined impasse in Japan's capitalism. Industrial rationalization seemed to offer no positive prospect; and no serious land reform was in the offing that could solve the problem of effective demand at the "base." Thus, he concluded, "at the same time that the incorporation of the 'wretched hovels' [cottage industry] was the fundamental factor in the flourishing of Japanese capitalism—the establishment of industrial capital—it also produced the fundamental cause of its own ruin."[33]

Yamada's Method: The Analysis of Reproduction

The distinct power of Yamada's text stems from its method of combining theoretical and historical perspectives in a single analysis. But in so doing, Uchida Yoshiaki has argued, Yamada disclosed a vital tension between the two elements of his intellectual will: the "unintending" Weberian sociologist, concerned to specify and typologize particulars, and the orthodox Marxian economist, determined to identify the "laws of motion" of a universal process.[34] Indeed, it is this tension that

---

31. *Bunseki,* 170–72.

32. Ibid., 182, 179. Yamada's treatment was drawn explicitly from Marx's *Eighteenth Brumaire* and its (in)famous characterization of the French peasantry as a "sackful of potatoes." See *The Marx-Engels Reader,* R. Tucker, ed. (New York: Norton, 1978), 608.

33. Yamada, *Bunseki,* 47.

34. Uchida Yoshiaki, "Yamada Moritarō to marukusu keizaigaku," in Uchida, *Wēbā to Marukusu: Nihon shakai kagaku no shisō kōzō* (Tokyo: Iwanami Shoten, 1978), 227–303.

generated both the light and the heat necessary for the work to be treated as a contestable classic.

As Yamada envisioned it, the *Analysis* was an attempt "to analyze the foundations of Japanese capitalism. It is the chief task of this work, by means of this analysis of fundamentals, to make clear the basic structure—i.e., antagonisms [*taikō*]—and prospects of Japanese capitalism. I view this task as a problem of grasping the reproduction process in Japanese capitalism; I hope, that is, to have *concretized the reproduction schema* in Japanese capitalism."[35]

The *Analysis* was also intended as a scientific demonstration of the schema's predictive power. Japanese capitalism, because it was capitalism, was destined to generate a crisis from which Yamada, at least, hoped it would not recover. Determining when that crisis would actually occur and what its effects would be, however, required an analysis of the specific conditions of reproduction in Japan.[36] It meant finding a way to relate the "visible" and "invisible" systems of Japan's modernity—agriculture, industry, and empire—on the one hand, to the morally problematic "something" called capitalism on the other. Yamada had to come to terms with history.

In analyzing actually existing capitalism in Japan, Yamada began with the notion of reproduction, that is, he took as his task the explanation not simply of how capitalist production and commodity circulation took place, but of how the *conditions* for such activity were reproduced. Yet the "reproduction schemas" (developed in the second volume of *Capital*) that provided Yamada's basic model were highly abstract. And particularly since he worked from the schema for simple reproduction,[37] certain critics were led to charge that Yamada conceived capitalism in equilibrium rather than dialectical terms.[38] By the time the articles that made up the *Analysis* appeared together in book form in 1934, Yamada had already published a theoretical study of reproduction that anticipated and responded, albeit unsatisfactorily for some, to the argument that the reproduction schema would harness any analysis to a Procrustean bed. Exactly so, was the reply. The reproduction schema, Yamada argued, "represents the most fundamental, most general grasp, and as such does not touch directly the particular, concrete capitalist structure of any specific country, or the structure of capitalism at any specific stage." Yet "insofar as it grasps this most fundamental dimension," the reproduc-

---

35. Yamada, *Bunseki*, 3; emphasis added.

36. Yamada Moritarō, *Saiseisan katei: Hyōshiki bunseki joron* (1931); hereafter *Joron*. *YMCS* I:111–16; Yamazaki, "*Nihon shihonshugi*," 186–89.

37. That is, a process in which the entire surplus product is consumed by the capitalist rather than being turned to accumulation; an equilibrium rather than expansive state.

38. See the review of criticisms of Yamada's use of the reproduction schema in Yamazaki, "*Nihon shihonshugi*," 226–31; also Iwasaki Chikatsugu, *Nihon marukusushugi tetsugakushi josetsu* (Tokyo: Miraisha, 1984 ed.), 353–61.

tion schema "assumes a concrete form that is present throughout the capitalist structure of any given country or at any given stage."[39]

At some level, yes, capitalism *was* the same everywhere. And, Yamada continued, it was no less important that it *did* the same thing everywhere—that is, in the process of "normal" operations, the capitalist system generated crises: even under the condition of perfect proportionality between departments of the economy, "the forms of motion of the totality of the social capital" brought with them their own antagonistic contradictions.[40] The reproduction schema, therefore, enabled one to determine "the ironlike necessity for change that runs through the structure at its base."[41]

Nevertheless, the "pure" capitalism laid bare in Marx's critique of political economy (even in its historical sections) could not have provided material sufficient to produce Yamada's *Analysis*. Although he strove mightily to follow *Capital*'s reproduction schemas, in formulating his model of "Japanese-type" capitalism Yamada was compelled to rely on "mediating links" derived from other instances of late development as a way of attaining the concreteness he sought. Lenin's notion of a "Prussian path" to capitalism, involving a "reconstruction from above, in which elements of a bourgeois system are incorporated into the *ancien régime* so as to ensure its survival in the context of a hostile international environment" offered what seemed a powerful, albeit qualified analogy to the "absolutist" Japanese state. *Imperialism* (1916) provided theoretical guidance in schematizing the reproduction process in a peripheral empire such as Japan's, in which an underdeveloped home market compelled the state to turn to colonialism as a substitute.[42] By the same token, the Physiocrat François Quesnay's *Table économique*, "as an embodiment of equilibrium [between feudal aristocracy and bourgeoisie], which is the basic condition of absolute monarchy," hinted at a method for analyzing what Yamada regarded as Japan's essentially precapitalist agrarian sector. Indeed Quesnay's *Table* allowed Yamada to set up a schema of capitalist reproduction that formally excluded the agricultural "base" on which capitalism rested: not because the production relations of agriculture were socially inconsequential, but because they were not, in Yamada's view, capitalist relations. Japanese agriculture was characterized by

land rent categories [*chidai hanchū*] that absorb all surplus labor, even eating into necessary labor itself; that do not permit any profit to materialize. In cases where the position of the landowner has overwhelming primacy, there is no space for the formation of capitalist farm operations aimed at realizing a profit. Thus, so-called owners

39. This particular formulation comes from a postwar text but in essence restates Yamada's original position: Yamada Moritarō, "Saiseisan hyōshiki" (1955), as cited in Yamazaki, "*Nihon shihonshugi*," 189.

40. Yamada, *Joron*, 55–56; see also Yamazaki, "*Nihon shihonshugi*," 232.

41. *Joron*, 56.

42. M. C. Howard and J. E. King, *A History of Marxian Economics*, vol. 1: *1883–1929* (Princeton: Princeton University Press, 1989), chaps. 11 and 13 (quote, p. 206).

of money, rather than being managers of agricultural leaseholds, tend generally to be parasitic landlords whose objective is the taking of land rent. Here we have a clear indication of the reasons for the strengthening, in the case of the development of Japanese capitalism, of the category of agricultural land rents that absorb all surplus labor and prevent the realization of profit; and of the regime of semi-serflike or parasitical landlordism. It is here that the limits to the capitalist transformation of Japanese agriculture are formed.[43]

CRITIQUE AND ASSESSMENT

In the process of "concretizing the reproduction schema in Japanese capitalism," the *Analysis* forged an iron link between the "special character"—the particularism—of Japan's capitalism and backwardness. For Yamada, particularism *was* backwardness.

It is not hard to see why Yamada's arguments, whether on Japanese agriculture, on capitalist development in general, or on the applicability of the reproduction schema to a specific instance, would have been controversial both in their own moment, and in ours. He made almost no direct response to criticisms of the *Analysis*. He did adjust his views, though not his basic approach, during the years between 1934 and the early postwar era, chiefly in the direction of giving much overdue attention to heavy industry in general, and especially in recognizing that a shift from textiles to heavy and petrochemical industries must have been well underway prior to 1931. Yet as of 1934, Yamada had clearly missed something, and not by oversight. He failed to grasp the capacity of Japanese capitalism to survive the depression, having essentially frozen his view of production relations in industry as of the decade between the two turn-of-century wars; he had virtually no grasp of the role of the state, especially after World War I (his assessment of industrial rationalization was narrowly drawn and essentially negative), no developed views of trade flows or state finance, or any conjunctural perspective more recent than that of his period of initial focus.[44]

In a sense, Yamada was too "faithful" a Marxist: where Marx had been forced to stop with a mere three volumes of *Capital*, dying with the more "conjunctural" aspects of his overall plan unrealized, so too Yamada stopped short of any attempt to treat the position of Japan in the capitalist world economy. Instead, his "types" developed within the histories of their national societies, each one running in isolation until it was exhausted or destroyed from outside. Indeed, criticism of Ya-

43. Yamada, "Saiseisan hyōshiki to chidai hanchū—Nihon keizai saiken no hōshiki to nōgyō kaikaku no hōkō o kimeru tame no ichi kijun" (1947), in *YMCS* 3:3–48, esp. 36–38 (quote, p. 41); the longer quote is from *Bunseki*, 166. See also Yamazaki, "*Nihon shihonshugi,*" 176–83, 198–99.

44. See also Ōshima Mario, "A Distant View of the Debate on Japanese Capitalism," *Osaka City University Economic Review* 26, no. 2 (July 1991); and Ōshima, "Kakuritsu ki Nihon shihonshugi no kōzō," in Yamamoto Yoshihiko, ed., *Kindai Nihon keizaishi: Kokka to keizai* (Kyoto: Mineruva Shobō, 1992).

mada's text has concentrated on the static, undialectical, and insufficiently historical character of his "types." In his use of equilibrium notions as the conceptual basis—not the normative or political end point—of analysis, Yamada had followed Nikolai Bukharin, whose *Historical Materialism* was avidly read in Japan. When Bukharin himself came under attack in the Soviet Union, equilibrium analyses such as Yamada's were branded "Bukharinist" and "right deviationist." While much of this criticism (which continued into the postwar years) was stridently dogmatic, it did have a germ of validity. As Iwasaki Chikatsugu commented:

> In the "type" [*kata*] itself, there is no movement or development. As molds are manufactured and then broken—which is the case with Yamada Moritarō's theory—there is only formation and disintegration. . . . As with the theory of equilibrium that is linked to it, the standpoint of "types" is by nature one of external causation. . . . In the theory of "types"—as in Yamada's *Nihon shihonshugi bunseki*—it is possible to recognize the product of a marriage between Weber and Bukharin performed on the basis of Marxism.[45]

These are not unfair, or necessarily unfavorable, observations. We may agree with the Rōnō-ha theoretician Sakisaka Itsurō, author of the first substantial criticism of the *Analysis*, that Yamada's capitalism "has no development"—that it hypostatized the past (= semi-feudal social relations) and refused to make any bow to the Rōnō-ha.[46] But when viewed from the perspective of the 1930s and the first half of the 1940s, it is hard to see how Sakisaka's own model of Japanese capitalism, drained of its specificity—based on what Sakisaka insisted *ought to have happened*—would have any more explanatory power than a static, structurally overdetermined model such as Yamada's. Yamada at least had his finger on a genuine, long-term problem: the disparity between sectors and the social and ideological consequences of that disparity. His problem was that he could find no theory that would allow him to move his finger.

Ultimately, for Yamada the analysis of Japanese capitalism came down to the problem of land and land rent—or, as one sympathetic critic, fed up with Yamada's penchant for nominalizations, put it, "the crisis of the land rent categories."[47] Here, of course, Yamada's views were vindicated, and therefore rendered honorable superfluities. Social scientists, if they are honest, should consider themselves lucky if their work meets such a fate. As Yamazaki Ryūzō noted, even though the *Analysis* may still be regarded as a key point of departure in the analysis of Japanese

45. Iwasaki, *Nihon marukusushugi*, 351, 355, 359. On Bukharin, see also Stephen Cohen, *Bukharin and the Bolshevik Revolution* (New York: Oxford University Press, 1980), 87–98, 107–22; Kenneth Tarbuck, *Bukharin's Theory of Equilibrium* (London: Pluto Press, 1989).

46. Sakisaka, *Nihon shihonshugi*, 17.

47. Uchida Yoshihiko, pseud. NNN, "'Shijō no ronri' to 'chidai hanchū no kiki,'" *Keizai hyōron*, nos. 3, 4, 6 (1949).

capitalism, it can no longer serve as a point of arrival.[48] And yet, if read not so much in terms of its own theoretical project, or of its flawed and truncated historical analysis, but as an inverted reflection of the particularism it sought to overthrow, the *Analysis* speaks still, and with a surprisingly powerful voice. If Japan's *kokutai*, its national polity, was "peerless throughout the world" in its inherent virtuousness, its "semi-feudal regime of parcelized cultivation" was likewise "peerless throughout the world . . . in its baseness and cruelty."[49] "Do not be deceived," Yamada seems to insist: "We live with a past already cruel enough for the masses of peasants in our society; a past now brought into and indeed indispensable to the present system of exploitation. This double cruelty speaks to us in a soothing voice of warm manners and beautiful customs, yet even now is arming itself for aggressive expansion, perhaps war; and I dare not even name him for whose sake our people toil and suffer."

In *Nihon shihonshugi bunseki*, Yamada Moritarō provided a theoretical analysis that both identified particularism with backwardness, and made Japanese capitalism *visible as such* (i.e., as capitalism) for the first time. The odd fate of this combination was that while capitalism advanced in the 1950s, it did not "universalize" as many analysts, whether of the Rōnō-ha, Uno school, or neoclassical lineages expected it would. Instead, "backwardness" metamorphosed into its obverse, the claim that particularism should now be linked with Japan's role as the *vanguard of postmodern capitalism*. Both positions share the feature of projecting back into the Tokugawa past and forward again those features of society thought to explain the present: for Yamada, the conditions of the late 1920s–early 1930s; for the upholders of Tokugawa Japan's postmodernity *avant la lettre*, the years of high growth from the mid-1960s through to the recent collapse of the bubble economy. In either case, the generality of capitalist relations remains insupportably abstract and undeserving of cultural imprimatur, while the link with the noncapitalist past remains the explanatory master-key.

But what past? That of Yamada's Marxian narrative? That of the peerless national polity and its happy and harmonious village communities? It is not enough to say that the two cancel each other out, or that they depend on one another. Yamada's Marxism may be frozen in time and, in a sense, in its social categories as well: but at least he did not renounce the attempt at serious comparison with cases outside Japan. Nor is it enough to observe that each present invents its past, for this begs the question: why does it do so when it does, why does it do so at all? Out of what strands of preexisting narrative and nonnarrative practices, and by what agents? As far as Japanese capitalism is concerned, we may say, in a twist on Barrington ("no bourgeois, no democracy") Moore: no tradition, no capitalism. We mean by this not what Yamada Moritarō meant, that the past controlled and

48. Yamazaki, "*Nihon shihonshugi*," 235–36.
49. Yamada, *Bunseki*, 151.

therefore in a sense created the present. Rather, while taking into account the long dominance of Kōza-ha over Rōnō-ha perspectives in Japanese Marxism, and the extensive influence of the Kōza-ha over Japanese social science generally, we must go beyond it to articulate the significance of a certain kind of *past-consciousness*. It was here, in the sphere of ideology and the production of meaning, that Yamada's analysis, and that of the Kōza-ha generally, was weakest—although that of the Rōnō-ha was weaker still. In this respect, neither grasped the real dynamic of Japanese capitalism, indeed of Japan's modernization as a whole. This lay in the invented—and *strategic*—character of the process through which "tradition" entered the present: not just "no tradition, no capitalism," but also "no capitalism, no tradition." No present, no past. Rather than laying bare capitalism's ideology as part of a "total grasp," Yamada's text effaced it and unwittingly reproduced the structure of concealment that was essential to its functioning.

The development of capitalism in Japan posed a double dilemma. It arrived, garbed in a morally problematic ideology of individual profit-seeking, and moreover in a global conjuncture in which Japan was placed at a radical disadvantage. Under these conditions, by making maximum demands on its semi-autonomous agrarian sector, Japan's leadership made its wager on backwardness. These original characteristics, in turn, were translated into the ideological virtues of national communalism and ceaseless self-sacrifice that informed and naturalized capitalism in Japan. As such, they have taken on a life of their own as normative orientations, indispensable not only for those whose interest lies in maintaining the political-economic regime, but for those who attempt to resist its powerful claims. Just as in economic analysis, where Rōnō-ha universalism has formed the subtheme to Kōza-ha particularism, in intellectual-moral discourse, globalism and individualism (two sides of the same coin) have operated under community constraint, relatively loose or tight as contemporary conditions dictate. Does the "internationalization"-cum-"liberalization" of the present economic moment or the disintegration of the Liberal Democratic political regime point to a fundamental national reorientation—a redefinition of the essential features of Japan's modernity? I am not sure that it does. Qualified though it has been by long-run transformations in Japanese capitalism and by challenges to its intellectual structure, the world of Yamada's *Analysis* has not yet passed into history.

SEVENTEEN

The Invention of Edo

Carol Gluck

EDO-MEMORY

Modernity, by definition, foresaw the future by setting itself off from the past. Newness was all, but it could only be grasped by juxtaposition to what was old. In France the ancien régime came to represent the whole of the old order, the very antithesis of the new revolutionary age. And in Europe the medieval past became the anterior otherness against which the modern historical imagination—even in America, which having had no Middle Ages of its own proceeded to borrow Europe's—defined itself *as modern*, whether by asserting utter difference or by evoking seductively selective affinities. In Japan the Edo period became just this sort of historical imaginary. "Edo" (meaning the Tokugawa era, not the city later named Tokyo) was the invented other in relation to which modernity posited itself. From early Meiji times, Japan's before-the-modern was imagined largely in terms of an Edo identified as Japanese "tradition." This grand conflation made it seem as if centuries of tradition had come to rest in the 300-year period immediately preceding the replacement of the old past with the new future. And it made Edo-as-tradition into the mirror of modernity. From the early 1870s to the mid-1990s, the reflections of Edo varied along with the ideas of what the modern was or ought to be. But the invented tradition of viewing Edo-as-tradition—"the way we (Japanese) once were"—remained the desired object of modern memory.

As a historical time, Edo was the immediately proximate past of Meiji, meaning that it was temporally linked to modernity by its beforeness as well as its pastness. Since history, in its modern telling, moved as if modernity were the only possible destination, accounts of modern Japan began by situating Edo, as roadblock or detour, straightaway or shortcut, on the historical highway leading to modern times. And the primacy of the nation-state meant that along the way both modernity and tradition had to be "nationalized" anew, saturated, as it were, with Japaneseness.

So Edo became not only a historical time but a cultural space, a repository of traditions (*dentō*) associated with Japanese distinctiveness, both positive and negative.

For such "Japanese-y culture" (*Nihonteki bunka*) as kabuki, sushi, zen, and tea ceremony, Tsuji Tatsuya gave four Edo-linked patterns: either these practices arose during Edo; took their full form during Edo; were established among the people during Edo; or acquired their "Japanese-y" character during Edo.[1] In this great ingathering of traditions, few mention how many of these were codified (and Edo-fied) during Meiji, when modern Japan did so much of its reinventing. It is also worth noting that the traditions enshrined in this Edo-as-storehouse of national identity centered more on practices and things than on politics or thought. The daily life of commoners, including rituals of peasant protest, pilgrimage, and travel, and also objects of material culture, hairstyles and (Japanese) clothing (*wafuku*), prints and pots, country haiku and city theater—all these were collected in an Edo archive of identity. Like the painted temples of earlier times that lodged in modern memory in their monochrome Edo forms, or the allegedly natural village presented in its historically Tokugawa shape, modern inscriptions of Japaneseness often had a distinctly Edo look to them.

Since my subject is Edo-as-tradition created in the mirror of the modern, I turn away from the cultural storehouse at its (no doubt) silkily worn wooden steps. And because memory, not history, is the issue here, it must be stressed that the changing Edo images were not figments fabricated in disregard for the absolute elsewhere that is the past. On the contrary, the agents of Edo-memory returned, almost obsessively, to that past to find in it whatever they were missing in the present or hoping for the future. Their views of the modern—defined not by doctrine but by what they were thinking and living through at the time—determined the light they cast on Edo. For Fukuzawa Yukichi, eager to escape from it, and for twentieth-century progressives committed to removing its oppressive social shadow, Edo loomed dark and feudal. Others, like Kitamura Tōkoku in mid-Meiji or Maruyama Masao at mid-century, saw rays of light that portended a liberal politics in the midst of mostly unmodern grayness. Some—Ōkuma Shigenobu in the 1900s and affirming modernizationists in the 1970s—saw the historical horizon lightening in a pre- or proto-vision of modern economic and political change. And in the postmodern 1980s rose-colored Edo appeared in dizzying sunlight, its play (*tawamure*) and freedom all the brighter for their being not before but beyond the modern. This ever-changing Edo chiaroscuro lit the past differently but did not invent a single Edo tradition like the now famous Scottish kilt. Less a product than a process, Edo-as-tradition opened a field of historical consciousness in which modern Japanese negotiated their path to the future by way of the past.[2]

1. Tsuji Tatsuya, *Edo jidai o kangaeru* (Tokyo: Chūkō Shinsho, 1988), 15–16.

2. See Michael Kammen, *Mystic Chords of Memory: The Transformation of Tradition in American Culture* (New York: Alfred A. Knopf, 1991); David Lowenthal, *The Past Is a Foreign Country* (Cambridge: Cambridge University Press, 1985); Robert Gildea, *The Past in French History* (New Haven: Yale University Press, 1994).

And they seldom agreed with one another about the route. Practically everyone was an Edo expert of one sort or another, their memory inventories rich with Edo images, analogues, and allegories, gathered from history books and school texts, family stories, local lore, popular entertainment, and later, films and television, cartoons, advertisements, and theme parks. In sense and sensibility, people's tastes had been Edo-trained to recognize this thatched roof and sedge hat, that loyal samurai and peasant rebel, these pastimes and travel paths, those virtues, vices, and follies as deeply, familiarly Japanese. Sometimes labeled as Edo, far more often just presumed as "tradition," Edo-memory thus appeared in many genres. Most fall, however, into three positional forms. The first and most obvious staked out its ground in narrating the nation-state. In the national Edo, the Tokugawa past became the matrix of national history, described as an impediment to or a resource for the modern nation-state. A good part of this linear story was instrumental, ideological production for the sake of imagining the national community, put forth not only by the state but by all those engaged in constructing "the story of the nation." But thinking the national past cannot be entirely subsumed under functionalist categories, which seem to suggest that the national story was always told for the sake of the nation. The tradition-to-modern plot could just as easily be told against the state, and in the second form of memory, it often was.

Oppositional Edo turned the Tokugawa past against the modern present. In what Nicholas Thomas calls "the inversion of tradition," those who dissent or are excluded from the hegemonic tradition as it is nationally sanctioned can use the same tradition in combat for their own cause.[3] While conservative avatars of cultural identity hailed community and harmony in the archetypal Edo village, political progressives invoked the tradition that inhered in the politics of protest. From peasant uprisings to the "ecological opposition" of Andō Shōeki, Edo-memories constituted a heritage of protest that animated the struggle to contest the power of the modern state.

Commodified Edo is the third form, which possessed, in quantity and reach, perhaps the largest share of the memory business. Ever since mid-Meiji, Edo was the favored site in the terrain of popular memory, whether in commercial media, historical fiction, museums and monuments, or the theming of Japan in history-lands like Genrokumura and Edomura. Like the heritage industry in Britain, Edo figured prominently in commodified nostalgia. It also provided the swashbuckling heroes of *chanbara* films, popular since the 1920s, and a reservoir of historical and visual allusions used to sell everything from *sake* to liver pills. In the recession of the early 1990s, an ad for the book *"Edogaku" no susume* (Encouragement of Edo-ology) promoted the wisdom of the Confucian Kaibara Ekken as a "survival strategy in these confusing times since the economic bubble burst." Other titles offered successful Edo exemplars of *risutora* (restructuring) as an inspiration for contempo-

3. Nicholas Thomas, "The Inversion of Tradition," *American Ethnologist* 19, no. 2 (May 1992).

rary corporate downsizing.[4] The ubiquity of this vernacular Edo both played off and added to the common stock of Edo images, in this case implying that the passage of time had not dulled the economic utility of tradition.

THE EMERGENCE OF "EDO"

Edo first emerged as a historical imaginary soon after the Meiji Restoration brought the historical Edo to an end. In a classic example of a new order reinventing the past to serve the future, participants in the Meiji national project asserted utter discontinuity between their age and what the Charter Oath of 1868 had called "evil customs of the past." The usages of Edo were judged instantly obsolete, as if ages, not moments, had passed in the course of the Restoration. This was the originary rupture typical of the modern: an epochal threshold had been crossed, a new age now began. Before 1868 restorationists such as Iwakura Tomomi described the shogun and his power as belonging to the past, destined to decline, but they had foreseen only a shift in government, not a change in time itself.[5] That came later, during the 1870s, when enlightenment figures like Fukuzawa Yukichi and Taguchi Ukichi judged the Edo past against the Meiji future, in terms both of difference and of progress. They used their own experience of the difference—Fukuzawa's "two lives in one"—to redraw Edo into the linear prehistory of the Meiji to come. Their word for progress, *kaika*, an opening toward the light of civilization, encompassed the modern sense of time characterized by Koselleck as ever advancing, always in transition, its newness marked out by contrast with the old.[6]

Because they saw the Meiji newness, called "civilization" (*bunmei*), as national and progressing, they depicted the Edo oldness as feudal and a hindrance to the march of time. Once named feudal, Edo never wholly shed the epithet. The "feudal system" (*hōken seido*) of Fukuzawa, Taguchi, Tokutomi Sohō, and many others in the 1870s and 1880s was the old Chinese term for decentralized government, which referred to the shogun-domainal Tokugawa polity. But—and this was far more important to them—they also used "feudal" to mean the hereditary status system that Fukuzawa described as his father's "mortal enemy." Later overlays first of European, then of Marxist definitions of feudalism complicated the historical question. But in Edo-memory, the tradition that modern Japan set itself against was, in a powerful word, "feudal," defined less in terms of political structure or land tenure than as a social system that oppressed and constrained the energies of the people. The people, in the Meiji context, were the national people

---

4. Kusumoto Fumio, *"Edogaku" no susume* (Tokyo: Kōsei Shuppansha, 1992); Kunimitsu Shirō, *Edo-bakumatsu daifukyō no nazo* (Tokyo: Kappa Books, 1994); Dōmon Fuyuji, *Edo no risutora shikakenin* (Tokyo: Shūeisha Bunko, 1993).

5. Osatake Takeshi, *Meiji ishin* (Tokyo: Munetaka Shobō, 1978), 1:53.

6. Reinhart Koselleck, " 'Neuzeit': Remarks on the Semantics of the Modern Concepts of Movement," in his *Futures Past: On the Semantics of Historical Time* (Cambridge, Mass.: MIT Press, 1985).

(*kokumin*) that the nineteenth-century nation-state everywhere demanded. Where the state wanted subjects, the popular rights movement wanted citizens, and the newspapers wanted common readers. But all soon envisioned the people in contradistinction to the hereditary four-class system represented by the feudal fetters of Edo.

Where to find the national people who would make the nation rich, the army strong, and the country civilized? Where else, of course, but Edo? The logic of Edo-as-tradition implies that even as modern Meiji strode purposefully away from its feudal past, it had nowhere else to turn for its national material. This selective reappropriation of elements of Edo did not compromise the sense of temporal rupture. Instead, through it Meiji writers reached across the chasm—always keeping arm's distance—to retrieve elements from the past that they thought the future required: in particular, popular energies and signs of progress. Even Fukuzawa, known in the 1870s for his categorical denunciations of the tyrannical Tokugawa regime and its politically supine population, could not dispense with Edo entirely. To remedy his own charge that "Japan had a government but no nation [*kokumin*]," he found a popular basis in Edo first for education and later for a parliament.[7] Taguchi, who viewed civilization as much in economic and social as in political terms, decried the Tokugawa feudal system and its samurai rulers but was heartened by the material and cultural developments (*kaika*) among the common people. And so "all things in society, tangible and intangible, could not but progress."[8] The author with enough bravado to reverse the Hegelian direction of history and posit "The Eastward Advance of Civilization" gave credit to Edo scholars who had managed to acquire Western knowledge even during seclusion, since it was they, he said, who had laid the basis for Meiji civilization.[9] Liberals like Yamaji Aizan found three hundred years of material progress among the nameless "heroes" of Edo villages and the development of human rights even within the feudal system.[10] Thus Edo, though largely viewed as a negative legacy, was at the same time pressed into service for the national modern.

Framed by the nation-state, "Edo" emerged locked in the temporal embrace of modernity, whether as the inverse of civilization or its supplier of usable national parts. Either way, Edo lay before, behind, gone and done with in the main line of national time. Revivals and retrievals occurred, but they took work and often lay across the contemporary grain. The former shogunal officials, for example, who

---

7. *Nihon ni wa seifu arite kokumin (nēshon) nashi.* Fukuzawa Yukichi, *An Outline of Civilization*, trans. David A. Dilworth and G. Cameron Hurst (Tokyo: Sophia University Press, 1973), 144.

8. Taguchi Ukichi, *Nihon kaika shōshi* (1877–82), in *Meiji bungaku zenshū*, vol. 14 (Tokyo: Chikuma Shobō, 1977), 49.

9. Fujita Mokichi, *Bunmei tōzen shi* (1884), in *Meiji bungaku zenshū*, vol. 77 (Tokyo: Chikuma Shobō, 1965).

10. Yamaji Aizan, "Kinsei busshitsuteki no shinpo" (1892) and "Nihon no rekishi ni okeru jinken hattatsu no konseki" (1897), in *Meiji bungaku zenshū*, vol. 35 (Tokyo: Chikuma Shobō, 1965).

had been written out of national history, staged a historical counteroffensive in the 1890s. But they had to do it on already-canonical terms, which had them arguing that the shogun had been the firmest imperial loyalist of them all. When an ex-shogunal group formed the Edokai in 1889 to redress the historical occlusion of the Tokugawa period, it argued—adopting the language of the occluders—that "the three hundred years of Tokugawa rule saw the greatest progress and development that Japanese civilization had ever known." And at the 1889 tricentennial commemoration of Tokugawa Ieyasu's entry into Edo, even the official name had been changed: it was no longer the establishment of the Edo shogunate but "the three-hundredth anniversary of the establishment of Tokyo," a patent absurdity remarked upon by the mayor, who commented that Tokyo was at that point all of twenty-two years old.[11]

Revivals of Genroku and *gesaku* literature, promotion of woodblock prints, and other signs of cultural redress occurred from the 1890s on, but it was after the turn of the century that Edo appeared in a temporally positive role. Uchida Ginzō was the first historian to call Tokugawa Japan *kinsei* (today rendered as early modern) in reference to European periodization rather than simply to the "near past." In 1903 he wrote praising Edo as stable, flourishing, and "preparatory" for the age to come, which he called the "nearest past" (*saikinsei*), meaning Meiji as the "most modern." His comparisons of the Tokugawa regime with European feudalism led him to conclude (like American historians a half-century later) that "centralized feudalism" was the most appropriate label for the shogunal state.[12] In public rhetoric, Ōkuma Shigenobu in 1909 stressed a similar preparatory service that Edo had rendered to the successful rise of the "New Japan."[13] For on the official side, this new Japan, once a project of the future, was now represented as already achieved, its "civilization" palpably writ in progress at home and empire abroad. By the end of Meiji, people were writing the story of modern Japan in the past tense, a change that gentled their narrative resistance to Edo. In nationally sanctioned memory—both official and demotic, in schoolrooms, newspapers, and comic routines—Edo now figured as a past past mobilized to tell the story of a modern nation well pleased with its present prospect.

A nearly parodic epitome of the triumphal view backward from the vantage point of the Great Empire Japan appears as the entry in the appropriately named *Great Japan Encyclopedia* of 1916. After some donnish throat-clearing about the different interpretations of its beginning and ending dates, followed by a fivefold internal periodization, the author gave the Tokugawa period a strong entrance as "the peak of samurai rule (*buke seiji*), indeed the last era of the old Japan." Its political system (shades of Uchida) was "centralized feudalism"; the central authorities

---

11. Ōkubo Toshiaki, *Sabakuha rongi* (Tokyo: Yoshikawa Kōbunkan, 1986), 74–75.

12. He dated the period 1616–1853. Uchida Ginzō, *Kinsei no Nihon—Nihon kinsei shi* ([1919, 1903]; Tokyo: Heibonsha, 1975).

13. Shigenobu Ōkuma, *Fifty Years of New Japan* (London: Smith, Elder, 1909), 1:38–42.

at Edo cleverly deployed the feudal lords through alternate attendance; and the positioning of domains and shogunal lands "was nearly ideal." Seclusionism (*sakokushugi*) was natural because it was necessary to preserve the shogunate and the nation; and since the shoguns maintained order and peace, culture flourished. It was the last age of adopting continental Asian civilization, and although Western civilization had been introduced, it had not yet established itself as dominant. Because "people high and low were no longer satisfied only with the culture of old Japan," Yoshimune lifted the ban on Western books. Western civilization flowed in and "prepared the way for the importation of that same civilization during Meiji." Because of seclusion, the people (*kokumin*) concentrated their energies within the country and reached a new self-awakening. Although Ieyasu conquered the realm with arms (*bu*), he also ruled through letters (*bun*). Learning was not confined to the aristocracy but reached the lower strata of society, and scholars could be employed by the shogunate, thus uniting politics and knowledge. Neo-Confucianism "combined with the essence of our *kokutai*" to become an independent Japanese learning that included loyalty and filial piety, *bushidō*, and finally emperor-centered thought. Slowly, imperceptibly (*shirazushirazu*), these came to contest the monopoly of shogunal military rule until "finally in the Bakumatsu era there was a surge of loyalist thought, and the shogunate collapsed of itself [*shizen ni metsubō suru*]."

And also, he continued—as if not to neglect a single Edo cliché—although the formal hereditary status system (*monbatsusei*) was strictly imposed, forces for its abolition had nonetheless grown in strength. The development of cities, too, made Tokugawa different from earlier times. And then, the activities of commoners were also important, for the "Edo period did not consist solely of the history of samurai but also witnessed the unfolding of the histories of peasants, artisans, and merchants, which then continued during Meiji." Nor, he allowed, "must one forget the rising power of the masterless samurai, the *shishi* men of spirit, and the wealthy peasants who contributed to the age." Literature, too, reached the lower strata of society. "In sum, the first half of the Tokugawa era maintained the forms of samurai rule and, in thrall to the customs established under Ieyasu's skillful policies, continued in its feudal daze. The latter half of the period saw the self-awakening of a sense of nation (*kokkateki kannen*) among the people, the restoration of our imperially centered *kokutai* to its original form, and with it the abolition of the classes (*kaikyū*) and finally the end of the shogunate and the beginning of the Meiji era."[14]

This tour de force of national narrative contained every ingredient of conventional Edo-memory, rearranged to celebrate both the statesmanship of the shogunate's rise and the stateliness of its collapse. It would have delighted the old shogunal types who had tried to rescue the Tokugawa from feudal oblivion in the

14. "Tokugawa jidai," *Nihon hyakka daijiten* (Tokyo: Nihon Hyakka daijiten Kanseikai, 1916), 7:952–53.

1890s (although the spume of national words never sprang so trippingly from their loyal tongues). Edo was now thoroughly populated by *kokumin*, national people *avant la lettre*, who were not only ready for Meiji but helped to bring it about. The old Japan looked to Asia; the new to the West, but no black ships sailed in with any real Westerners in them. Samurai belonged to the past, commoners to the future. Everyone thought and read and studied; no one seemed to work, except perhaps by extrapolation from the mention of peasants, artisans, and merchants. And none of these hungered, suffered, or rose up. Indeed, Edo had so well set the stage for civilization by shaking itself free of its feudal daze that Meiji seemed inevitable, arising as if "of itself." Such was the national folktale of modern Japan.

While such views are now deadeningly familiar, it bears pointing out, first, that Edo-as-tradition began its Meiji career as the bygone old order, which excited little favorable comment or nostalgia except perhaps among former shogunal retainers and other chronological exiles, and, second, when Edo tradition was later re-dressed as fore-modern, it could only strut its preparatory stuff in the single storyline of the national modern. For once modernity constructs its temporal tradition, the narrative holds. And even those who would deny it must dispute it in order to do so, thereby incising it ever deeper in the national memory of time past and future.

CHANGING TIMES

That being said, times change. While invented traditions, once invented, remained traditional (at least for the modern moment under scrutiny here), they did not on that account stay just the same (because the modern moment changed). No single proprietary interest controlled the range of Edo images that coexisted in any period, including the Meiji years I have too neatly chronicled. One constructs a narrative of Edo-memory at peril of erasing the kind of floating signifier that "Edo" always was, and always is. Edo-as-tradition could work no other way. Still, there were times when Edofying grew more intense, when the discursive field of Edo-memory seemed to shift its topology. After the initial emergence, from the 1870s through the 1890s, another significant eruption occurred during the 1920s and 30s, when waves of discontent with post-Meiji modernity brought a seachange in the views of Edo.

In the years after the First World War, the social dislocations wrought by capitalism, war, and empire consumed the energies of numbers of intellectuals, activists, and commentators, in Japan as in Europe. Responding to the human costs exacted by the Meiji pursuit of national civilization, they sought a different and better social future—which impelled them to invoke a different Edo past. The left brought forth Edo images in such profusion that it appeared to one writer as if the Tokugawa era monopolized all historical research because, he knew, "the rise of democratic movements demanded a criticism of feudalism" to bring out the political possibilities latent in the past.[15] Animated by a critique of capitalist modernity, the needs of present politics coursed through the fierce and often exhausting debates among Marxists over the nature of Tokugawa history. Noro Eitarō, the historian-activist, found three contradictions within "centralized feudalism" that might have been capable of bringing the system down: the impoverishment of the samurai, the exploitation of the peasants, and the wealth of the merchants. In this oppositional Edo the left located a tradition of protest that could be turned against the "feudal remnants" that beset modern society—whether by means of land reform, social democracy, or a communist revolution.

The Edo of the left seemed even darker than that of their early Meiji predecessors, for it bore the allegorical weight of the oppressions of both Tokugawa feudalism and the modern capitalism that succeeded it. But they looked, too, to the pre-proletariat of Edo for the precursors of the new age they hoped to help bring about. Some saw bright spots. In his prison notes the Communist Fukumoto Kazuo wrote of a "Japanese Renaissance" of Edo thought and culture from 1651 to 1850, an era that was "one great long bridge arched like a rainbow over the several hundred years of medieval feudalism to link ancient Japanese and Chinese culture with *kinsei* and then with the Meiji Restoration."[16] More poetic than most, his historical rainbow bridge, which bypassed the medieval to connect ancient culture directly to Edo, shared a temporal orientation with others of the left. For their Edo was no less a captive of time than the Edo of Meiji, only in a different way. The road to the future now moved dialectically rather than linearly, but Edo had nonetheless to be aligned on a single path toward the modern. And since those on the left were treading a path decreed either by European historical example or by the Comintern in Moscow, their views of Japan's past produced the logic of deviation and backwardness that itself became traditional in historical depictions of Japan's tradition.[17]

Another oppositional Edo arose during the same years, from the 1910s through the 1930s, again in response to a modernity found wanting but in a different register. Like their counterparts in Germany and France, a portion of the cosmopolitan cultural elite judged the modern condition to be spiritually vacuous, moving at ever-higher speeds toward greater individual alienation, sunk in materialist and commodified values that were the enemy of true culture and inner authenticity. They looked around them at the mass culture on the teeming streets of the modern city and wanted to be somewhere else—Edo. For figures as unlike as Yanagita Kunio, Kuki Shūzō, Nagai Kafū, and Tsuda Sōkichi, Edo became a refuge, a

15. Izu Kimio, "Gendai no rekishigaku" (1947), in *Shinpan Nihon shigaku shi* (Tokyo: Azekura Shobō, 1972), 42.

16. Fukumoto Kazuo, "Nihon runessansu shiron no daiichiji sōkō kara," in *Fukumoto Kazuo shoki chosakushū* (Tokyo: Kobushi Shobō, 1972), 4:316.

17. See Andrew Barshay, "'Doubly Cruel': Marxism and the Presence of the Past in Japanese Capitalism," in this volume.

place of utter difference. Its attraction was that it led nowhere but to itself: no straight path, no lurching dialectic, no rainbow bridge toward the past, indeed no time at all. This Edo-as-tradition offered a cultural space, timeless and unchanging, where the spirit abraded by the masses, machines, and modish modernism could "return" to be refreshed and re-Japanned.

Think of Tokutomi Sohō's paean to Tokyo in 1886, when he proposed to bring the people of Shogun Ienari's time "back from the tomb and let them stand in the Ginza today. . . . They certainly could not comprehend even in their dreams that this is what was known to them as Edo."[18] Then Kafū some forty years later, in his nostalgia for lost low-city pleasures: "Let me list a few of the things I dislike about the Ginza: the enormous cupid dolls, the dolls of the Tengadō, and the girls of the Lion Cafe."[19] The young Sohō was the H. G. Wells of his Meiji day, a true contemporary celebrating smokestacks, parliaments, and "the downfall of our feudal society." The middle-aged Kafū had more in common with Baudelaire (whose poetry he translated), at least in his revulsion against the debased tastelessness of the common man—and the modern girl.

Closer to the Baudelairean high modernist who could not abide the real modernity that surrounded him was Kuki Shūzō, who virtually hallucinated a new cultural Edo in the tradition of taste he identified as *iki*.[20] But this urbane aesthetic theorist was not alone in his retreat to Edo. Yanagita Kunio enshrined as timeless rural tradition what, by visual and performative definition, were chiefly the folkways of Edo, the less tainted by Meiji civilization the better. The folkcraft movement, too, often evoked latter-day Edo-like objects, not because they recalled Tokugawa lives, but because they materialized the authenticity of tradition. Some, like Watsuji Tetsurō, chose earlier periods in which to take refuge from the present. But for the story of Edo-as-tradition, this twentieth-century distaste for modern times proved decisive. It provided a parallel to Edo as historical consciousness, which remained lodged in time, in Edo as a cultural unconscious, a space that appeared eternally the same and essentially Japanese.

The Japanizing of Edo owes much to the same interwar years. The contrast between the "closed country" and the "open country" had of course been starkly felt since the mid-nineteenth century, as had the dichotomous division between things Western and things Japanese that, since Meiji, operated in every iterated domain of theoretical and practical life. But the original inventors of Edo-as-tradition had been hastening toward civilization in a national progress they called "Euro-Americanization." So while they emphasized the native resources Edo

18. Tokutomi Sohō, *The Future Japan*, trans. Vinh Sinh (Alberta: University of Alberta Press, 1989), 16.

19. Edward Seidensticker, *Kafū the Scribbler: The Life and Writings of Nagai Kafū, 1879–1959* (Stanford: Stanford University Press, 1965), 65.

20. *Iki no kōzō* (1930). See Leslie Pincus, *Authenticating Culture in Imperial Japan: Kuki Shūzō and the Rise of National Aesthetics* (Berkeley and Los Angeles: University of California Press, 1996).

offered, they frequently included Western knowledge among them. In wholesale terms, Edo became Japan's native place only later, once that Euro-American modernity had become a reality. For when that modernity disappointed, the disappointment attached itself to the West. A syllogism had formed: Modernity is Westernization. Japan is now modern. Therefore, Japan is Westernized: Japan is no longer Japan. This elision between modernity and the West affected high cosmopolites like Kuki Shūzō, who was as much at home in Paris as in Kyoto, and low ideologues like the Japanists of the fascist 1930s, who wanted to purify Japan of its Western-style material modernity and seek a more spiritual because more martial Japanese kind. Applying the syllogism to history increasingly meant that Japaneseness inhered in Edo, the period before the West appeared and seduced Japan with the siren-calls of a false modern.

Edo nativism also aligned with national identity in another way. In 1918 Shimazaki Tōson, himself not displeased with what he called "the spirit of modernity," made the derogatory observation that "fortunately for us, Nagasaki escaped becoming Singapore," by which he meant that Japan had preserved its independence from colonial rule. His explanation? Japan, unlike India, Egypt, and Turkey, had experienced a feudal age, from Kamakura through Edo. And "from the late eighteenth through the mid-nineteenth century, an extremely conservative spirit flourished," which through its nativism, learning, and patriotism was able to turn Western influence back from the door. "Our country as it is today is a gift of the feudal age."[21] This retro-nativism reserved for Edo the power to repel both the cross and the gunboats and keep Japan Japanese.

The stock of Edo images expanded exponentially during the 1920s, not because of high Edo tastes or low-city Edo connoisseurship but because of the explosion in mass culture. In films and historical fiction, in performances and exhibits, Edo provided the stuff of much of popular entertainment. In kinesic and material terms, everything Edo looked "Japanese": clothes, food, architecture, transport, and the rest. The widely read novels serialized in the newspapers, such as the famous *Daibosatsu tōge* (1913–44) and *Fuji ni tatsu kage* (1924–27) took Edo as their setting, the former as a generalized ambiance for its nihilist samurai protagonist, the latter as an eighty-year historical frame (from Bunka-Bunsei into Meiji) for the interwoven saga of two families. The sixtieth anniversary of the Restoration in 1928 brought a spate of Bakumatsu works, and the perennial tale of the forty-seven *rōnin*, in Osaragi Jirō's new version, was a best-seller at the same time. Quantity made the difference: the vast array of small and large magazines, cheap books, newspapers, and radio broadcasts brought Edo to mass audiences, flooding the media with "traditional" images even as the female icons of *modanizumu* walked the Ginza in flapper fashions. When the wartime government later removed such

21. Shimazaki Tōson, "Umi e," quoted in Kotani Hiroyuki, "Kindai Nihon no jiko ninshiki to Ajiakan," in Arano Yasunori et al., eds., *Ajia no naka no Nihon shi* (Tokyo: Tōkyō Daigaku Shuppankai, 1992), 1:62–64.

extravagances by fiat and patriotic women wore *monpe*, the iconic ground had already been plowed. Extravagance was not the only enemy; overcoming modernity meant folding up the signs of the West and putting them away for the duration.

After the war, Edo-memory, still the same song, resumed in a different key. Under the occupation the bad parts of the past, Tokugawa and imperial Japan included, were labeled "feudal" and rejected. The occupation authorities even locked the Edo culture cabinet for a time, its "feudal" tales of revenge, "militaristic" swordplay, and exploitative hierarchy deemed the enemy of American-style democracy. Equally set against all things "feudal," Japanese of the day also evoked the metaphor of *sakoku*, the closed country, and its opposite, the open country (*kaikoku*). In his book on *sakoku*, subtitled "Japan's tragedy," Watsuji Tetsurō argued that the shogunal policy had been a grave mistake, depriving the Japanese people of the opportunity to develop a "scientific spirit." His was no great revision, since the policy had not been recently defended, even in the wartime textbooks.[22] The evocation of the postwar reforms as the second (or third) opening of the country became the stronger theme, tying postwar Japan not to Edo but to Meiji. Indeed, because so many conceived of postwar goals in terms of a reformed and revamped modernity, the historical uses of Edo resembled those of the Meiji apostles of enlightenment. That is, Edo-as-tradition became temporal again, a period of premodernity to be assessed for its contributions to or blockades against a more perfect modern. But now positions appeared more evenly distributed on both sides than they had been in early Meiji; the Edo chiaroscuro was mottled while the black darkness fell on the imperial years of fascism and war. Then as the postwar period wore prosperously on and conservative voices grew stronger, Edo brightened considerably, stepping back by the 1970s into the "preparatory" role that Uchida Ginzō had assigned it when modernity was looking good after the turn of the century.

Something rather different happened during the 1980s when the so-called Edo boom hit and Tokugawa times received more attention—and more hype—than probably ever before. Once again a cultural storehouse, Edo escaped time as it had in the 1920s, only now it became a space of postmodern freedom, play, and infinite *baraechii* (variety). "No truth or ego needed! Edo-style playfulness" beckoned.[23] Edo-ologists like Tanaka Yūko celebrated Edo-the-city—its energies of cultural overripeness and *nettowaaku* (networks) of information, poetry, and science, in which culture passed from person to person in a series of endless, structureless links (*tsurane*). Her contributions to the "Edo Renaissance" of the mid-1980s featured creative eccentrics like Hiraga Gennai and Santō Kyōden (in her

22. Watsuji Tetsurō, *Sakoku: Nihon no higeki* (Tokyo: Chikuma Sōsho, 1964). See also Kobori Keiichirō, *Sakoku no shisō* (Tokyo: Chūkō Shinsho, 1974).

23. "Tokushū: Edo runessansu," *Asahi jānaru* (January 2–9, 1987). "Ō-Edo mandara waido," *Asahi jānaru* (October 2, 1987).

words "the Warhol of Edo") rather than shogunal reformers or Confucian heavy thinkers. Gennai appealed precisely because, unlike the scholars of Western learning who "contributed to modernity, Hiraga Gennai did not contribute to anything" but through his "clattering about" exemplified the "swirling ambiance of eighteenth-century Edo."[24] Escape to Edo thus trumped the tyranny of the linear, rationalist modern.

In this image of "happy feudalism," the "Genroku salaryman" indulged himself in leisure, pleasure, and, above all, things—a commodified reflection of the bubble consumerism of the 1980s. Not so the Genroku women, who though they were accorded attention and a greater measure of subjectivity, remained largely trapped in the still perennial Edo image of the pleasure quarters. The freedom implied by the phrase "Edo girls with no fear of flying" in fact referred to amateur concubines of foreigners (*rashamen*), a not-unfamiliar male preoccupation. And women scholars acknowledged the challenge of writing about Edo culture, "based as it was on theater and the licensed quarters."[25] Meanwhile Edo-the-city became a media fetish, its "*yaminabe* culture" described as a bubbling social stew of who-knows-what, preferable to present-day society, which separates people by clear partitions like a pot of *oden*.[26] Ō-Edo mandala, Ō-Edo recycling, Ō-Edo technology—the networks of mass information filled with paeans to a Great City of Edo that Tokutomi Sohō and Nagai Kafū would have neither recognized nor approved of.

In its postmodern modes Edo-memory sometimes eliminated the tradition-modernity divide altogether. Modern times, located somewhere between the Meiji Restoration and postwar High Growth, disappeared from the historical frame. One could almost see them go: "'Edo' is definitely not our 'past' because the 'past' is not simply a temporal relation between before and after. It is up to us now to encounter 'Edo.' In this sense 'Edo' is really the future." By this sleight of (somewhat silly) historical hand, Edo became tomorrow.[27] For Karatani Kōjin, Edo was more appropriately compared to today. He described the postmodern 1980s as a cultural revival of Bunka-Bunsei (1804–30), which by such standards as decentering, spatiality, simulacra, and the like, had already reached postmodernity. The historical prescience that enabled Edo to reach the postmodern before the modern had even arrived suggested a new nativist narrative. Karatani asserted a nearly exact parallel between Chinese thought in Edo and Western ideas

24. For Gennai, Tanaka Yūko, *Edo no sōzōryoku: 18-seiki no media to hyōchō* (Tokyo: Chikuma Shobō, 1986), 50. For Warhol, Tanaka Yūko, *Edo wa nettowaaku* (Tokyo: Heibonsha, 1993), 143–85.

25. Araki Seizō, "Tonderu Edo no musumetachi," in *Rashamen* (Tokyo: Tairiku Shobō, 1982); Itasaka Yōko, *Edo no onna, ima no onna* (Fukuoka: Ashi Shobō, 1993), 222.

26. Tanabe Seiko and Sugiura Hinako, "Motto funwaka shita warai ga hoshii," *Ushio* 353 (September 1988): 162–63.

27. "Edogaku no susume," *Gendai shisō, Sōtokushū* (1986). See Noguchi Takehiko, *Edojin no rekishi ishiki* (Tokyo: Asahi Shinbunsha, 1987), 3–12.

since Meiji: a logocentric, rationalist stance characterized them both. But Edo thinkers from Itō Jinsai to Motoori Norinaga had already begun to "deconstruct" the dominant discourse of Chu Hsi Confucianism, producing an alternative tradition that was lost when modern Western reason usurped the epistemological center in Meiji.[28] Thus Karatani's newly Derridean Edo suggested an ahistory in which Japan's premodern was in fact already post-.

The pomo Edo of the 1980s emerged from a larger postmodern move to grasp the cultural logic of a modernity that had altered enough in late capitalist societies so as to seem a different animal. As in earlier periods of rethinking, Japan shared the historical challenge with other places. That Edo became an archival site of this postmodern mapping owed to the long-ago invented and longtime naturalized tradition of Edo as modern Japan's historical imaginary of first and last resort. The Japanizing of preternaturally postmodern Edo retained the old Japan-West division but changed the terms of the earlier syllogism to make (post) modernity Japanese. And after the word *posutomodan* faded from popular (not theoretical) ubiquity in the 1990s, Edo remained somehow "transmodern," in that its modernity seldom any longer suffered the prefix "pre-." This was not because Edo had become tomorrow but because the term "modern" had everywhere destabilized, turned fluid, lost the solidity of its earlier referents. In the steady stream of commentary about the fate of *fin-de-siècle* Japan, the search for a new future that did not depend on Western definitions entailed, as before, evocations of Edo.

And in the conservative, neo-nationalist, and uncertain 1990s, Edo had never looked better. Celebration came in many varieties, including the considerable literature pitched at businessmen who, if they followed the "Genroku way of the samurai," would find their way to prosperity in the present.[29] Hailing Edo in this way was not new. Historians such as Ōishi Shinzaburō, Hayami Akira, and Haga Tōru had long argued for a more positive, because proto-modern, view of Edo.[30] "What is Edo?" asked Bitō Masahide in 1992, answering: Japanese modernity (*Nihonteki kindai*), which was succeeded by Western modernity after the Restoration. He then began with the prehistoric Yayoi period to make the long historical point that the transition to the modern had occurred "of itself" (not from outside) in the fifteenth and sixteenth centuries. Everything before Edo he called "ancient," everything after Edo "modern." As for that once epochal event, the Meiji

28. Karatani Kōjin, "Ri no hihan: Nihon shisō ni okeru puremodan to posutomodan," *Gendai shi techō* 29, no. 5 (May 1986): 36–47.

29. "Genroku bushi (sararīman) gaku–*Budō shoshinshū* o yomu," *Will* (May 1986).

30. E.g., Ōishi Shinzaburō, Nakane Chie, et al., *Edo jidai to kindaika* (Tokyo: Chikuma Shobō, 1986). Also Nakane and Ōishi, eds., *Tokugawa Japan: The Social and Economic Antecedents of Modern Japan* (Tokyo: University of Tokyo Press, 1990); Hayami Akira, *Rekishi no naka no Edo jidai* (Tokyo: Tōkyō Keizai Shinpōsha, 1977); Haga Tōru, ed., *Bunmei toshite no Tokugawa Nihon. Sōsho hikaku bungaku hikaku bunka*, vol. 1 (Tokyo: Chūō Kōronsha, 1993).

Restoration, unlike the bloody revolutions in other places, it occurred "without a hitch" (*junchō ni*): "the Edo shogunate self-destructed in a relatively smooth manner (*junchō ni*)" and the modern state was easily established (*junchō ni*).[31] And the reason for this "piece-of-cake" transition, of course, was already-modern Edo.

The civilization theorists of the 1990s found in Edo a modernity not only for Japan but for the world. "Was Edo a dream?" No, it was "a kind of socialist paradise" based on policies of economic equality.[32] Did Tokugawa Japan lag behind the West? Not a bit: in seclusion it experienced an "industrious revolution" of its own, gave up the gun, and lived peaceably in Asia while Europe tore itself apart.[33] Indeed, "the new civilization rising from Japan" at the beginning of a new millennium would owe everything to Edo, when Japanese, "living in a limited space, maintained a balance in power, preserved the environment, and achieved a relatively affluent society." Now with resources and space everywhere in short supply, the "world is Edo-izing" (*sekai wa Edoka suru*), and Japan would be a model for the globe.[34] This civilizational puffery crested on a surge of nationalist self-satisfaction, but it may also have signified what one writer called an eschatological sense of the impending end of the forever forward-pressing modern, a "long historical sigh" that found refuge once again in Edo.[35]

TOKUGAWA TROPES

However varied the sighs and glows that fell on Edo across the changing times, the historical inventory of Edo images remained remarkably constant, from the beginning of Meiji to the end of the twentieth century. As examples of the lost-wax process by which tradition was molded of modernity, here are four fundamental figures of Edo discourse and the aspects of the modern from which they took their inverted shape.

First, the trope that re"class"ified Edo by fastening on the status hierarchy only to undo it. Known in Meiji as "the relations between high and low" and more recently as the Tokugawa "status system" (*mibun seido*), the four-class hereditary division of samurai, peasant, artisan, and merchant (*shinōkōshō*) was the primordial and is perhaps still the preeminent construction of Edo-as-tradition. "Feudalism," in its affective Meiji meaning, evoked the economic fetters and social shackles that Tokutomi Sohō said had divided the people into slavelike commoners and samu-

31. Bitō Masahide, *Edo jidai to wa nani ka: Nihonshijō no kinsei to kindai* (Tokyo: Iwanami Shoten, 1992), vi–xv, 1–16.

32. Mizutani Mitsuhiro, *Edo wa yume ka* (Tokyo: Chikuma Shobō, 1992), 2.

33. Kawakatsu Heita, *Nihon bunmei to kindai seiyō: "Sakoku" saikō* (Tokyo: NHK Bukkusu, 1991). "Industrious revolution" is Hayami Akira's phrase. See also Kawakatsu, *Atarashii Ajia no dorama* (Tokyo: Chikuma Shobō, 1994).

34. Irie Takanori, *Nihon ga tsukuru shinbunmei* (Tokyo: Kōdansha, 1992), 27, 258.

35. Kawahara Hiroshi, *"Edo" no seishin shi* (Tokyo: Perikansha, 1992), 9.

rai masters and inhibited their nascent entrepreneurial spirit.[36] By the 1920s the left called the same system institutionalized serfdom and exploitative class collusion. But in nearly every inflection, this feudal tradition stood in juxtaposition to the social illusions of modernity, which posited a leveling of hereditary status or a co-equalization of access and obligation. For some, like the Meiji popular rights activists, the progressive left, and the agrarianist right of the interwar period, the social leveling took political shape. For Edo in popular culture, it gestured rather to the social homogenization that underlay the twentieth-century myth of society as one vast middle class.

The feudal fetters, one sees, were there to be metaphorically loosed, so that a view of emancipatory Edo accompanied the insistence on hierarchy. As a counter-trope to Fukuzawa's image of millions of Japanese "closed up inside millions of individual boxes" separated by class walls "as strong as iron," there came forth the image of Tokugawa society as flexible, permeable, and free.[37] Spaces of autonomy appeared in village festivals, urban gay quarters, on the roads and along the edges of the status compartments. In the interstices of the four-class system existed pockets of entirely "democratic society." Equality in human relationships was said to offset differences in hierarchical status. Even work, the very sign of hereditary occupational status, could come unchained: "Edo commoners, all *furii-arubaitaa* (freelancers)," in the words of the happy postmodern.[38] The civilizationist Umehara Takeshi, ever reaching beyond the reasonable, wrote that the free hunting culture of prehistoric Jōmon and its preference for equality had revived with the rise of the city of Edo.[39] Edo images stressed mobility, especially for townsmen and peasants, at times for lower samurai as well. Then there was Nakane Chie's astonishing comment on the virtues of social oppression: "the Tokugawa social system encouraged those on the bottom to strive to better themselves and thereby raised the general sophistication of the masses."[40] Two contrary molds were being cast here: the first served the modern social ideology of rising in the world through one's own efforts by making self-help an Edo tradition; the second saw modernity itself as the iron box and sought an escape hatch in an Edo where commoners enjoyed a freedom that had now been lost.

Commoners, always commoners: Edo, in social epithet, appeared as a *shomin shakai*, commoner society. Here memory performed a kind of ideological *gekokujō*, where the lowly came out on top. Despite—or more likely, because—everyone knew that the small samurai elite ruled during Tokugawa, one of the strongest images of Edo depicted commoner vitality, popular creativity, and sometimes civil

---

36. Tokutomi, *Future Japan*, 16.
37. Fukuzawa, *An Outline of Civilization*, 160.
38. Tanabe and Sugiura, "Motto funwaka shita," 154–55.
39. Umehara Takeshi, "Edo, Jōmonteki naru mono no fukkatsu," *Asahi jānaru* (January 2–9, 1987).
40. Nakane Chie, "Tokugawa Society," in Nakane and Ōishi, *Tokugawa Japan*, 231.

society (*shimin shakai*), mass society, or even a humane society in an "age of humanity" (*ningen no jidai*). Chafing under Meiji authoritarianism, Kitamura Tōkoku found the beginnings of democratic society (*heimin shakai*) in "the voices of the people" first raised in Genroku literature.[41] Others looked to the plebeian society of the city of Edo in the eighteenth century, when the period was at its "most Edo-like."[42] Townsmen, or peasants acting like them, represented entrepreneurial and consumerist Edo but received equal credit for the efflorescence of their cultural production. And the enormous popular stock of Edo images associated with material culture and the practices of daily life emerged largely from the houses and shops of commoners, a term that included (and leveled) peasants, artisans, merchants, and townsmen. In this way the ideological nation of samurai that Yanagita Kunio evoked in the Meiji period became instead a cultural nation of commoners. Here modern memory made its homogenizing social myths out of hierarchical Edo cloth, as if dismissing the aristocracy in the process.

But where have all the *bushi* gone? The samurai certainly appeared in the precincts of Edo-memory, sometimes negatively as idle parasites, often positively as shogunal reformers, men of talent, or sage officials like Ōoka Echizen no Kami, famous for dispensing a trans-Solomonic judgment that resulted in each of the two parties to the dispute—and also the judge himself—losing an equal sum of money. The shogunal official Tanuma Okitsugu, once viewed as a one-man "swamp of corruption," reappeared in the administrative mood of the early 1990s as a brilliant financial bureaucrat.[43] But the most popular and perduring Edo samurai appeared as the heroes and anti-heroes of film and fiction: the forty-seven *rōnin* of Chūshingura, which remained the best known and most told tale of Edo, the nameless cinematic swordsmen of *chanbara*, and the named Bakumatsu "men of spirit" epitomized by Sakamoto Ryōma. For ideological and militaristic purposes, the samurai models came from earlier feudal eras, with Kusunoki Masashige the favored choice in imperial schoolbooks. Edo supplied only the forty-seven *rōnin*, and even they fell victim to wartime moralism in the 1940s.

Business magazines in the 1990s still sounded the call of *bushidō*—"There's no future in a Japan that has lost its samurai *maindo*. Men, take back your pride and your will!"[44] After Prime Minister Hosokawa quoted Nitobe Inazō in a speech at the United Nations in 1993, a reprint of Nitobe's Meiji book on *bushidō* was advertised as providing the key to the "national mind" and the "driving force in Japan's

41. Kitamura Tōkoku, "Tokugawa shi jidai no heiminteki risō," in *Tōkoku zenshū* (Tokyo: Iwanami Shoten, 1950), 1:358–64.

42. Nakano Mitsutoshi, *Uchinaru Edo: Kinsei saikō* (Tokyo: Yudachisha, 1994), 8.

43. Ōishi Shinichirō, *Tanuma iyoku no jidai* (Tokyo, 1992). For a post-bubble view, "from Tanuma Okitsugu's bubble to Matsudaira Sadanobu's *risutora*," see Dōmon Fuyuji, *Numa to kawa no aida de* (Tokyo: Mainichi Shinbunsha, 1995).

44. "Otoko wa ikani ikubeki ka: Ima 'bushidō' ni manabu," *Purejidento* (October 1992; special issue).

development."[45] But while this sort of generalized samurai aura lived on in popular discourse, when it came to Edo, the *bushi* seldom appeared as the main protagonists of tradition. That role belonged to commoners—who were all samurai now. With this trope the historical lineaments of the modern arrangements of power, which had originated in the redeployment of Edo samurai as Meiji bureaucrats, disappeared from collective view.

The second trope established the modern visions of, and divisions between, the country and the city. During Meiji the village became identified as the Japanese Ur-community, as if from time immemorial, when in fact it was almost always described in its specific Tokugawa forms. The household (*ie*) system, the patriarchal family, the "traditional Japanese woman" were all Meiji refabrications that partly drew on Edo images and partly retrojected backward phenomena, such as the "good wife, wise mother" that most of Edo had never known. In the manner of Bashō and Buson, whose poetic images of nature in the eighteenth-century countryside had owed much to their lives in the city, the good life later imputed to the so-called natural village came mostly from modern metropolitan minds.[46] The sets of the *Edo-mono* on television with their decidedly ungorgeous buildings of wood, tile, and thatch—or for that matter, a visit to any rusticated *soba* shop—gave the latter-day urbanite a whiff of what Yanagita Kunio had long ago sought in the valley of Tōno: the evocation of a folkish rural past.

Edo-memory also repositioned the peasants, not only as the carriers of folk tradition but as agents of their own history. Some, like Hayami Akira and others drawn by the "appeal of Edo," characterized the Tokugawa peasant as a commercializing, profit-maximizing, family-planning, rational head-of-household farmer. They represented what Eric Hobsbawm once called "the cheerful historians," whose view of the past explained away the miseries they preferred not to see. Their number grew larger and their tone more cheerful with the expanding economic self-satisfaction of the 1970s and 1980s. The uncheerful historians, who constituted the majority for much of the century, preferred to chronicle the ritually or violently uprising, exploited peasant or the socially creative, morally economical communitarian peasant.[47] But whether described as powerless against oppression or empowered by its social forms and religious beliefs, the peasantry became the protagonist of the Edo countryside. This particular reinvention suited social modernity in Japan, which in demographic fact, at least, was a nation composed largely of peasants.

But the Edo period possessed an urban and urbane side as well, celebrated in memory as a cultural space rather than a historical time. Modern ideology and

45. Ad and jacket copy for *Gendaigo de yomu saikō no meichō: Bushidō*, ed. Naramoto Tatsuya (Tokyo: Mikasa Shobō, 1993).

46. See Kurachi Katsunao, "Shizen to ningen, karada to kokoro," in Hirota Masaki, ed., *Minshū no kokoro, Nihon no kinsei*, vol. 16 (Tokyo: Chūō Kōronsha, 1993).

47. E.g, "Edo jidai no miryoku," *Shokun!* (September 1976); Nakane and Ōishi, *Tokugawa Japan*; Hayami Akira, *Atarashii Edo jidaishi zō o motomete* (Tokyo: Tōyō Keizai Shinpōsha, 1976).

social policy preferred the village to the city, which harbored so many elements that seemed iniquitous to the state. Edo-as-tradition also located the ethnographic folk and the socioeconomic peasantry in the countryside, poised along a time-line toward Meiji and the modern. But in an often-countermodern move, twentieth-century intellectuals imagined the cities as (free) spaces of culture, consumption, and desire. From *ikki* to *iki*, from peasant uprisings to urban chic, the move from countryside to city expressed a cultural secession from the modern present, both in the interwar years and in the postmodern 1980s. In this trope, Osaka, the merchant city, and Edo, the shogunal city with its thriving plebeian society, appeared as zones of cosmopolitanism and commodification, associated with images of Genroku culture, the pleasure quarters, and *chōnin* (townsman) canniness. Edo-the-city became a prime site of cultural nostalgia, a kind of phantasmic counter-Tokyo and a synecdoche of commoner culture. The visitor to Edomura theme park, after purchasing a shogun (eleven pavilions), daimyo (four pavilions), or townsman (one pavilion) pass, could wander through this "special period in world history," stopping at the iconic sites of both the city and the era—the Yoshiwara, the residence of Lord Kira of Chūshingura, an Edo tenement, a *ninja* mansion, an Edo theater, courthouse, and jail—while street entertainers performed "typical Japanese arts" and vendors hawked "the tastes of traditional Japanese cuisine," with nary a peasant or a paddyfield in sight.[48]

The third trope centered on the Tokugawa shogunate—the realm, the system, the state—in short, the institutional arrangements of the political ancien régime. Here feudalism meant the oxymoronic "centralized feudalism" of the shogun-domainal system (*bakuhan taisei* in current usage). Its modern referent was always the centralized imperial nation-state, which, depending on the interpreter, had either abolished the Tokugawa polity or continued its centralizing momentum while shedding its feudalism. The issue had bifocal importance: For the cheerful historians who saw the shogunal state as already unified, public, and territorially, ideologically "Japanese," Edo was already modern. The Meiji state amounted only to a seasonal "change-of-clothes" (*Meiji koromogae kokka*) from Japanese to Western style.[49] The real centralizing work had been done under the Tokugawa. On the other side stood the progressives, uncheerful, who insisted on the unmodern feudal character of Edo that had hobbled the modern state by surviving the Restoration, in remnants if not in entire garments. Looking through the historical lens at a different angle, these same groups measured Japan's "traditional" institutions against versions elsewhere in the world, calling them absolutist, proto-nationalist, or fully feudal, and judging their strengths and failings—but always in relation to the temporal sequence leading nowhere else but to the modern.

48. Nikkō Edomura is located in Karakura, Tochigi Prefecture, near Kinugawa *onsen*.
49. Kimura Shōzaburō, in Hayami Akira, *Rekishi no naka*, 205–6. See also Bitō, *Edo jidai*; Tsuji, *Edo jidai*.

Perhaps the most indelible impression of the Tokugawa polity was its character as a "system" (*taisei*)—not merely a regime but a totality that assumed, or attempted to assume, control of "all under heaven." The modern stamp here derived first from imperial Japan, which proceeded to assert its own kind of systematic control over everything and everybody. But the sense of system also reflected the feeling that history happened from above, both then and now. Indeed, politics appeared far less prominently in Edo-memory than did society, which seemed to operate best in the loopholes it created in the system, and culture, which flourished as an almost independent realm. This displacement of politics from the historical imaginary said as much (or more) about the relation between the ruler and the ruled in modern Japan as it did about the Edo past.

Tales of the unifiers were a staple of popular culture, which thrived on squabbles over which of the three, Hideyoshi, Nobunaga, or Ieyasu, deserved most credit or blame. And people knew about the shogunal "three great reforms" of Yoshimune, Matsudaira, and Mizuno. But the political achievement of the shogunate that outweighed all others, from Meiji to Heisei, was the so-called Pax Tokugawa. In 1882 Taguchi Ukichi, who had few good words for the shogunate, praised the "era of great peace" for enabling society to progress "without government protection or foreign borrowing."[50] In 1986 Haga Tōru, who had nothing but good to say for the "Pax Tokugawana," compared the "ingenious" alternate attendance system to international organizations like UNESCO. And his colleague added, with a straight face, that "the Tokugawa system did a spectacular job of ending. Japan did not become a colony, and its human resources and wisdom passed to Meiji," which—he neglected to add—promptly used the tradition of peace to go to war.[51]

The fourth trope was *sakoku*, the closed country (and its historical opposite *kaikoku*, the open country)—the most pervasive Edo image after the four-class social hierarchy and surely the single most evoked metaphor from the Edo past. From the beginning, even before the closed country was opened, *sakoku* stood both for Japan's relations with the world and the achievement of modernity on Western versus native terms. Some disputed the meaning of *sakoku*, insisting that Edo, while closed in some ways, remained open in others, including trade with Asia and the absorption of Western learning. Others gainsaid its effect, portraying Edo as a hothouse of national culture, which enabled Japanese to assert its cultural independence from China and ready itself for the challenge from the West. Some, like Tokutomi Sohō in his hundred-volume history of the Tokugawa era, judged *sakoku* a grand shogunal error that had turned Japan into a "bagworm," which by the time it emerged from its case in the mid-nineteenth century had missed the world-historical moment for imperial expansion.[52] Others thought the policy reasonable, effective, or smart: it

50. Taguchi, *Nihon kaika*, 49–60.

51. Haga Tōru, "Idai naru kana 'Pakkusu-Tokugawana,'" in Ōishi, Nakane, et al., *Edo jidai*, 443; Tanizawa Eiichi on the spectacular ending, in ibid., 451.

52. Tokutomi Sohō, *Kinsei Nihon kokuminshi* (Tokyo: Meiji Shoin, 1935), 14:2.

prevented Western colonization, protected bullion resources, and, above all, kept the peace. *Sakoku* was Japan's tragedy—or its triumph, a creation economically comparable with the European world system established at the same time.[53]

While no single view ever held the entire stage, the perturbations in Japan's modern international relations can be traced in the changing evocations of *sakoku*. As national pride waxed in the course of the 1970s, the lack of direct Western contact seemed advantageous: Edo Japanese had acquired what they wanted from the West in the felicitous condition of having access to the West without Westerners having had access to them. As international conditions grew uncertain in the 1990s, nostalgia for the closed country returned. Once, in the vexed year of 1932, locked-away Edo had appeared like "spring in an island paradise." And again in 1992, amid trade frictions, immigrant workers, and international peacekeeping operations, people looked with affection on the self-sufficiency of Edo, cozy "inside the threshold of *sakoku*."[54]

The open/closed country also served the cause of separating Japan from the West, uncoupling the old syllogism that made modernity Western. In the 1980s cheerful historians and cheering conservatives promoted indigenous Edo by contrasting it with the West in the same centuries. The Edo economy was as advanced as the European economies in the seventeenth and eighteenth centuries; it emerged from the yoke of religion a century ahead of Europe; and while Japanese culture flourished "during the Edo era, there wasn't anything but buffalo in America."[55] Because all this had allegedly occurred while the country was closed to the West, *sakoku* provided support for the argument that Japan had become modern in its own way, on its own terms, "of itself." But since the West was never Japan's only Other, the closed-country image also continually shifted in reference to relations with Asia. Edo's openness to Western ideas figured in Meiji explanations of why Japan ranked ahead of China and Korea on the civilizational scale. Edo's resistance to Western imperialism played a rhetorical role in justifying Japan's own imperialism on pan-Asian grounds. When Japanese rediscovered Asia during the 1980s, historians stressed that Edo had always been open to the region. To make the point, they replaced the term *sakoku* with a Japanese version of the Sinic "order of the civilized and the barbarian."[56] Yet in spite (or because) of the fact that closing off the country was no longer possible in reality, the metaphor retained its power in the historical imaginary expressed by the familiar Tokugawa tropes.

53. Watsuji, *Sakoku*; Kawakatsu, *Nihon bunmei*, 127.

54. "Edo jidai," *Daihyakka jiten* (Tokyo: Heibonsha, 1932), 3:266; Kawahara, *"Edo,"* 10.

55. Ōtani Mizuo, *Rekishi no ronri: "Hōken" kara kindai e* (Tokyo: Tōsui Shobō, 1988), 36; Ōishi Shinzaburō, "Gendai Nihon no genkei wa Edo jidai ni aru ka," in Ōishi and Nakane, et al., eds., *Edo jidai*, 10; Ishihara Shintarō, quoted in *Wall Street Journal* (November 7, 1989).

56. Arano Yasunori, *Kinsei Nihon to higashi Ajia* (Tokyo: Tōkyō Daigaku Shuppankai, 1988). See also Ronald P. Toby, *State and Diplomacy in Early Modern Japan: Asia in the Development of the Tokugawa Bakufu* (Princeton: Princeton University Press, 1984).

EDO ALLEGORIES

Edo-as-tradition lived its rhetorical life in prefixes to modernity. Edo was un-pre-proto-post–modern, always in teleological relation to what came after it. Structurally unmodern Edo might be feudal, semi-civilized, or reactionary, requiring a revolution to eliminate obstacles like Confucianism, parasitic landlords, or authoritarian elites. Seductively unmodern Edo could be prelapsarian, arcadian, a garden of urban delights before the fall to Western modernity. Presciently premodern Edo prepared the way for modernity in commercialization, urbanization, centralization, and the other "-izations" that comprised the gradual, evolutionary scenario of becoming modern. Proto-modern Edo did the same thing, primarily in economic processes like proto-industrialization. Partly premodern Edo showed signs, or sprouts, of modernity, as defined by Western models of Marxism or liberalism, but the soil proved infertile either because its balance was predominantly un-modern and the sprouts withered or because they were crushed by the Meiji state.

Edo could also be potentially modern, the breezes of political and social change blowing in Japanese directions, only to be halted by the Western gale that swamped the trends of indigenous change occurring in commoner society. For some, Edo contained the origins (*genten*) or original form (*genkei*) of the modern, so that the national state, for example, "emerged" after the Restoration but had been created during Tokugawa. For others, Edo was already modern because the moment of transition had occurred earlier, usually in the fifteenth and sixteenth centuries. Postmodern Edo went modernity one better by getting there first, so that the Restoration period marked the end of the Edo postmodern rather than the beginning of modern Meiji. All of these teleological Edos posited a historical "tradition" that lived, as it were, for the modern.

The relation of Edo-as-tradition to modernity was stated not only in prefixes of linear history but also through the medium of difference and identity. At one extreme Edo was imagined as alterity, a place utterly different from the present. When Meiji Japanese turned their back on the past in pursuit of a wholly new age, they took up the challenge of overcoming tradition, which they defined as the opposite of the future they envisioned. When interwar Marxists elaborated their critique of feudalism, they articulated the differences that ought to have obtained between the feudal past and capitalist present, and found those differences incomplete: hence, the feudal remnants. When moderns and postmoderns sought refuge in the byways of bygone Edo, it was the thrill of difference they desired. In these instances Edo was the historical other, the past.

At the other extreme, Edo was imagined as essentially, identically the same time as today. Japanese traditions, cultural identity, social and economic foundations were all established in Edo, and "despite the major upheaval of the Meiji Restoration and the modernization process that followed, society has experienced no fundamental structural change."[57] This aboriginal Edo was the ground of

57. Nakane Chie, "Introduction," in Nakane and Ōishi, *Tokugawa Japan*, 7.

identity, an ahistorical, essentialist Japan that knew neither modernity nor tradition. The historical Edo became a space between two times. Change occurred before its beginning in sixteenth-century Sengoku and at its end, in mid-nineteenth-century Bakumatsu. In between spread a synchronic panorama of Japaneseness, an Edo frozen as national tradition. In these instances, memory displaced history, and Edo the storehouse of identity lay entirely outside time.

As the master trope for tradition, Edo was an allegory that evoked what was other to the modern. It was both gone and not gone, both the world that was lost and the world that never was. Like the Middle Ages in European memory, Edo was modernity's way of pinching itself to be sure it was real. And as modernity continued the colonization of the past by the future, Edo-as-tradition remained forever trapped in the mirror of the modern.

EIGHTEEN

Afterword

Revisiting the Tradition/Modernity Binary

Dipesh Chakrabarty

I have organized my response to this volume in three parts. The first part argues how and why this book extends the original framework of "the invention of tradition." In the second part, I read the contributions to this volume to highlight certain themes that, for me, have strong resonances in my own area of research, modern Indian history. In the third part, I utilize the reading in the preceding section to discuss a few questions that this book raises for an outsider looking into the history of modernity in Japan.

The essays collected here exceed—as indeed they should—the intellectual charter of the problematic of "the invention of tradition" as it was set out by Eric Hobsbawm more than ten years ago. That original charter stayed well within the problematic of analyzing "ideologies"—in this case, ideological uses of the past. And the exposition of the framework by Hobsbawm was not without some ambiguities and difficulties.

Hobsbawm, readers will recall, saw it as one key characteristic of all "invented traditions" that they each claimed to represent some invariant quality of the past. This was the ground on which he distinguished "tradition" from "custom":

> The object and characteristic of "traditions," including invented ones, is invariance. The past, real or invented, to which they refer imposes fixed (normally formalized) practices. . . . "Custom" in traditional societies has the double function of motor and fly-wheel. It does not preclude innovation and change up to a

I am grateful to Rajyashree Pandey, Anne Hardgrove, and Jonathan Mee for discussions and comments.

point. . . . "Custom" cannot afford to be invariant, because in "traditional" societies life is not so.[1]

Hobsbawm's distinction between pasts "real or invented" is easily explained: "real past" must allude to something that demonstrably happened, while "invented" refers to a "false" (i.e., proved false by professional historians' methods of proof) claim made about the past. "Myths," by this account, would have to be classified under "customs," for myths change and do not preclude innovation. But then how does one distinguish between "invented" and "noninvented" traditions? "The term 'invented tradition,'" Hobsbawm writes,

> includes both "traditions" actually invented, constructed and formally instituted and those emerging in a less easily traceable manner within a brief and dateable period—a matter of a few years perhaps—and establishing themselves with great rapidity. The royal Christmas broadcast in Britain (instituted in 1932) is an example of the first; the appearance and the development of the practices associated with the Cup Final in British Association Football, of the second.[2]

At first sight, the typology of "invented traditions" may look neat, but on closer inspection it reveals certain problems. When do we, for instance, call a tradition "real," that is, noninvented? And how would real traditions be different from "customs"? Clearly, datable and formally instituted cultural practices or rituals, and rituals of recent origin enjoying a rapid rise to the status of something time-honored, fall within the category of invented traditions. But this is not enough for a definition: we have to add the other requirement insisted on by Hobsbawm, that these invented traditions, in order to be classifiable as "invented," must also claim to stand for invariant pasts. At this point, the system of nomenclature begins to encounter difficulties. For if a noninvented tradition is one that does not show these characteristics, it would be difficult to separate it from what Hobsbawm has called "custom." Second, the picture of a changeless or static past is usually itself a construction of early-modern European historical or sociological thinking. It has seldom been a non-Western society's way of describing itself until recent times. Just as "traditional" societies do not usually see themselves as "traditional," similarly societies ascribed to have changeless pasts—such as Indian society before British rule or the Australian Aboriginal society before European occupation—seldom saw themselves in those terms until their subjugation by Europeans or European modes of thought. Both the arguments for and the arguments against the tendency to see any history or culture as static, are themselves modern. The idea that "change" is intrinsic to the nature of the historical process itself and that therefore any ascription of "changelessness" to a society must constitute an error of judgment, is fundamentally a feature of the thought apparatus of both eighteenth/nineteenth-

---

1. Eric J. Hobsbawm and Terence O. Ranger, eds., *The Invention of Tradition* (Cambridge: Cambridge University Press, 1994), 2.
2. Ibid., 1.

century philosophers such as Hegel and recent modernization theorists that we, historians and social scientists, fight against today. It is easy to agree with Hobsbawm when he argues, "against both nineteenth-century liberalism and . . . modernization theory," that "invented traditions" are a ubiquitous feature of modern societies. But he seems to be on much less certain grounds when he says that "there is probably no time and place with which historians are concerned which has not seen the 'invention' of tradition in this sense."[3] It may indeed be anachronistic to talk about "traditional," nonmodern societies inventing traditions for themselves.

In other words, the "invention of tradition" framework, as explained by Hobsbawm, appears to be theoretically innocent with regard to its own implication in modern systems of thought. Its more positive contribution may have been to raise a functionalist, but nevertheless interesting, question about why "tradition" is called into being by the very demands of modernity itself: how do "traditionalizing" claims function as "ideology" in times of rapid social change (such as those produced by capitalist transformation or the genesis of a nation-state)?[4] This is what Stephen Vlastos seems to have taken as one of his guiding questions in putting together this volume. He and several of his collaborators in this volume use, with great effect, the historian's capacity to "surprise" and "startle" the reader by documenting the relatively recent appearance in Japan of cultural and social practices (such as "weak legal consciousness" or industrial paternalism) presumed to predate modernization.[5] Vlastos's introduction summarizes these aspects of the contributions to this volume, and I do not wish to repeat his points here.

But the papers in this volume, to the extent that they take their cue from Hobsbawm, all go to show both the strengths and the limitations of his framework. They demonstrate, for example, how powerful the "invention of tradition" framework can be when used as a tool for unmasking "ideology," in particular the ideologies of the nation-state and capitalism. In that sense, Itō Kimio strikes a note characteristic of this volume as a whole when he declares that the spirit of *wa* "took on the ideological function of state integration."[6] The very use of the category "ideology," however, entails a theoretical dilemma of which we are more aware in the 1990s. Having "demystified" a particular ideology, what does one put in its place—the "real"? There thus remains a problematic tendency to oppose "invented traditions" to the historical realities these traditions are seen as trying to cover up, to see the former as a denial of the latter. Thus Scheiner writes that "an attempt to reify images of Japan as a community united by elemental themes . . . ignores the problematic of the past, its authoritarianism and status hierarchy, and

3. Ibid., 4–5.
4. Ibid., 3–13.
5. Ibid., 1.
6. Itō Kimio, "The Invention of *Wa* and the Transformation of the Image of Prince Shōtoku in Modern Japan."

inevitably suppresses the role of conflict," or Vlastos says of Yokoi Tokiyoshi's *Studies Concerning Small Farming* (1927) that, for all its double-voiced critique of industrial capitalism and its projection of a compelling vision of harmony, economic revitalization and spiritual cohesion, it "required a massive denial of the actual social divisions in Japanese agriculture."[7] In a similar spirit, Young invokes the imaginary/reality distinction in critiquing the nationalist tendency to "imagin[e] a harmony of community interests against the reality of mounting class tensions."[8]

At the same time, however, the contributions in this volume move us significantly beyond the useful but functionalist task of unpacking "ideologies" and connect the question of "inventing traditions" both to certain methodological propositions that have been with us since Foucault and to some larger questions of modernity itself. This volume, one might say, is far more aware than the Hobsbawm-Ranger volume was, of how modernity itself might be a researchable problem. Vlastos himself provides the lead by raising a question about the role of "affect" in Japanese modernity: he relates the tendency to invent traditions to pervasive feelings of "anxiety over new, more sharply delineated and disturbing social divisions."[9] Andrew Gordon introduces echoes of Michel Foucault in thinking of "invented tradition"—in his case, the tradition of Japanese management—as "a discursive structure."[10] Both Miriam Silverberg and Inoue Shun raise the question of why while some "invented traditions" work, there are many others that do not. Silverberg writes: "Traditions do not of course spring up ex nihilo; genealogies, if not origins, can be found."[11] In the case of the martial arts tradition, Inoue documents the way invented traditions depended for their efficacy on "judo's connection to the older tradition of *bujutsu*."[12]

Taken together, these essays address the larger question of the relationship between capitalist and statist modernity and different ways of framing the past in a non-European context. As might be imagined, there are strong resonances in modern Indian history of the Japanese experiences in this regard. It is a global process within which countries acquire their specific relationship to certain general features of modernity as much as they introduce their particular twists and spins into the process. In the rest of this short essay, I will endeavor to highlight certain themes in this global history that cut across the historical differences invoked by the names "India" and "Japan."

There are three particular themes in this collection that strike me with some force for their resemblances to issues in Indian modernity: heterogeneity or plural-

7. Irwin Scheiner, "The Japanese Village: Imagined, Real, Contested"; Stephen Vlastos, "Agrarianism Without Tradition: The Radical Critique of Prewar Japanese Modernity."
8. Louise Young, "Colonizing Manchuria: The Making of an Imperial Myth."
9. Stephen Vlastos, "Tradition: Past/Present Culture and Modern Japanese History."
10. Andrew Gordon, "The Invention of Japanese-Style Labor Management."
11. Miriam Silverberg, "The Cafe Waitress Serving Modern Japan."
12. Inoue Shun, "The Invention of the Martial Arts: Kanō Jigorō and Kōdōkan Judo."

ity in the experience of time by the subject of modernity; cultural differences and the politics of the tradition/modernity binary; and romantic and realist modes of perception of the past and their relationships to state and subject formation.

The experience of dislocations in the flow of time stands out as one of the central motifs of both Japanese and Indian modernities. For all their obvious tendency to absorb Japanese pasts into the culturally homogenizing project of building a militaristic nation-state in the twentieth century, the Japanese intellectuals and institutions discussed in this volume give ample evidence to suggest this. The existence of the "peasant" in the consciousness of the urban intellectual, the presence, or as Yanagita Kunio put it, "the countryside [existing] in the capital," "all kinds of archaisms enter[ing] into and mix[ing] with the modern," are all experiences with parallels in South Asian modernity.[13] To what degree this language speaking of duality or plurality of time actually measures the "reality" of the experience is not a question that engages me here. I am interested in the rhetoric that frames the experience, a language that speaks of different times as the simultaneous existence of the nonsimultaneous and sees this as a *problem* in the identity of the modern (as did Yanagita and his cohorts, to go by Harootunian's and Hashimoto's illuminating discussions in "Figuring the Folk" and *"Chihō"*). Why belonging to a field of simply different temporalities should appear as an acute experience of disjuncture in the identity of the modern, as a theme of loss in the history of modernity, is something we will discuss shortly.[14] For the present, I simply want to note, on the basis of the discussion presented in this volume, two kinds of ethnographic practices by which the experience of plurality of times is handled by modern intellectuals in their search for a relationship to the past. Here Indian history has strong parallels to Japanese history.

These two practices correspond to two different modes of looking at "tradition." Both of them involve what Harootunian calls "depth hermeneutics" in his discussion of the category "folk"—that is, a training to see beyond the "surface" into the "depths" of identities (historical or otherwise).[15] One of these modes of viewing I shall call "nostalgia," the other one "epiphanic." The latter, for our purpose, refers to the practice of viewing the traditional as something that is always present but hidden except to a poetic, nonrealist gaze, as some vision of eternity itself. While collapsible into one another and often present in the same person or piece of writing, these two visions call for different kinds of political relationship to the "traditional." Nostalgia is located in an experience of loss and calls for a politics of recovery and recuperation, and for a political agency adequate to that task.

13. H. D. Harootunian, "Figuring the Folk: History, Poetics, and Representation."
14. Cf. Harootunian, "Figuring": "The discipline of native ethnology could only seek to compensate for the loss experienced in modern life."
15. Ibid.

That agency could be the state. It could also be the individual. The political task of nostalgic memory, whether individual or collective, is to recover and preserve, make the past a part of the present.

The discussion of Yanagita Kunio by Harootunian and Hashimoto illustrates this. Consider Yanagita's tendency to collect artifacts or to narrate pre-capitalist subjectivities as personal and generational memories. We have to remember that to name such subjectivities "memory" is as much an act of categorization as the labeling of something as "pre-capitalist." Yet, clearly, recourse to the language of "memory" and "generations" is one way the moderns have for handling the experience of heterogeneous temporalities that marks their very constitution as subjects. If I say that I have access via memory to the meaning of some actions of my grandfather (to stay with Yanagita's metaphorization of patriliny into national ancestry), actions that "I" as a modern person might distance myself from, then the gesture of separation of "my" modern subjectivity from that imputed to "my grandfather" works only because we bracket for the time being the question of intersubjectivity between the two figures, "me" and "*my* grandfather," both figures of "my" mind. This bracketing itself then becomes a legitimate way of *being* pre-capitalist while ascribing the practice in question to somebody else from another time (marked here by "generational change"). For the label "another time/generation" is precisely what allows other times to be both subsumed under and be disruptive of our experience of a uniform or unilinear capitalist temporality. The condition for experiencing a pure capitalist temporality, one might say, would be the loss of all "memories." When Yanagita Kunio begins the story of a murder with the statement, "This lives in no one's memory but mine today," the invocation of a dying memory acts as a ruse that is nothing but performative, for Yanagita's very telling of the story implants it into somebody else's "memory" and thus makes it part of that person's present subjectivity as well.[16] Yanagita, in effect, demonstrates for us—as have countless others in the history of capitalist modernity—some of the narrative techniques available to the modern for managing and living with "archaic" parts of the self that do not easily fall in line with avant-gardist ideas of history, progress, and self-making. Yanagita's projects of public collecting of folk artifacts display the same politics of nostalgia. This politics, while romantic, remains wedded to both historicism and objectivism—witness, for instance, Yanagita's search for positive evidence for the *jōmin* ("the original people") among the *sanka* and later on in Okinawa, his commitment to "scientific rigor," his evolutionist talk of "vestiges" and "survivals."[17]

The moment of eternity, however, is born of an epiphanic optics and, while it involves its own kind of depth hermeneutics, is nevertheless to be logically distinguished from the moment of nostalgia. An epiphanic vision does not necessarily call for the realization of a future that is also a gesture of return to a historical

---

16. Hashimoto Mitsuru, "*Chihō*: Yanagita Kunio's 'Japan.'"
17. Harootunian, "Figuring"; Hashimoto, "*Chihō*."

past. Unlike the moment of nostalgia, the epiphanic vision is not located in a thematic of loss. Epiphany is precisely the capacity to get out of historical time and hence out of the idea that a loss has happened in history. This is what I would read into Yanagita's vision of a "timeless folk," his dismissal and distrust of photography and realistic representation. The tension between the nostalgic mode (which allows for historical-ethnographic realism) and the epiphanic mode is visible in Yanagita's troubled relationship to the question of evidence. There is, on the one hand, his stance of being a scientific researcher. But there are also instances of his unwillingness to conflate the *jōmin* with historical reality. Hashimoto mentions Yanagita's suspicion of his follower Orikuchi Shinobu's search for the *jōmin* in ancient Japan. Hashimoto writes: "Yanagita sought to locate the 'mountain people' even though he realized that their world could not exist except as a 'phenomenon of the mind' [*shin'i genshō*]," for it was simultaneously a category expressing both truth and desire. "The spiritual life of the *jōmin* could appear only when folklore studies reconstituted it in the present. *Jōmin*, existing 'everywhere and nowhere,' were the latent potential of all Japanese, and therefore not limited to historical, geographical, or social specificity."[18]

In both nationalist nostalgia and epiphany, however, there is a question of political agency. In nostalgia, as I have already said, it is the agency that sets as its own historical task the recovery of the lost past. This agency could be the state or a political party. The question of agency in modern nationalist epiphany is hinted at in Yanagita's statement that such epiphanic resistance to the time of history—one that places "tradition" beyond historical representation—is itself a matter of will, as it is a "phenomenon of the mind." The agency here is involved in the work of the vision; the poetry itself is the work needed to bring into presence the eternity that remains hidden to the ordinary eye. This agency is performative and does not call for an institution—such as the state—outside the performance. However, one may read Yanagita's reference to will as a reference to the work of resistance that this agency has to perform against the representation of history. In other words, historical representation belongs to the field of force within which this epiphanic will-to-resist arises. We need to ask: what is the field of force to which historical representation belonged in Japanese modernity?

Or the question could be put another way. Why could not the different temporalities that marked Japanese modernity remain, for nationalist intellectuals such as Yanagita, just that, a collage of times? Why could not they, the nationalist intellectuals, celebrate the hybridities and disjunctures that characterize the modern everywhere? Why was the collage experienced as a problem of identity and made part of an attempt to center and ground the modern Japanese subject? Why were heterogeneities hierarchized into the polarities of inside/outside, depth/surface, tradition/modernity? Why did such binaries arise in what, theoretically, could have been a distribution of pure and inert differences?

18. Hashimoto, "*Chihō*."

Part of the answer, it seems to me, can be gleaned from the contributions of
Miriam Silverberg, Jennifer Robertson, and Jordan Sand in this volume. Silverberg's sophisticated analysis of the history of the figure of the modern Japanese
cafe waitress, the *jokyū*, treats that figure genealogically. Silverberg does not look
for a fixed origin in which its meaning is securely anchored. Its history contains an
eclecticism typical perhaps of modernity anywhere. The *jokyū* was part of "the
new customs of the 1920s and 1930s—which encompassed foreign words, consumer items, and most of all, media images," but it belongs to "comparisons
. . . within Japanese history" itself, for its meaning was unintelligible except by a
comparison of its differences with other Japanese words having to do with women
in public arenas, such as *meshimori onna, yūjo, inbaita*, and so on.[19] The modernity of
the cafe waitress thus belonged to something like a Saussurean sign-chain with no
absolute separation or rupture distinguishing the new from the old, the origin of
the new being dispersed—to remember Foucault's description of the project of
genealogical history—in a field of differences.[20]

The erection of polarities such as tradition and modernity has to ignore these
carry-overs between categories. The modern, like any other historically evolved
structure, is hybrid. It contains the polysemy and the uneven temporalities that
Robertson reads in *furusato*, with its combination of different connotations of
place and time.[21] Why then do binaries arise, binaries that seem precarious and
enduring at the same time? What transforms differences into hierarchies?

Jordan Sand's discussion of "the Japanese home" is instructive on this point. In
its actual architecture, as Sand shows, the ideal Japanese house had incorporated
by the 1890s both Western and Japanese features, the semiotics of the older conception of the *ie sei* carrying over—in Silverberg's sense of this expression—into
the more European-derived neologism of the *hōmu*.[22] Yet this ambiguity was over-
ridden by the binaries of modernity. The word *hōmu*, Sand writes, "began its career [in the hands of Protestant social reformers] as a weapon against *ie sei*, or
against conservative mores generally."[23] The words were caught up in debates to
do with the virtues of the nuclear family (as against extended ones), with new
structures of emotion, privacy, personal hygiene, selfhood, and so forth. *Ie* and
hōmu "thus appeared to be antitheses—indigenous and foreign, feudal and modern," continues Sand, and adds: "But they were not, *in fact* [emphases added], mutually exclusive."[24]

19. Silverberg, "Cafe Waitress."
20. Michel Foucault, "Nietzsche, Genealogy, History," in his *Language, Counter-Memory, Practice: Selected Essays and Interviews*, ed. and trans. Donald F. Bouchard and Sherry Simon (Ithaca, N.Y.: Cornell
University Press, 1977).
21. Jennifer Robertson, "It Takes a Village: Internationalization and Nostalgia in Postwar Japan."
22. Jordan Sand, "At Home in the Meiji Period: Inventing Japanese Domesticity."
23. Ibid.
24. Ibid.

Here the word "feudal" is tell-tale. The field of differences in which institutions of Japanese modernity arose was cut across by another structure, a temporal slope (to use Johannes Fabian's expression), the progressive, developmentalist meta-narratives of history that no modernity has ever escaped, for this meta-narrative has been the sure sign, in every single instance of modernization, that modernity happens within a global context, brought into being and kept in place by discourses and practices of institutional power.[25] Indeed, if Fabian's argument is to be heeded, then we cannot picture a before-after scenario in which a certain preexisting field of neutral differences gets washed over by a rush of meta-narratives that modernity introduces. Fabian's argument regarding the binaries (e.g., feudal/capitalist) that operate as the founding taxonomic principles of the social sciences, is quite to the contrary. He writes:

> Far from merely reflecting relations of order, it [the founding taxonomy] creates them. The founding classificatory act, the first binary (or in Bateson's famous terms, the difference that makes the difference) is the one between the native text and the taxonomic difference about that text.[26]

So there is no talk of difference located completely outside of the oppression of the meta-narratives. The meta-narratives of progressive history were the "founding classificatory acts" within which a question such as "what were Japan's traditions?" could be asked, answered, and contested. This is not to say that the answers were predictable or that the room for debate had been in any way foreshortened. The play of ambiguities and polysemy in the very categories constitutive of Japanese modernity—as discussed by most contributors to this volume—reveals to us the space of contingency within which traditions were "invented." We lose sight of this space in veering to the two extremes of vision—one of a world structured by the meta-narratives of capitalism and the nation-state alone, and the other a vision of pure hybridity. The space that I have called "contingency" contains both, but I do not think of it as a half-way house, an arithmetic average of the two extremes, or something that is defined by possessing "a bit of this and a bit of that." By contingency, I mean moments of openness, of undecidability, of movements that speak to no pre-given horizons—yet movements that have to negotiate the opposition of structures we legitimately call "meta-narratives" and "hybridities."

I want to conclude by asking a few questions of this volume with an eye to this space of contingency in the history of Japanese modernity. My questions arise from my involvement in Indian history and from my ignorance of corresponding

25. Johannes Fabian, *Time and the Other: How Anthropology Makes Its Object* (New York: Columbia University Press, 1983), 103.
26. Ibid., 99.

Japanese material. These are questions prompted by issues in another history, and I apologize in advance if I end up only trying the specialist reader's patience.

There is an overall tension that structures this volume. Individually, all the contributions are assiduously open to the empirics of Japanese modernity and the ambiguities of meanings that haunt the historical experiences analyzed here. Yet the pursuit of ambiguities is often cut short by the falling shadows of teleological structures of two meta-narratives, of capitalism and of the nation-state. As a result, some very important questions of (Japanese) modernity seem to get closed off almost as soon as they are opened up. Let me explain.

One of the most critical ways in which this collection furthers and enriches the framework of "the invention of traditions," it seems to me, is by explicitly raising the question of affect and its role in modernities. Several of the contributions draw our attention to the fact that many of the invented traditions of Japanese nationalism expressly used categories of sentiment and spoke of the "harmony," "beauty," and the "spirit" of "traditional" Japaneseness. Yet the discussion is short-circuited in many places by the assumption that such talk was always and necessarily compensatory, that it simply made up for the "anxiety" produced by the speed of changes brought about by the introduction of capitalism and an increasingly militarizing state. Vlastos has recourse to the idea of anxiety in ruling circles in order to contextualize the "reassuring image of harmonious and productive farm families [that] served the ideological needs of many sectors of Japanese society."[27] Harootunian refers to an affect similar to that of anxiety in explaining why native ethnologists like Yanagita Kunio, Orikuchi Shinobu, and their followers' poetics created a "timeless folk"—it was, he says, meant to provide "protection against the dizzying experience of shock, speed and sensation generated by capitalist modernization."[28] In effect, "anxiety," "shock," and "fear" circulate in this volume as the most uninterrogated categories, while serving, most usefully, to remind us that no "invention of tradition" is effective without a simultaneous invocation of affect, of sentiments, emotions, and other embodied practices.

Kären Wigen's contribution draws attention to this point by discussing, though only in passing, the role of singing in the diffusion of a regional identity.[29] Jennifer Robertson similarly alludes—alas, only too briefly—to "the nostalgic feelings aroused" by the mention of the word *furusato*.[30] These are two of the very few places where the history of embodied practices of subjectivity in Japan—the history of the cultural training of our senses, of "sensuous practical activity" (to imitate the voice of the young Marx critiquing Feuerbach), of smelling, tasting and touching, of seeing and hearing—makes its presence felt in this book. My point is simple. If even invented traditions need genealogies for their own effectiveness, no

---

27. Vlastos, "Agrarianism."
28. Harootunian, "Figuring."
29. Kären Wigen, "Constructing Shinano: The Invention of a Neo-Traditional Region."
30. Robertson, "It Takes a Village."

such genealogy can ever consist of an inventory of ideas alone. Ideas acquire materiality through the history of bodily practices. They work not simply because
they persuade through their logic; they are also capable, through a long and heterogeneous history of the cultural training of the senses, of making connections
with our glands and muscles and neuronal networks. This is the work of memory,
if we do not reduce the meaning of that word to the simple and conscious mental
act of remembering. The past is embodied through a long process of training the
senses, and it is this deep history of the subject of Japanese modernity that I miss
in the otherwise illuminating selection of articles presented in this volume.

If my point is right, then the "nostalgic" and the "epiphanic" modes of viewing that we detect in somebody like Yanagita Kunio must be seen as belonging, at
least in part, to this deep history of the subject. In other words, we must make sure
that the words "nostalgia" and "epiphany" in this case are not completely assimilated into the narratives and understandings that enclose these words in European
or Biblical history. We should be able to open up these necessary but unsatisfactory words so as to insert into them histories of "practical sensuous activities," of
the cultural training of the senses, as they unfolded in Japan. For the subject that
negotiates capitalism and the nation-state has a much longer history than those of
the latter two, much more datable, global formations. This is not to deny the
many and profound ways in which both capital and the state mold us as subjects—this volume in fact bears ample testimony to those processes. It is to argue
that the subject of a historically situated modernity is always in excess of the universal teleologies imputed to capital and the state by the languages and methods
of the social sciences.

I say this because, for very understandable historical reasons, the shadows of
both capitalism and the nation-state fall much more heavily and lengthily on our
discussions of Japanese history than they do in my own area of studies, modern
South Asia. Of course, the strength of Japanese capitalism, the militarism of the
prewar Japanese state, and the absorption of modern Japanese intellectual life in
the life of the state itself cannot be denied.[31] It makes much sense, therefore, to see
Japanese nationalist intellectuals' tendency to "aesthetic romanticism" in political-
public life through the filter of the history of European fascism. The value of this
exercise is attested to by this volume and others. A note of Benjaminian suspicion—that the "aestheticization of the political . . . [is a] distinguishing mark of
fascism"—sounds naturally legitimate in discussions of modern Japanese nationalist thought.[32] Yet I know from the Indian examples of Gandhi and Tagore that
there is no inexorable logic or process of historical inevitability that must always,

31. I have benefited much on this from Andrew Barshay's essay, "'Doubly Cruel': Marxism and
the Presence of the Past in Japanese Capitalism."

32. See Leslie Pincus, "In a Labyrinth of Western Desire: Kuki Shūzō and the Discovery of Japanese Being," *Boundary 2* (Fall 1991; special issue: Masao Miyoshi and H. D. Harootunian, eds., *Japan in
the World*), 155.

anywhere and everywhere, lead romantic/aesthetic nationalism into statist and fascist jingoism. This happened in Japan, and happened in particular instances in Indian history, but these were instances in which, in my terms, the state was able to assimilate to its own ends the much richer, older, and more complex histories of the training of the senses that the subject of modernity embodied. How this happened, and where, is for the historian to explain.

My plea for the insertion of a deeper history of the subject—of the past as a series of embodied practices (including practices of affect)—into our studies of invented traditions under conditions of capitalist and statist modernities, can then be reduced to three questions: (a) what is the history of the embodied subject?, (b) how does it connect to the history of state-formation?, and (c) what are the moments where one history exceeds the other (for it is in these moments of excess that we glimpse the possibilities of other and alternative developments)?

These questions do not constitute a critique; they are my tribute to this stimulating volume. They are questions that I will take back to my studies in Indian history.

GLOSSARY

Bakufu	military government of the shogun
Bakumatsu	end of the Tokugawa Bakufu; period from 1853 to the Meiji Restoration of January 3, 1868
banzuke	"line-up" of sumo matches published daily during tournaments
budō	modern term for the Japanese martial arts
bujutsu	Tokugawa-era martial arts
Burakumin	outcast communities (of ethnic Japanese) juridically constituted in the Tokugawa period; granted equal status by decree after the Meiji Restoration but continue to face discrimination
chabudai	short-legged dining table
chanbara	popular genre of plays and movies featuring furious sword fights
chihō	(remote) rural areas
chō	square measure equal to 2.45 acres
Chōshū	powerful fief in southwestern Honshū; with Satsuma, dominated top offices in the Meiji government
dan-kyū	ranks and steps; the "belt" system of the modern martial arts
eboshi	colorful cap of the ancient period
Edo	old name for Tokyo; *see* Tokugawa
furusato	native place
furusato-zukuri	development of rural villages as tourist sites
gekokujō	revolt by subordinates
gōmyō	Tokugawa-period term for wealthy farmers

gun	county
hōmu	phonetic neologism for "home"
hoshitorihyō	table recording the outcome of sumo tournament matches
ie sei	the patriarchal stem-family
ikka danran	gathering of family for food and conversation
iriaiken	right to use of common lands
jokyū	cafe waitress
jōmin	"abiding folk"
kamishimo	Tokugawa-period formal dress
Kantō	Tokyo and surrounding prefectures in eastern Japan
kata	(practice of) set forms in martial arts
katei	character neologism for "home"
kazoku-shugi	"family-ism"
Kenseikai/Minseitō	mainstream political party of the prewar period
Kinki	Kyoto, Osaka, and Kobe and the surrounding prefectures in western Japan
kobyakushō	Tokugawa-period term for small farmers
kokusaika	"internationalization"
kokutai	concept of a uniquely Japanese emperor-centered policy based on the idea of unbroken imperial succession
komae	Tokugawa-period term for poor rural households, including but not limited to tenant farmers
Kōza-ha	"lectures" stream of Marxism; argued that modern Japan had not undergone a thorough bourgeois revolution
kumi	ward; administrative subdivision of village or town
kyōdōtai	village community (Gemeinschaft) signifying the corporatist character of Tokugawa rural society
makunouchi	main bouts of a sumo tournament
Manchukuo	puppet state created by Japan in 1932
Manchurian Incident	onset of the military occupation of all of Manchuria, beginning September 17, 1931
Meiji period	reign of the Meiji Emperor, 1868–1912; often broken into an "early" period (ca. 1868–89) and a "late" period (ca. 1890–1912)
Meiji Restoration	military overthrow of the Tokugawa shogun and subsequent modernizing reforms

minzokugaku	native ethnology
monpe	Japanese-style women's work pants
nichirin heisha	"sun-shaped" barracks built on the grounds of the Uchiwara training center for Manchurian colonization
onjō-shugi	"warm-heartedness-ism"; ideology of Japanese-style labor management
oyakata / kokata	patron/client
ōzeki	second highest rank in sumo
Pacific War	war with China and then with the Allied Powers, 1937–45
randori	free-style sparring in martial arts
Rōnō-ha	"worker-farmer" stream of Marxism; argued that Japan was already a bourgeois society
sanka	"mountain people"
Satsuma	powerful feudal domain in southern Kyūshū; with Chōshū, dominated the top offices in the Meiji government
sechie	ancient form of wrestling, precursor to sumo
seikatsu	life-style
Seiyūkai	mainstream political party of the prewar period
sekiwake	third highest rank in sumo
Seventeen-Article Constitution	foundational political document of laws and political precepts of the early seventh century attributed to Prince Shōtoku
shikiri	stylized "face-off" between sumo wrestlers
Shōwa	reign of the Shōwa Emperor, 1926–89; often divided into "early" (1926–37), "wartime" (1937–45), and "postwar" periods
Social Policy Association	influential public policy "think tank" founded in the late Meiji period; members included bureaucrats, businessmen, and intellectuals
suō	colorful gown of the medieval period
Taishō	reign of the Taishō emperor, 1912–26; period of the extension of democracy and mass culture
tatami	tightly woven straw mats used as flooring
Tokugawa	period from 1600 to 1867, when the Tokugawa house ruled; often referred to as the Edo period

wa no seishin	"spirit of peace and harmony"
yokozuna	highest rank in sumo
yonaoshi	world renewal or rectification
yūjo	courtesan
yūtoku no mono	wealthy village households

SELECTED BIBLIOGRAPHY

Allison, Anne. *Nightwork: Sexuality, Pleasure, and Corporate Masculinity in a Tokyo Hostess Club*. Chicago: University of Chicago Press, 1994.

Anderson, Benedict R. *Imagined Communities*. London: Verso, 1991.

Anderson, Perry. "Modernity and Revolution." In Cary Nelson and Lawrence Grossberg, eds., *Marxism and the Interpretation of Culture*. Urbana and Chicago: University of Illinois Press, 1988.

Andō Kōsei. *Ginza saiken*. Tokyo: Chūō Kōronsha, 1977.

Arano Yasunori. *Kinsei Nihon to higashi Ajia*. Tokyo: Tōkyō Daigaku Shuppankai, 1988.

Awazu Kiyoshi, Ii Tarō, and Hosaka Kunio, *Abe Sada: Shōwa jūichinen no onna*. Tokyo: Tabata Shoten, 1976.

Bailey, Peter. "Parasexuality and Glamour: The Victorian Barmaid as Cultural Prototype." *Gender and History* 2, no. 2 (Summer 1990).

Bitō Masahide. *Edo jidai to wa nani ka: Nihonshijō no kinsei to kindai*. Tokyo: Iwanami Shoten, 1992.

Bolitho, Harold. "Sumō and Popular Culture: The Tokugawa Period." In Gavan McCormack and Yoshio Sugimoto, eds., *The Japanese Trajectory: Modernization and Beyond*. Cambridge: Cambridge University Press, 1988.

Bommes, M., and P. Wright. "'Charms of Residence': The Public and the Past." In R. Johnson, G. McLennan, B. Schwarz, and D. Sutton, eds., *Making Histories: Studies in History-Writing and Politics*. London: Hutchinson, 1982.

Buck-Morss, Susan. *The Dialectics of Seeing: Walter Benjamin and the Arcades Project*. Cambridge: MIT Press, 1991.

Chen Xiaomei. "Occidentalism as Counterdiscourse: 'He Shang' in Post-Mao China." *Critical Inquiry* 18, no. 4 (1992).

Christy, Alan S. "The Making of Imperial Subjects in Okinawa." *Positions: East Asia Cultures Critique* 1, no. 3 (1993).

Clarke, T. J. *The Painting of Modern Life: Paris in the Art of Manet and his Followers*. Princeton: Princeton University Press, 1984.

Cohen, Stephen D. *Bukharin and the Bolshevik Revolution.* New York: Oxford University Press, 1980.

Comaroff, John, and Jean Comaroff. *Ethnography and the Historical Imagination.* Boulder: Westview Press, 1992.

Cuyler, P. L. *Sumo: From Rite to Sport.* New York and Tokyo: Weatherhill, 1985.

Davis, Fred. *Yearning for Yesterday: A Sociology of Nostalgia.* New York: Free Press, 1979.

de Becker, J. E. *The Nightless City.* Yokohama: Z. P. Maruya, 1899. Reprint of 1905 edition; Rutland, Vt.: C. B. Tuttle, 1971.

de Certeau, Michel. *Heterologies.* Trans. Brian Massumi. Minneapolis: University of Minnesota Press, 1986.

de Lauretis, Teresa. *Technologies of Gender: Essays on Theory, Film, and Fiction.* Bloomington: Indiana University Press, 1987.

Desai, Gaurav. "The Invention of Invention." *Cultural Critique,* no. 24 (Spring 1993).

Devi, Mahasweta. "Draupadi." Trans. and with a foreword by Gayatri Chakravorty Spivak. In Gayatri Chakravorty Spivak, *In Other Worlds: Essays in Cultural Politics.* New York and London: Methuen, 1987.

Dirks, Nicholas B. "History as a Sign of the Modern." *Public Culture* 2, no. 2 (Spring 1990).

Dirlik, Arif. "The Past as Legacy and Project: Postcolonial Criticism in the Perspective of Indigenous Historicism." *American Indian Culture and Research Journal* 20, no. 2 (1996).

Dore, Ronald P. "The Modernizer as a Special Case: Japanese Factory Legislation, 1882–1922." *Comparative Studies in Society and History* 11, no. 4 (October 1969).

Dore, Ronald P., and Ouchi Tsutomu. "Rural Origins of Japanese Fascism." In J. W. Morley, ed., *Dilemmas of Growth in Prewar Japan.* Princeton: Princeton University Press, 1971.

Dower, John. *War Without Mercy: Race and Power in the Pacific War.* New York: Pantheon, 1986.

Fabian, Johannes. *Time and the Other: How Anthropology Makes Its Object.* New York: Columbia University Press, 1983.

Featherstone, Mike, Scott Lash, and Roland Robertson, eds. *Global Modernities.* Thousand Oaks, Calif.: SAGE Publications, 1995.

Field, Norma. *In the Realm of a Dying Emperor.* New York: Pantheon, 1990.

Foucault, Michel. "Nietzsche, Genealogy, History." In Michel Foucault, *Language, Counter-Memory, Practice: Selected Essays and Interviews.* Ed. and trans. Donald F. Bouchard and Sherry Simon. Ithaca, N.Y.: Cornell University Press, 1977.

Fujikawa Seikatsu. "Sumō no gaiyō." In *Gendai taiiku supōtsu taikei,* vol. 20. Tokyo: Kōdansha, 1984.

Fujimori Terunobu, Hatsuda Tōru, and Fujioka Hiroyasu, eds. *Ushinawareta teito Tōkyō: Taishō Shōwa no machi to sumai.* Tokyo: Kashiwa Shobō, 1991.

Fujitani, T[akashi]. *Splendid Monarchy: Power and Pageantry in Modern Japan.* Berkeley and Los Angeles: University of California Press, 1996.

Fukaya Katsumi. *Hyakushō ikki no rekishiteki kōzō.* Rev. ed. Tokyo: Azekura Shobō, 1986.

Fukuzawa Yukichi. *"Nihon ni wa seifu arite kokumin (neeshon) nashi": Fukuzawa Yukichi, An Outline of Civilization.* Trans. David A. Dilworth and G. Cameron Hurst. Tokyo: Sophia University Press, 1973.

Garon, Sheldon. *Molding Japanese Minds: The State in Everyday Life.* Princeton: Princeton University Press, 1997.

———. *The State and Labor in Modern Japan.* Berkeley and Los Angeles: University of California Press, 1987.

————. "The World's Oldest Debate?: Prostitution and the State in Imperial Japan, 1868–1945." *American Historical Review* 98, no. 3 (June 1993).

Giddens, Anthony. *Modernity and Self-Identity*. Stanford: Stanford University Press, 1991.

Gluck, Carol. *Japan's Modern Myths: Ideology in the Late Meiji Period*. Princeton: Princeton University Press, 1985.

Gordon, Andrew. "Business and the Corporate State: The Business Lobby and Bureaucrats, 1911–1941." In William D. Wray, ed., *Managing Industrial Enterprise: Cases from Japan's Prewar Experience*. Cambridge, Mass.: Harvard Council on East Asian Studies, 1989.

————. "Contests for the Workplace." In Andrew Gordon, ed., *Postwar Japan as History*. Berkeley and Los Angeles: University of California Press, 1993.

————. *The Evolution of Labor Relations in Japan: Heavy Industry, 1853–1955*. Cambridge, Mass.: Harvard Council on East Asian Studies, 1985.

————. *Wages of Affluence*. Cambridge, Mass.: Harvard University Press, 1998.

Haga Tōru, ed. *Bunmei toshite no Tokugawa Nihon. Sōsho hikaku bungaku hikaku bunka*, vol. 1. Tokyo: Chūō Kōronsha, 1993.

Haley, John O. "The Myth of the Reluctant Litigant." *Journal of Japanese Studies* 4 (1978).

————. "The Politics of Informal Justice: The Japanese Experience, 1922–1942." In Richard Abel, ed., *The Politics of Informal Justice*, vol. 2. New York: Academic Press, 1982.

Handler, Richard, and Joyce Linnekin. "Tradition, Genuine or Spurious." *Journal of American Folklore* 97 (1984).

Hane, Mikiso. *Reflections on the Way to the Gallows: Rebel Women in Prewar Japan*. Berkeley and Los Angeles: University of California Press, 1988.

Harootunian, H. D. *Things Seen and Unseen: Discourse and Ideology in Tokugawa Nativism*. Chicago: University of Chicago Press, 1988.

Hashimoto Mitsuru. "Kindai Nihon ni okeru dentō no hatsumei shinpojiumu." *Sochioroji* 37, no. 1 (May 1992).

Havens, Thomas R. H. *Farm and Nation in Modern Japan: Agrarian Nationalism, 1870–1940*. Princeton: Princeton University Press, 1974.

Hayashi Fumiko. *Hōrōki*. Tokyo: Shinchōsha, 1974.

Hazama Hiroshi. *Nihon no rōmu kanri shi kenkyū*. Tokyo: Ochanomizu Shobō, 1978.

Heilbroner, Robert. *The Nature and Logic of Capitalism*. New York: Norton, 1985.

Henderson, Dan Fenno. *Conciliation and Japanese Law, Tokugawa and Modern*. 2 vols. Seattle: University of Washington Press, and Tokyo: University of Tokyo Press, 1965.

Hirotsu Kazuo. "Jokyū." In *Hirotsu Kazuo zenshū*, vol. 5. Tokyo: Chūō Kōronsha, 1988.

Hobsbawm, Eric J., and Terence O. Ranger, eds. *The Invention of Tradition*. Cambridge: Cambridge University Press, 1983.

Hoston, Germaine. *Marxism and the Crisis of Development in Prewar Japan*. Princeton: Princeton University Press, 1986.

Howell, David L. "Ainu Ethnicity and the Boundaries of the Early Modern Japanese State." *Past and Present*, no. 142 (1994).

Igarashi Tomio. *Nihon josei bunka shi*. Tokyo: Agatsuma Shōkan, 1984.

Iizuka Ichiyō. *Jūdō o tsukutta otokotachi*. Tokyo: Bungei Shunjū, 1991.

Ikeda Masao. *Sumō no rekishi*. Tokyo: Heibonsha, 1977.

Inouye, Jukichi. *Home Life in Tokyo*. 1910; London: Routledge and Kegan Paul, 1985.

Irie Katsumi. *Nihon fashizumu-ka no taiiku shisō*. Tokyo: Fumaidō Shuppansha, 1986.

Irie Takanori. *Nihon ga tsukuru shinbunmei*. Tokyo: Kōdansha, 1992.

Irokawa, Daikichi. "Japan's Grass-Roots Tradition: Current Issues in the Mirror of History." *Japan Quarterly* 20, no. 1 (1973).

———. *The Culture of the Meiji Period.* Ed. and trans. Marius B. Jansen. Princeton: Princeton University Press, 1985.

———. "The Survival Struggle of the Japanese Community." In J. Victor Koschmann, ed., *Authority and the Individual in Japan: Citizen Protest in Historical Perspective.* Tokyo: University of Tokyo Press, 1978.

Ishii Ryōsuke. *Nihon hōsei shi gaisetsu.* Tokyo: Kōbundō, 1960.

Itasaka Yōko. *Edo no onna, ima no onna.* Fukuoka: Ashi Shobō, 1993.

Itō Masanao, Ōkado Masakatsu, and Suzuki Masayuki. *Senkan ki no Nihon nōson.* Tokyo: Sekai Shisōsha, 1988.

Ivy, Marilyn. *Discourses of the Vanishing: Modernity, Phantasm, Japan.* Chicago: University of Chicago Press, 1995.

Iwasaki Chikatsugu. *Nihon marukusushugi tetsugaku shi josetsu.* Tokyo: Miraisha, 1984.

Jackson, Laura. "Bar Hostesses." In Joyce Lebra, Joy Paulson, and Elizabeth Powers, eds., *Women in Changing Japan.* Stanford: Stanford University Press, 1976.

Japan Ministry of Education. *Kokutai no hongi: Cardinal Principles of the National Entity of Japan.* Trans. John Owen Gauntlett; ed. with an introduction by Robert King Hall. Cambridge, Mass: Harvard University Press, 1949.

Jinnai Hidenobu. *Tokyo: A Spatial Anthropology.* Trans. Kimiko Nishimura. Berkeley and Los Angeles: University of California Press, 1995.

Kajiki Gō, ed. *Yanagita Kunio no shisō.* Tokyo: Keiso Shobō, 1989.

Kami Shōichirō. *Manmō kaitaku seishōnen giyūgun.* Tokyo: Chūō Kōronsha, 1973.

Kammen, Michael. *Mystic Chords of Memory: The Transformation of Tradition in American Culture.* New York: Knopf, 1991.

Kanō Jigorō. *Kanō Jigorō taikei.* Tokyo: Honnotomosha, 1988.

Kano Masanao. *Senzen "ie" no shisō.* Tokyo: Sōbunsha, 1983.

Kaplan, Alice Yaeger. *Reproductions of Banality: Fascism, Literature, and French Intellectual Life.* Minneapolis: University of Minnesota Press, 1986.

Karatani Kōjin. "Ri no hihan: Nihon shisō ni okeru puremodan to posutomodan." *Gendai shi techō* 29, no. 5 (May 1986).

Kawahara Hiroshi. *"Edo" no seishin shi.* Tokyo: Perikansha, 1992.

Kawakatsu Heita. *Nihon bunmei to kindai seiyō: "Sakoku" saikō.* Tokyo: NHK Bukkusu, 1991.

Kawamura Minato. *Ikyō no Shōwa bungaku: "Manshū" to kindai Nihon.* Tokyo: Iwanami Shoten, 1990.

Kawashima Takeyoshi. *Nihonjin no hō ishiki.* Tokyo: Iwanami Shoten, 1967.

Kelly, William W. *Deference and Defiance in Nineteenth-Century Japan.* Princeton: Princeton University Press, 1985.

Kitamura Tōkoku. "Tokugawa shi jidai no heiminteki risō." In *Tōkoku zenshū*, vol. 1. Tokyo: Iwanami Shoten, 1950.

Kobori Keiichirō. *Sakoku no shisō.* Tokyo: Chūkō Shinsho, 1974.

Kōda Rohan. "Kaoku." In *Rohan zenshū*, vol. 29: *Zuihitsu*, pt. 1. Tokyo: Iwanami Shoten, 1954.

Koizumi Kazuko. *Kagu to shitsunai ishō no bunka shi.* Tokyo: Hōsei Daigaku Shuppan, 1979.

Kotani Hiroyuki. "Kindai Nihon no jiko ninshiki to Ajiakan." In Arano Yasunori et al., eds., *Ajia no naka no Nihon shi*, vol. 1. Tokyo: Tokyo Daigaku Shuppankai, 1992.

Kumakura Isao. "Enkyo to shite no shokutaku." In Umesao Tadao, ed., *Gendai Nihon bunka ni okeru dentō to henyō*, vol. 8: *Shōwa no sesō shi*. Tokyo: Domesu Shuppan, 1993.

Kurita, Isamu. "Revival of the Japanese Tradition." *Journal of Popular Culture* 17, no. 1 (1983).

Larsen, Neil. *Modernity and Hegemony*. Minneapolis: University of Minnesota Press, 1990.

Lincicome, Mark. "Nationalism, Internationalization, and the Dilemma of Educational Reform in Japan." *Comparative Education Review* 37, no. 2 (1993).

Linnekan, Jocelyn. "The Politics of Culture in the Pacific." In Jocelyn Linnekan and Lin Poyer, eds., *Cultural Identity and Ethnicity in the Pacific*. Honolulu: University of Hawaii Press, 1990.

Lowenthal, David. *The Past Is a Foreign Country*. Cambridge: Cambridge University Press, 1985.

Magagna, Victor V. *Communities of Grain: Rural Rebellion in Comparative Perspective*. Ithaca, N.Y.: Cornell University Press, 1991.

Mandell, Richard D. *Sport: A Cultural History*. New York: Columbia University Press, 1984.

Mann, Michael. *The Sources of Social Power*, vol. 1: *A History of Power from the Beginning to a.d. 1750*. Cambridge: Cambridge University Press, 1986.

———. *The Sources of Social Power*, vol. 2: *The Rise of Classes and Nation-States, 1760–1914*. Cambridge: Cambridge University Press, 1993.

Manshū Kaitakushi Kankōkai. *Manshū kaitakushi*. Manshū Kaitakushi Kankōkai, 1966.

Maruyama, Masao. *Thought and Behavior in Modern Japanese Politics*. Trans. Mikiso Hane. Reprint of 1963 ed.; London: Oxford University Press, 1969.

Marx, Karl. *Capital*. Harmondsworth: Penguin, 1992.

———. *Political Writings*, vol. 3: *The First International and After*. Harmondsworth: Penguin, 1992.

Matsuzawa Tetsunari. *Tachibana Kōzaburō: Nihon fuashizumu genshi kaiki ron ha*. Tokyo: San'ichi Shobō, 1973.

Minami Hiroshi. "Nihon no ryūkōka." In Kata K. and Tsukuda S., eds., *Ryūkōka no himitsu*. Tokyo: Bunwa, 1980.

———, ed. *Shōwa bunka*. Tokyo: Keisō Shobō, 1987.

Mitchell, W. J. T. "Imperial Landscape." In W. J. T. Mitchell, ed., *Landscape and Power*. Chicago: University of Chicago Press, 1994.

Miwa Ryōichi. "Rōdō kumiai hō seitei mondai no rekishiteki ichi." In Andō Yoshio, ed., *Ryōdaisenkan no Nihon shihonshugi*. Tokyo: Tōkyō Daigaku Shuppankai, 1979.

Miyake, Yoshiko. "Doubling Expectations: Motherhood and Women's Factory Work Under State Management in Japan in the 1930s and 1940s." In Gail Bernstein, ed., *Recreating Japanese Women, 1600–1945*. Berkeley and Los Angeles: University of California Press, 1991.

Mizutani Mitsuhiro. *Edo wa yume ka*. Tokyo: Chikuma Shobō, 1992.

Morisaki, Kazue. "Two Languages, Two Souls." *Concerned Theater Japan* 2, no. 3/4 (1973).

Morishima, Michio. *Why Has Japan "Succeeded"?* Cambridge: Cambridge University Press, 1982.

Morris-Suzuki, Tessa. *Beyond Computopia: Information, Automation, and Democracy in Japan*. London: Kegan Paul International, 1988.

Mouer, Ross, and Yoshio Sugimoto. "Internationalization as an Ideology in Japanese Society." In Hiroshi Mannari and Harumi Befu, eds., *The Challenge of Japan's Internationaliza-*

tion: Organization and Culture. Tokyo: Kwansei Gakuin University and Kodansha International, 1983.

Mukai, K., and N. Toshitani. "The Problems and Progress of Compiling the Civil Code in the Early Meiji Era." Trans. Dan Henderson. In *Law in Japan: An Annual* 1 (1967).

Murakami, Yasusuke. "Ie Society as a Pattern of Civilization." *Journal of Japanese Studies* 10, no. 2 (Summer 1984).

Muta Kazue. "Images of the Family in Meiji Periodicals: The Paradox Underlying the Emergence of the 'Home.'" *U.S.-Japan Women's Journal* (English Supplement), no. 7 (1994).

Naff, William. "Shimazaki Tōson's *Before the Dawn*: Historical Fiction as History and as Literature." In James W. White, Michio Umegaki, and Thomas R. H. Havens, eds., *The Ambivalence of Nationalism: Modern Japan Between East and West*. Lanham and New York: University Press of America, 1990.

Nagahara Kazuko. "Heiminshugi no fujinron: 'Kokumin no tomo' to 'Katei zasshi' ni tsuite." *Rekishi hyōron* 311 (March 1976).

Nagazumi, Akira. "The Diffusion of the Idea of Social Darwinism in East and Southeast Asia." *Historia Scientiarum* 24 (1983).

Najita, Tetsuo. *Visions of Virtue: The Kaitokudō Merchant Academy in Tokugawa Japan*. Chicago: University of Chicago Press, 1987.

Najita, Tetsuo, and H. D. Harootunian. "Japanese Revolt Against the West: Political and Cultural Criticism in the Twentieth Century." In Peter Duus, ed., *Cambridge History of Japan*, vol. 6: *The Twentieth Century*. Cambridge: Cambridge University Press, 1988.

Nakamura Sadenji. *Kenka 'Shinano no kuni' o kangaeru*. Nagano-shi: Shinano Kyōikukai, 1976.

Nakamura Takafusa. "Nihon shihonshugi ronsō ni tsuite." *Shisō*, no. 624 (June 1976).

Nakano Mitsutoshi. *Uchinaru Edo: Kinsei saikō*. Tokyo: Yudachisha, 1994.

Nakazawa Yōko. "Katei, uchi, kanai, hōmu." In Satō Kiyoji, ed., *Kōza nihongo no goi*, vol. 9: *Goshi*, pt. 1. Tokyo: Meiji Shoin, 1983.

Nimura Kazuo. *Ashio bōdō no shiteki kenkyū*. Tokyo: Tōkyō Daigaku Shuppankai, 1986. Trans. as *The Ashio Copper Mine Dispute*. Durham: Duke University Press, 1997.

Nippon Sumō Kyōkai Hakubutsukan Un'ei Iin, ed. *Kinsei Nihon sumō shi*, 5 vols. Tokyo: Bēsubōru Magajinsha, 1975–81.

Nishikawa Yūko. "The Changing Form of Dwellings and the Establishment of he *Katei* (Home) in Modern Japan." *Nichibei josei jaanaru* [U.S.-Japan Women's Journal] English Supplement, no. 8 (1995): 3–36.

———. "Otoko no ie, onna no ie, seibetsu no nai heya." In Wakita Haruko and Susan Hanley, eds., *Jendaa no Nihon shi*, vol. 2. Tokyo: Tōkyō Daigaku Shuppankai, 1995.

Nishinarita Yutaka. *Kindai Nihon rōshi kankei shi no kenkyū*. Tokyo: Tōkyō Daigaku Shuppankai, 1988.

Noguchi Takehiko. *Edojin no rekishi ishiki*. Tokyo: Asahi Shinbunsha, 1987.

Norman, E. H. *Japan's Emergence as a Modern State*. Reprinted in John W. Dower, ed., *Origins of the Modern Japanese State*. New York: Pantheon, 1975.

Ōbayashi Munetsugu. *Jokyū seikatsu no shinkenkyū: Ōsaka shi ni okeru kafee jokyū chōsa*. Tokyo: Ganshōdō, 1932.

Ōdachi Uki. *Bakumatsu shakai no kiso kōzō: Bushū yonaoshi no keisei*. Saitama: Saitama Shinbunsha, 1981.

Ōkawa Naomi. *Sumai no jinruigaku*. Tokyo: Heibonsha Imeeji Riidingu Sōsho, 1986.

Ōkuma, Shigenobu. *Fifty Years of New Japan*, vol. 1. London: Smith, Elder, 1909.

Ooms, Herman. *Tokugawa Village Practice: Class, Status, Power, Law.* Berkeley and Los Angeles: University of California Press, 1996.

Ōshima, Mario. "A Distant View of the Debate on Japanese Capitalism." *Osaka City University Economic Review* 26, no. 2 (July 1991).

Otaki Tadao. "Gakusei jūdō no genryū." In Zen Nihon Gakusei Jūdō Renmei, ed., *Gakusei jūdō sanjūnen no ayumi.* Tokyo: Mainichi Shinbunsha, 1981.

Ōuchi Tsutomu, ed. *Shonō hogo no mondai.* Tokyo: Nōsangyoson Seisaku Gakkai, 1976.

Ōya Sōichi, "Modan sō to modan sō." *Chūō Kōron,* February 1929. Reprinted in *Ōya Sōichi zenshū,* vol. 2. Tokyo: Eichōsha, 1981.

Pincus, Leslie. *Authenticating Culture in Imperial Japan: Kuki Shūzō and the Rise of National Aesthetics.* Berkeley and Los Angeles: University of California Press, 1996.

———. "In a Labyrinth of Western Desire: Kuki Shūzō and the Discovery of Japanese Being." *Boundary 2* vol. 18, no. 3 (Fall 1991). Special issue: Masao Miyoshi and H. D. Harootunian, eds., "Japan in the World."

Rimmer, P. J. "Japan's 'Resort Archipelago': Creating Regions of Fun, Pleasure, Relaxation, and Recreation." *Environment and Planning A* 24 (1992).

Robertson, Jennifer. "Gender Bending in Paradise: Doing 'Female' and 'Male' in Japan." *Genders,* no. 5 (Summer 1989).

———. "Mon Japon: The Revue Theater as a Technology of Japanese Imperialism." *American Ethnologist* 22, no. 4 (1995).

———. *Native and Newcomer: Making and Remaking a Japanese City.* Berkeley and Los Angeles: University of California Press, 1991.

Roden, Donald. "Taishō Culture and the Problem of Gender Ambivalence." In J. Thomas Rimer, ed., *Culture and Identity: Japanese Intellectuals During the Interwar Years.* Princeton: Princeton University Press, 1990.

Rubin, Gayle. "Thinking Sex." In Ann Snitow, Christine Stansell, and Sharon Thompson, eds., *Powers of Desire: The Politics of Sexuality.* New York: Monthly Review Press, 1983.

Sakai, Naoki. "Return to the West / Return to the East: Watsuji Tetsuro's Anthropology and Discussion of Authenticity." *Boundary 2* 18, no. 3 (1991).

Sakai Tadaichi. *Shi to kokyō.* Tokyo: Ōfūsha, 1971.

Sakuramoto Tomio. *Manmō kaitaku seishōnen giyūgun.* Tokyo: Aoki Shoten, 1987.

Sand, Jordan. "House and Home in Modern Japan, 1880s–1920s." Ph.D. diss., Columbia University, 1995.

Sasaki Junnosuke. "Bakumatsu no shakai jōsei to yonaoshi." In Sasaki Junnosuke, ed., *Nihon no rekishi,* vol. 13. Tokyo: Iwanami Shoten, 1977.

———. *Bakumatsu shakai ron.* Tokyo: Hanawa Shokyoku, 1969.

———. "Epilogue." In Sasaki Junnosuke, ed., *Murakata sōdō to yonaoshi,* vol. 1. Tokyo: Aoki Shoten, 1972.

Sasaki Tadamasa. *Nippon sumō shi,* 2 vols. Tokyo: Bēsubōru Magajinsha, 1956, 1964.

Schattschneider, Ellen. "The Labor of Mountains." *Positions: East Asia Cultures Critique* 4, no. 1 (1996).

Seidensticker, Edward. *Kafū the Scribbler: The Life and Writings of Nagai Kafū, 1879–1959.* Stanford: Stanford University Press, 1965.

Shils, Edward. *Tradition.* Chicago: University of Chicago Press, 1981.

Shively, Donald H., ed. *Tradition and Modernization in Japanese Culture.* Princeton: Princeton University Press, 1971.

Sievers, Sharon. *Flowers in Salt: The Beginnings of Feminist Consciousness in Modern Japan.* Stanford: Stanford University Press, 1983.

Silverberg, Miriam. "Constructing a New Cultural History of Prewar Japan." In M. Miyoshi and H. Harootunian, eds., *Japan in the World.* Durham: Duke University Press, 1993.

―――. "Nihon no jokyū wa buruusu o utatta." In Wakita Haruko and Susan Hanley, eds., *Jendā no Nihon shi,* vol. 2. Tokyo: Tōkyō Daigaku Shuppankai, 1995.

―――. "Remembering Pearl Harbor, Forgetting Charlie Chaplin, and the Case of the Disappearing Western Woman: A Picture Story." *Positions: East Asia Cultures Critique* 1, no. 1 (Spring 1993).

―――. "The Modern Girl as Militant." In Gail Lee Bernstein, ed., *Recreating Japanese Women 1600–1945.* Berkeley and Los Angeles: University of California Press, 1991.

Smith, Henry D., II. "Tokyo as an Idea: An Exploration of Japanese Urban Thought Until 1945." *Journal of Japanese Studies* 4, no. 1 (1978).

Smith, Robert J. "The Cultural Context of the Japanese Political Economy." In S. Kumon and H. Rosovsky, eds., *The Political Economy of Japan,* vol. 3. Stanford: Stanford University Press, 1991.

―――. "Town and City in Pre-modern Japan." In A. Southall, ed., *Urban Anthropology.* Oxford: Oxford University Press, 1973.

Smith, Thomas C. *Native Sources of Japanese Industrialization.* Berkeley and Los Angeles: University of California Press, 1988.

―――. "The Right to Benevolence." In Smith, *Native Sources of Japanese Industrialization.* Berkeley and Los Angeles: University of California Press, 1988.

Sone Hiromi. "Baitakō—kinsei no baishun." In Josei Shi Sōgō Kenkyūkai, ed. *Nihon josei shi seikatsu shi,* vol. 3: *Kinsei.* Tokyo: Tōkyō Daigaku Shuppankai, 1991.

Steffensen, Sam. "Regional Development Issues, Localism, and the Emergence of New Social Dynamics in Contemporary Japan: An Inquiry into the 'Era of Localities.'" Ph.D. diss., University of Copenhagen, 1994.

Sugita Fusako. "Mini dokuritsukoku (ginnankoku) kenkoku ni tsuite." In Nōringyogyō Taiken Kyōkai, ed., *Furusato saihakken.* Tokyo: Nōrin Tōkei Kyōkai, 1986.

Sumiya Mikio. "Kōjō hō taisei to rōshi kankei." In Sumiya Mikio, ed., *Nihon rōshi kankei shi ron.* Tokyo: Tōkyō Daigaku Shuppankai, 1977.

Tachibana Kōzaburō. *Kōdō kokka nōhon kenkoku ron.* Tokyo: Kensetsusha, 1932.

―――. *Nōsongaku.* Tokyo: Kensetsusha, 1932.

Takagiwa Hiroo. *Nihonjin ni totte wa to wa nani ka: Shūdan ni okeru chitsujo.* Saitama-ken, Niizashi: Shōgaku Kenkyūsha, 1987.

Tamanoi, Mariko. *The Politics and Poetics of Rural Women in Modern Japan: The Making of a National Subject.* Honolulu: University of Hawaii Press, 1998.

Tanaka Yūko. *Edo no sōzōryoku: 18-seiki no media to hyōchō.* Tokyo: Chikuma Shobō, 1986.

―――. *Edo wa nettowaaku.* Tokyo: Heibonsha, 1993.

Thomas, Nicolas. "The Inversion of Tradition." *American Ethnologist* 19, no. 2 (May 1992).

Toby, Ronald P. *State and Diplomacy in Early Modern Japan: Asia in the Development of the Tokugawa Bakufu.* Princeton: Princeton University Press, 1984.

Togawa Yukio. *Shōsetsu Kanō Jigorō.* Tokyo: Yomiuri Shinbunsha, 1992.

Tomlinson, John. *Cultural Imperialism.* Baltimore: Johns Hopkins University Press, 1991.

Trevor-Roper, Hugh. "The Invention of Tradition: The Highland Tradition of Scotland." In Eric Hobsbawm and Terence Ranger, eds., *The Invention of Tradition.* Cambridge: Cambridge University Press, 1983.

Tsuji Tatsuya. *Edo jidai o kangaeru*. Tokyo: Chūkō Shinsho, 1988.

Tsunasawa Mitsuaki. *Nihon no nōhonshugi*. Tokyo: Kinokuniya Shinsho, 1971.

Turnbull, Stephen. *The Lone Samurai and the Martial Arts*. London: Arms and Armour, 1990.

Uchida Seizō. "Meiji ki no jūtaku kairyō ni mirareru puraibashii no ishiki ni tsuite." *Nihon kenchiku gakkai taikai gakujutsu kōen kōgaishū* (Kantō), no. 8088 (October 1975).

———. *Nihon no kindai jūtaku*. Tokyo: Kajima Shuppan, 1992.

Uchida Yoshiaki. "Yamada Moritarō to marukusu keizaigaku." In Uchida, *Vēbā to marukusu: Nihon shakai kagaku no shisō kōzō*. Tokyo: Iwanami Shoten, 1978.

Ueno, Toshiya. "Tasha to kikai / The Other and the Machine." In Yukio Fukushima and Marcus Nornes, eds., *Media Wars: Then and Now*. Yamagata International Documentary Film Festival '91. (Tokyo: Sōjinsha, 1991).

Upham, Frank. *Law and Social Change in Postwar Japan*. Cambridge, Mass.: Harvard University Press, 1987.

Vlastos, Stephen. "Opposition Movements in Early Meiji." In Marius B. Jansen, ed., *The Cambridge History of Japan*, vol. 5: *The Nineteenth Century*. Cambridge: Cambridge University Press, 1989.

———. *Peasant Protests and Uprisings in Tokugawa Japan*. Berkeley and Los Angeles: University of California Press, 1986.

Vogel, Ezra F. *Japan's New Middle Class*. 2d ed. Berkeley and Los Angeles: University of California Press, 1971.

Waswo, Ann. *Japanese Landlords: The Decline of a Rural Elite*. Berkeley and Los Angeles: University of California Press, 1977.

———. "The Transformation of Rural Society, 1900–1950." In Peter Duus, ed., *Cambridge History of Japan*, vol. 6: *The Twentieth Century*. Cambridge: Cambridge University Press, 1988.

Watanabe Tōru. "Nihon ni okeru rōdō kumiai hōan no tōjō o megutte," pt. 1. *Nihon rōdō kyōkai zasshi*, no. 87 (June 1966).

White, James W. *Ikki: Social Conflict and Political Protest in Early Modern Japan*. Ithaca, N.Y.: Cornell University Press, 1995.

Wigen, Kären. "Politics and Piety in Japanese Native-Place Studies: The Rhetoric of Solidarity in Shinano." *Positions: East Asia Cultures Critique* 4, no. 3 (1996).

———. *The Making of a Japanese Periphery, 1750–1920*. Berkeley and Los Angeles: University of California Press, 1995.

Williams, Raymond. *The Politics of Modernism*. London and New York: Verso, 1989.

Yamada Moritarō. *Nihon shihonshugi bunseki*. Tokyo: Iwanami Shoten, 1934. Reprinted in *Yamada Moritarō chosakushū*, vol. 2. Tokyo: Iwanami Shoten, 1983.

———. "Saiseisan hyōshiki to chidai hanchū—Nihon keizai saiken no hōshiki to nōgyō kaikaku no hōkō o kimeru tame no ichi kijun" (1947). Reprinted in *Yamada Moritarō chosakushū*, vol. 3. Tokyo: Iwanami Shoten, 1983.

———. *Saiseisan katei: Hyōshiki bunseki joron* (1931). Reprinted in *Yamada Moritarō chosakushū*, vol. 1. Tokyo: Iwanami Shoten, 1983.

Yamada Shōji. "Furikaeru Nihon no mirai: Kaisetsu Manshū imin no sekai." In Yamada Shōji, ed., *Kindai minshū no kiroku*, vol. 6: *Manshū imin*. Tokyo: Shin Jinbutsu Ōraisha, 1978.

Yanagita Kunio. *Densetsu* (1940). Reprinted in *Yanagita Kunio zenshū*, vol. 4. Tokyo: Chikuma Shobō, 1989.

————. *Jidai to nōsei* (1910). Reprinted in *Yanagita Kunio zenshū*, vol. 29. Tokyo: Chikuma Shobō, 1989.

————. *Kaijō no michi* (1961). Reprinted in *Yanagita Kunio zenshū*, vol. 43. Tokyo: Chikuma Shobō, 1989.

————. *Kainan shoki*. Tokyo: Ōokayama Shoten, 1939.

————. *Kyōdo seikatsu no kenkyū hōhō* (1935). Reprinted in *Yanagita Kunio zenshū*, vol. 28. Tokyo: Chikuma Shobō, 1989.

————. *Kyōdo shi ron* (1914). Reprinted in *Yanagita Kunio zenshū*, vol. 27. Tokyo: Chikuma Shobō, 1989.

————. *Meiji Taishō shi sesōhen*. 2 vols. Tokyo: Kōdansha, 1992.

————. *Minkan denshō ron* (1934). Reprinted in *Yanagita Kunio zenshū*, vol. 28. Tokyo: Chikuma Shobō, 1989.

————. *Teihon Yanagita Kunio zenshū*. Tokyo: Chikuma Shobō, 1968–71.

————. *Tōno monogatari* (1910). Reprinted in *Yanagita Kunio zenshū*, vol. 4. Tokyo: Chikuma Shobō, 1989.

————. *Toshi to nōson* (1929). Reprinted in *Yanagita Kunio zenshū*, vol. 29. Tokyo: Chikuma Shobō, 1989.

————. *Yama no jinsei* (1926). Reprinted in *Yanagita Kunio zenshū*, vol. 4. Tokyo: Chikuma Shobō, 1989.

Yasuba, Yasukichi. "Anatomy of the Debate on Japanese Capitalism." *Journal of Japanese Studies* 2, no. 1 (Autumn 1975).

Yasumaru Yoshio. "Minshū hōki sekaizō." *Shisō*, April 1973.

————. *Nihon kindaika to minshū shisō*. Tokyo: Aoki Shoten, 1974.

Yokoi Tokiyoshi. "Nōhonshugi." In *Yokoi hakushi zenshū* 8. Tokyo: Yokoi Zenshū Kankōkai, 1925.

————. *Shonō ni kansuru kenkyū*. Tokyo: Maruzen, 1927.

Young, Louise. *Japan's Total Empire: Manchuria and the Culture of Wartime Imperialism*. Berkeley and Los Angeles: University of California Press, 1997.

Young, Robert. *White Mythologies: Writing History and the West*. London: Routledge, 1990.

CONTRIBUTORS

ANDREW E. BARSHAY is an Associate Professor in the History Department of the University of California, Berkeley. His recent publications include *State and Intellectual in Imperial Japan* (1988) and "Toward a History of the Social Sciences in Japan," *Positions* (1996). His current project is an intellectual history of capitalism in postwar Japan.

DIPESH CHAKRABARTY is a Professor in the Department of South Asian Languages and Civilizations of the University of Chicago. His recent publications include *Rethinking Working-Class History: Bengal, 1890–1940* (1989) and, as co-editor, *Subaltern Studies*, vol. 9. A book, *The Unworking of History*, is forthcoming.

CAROL GLUCK is George Sansom Professor of History at Columbia University. Her recent publications include *Japan's Modern Myths* (1985) and, as co-editor, *Asia in Western and World History* (1997). A study of twentieth-century Japanese views of modern Japanese history is forthcoming.

ANDREW GORDON is a Professor in the History Department of Harvard University. His recent publications include *Labor and Imperial Democracy in Prewar Japan* (1991) and, as editor, *Postwar Japan as History* (1993). A book, *Wages of Affluence*, is forthcoming.

H. D. HAROOTUNIAN is a Professor in the Department of East Asian Studies of New York University. His recent publications include *Things Seen and Unseen: Discourse and Ideology in Tokugawa Nativism* (1988) and, as co-editor, *Japan in the World* (1993). He is completing a book, *Overcome by Modernity: Historical Surplus and Cultural Authenticity in Interwar Japan.*

HASHIMOTO MITSURU is a Professor in the Faculty of Human Sciences of Osaka University. His recent publications include *Monogatari toshite no 'ie'* (1994) and

"Chūō to chihō," in *Nihon bunka no shakaigaku* (1996). He is writing a book on the concept of tradition in the Japanese social sciences.

INOUE SHUN is Professor of Sociology in the School of Letters of Kyoto University. His recent publications include *Bungaku to geijutsu no shakaigaku* (1996) and *Nihon bungaku no shakaigaku* (1996). He is currently researching popular culture in modern Japan.

ITŌ KIMIO is a Professor of Sociology in the Faculty of Human Sciences of Osaka University. His recent publications include *Danseigaku nyūmon* (1996) and *Otokorashisa no yukue* (1993). He is preparing a book on popular culture in the Shōwa period.

JENNIFER ROBERTSON is a Professor in the Anthropology Department of the University of Michigan, Ann Arbor. Her recent publications include *Native and Newcomer: Making and Remaking a Japanese* City (1991; 1994) and "Mon Japon: The Revue Theater as a Technology of Japanese Imperialism," *American Ethnologist* (1995). Her next book, *Takarazuka: Sexual Politics and Popular Culture in Modern Japan,* is forthcoming.

JORDAN SAND is an Assistant Professor in the Department of East Asian Languages and Cultures of Georgetown University. His recent publications include, as co-author, *Tsukuda ni watashi ga atta* (1994), a history of the fishing community on Tsukuda Island in Tokyo. He is currently revising his dissertation, "House and Home in Modern Japan, 1880s–1920s" (Columbia University, 1995).

IRWIN SCHEINER is a Professor in the History Department of the University of California, Berkeley. His recent publications include "Socialism, Liberalism and Marxism," in *The Cambridge History of Japan*, vol. 6 (1989). He is completing a book, *Yonaoshi Rebellion and Its Enemies.*

MIRIAM SILVERBERG is an Associate Professor in the History Department of the University of California, Los Angeles. Her recent publications include *Changing Song: The Marxist Manifestos of Nakano Shigeharu* (1990) and "Constructing the Japanese Ethnography of Modernity," *Journal of Asian Studies* (1992). She is currently completing a history of the politics of Japanese cultural consciousness.

LEE A. THOMPSON is an Associate Professor in the Faculty of International Studies of Osaka Gakuin University. He has published articles in Japanese on Western-style professional wrestling in Japan and the modernization of sumo. His other publications include "Nichijō seikatsu ni okeru 'Nihonjin' to teiji no stiguma toshite no gaikokujin," in *Sabetsu no shakai riron* (1996).

FRANK K. UPHAM is a Professor in the School of Law of New York University. He is the author of *Law and Social Change in Postwar Japan* (1987). His recent publications include "Privatized Regulation: Japanese Regulatory Style in Comparative and International Perspective," *Fordham International Law Journal* (1997). He is writing a comparative study of land use law, policy, and politics in New York and Tokyo.

STEPHEN VLASTOS is a Professor in the History Department of the University of Iowa. His recent publications include *Peasant Protests and Uprisings in Tokugawa Japan* (1986) and "Opposition Movements in Early Meiji," in *The Cambridge History of Japan*, vol. 5 (1989). He is writing a book on radical agrarian movements in prewar Japan.

KÄREN WIGEN is an Associate Professor in the History Department of Duke University. Her recent publications include *The Making of a Japanese Periphery, 1750–1920* (1995) and, as co-author, *The Myth of Continents: A Critique of Metageography* (1997). Her current research focuses on the ongoing process of regional identity formation in modern Japan.

LOUISE YOUNG is an Assistant Professor in the History Department of New York University. Her recent publications include *Japan's Total Empire: Manchuria and the Culture of Wartime Imperialism* (1997). Her current research is on urban modernism in interwar Japan.

INDEX

emperors, 1, 12, 45–46; Meiji, 38; Prince
Shōtoku and, 40, 43–45; Yanagita and,
135–36, 139–41
empire building, 109
employment, 70, 74, 93; by-, 9, 70, 84; lifetime,
20, 33; wage, 70
Endō Arata, 206
Engels, Friedrich, 73, 75
England, 56, 68, 93, 154, 192, 196; domesticity
in, 205. *See also* Britain
entertainment, 14, 219, 264, 272
epiphanic (mode of viewing), 15, 289–91, 295
Equal Employment Opportunity Act, 60,
62, 63
eroticism, 211–25
ethics, 253
ethnography, 154–155
Europe, 11, 34, 45–46, 210–11, 236, 241, 269, 276,
286; culture in, 209; disparity of wealth in,
83; eating rituals in, 200n; economics in,
282; factories in, 20; fascism in, 295; feudalism in, 265, 267; folklore of, 142; Middle
Ages in, 262, 284
exceptionalism, 8, 154n, 155
expansion, 281
exports, 90, 249

Fabian, Johannes, 293
factories, 13, 18–19
factory law, 8, 20–27
families, 10, 59, 92, 116, 191–93, 196, 198, 206–7,
239; eating rituals, 198–201, 205, 209; extended, 57, 158; farm, 80, 83–84, 87, 90,
92–93, 108, 156–57, 294; houses and, 203–5,
207; Meiji, 279; middle class, 83; nuclear,
292; Osaka, 197; Tokugawa, 246
Family Court, 60
family-state, 1, 11, 127
farmers, 49–51, 68, 70, 79, 81–94, 98, 157; emigration of, 96–97, 108; small, 83–87
Farm Tenancy Conciliation Law of 1924, 59
fascism, 15, 16, 34, 150, 273, 295
femininity, 214, 222
feminism, 127
feudalism, 13–14, 23, 29–30, 209, 250, 255, 272,
283, 292–93; capitalism and, 243; centralized, 267–68, 270, 280; corporate, 31; eating
rituals and, 199; Edo period and, 15, 265–66;
European, 265, 267; medieval, 270; Meiji,
276–77; Tokugawa, 73–74, 81, 266, 268–70,
280
Finance Ministry, 22

folk, 16, 144–59, 280, 289; artifacts, 290; arts,
236; beliefs, 137; ethnology, 154; studies, 154,
156
folkcraft movement, 271
folklore studies, 15, 133, 136, 138, 142–43, 153
Foucault, Michel, 288, 292
France, 15, 58, 236n, 237, 262, 270
Frazer, James George, 12, 142
Fujin kōron, 217
Fujin kurabu (Woman's club), 219
Fujin no tomo (Woman's friend), 205n, 206, 219
Fujitani, Takashi, 11
Fujo kai (Woman's world), 219
fukoku kyōhei (Rich Country, Strong Army),
245–47
Fukuda Hachinosuke, 164
Fukuda Kiyohito, 107
Fukuda Tokuzō, 85
Fukumoto Kazuo, 270
Fukushima prefecture, 99
Fukuzawa Yukichi, 194n, 245, 263, 265–66, 277;
Katei sōdan, 194n
furusato, 16, 67–68, 110–12, 114–21, 125–28, 294;
"Ambassadors," 118; defined, 297; mother
and, 124; -*mura*, 119–21; parcel post, 118–20;
Plaza, 120; temporality and, 292. *See also* na-
tive place
Furusato: Family, 116; Information Center, 116,
121, 125; *Jōhō*, 120; Miss Furusato contests,
125–27; parcel post, 118–20; Plaza, 120;
Tokyo Festival, 119
Furusato (movie), 14, 124
furusato-zukuri, 14, 77–78, 110, 115–19; Comprehensive Development Plans, 123; defined,
297. *See also* native place
Futahaguro, 174, 177, 184–86

Gakushūin University, 167
Gandhi, Mahatma, 15, 295
geisha, 209, 212–13, 224
gekokujō, 277; defined, 297
gender, 222, 239; difference, 125; domination,
222–23; hierarchy, 93; inequalities, 116; *jokyū*
and, 212, 216–17, 221; male-female relationships, 222; norms, 14; nostalgia and, 124–27;
relations, 14, 92, 150; roles, 93, 124–27, 193,
214–15
Genrokumura, 264
Genroku period, 267, 274–75, 278, 280
geography: administrative, 242; feudal, 236; historical, 239; Nagano's, 241; political, 232, 237
German Peasant Wars, 73, 75

Germany, 26, 28, 58, 143, 196, 242, 270
GHQ, 173
Giddens, Anthony, 2, 6
Gifu, 99
Gilroy, Paul, 210
Ginkgo Nut Nation (Ginnankoku), 126–28
Ginkgo Tree Festival, 126
Ginza, 213, 215, 217, 221, 224, 271–72
globalism, 261
globalization (*gurōbarizeshon*), 113
glocalization, 128
Gluck, Carol, 11, 15, 237–38, 262–84
The Golden Bough (Frazer), 12, 142
gōmyō, 50–51; defined, 297. *See also* farmers
Gordon, Andrew, 8, 16, 19–36, 288
Greater East Asia Co-Prosperity Sphere, 123n
Great Japan Encyclopedia, 267
Grundrisse (Marx), 145
gun, 232, 240: defined, 297

habitus, 4n, 245
Hachiōji, 126
Haga Tōru, 275, 281
Haley, John, 59
Hamaguchi Osachi, 219
Hanada family, 186
Hanayama Shinshō, 41, 43–44
Hani Gorō, 73, 158
Hani Motoko, 205–6
harmony, 8, 15, 26, 49, 57, 59, 63, 87, 92, 288, 294; group, 1, 68, 78; rural, 80. *See also wa*
Harootunian, H. D., 10, 15–16, 69, 144–59, 289–90, 294
Hashimoto Mitsuru, 10, 12, 15, 133–43, 289–91
Hattori Shisō, 250
Havens, Thomas, 83
Hawaii, 96, 219
Hayami Akira, 275, 279
Hayashi Fumiko, 221–23
Hayashi Razan, 41
Hayashi Shōzō, 88
Hegel, G. W. F., 244, 266, 287
Heian period, 41, 175
Heian Shrine, 171
Heidegger, Martin, 156, 159
Heisei period, 281
Hida, 231
Hideyoshi. *See* Toyotomi Hideyoshi
Hiraga Gennai, 272–73
Hirano Yoshitarō, 249
Hirata Atsutane, 41, 140
Hirose Takeo, 167

Hirotsu Kazuo, 217–18
historicism, 290
historiography, 13, 143, 151, 247
Hitachiyama, 183
Hobsbawm, Eric, 2–4, 37, 169, 279, 285–88
Hōchi shinbun, 206
Hofstadter, Richard, 68
Hokkaido, 95–97, 235n
Hokutoumi, 185–86
Holland Village, 114
home, 10, 14–15, 92, 110n, 191–207, 292. *See also katei*
Home Ministry, 24, 26–27, 33n, 54, 233; Nagano and, 241
Homi Bhabha, 215
hōmu, 192–94, 292; defined, 297
Honshu, 229, 231, 239
Horikawa Kiyomi, 106
hoshitorihyō, 179–81; defined, 297
Hosokawa, Prime Minister, 278
houses, 201–7
Housewife's Friend (Shufu no tomo), 216, 219
housewives, 195, 204–5, 216
Hozu, 16, 49–55
Hozumi Yatsuka, 58, 192
Huis Ten Bosch, 114

Ibaraki prefecture, 10, 88, 107
Ichō Festival, 126
identity, 144, 158, 207, 289, 291; cultural, 5, 7–9, 112–13, 115, 122, 125–26, 128, 264, 283; Edo, 263, 283–84; eroticized, 217; ethnic, 215; gendered, 217; inherited, 237; local, 235, 238; modern, 143; prefectural, 239; regional, 13, 229–30, 236, 239, 294; Shinano, 13, 238; territorial, 242. *See also* national identity
ie, 16, 67, 191–92, 195, 207, 292; Tokugawa and, 245, 279
Ie (publication), 200
Iemitsu. *See* Tokugawa Ieyasu
Ienari, 176, 271
Ie no hikari, 210, 216
ie sei, 92, 192, 292; defined, 297
Ieyasu. *See* Tokugawa Ieyasu
Igarashi Tomio, 211
Ihara Saikaku, 163
Iikubo Tsunetoshi, 164, 169
Iinmaku Kyūgorō, 177
ikka danran, 198; defined, 297
ikkoku minzokugaku, 12, 142
Ikota Jundō, 72

247; of sports, 170–72; of sumo, 178, 187; theory, 3, 287; tradition and, 182, 287; Yanagita and, 143
moga, 14
Moore, Barrington, 260
Morisaki Kazue, 113
Morishima Michio, 247
Morita Akio, 33
Motoori Norinaga, 140, 275
mountain people (*sanka*), 135–38, 290
Mutō Sanji, 35
mythology: imperial, 108–9
myths, 11, 175, 230, 286; social, 278

Nagai Kafū, 270–71, 274
Nagano, 13, 98–99, 105, 229–35, 238–41; Gijuku (Nagano Normal School), 234–35; Seven Roads Project, 234
Nagasaki, 114, 119n
Nagayama Moriteru, 231
Nakabayashi Shinji, 163
Nakai Riken, 41
Nakane Chie, 277
nakarōka, 14, 203
Nakasendō, 238
Nangaku Eshi, 41
Nara period, 41, 156
national identity, 9–12, 112–13, 115, 122, 125–26, 136, 236; capitalism and, 244; Edo and, 263, 272; martial arts and, 164, 169
nationalism, 15–16, 74, 127, 242, 294, 296; Chinese, 109; in Meiji period, 235–42; Prince Shōtoku and, 39, 42, 44; Taishō and, 45
nation-states, 8, 11, 15–16, 37, 83, 134, 140, 287, 289, 293–95; *budō* and, 171; colonization and, 96; culture and, 143; Edo and, 262, 264, 266, 280; emperors and, 140; farming and, 82; *furusato* and, 115; globalization and, 113; nation-building, 96, 125; political traditions and, 9
native ethnology (*minzokugaku*), 10, 12, 16, 144–46, 150, 152–55, 158, 289n
native place, 16, 67–68, 110–12, 114–21, 125, 146, 148–49, 151, 153–54, 157; Edo as, 272; place-making, 14, 110, 112, 115–19, 121, 123–24, 127–28. See also *furusato*
nativism (*kokugaku*), 145, 153–54, 272, 274; new, 155–57
Naval Academy, 167
Nazi Labor Front (DAF), 28
Nehru, Jawaharlal, 13

Neo-Confucianism, 41, 58, 81, 268
Netherlands, 114
New Zealand, 96–97
nichirin heisha, 107–8; defined, 298
Nihonjinron, 153
Nihonmatsu, 123
Nihon shihonshugi bunseki (Yamada), 13, 248–61
Nihon shoki, 41, 175
Niigata, 99
Nikkeiren, 29–30
Nikkō, 69, 71
Ninomiya Sontoku, 104
Nippon Kōkan (NKK) steel works, 29
Nishikawa Yūko, 215
Nishinoumi, 177
Nitobe Inazō, 45, 145, 278
Nogi, General, 219
Noguchi Genzaburō, 172
nōhonshugi, 10. See also agrarianism
"*Nōhonshugi*" (Yokoi), 82–83
Noro Eitarō, 250, 270
Nōson kenkyū, 88–91
nostalgia, 110–29, 264, 280, 294; as mode of viewing, 15, 289–91, 295

Ōbayashi Munetsugu, 220, 222
Odaka Kunio, 30
Oda Makoto, 76
Oda Mikio, 170
Ogasawara school, 204–5
Ogyū Sorai, 80–81
Ohara Institute for the Study of Social Problems, 218
Ōhinata village, 105–6
Ōishi Shinzaburō, 275
Okada Masayuki, 45
Oka Minoru, 22
Ōkawa Shūmei, 43
Okayama, 101
Okinawa, 138, 140, 142, 155–56, 235, 290
Ōkubo Toshimishi, 81
Ōkuma Shigenobu, 263, 267
Olympics, 170–71, 173
onjō-shugi, 8, 12, 19, 29; defined, 298
Onokawa Kisaburo, 176
Ono Seiichirō, 46
oppression, 74, 83, 158, 279, 293; social, 277
Orii Hyūga, 29–30
Orikuchi Shinobu, 10, 141–42, 144–45, 147, 155, 158, 291, 294
Osaka, 210n, 213, 217, 219–21, 280; Dōtonburi, 217

Index: Laurie Reith Winship
Composition: Impressions Book and Journal Services, Inc.
Text: 10/12 Baskerville
Display: Baskerville
Printing and binding: Edwards Brothers